B$ 5.95

The Search for Modern Europe

The Search for Modern Europe

Henry Grosshans

Washington State University

HOUGHTON MIFFLIN COMPANY · BOSTON

New York   Atlanta   Geneva, Illinois   Dallas   Palo Alto

Table of Contents

Preface

This book attempts to present a direct and challenging analysis of the major problems of European history during the last two hundred and fifty years. It has been written for Americans, and the focus is upon what is necessary and important for American students to know about Europe's recent historical past. The emphasis is upon those subjects — revolution, secularism, industrialization, nationalism, war, the relation of America to Europe — that are the basic ingredients of modern European civilization.

The book is organized so that readers may make immediate contact with these subjects. An introduction entitled "The Idea of Europe" provides a short general description of European civilization at the beginning of the modern age. This introduction is followed by ten sections — each devoted to one of the traumatic experiences or periods in modern European history. The book concludes with "The Idea of America."

Each of the ten sections consists of several parts. There is a background chapter that describes the event, the subject, or the period and sets the general historical problem. This is followed in every case by three short chapters devoted to individuals or historical occurrences that illustrate attitudes toward and implications of the problem. Each section also contains a chronology of important events. The chronologies are designed as convenient guides to the reader and include, where appropriate, explanatory comments. A short bibliographical essay is included in each section.

The choice of subjects and the method of discussing them make this book somewhat different than the usual history text. First, there is a concentration upon those historical problems that have continued throughout the modern period, have stimulated persistent conflict, hope, and fear, and have contributed to our ideas of modernity. Thus I have avoided those largely artificial divisions that so often make history appear as a series of separate events that took place in the past but with little present relevance. Second, I have largely concerned myself with the Europe that has been significantly influenced by the eighteenth-century Enlightenment, industrialization, nationalism, secularization, and, to a lesser or greater degree, the democratic revolution. The great majority of the important events of modern European history took place in England, France, and Germany, and the problems of modern European civilization can best be examined through an emphasis upon this part of Europe. Such an emphasis does not imply that other European societies are inferior or uninteresting. They are, however, not as useful to my purpose.

Third, I have not written an exclusively political history. Politics is important, but it is only one aspect of history, and I have included a great deal of material drawn from literature, science, philosophy, and other disciplines. Fourth, I have presented judgments for the reader's consideration. Meaningful history cannot be dispassionate or without moral and ethical considerations. There are historical crimes and historical stupidities, and they should be identified as such.

The Search for Modern Europe is designed as an instrument for active teaching and learning. Its approach and organization have been influenced by student interest, student demands, and student response. Every section can be expanded and developed as the teacher and the students desire. The book provides scope for imaginative speculation on the part of the reader, and even the opportunity for him to engage in great part in his own education. It attempts to liberate his thought, not confine it, and to invite him to participate in his own history.

King Edward I in Parliament, Wriothesley Manuscript, Royal Collection, Copyright Reserved, London.

1

The Idea of Europe

In 1957, Denys Hay, Professor of Medieval History at the University of Edinburgh, published a small book entitled *Europe: The Emergence of an Idea.* Near the end of his book he quoted from two important Europeans. One was the Frenchman Voltaire who in 1751 in his *Age of Louis XIV* wrote that Europe is "a kind of great republic divided into several states, some monarchical, the others mixed; the former aristocratic, the latter popular; but all corresponding to one another. They all have the same religious foundations, even if divided into several confessions. They all have the same principles of public law and politics, unknown in other parts of the world." The second was the Englishman Edmund Burke who in 1796 said: "No European can be a complete exile in any part of Europe." Professor Hay himself then added: "With these words of Burke we come to the final realization of the idea of Europe."

What Professor Hay is suggesting is that by the eighteenth century Europeans had become aware of themselves as members of a distinctive historical group united by similar institutions and experiences. They had developed common patterns of domestic life, styles of architecture, music, literature, and art, methods of military and economic organization, philosophies of space and time, and ideas of human destiny. They were participants in a culture or civilization that was significantly different from any other in the world.

There have been many attempts to define Europe and the Europeans. Some authorities have regarded race as the important distinguishing aspect of European civilization. Others have stressed climate, practices of land cultivation, and systems of philosophical inquiry. Europe has been identified with the Mediterranean area of the Roman Empire and with Charlemagne's empire of the early ninth century, or defined as those peoples and areas that had been influenced by Roman Catholic Christianity.

The European Continent

All these interpretations are more or less valuable, and at least some manifestation of each of them is incorporated in the principal features of the idea of Europe as Voltaire, Burke, and their contemporaries thought of it. First there was the continent of Europe itself. A series of historical circumstances had tied the European closely to his land. By the twelfth century all those we think of as Europeans had been converted to Christianity. But after that success and until the period of significant overseas colonization in the sixteenth and seventeenth centuries, every European attempt to expand farther out into the world had failed. In fact, during a great part of their history, Europeans had been on the defensive and had been forced to withstand military pressures from the Moslems, who moved across north Africa and into Spain, from the Mongols, who conquered Russia and came as far west as the Hungarian plains, and from the Turks, who in 1453 took Constantinople, invaded the Balkans, and in 1683 besieged Vienna. Late in the fifteenth century, however, the Moslems were forced from Spain and Russia freed herself from Mongol control. The Turks, too, were thrown back near the end of the seventeenth century, and while they continued to rule a large part of the Balkans, they were no longer a threat to European security.

Situated in a small area of the world that had been spared invasion by outsiders and forced to devote their attentions and energies to their native environment, Europeans, and particularly those we think of as Western Europeans, had become conditioned by their geographical circumstances to look at themselves and their surroundings in a particular way. Europe seemed to them a most appropriate place for men to live, in many ways the only habitable part of the planet. Only in Europe, they believed, had men brought their physical conditions under control and had mastered nature. Other parts of the earth might be wild and untamed. But in Europe all was measured and in order. Everywhere else men appeared to be largely nomads who had not found a suitable place in which to settle. But in Europe, Englishmen, Frenchmen, Germans, and others had taken possession of the land, which they had "fortified with castles, edified with towns, crowned with cities." The rich, sustaining soil and the temperate climate gave a sense of geographical permanence that Europeans thought lacking elsewhere. Historical experience and the land were united in a patriotic affection that made statements such as "this fair France" a testimonial to a physical attraction as well as to a treasured memory. The speech that William Shakespeare put into the mouth of John of Gaunt in *Richard II* was only one of the many poetic expressions in which Europeans stressed the unity of their history and their land.

This royal throne of kings, this scept'red isle,
This earth of majesty, this seat of Mars,
This other Eden, demi-paradise,
This fortress built by Nature for herself
Against infection and the hand of war,
This happy breed of men, this little world,
This precious stone set in the silver sea,
Which serves it in the office of a wall,
Or as a moat defensive to a house,
Against the envy of less happier lands;
This blessed plot, this earth, this realm, this England.

On this land the Europeans had developed what we would call a way of life. In the early seventeenth century Francis Bacon said that the difference between Europe and other parts of the world was not climate, soil, or race but "the arts," the acts of creative imagination whereby men recognize and interpret their experiences. At the beginning of the eighteenth century the Frenchman Bernard de Fontenelle made something of the same argument when he wrote that "there is a certain specific quality of mind or genius which you meet with nowhere but in Europe, or at any rate not far beyond it." This belief in the uniqueness of Europe was dramatically expressed in illustrated books of the sixteenth and seventeenth centuries that showed the divisions of the earth. Europe was traditionally portrayed as a gracious and commanding figure with a scepter and an orb, with weapons, scientific instruments, books, and Christian symbols. Asia was presented as a richly dressed, forbidding ruler, holding an incense burner and supported by camels and donkeys. Africa was naked and surrounded by elephants, lions, snakes, and palm trees, while America was equally naked but with a feathered head dress and bows and arrows. Comparisons of Europe and Asia were particularly common. Europe stood for political and religious order, for progress, and for the absence of tyranny. Asia represented stagnation, luxurious splendor, despotic rule, and ethnic peculiarities. That Europeans had little knowledge of other parts of the world was beside the point. The significant thing was that they were convinced of the correctness of their view. Europe was the true home, and other lands remained to the general European consciousness exotic and mysterious places.

Christian Europe

European civilization can be examined as a series of great forms — interpretations of life, patterns of conduct, definitions of existence. Without these interpretations, patterns, and definitions the European believed that life was not only insecure but without value. The most important of these forms were the Christian religion, the classical heritage, a tradition of political theory that sought to combine order with freedom, a searching intellectualism, and a flexible but recognizable class structure.

We casually speak of European civilization as a Christian civilization. Many have quarreled with this generalization. Actions of Europeans often seemed to deny rather than to affirm Christian principles, and European history had not been a particularly happy account of how Christian men should live. Moreover, the peoples of Europe had slaughtered each other in a long series of religious wars, and there were deep divisions caused by doctrinal disputes. Paris, Tours, Antwerp, and other cities had been the scenes of bloody acts perpetrated by one group of Christians on another. Pieter Brueghel in his *Massacre of the Innocents* had immortalized the horror of religious fanaticism in the Netherlands, while John Milton in his "On the Late Massacre in Piedmont" had called on God:

> Forget not: in thy book record their groans
> Who were thy sheep, and in their ancient fold
> Slain by the bloody Piedmontese, that rolled
> Mother with infant down the rocks.

Entire areas had been devastated by religious terror, and in every European country those who dissented from the accepted method of Christian worship were subjected to political, economic, and social disabilities. Great numbers of people were forced to depart their homes. In the early seventeenth century James I announced his intention of "harrying" the Puritans out of England, and the soldier, statesman, and writer Saint-Simon declared that Louis XIV's decision in 1685 to force the Protestant Huguenots from France offered Europe "the spectacle of a most prodigious people proscribed, naked, and fugitive, vagrant and yet innocent, seeking asylum far from its native land."

Despite these religious controversies, however, the great majority of Europeans thought of themselves as Christian. All rulers believed that they were "Defenders of the Faith," and most political arrangements were based upon the principle that "he who lives within my system of law must be an adherent of my faith." Christian symbols were everywhere, there was general reverence for the Christian holy book (or perhaps we should say holy books), and there was a common belief that the mortal world would be redeemed through Jesus Christ. Christian ceremonies attended the crises of life that stretched from birth to death. Law, politics, literature, and education all drew heavily upon Christian doctrine, and the greatest of European painters turned repeatedly to biblical sources. The Christian churches — both Catholic and Protestant — were visible indications of order, of a purpose to human history that ran from the world's beginning to some great end when all believers would be united in "one feast, one home, one mutual happiness." The promise of a Christian heaven and the fear of a Christian hell were underlying premises of European life, as much for the high as for the low, for the learned as for the ignorant. "I am afraid I may be one of those who shall be damned," said Samuel Johnson, the literary critic and compiler of the dictionary of the English language, in the latter half of the eighteenth century. "What do you mean by damned?" asked a friend. "Sent to hell, sir, and punished everlastingly," replied Johnson. Christianity was the hard rock of European existence, and the Frenchman Blaise Pascal in the middle of the seventeenth century wrote of the role that Christianity played in the European scheme of things:

> It illuminates our nature and experience. It draws into a unity the scattered elements of our life. It guides our minds and controls our science, because it alone can unfold the full mystery of nature. It answers the questions that reason can only raise, and it brings us to that fulfillment of life toward which science in its more limited way is struggling. It cannot be set in opposition to reason or science, because it includes yet transcends both.

The Classical Heritage

Thus Christianity penetrated every level of European life. But for the educated European the classical heritage was almost as important. In 1620 Francis Bacon in his *Novum Organum*, a discussion of the principles of scientific inquiry, quoted a three-line verse that expressed the reverence in which the classical world was held:

> To man's frail race great Athens long ago
> First gave the seed whence waving harvests grow,
> And re-created all our life below.

What has been called "the glory that was Greece and the grandeur that was Rome" exercised a continual fascination, and the Greek and Roman classics provided the basis for a learned community that stretched from the Mediterranean to the Baltic, from England to Poland. The widespread use of Latin, the sacred language of Christianity and the medium of secular intellectual communication, created a bond between educated Europeans and the Roman world of literature, law, and philosophy. An acquaintance with the works of Plato and Aristotle and with the great Roman writers was a prerequisite for inclusion in the intellectual life of Europe. The classics were the recorded accounts of a heroic age, "writings," in the words of the historian Edward Gibbon, that "will interest the last generation of mankind." To speak simply and strongly as a Roman and to see with the clear eye of the Greek — these were the aspirations of the educated European, and for several hundred years the argument of William Adlington in 1566 that students of the classics would gain "the knowledge of the present state, and thereby transform themselves into the right and perfect shape of men" was accepted almost without question.

The Political Order

Politically, too, Europe had by the eighteenth century assumed a certain form. There were important political differences among the European countries, and there were controversies over the type of political arrangement that was most beneficial. But the European political communities, particularly in Western Europe, were more like each other than they were like such communities elsewhere in the world.

The common European political organization was the monarchy, and the state was identified with the sovereign. Political authority, and in some cases religious authority as well, was vested in kings who assumed their positions by hereditary right. Some monarchs ruled personally and claimed absolute authority. Louis XIV of France is usually regarded as an absolute monarch from 1661 to 1715 and is reported to have said, "The state, it is I." In England after the middle of the seventeenth century, on the other hand, the monarch reigned but actually ruled in company with the powerful landed nobility and other officials. Noble birth, high position in the official church, and outstanding talent were the prerequisites for political influence, and the European political system could perhaps best be described as one where monarchs, often allied with gifted commoners who were usually given titles for services rendered, and hereditary nobles exercised authority, with the balance of power ill-defined and liable to shifts in one direction or the other.

The primary responsibility of anyone possessing political power was to preserve order. Europeans had a highly developed regard for political order and a justified horror of political instability. During the sixteenth and seventeenth centuries every European country had been subjected to civil strife — Puritan against Royalist in England, Protestant against Catholic in the Netherlands, Catholic against Lutheran in Germany, Catholic against Protestant and the king against the nobles in France. Religious fanaticism, conflicting claims to political power, and national quarrels had threatened to reduce European life to a condition described by the English political philosopher Thomas Hobbes as "solitary, poor, nasty, brutish, and short." In 1601 Queen Elizabeth of England had said in a speech to the members of Parliament that her duty was "to preserve you from envy, peril, dishonour, shame, tyranny, and oppression." This was the responsibility of anyone claiming political power, and Europeans expected their rulers to maintain public order and internal peace.

Power was often used brutally. Dismemberment, mutilation, confiscation of property, and exile were common punishments for those thought dangerous to public order. But in the mainstream of European political theory was the idea that authority was in some way restrained, and in all European political literature there was no more derogatory term than tyrant. Europeans saw themselves as citizens, compared with people elsewhere who were only subjects. When the Italian political philosopher Niccolo Machiavelli in the early sixteenth century wrote of "the Turk and the King of France," he was certain that his readers would know that he was contrasting a tyrant with a proper ruler. Government might be aristocratic or even claim to be absolutist. But it was not to be arbitrary or despotic. In the introduction to his *Leviathan* in 1651, Hobbes, who is usually regarded as the great advocate of strong and undivided political authority, argued that no political philosophy should do anything "to countenance either the barbarous state of men in power towards their inferiors, or to encourage men of low degree to a saucy behavior towards their betters."

Political order was not to serve so much the interest of those in power but to forward the individual welfare of the citizens. European political literature abounded in eloquent statements about the virtues of freedom, and about the rights of Europeans to protection of laws that were equitably applied. The English, the Dutch, and the French had a history of persistent claims to live as free men, and there was continual reference to the belief that rulers must rule by law and not by whim. In the late seventeenth century Sir William Temple, the English ambassador to the Netherlands, wrote admiringly of the Dutch: "The people here live like citizens of the world, bound to each other by the ties of civility and peace, under the impartial protection of moderate laws." In England there was continual pressure for the extension of civil liberties. In 1669 "Jews, heathens, and dissenters" were granted liberty of conscience in the Carolina colony in America, and in 1689 John Locke published his *Letters Concerning Toleration*, where he wrote: "The toleration of those that differ from others in matters of religion is so agreeable to the Gospel of Jesus Christ and to the genuine reason of mankind, that it seems monstrous for men to be so blind as not to perceive the necessity and advantage of it, in so clear a light." Locke's argument was undoubtedly too extreme for many, but there was an increasing tendency to accept, at least in part, the suggestion set down by Laurence Sterne in his novel *Tristram Shandy*: "So long as a man rides his hobby-horse peacefully and quietly along the King's highway, and neither compels you or me to get up behind him, — pray, Sir, what have either you or I to do with it?"

Europe was not democratic in our sense of the word, and both in theory and practice the "liberties of the people" were restricted to a limited number. The French poet François Villon had written in the fifteenth century:

> Upon the graves of my ancestors,
> Whose souls may God embrace,
> One sees neither crowns nor scepters.

And what had been true of Villon's ancestors was largely true of his descendants. The great European debate about liberty was carried on among a small group of people and was meant to apply to them alone. In 1551 Sir Thomas Smith, in his *The English Republic*, divided English society into nobles, knights and squires, gentlemen, those "who can live idly and without manual labour"; citizens "of some substance"; yeomen; and finally "day labourers, poor husbandmen, yea merchants and retailers which have no free land, copyholders, and all artificers who have no voice nor authority in our commonwealth, and no account is made of them but only to be ruled." The last-named group consisted of those whom Lord Clarendon a century later called the "dirty people of no name." The peasants — the great majority of Europeans — were victimized by tax collectors, noblemen, church officials, and military functionaries. Philippe Erlanger, in his *The Age of Courts and Kings*, writes of this almost silent historical majority:

> Every imagination hesitates before these millions of beings isolated by their ignorance, the scorn in which they were held, their almost complete inability to circulate, their fear of a hostile society. What ideas did they have of their country, of politics, of the wars they suffered from, of the castes they fed, or the religion, sometimes mingled with pagan superstitions, which inspired them?

Those writing of European freedom were largely uninterested in the peasants, except when they broke out in wild and vicious fits of rage. Locke was careful to point out that liberty was closely related to "the possession of outward things, such as money, lands, houses, furniture and the like." In 1773 the Frenchman Paul d'Holbach, in his book *The Social System*, defined the limits of the European idea of liberty:

By the word people I do not mean the stupid population which, being deprived of enlightenment and good sense, may at any moment become the instrument and accomplice of turbulent demagogues who wish to disturb society. Every man who can live respectably from the income of his property and every head of a family who owns land ought to be regarded as a citizen. The artisan, the merchant, and the wage-earner ought to be protected by a state which they serve usefully after their fashion, but they are not true members until by their labor and industry they have acquired land.

Intellectual Activity

As important as any distinguishing mark of European civilization was a new form of restless intellectual activity. A great deal of purple prose has been written about the Renaissance period and about the glamorous and not-so-glamorous giants of the age. Phrases such as "the humanistic spirit," "the discovery of man," "the development of the individual" have become cliches. At one time a common interpretation of European history held that after an extended period of darkness, ignorance, and superstition, Europeans suddenly brushed the cobwebs from their eyes and saw the sunlit world. Such a description strikes us now as naive and misleading. Change was gradual, and there was a continuity to Europe's history.

Yet a new form of intellectual exuberance had entered into European life during the fifteenth and subsequent centuries and became a permanent part of European history. Overseas explorations drastically changed the European vision of the world, and the voyages of Columbus, Magellan, da Gama, and others stimulated new ideas about the nature of the earth and its inhabitants. The invention of the microscope, the thermometer, the pendulum clock, the telescope, the barometer, and a host of other devices in the sixteenth and seventeenth centuries increased the power of the human eye and provided new methods of measuring the environment. Gutenberg's invention of printing from movable type in the fifteenth century made possible the dissemination of knowledge on a previously unimagined scale.

This new knowledge and these new ideas created what John Locke called "a commonwealth of learning" — political writers, scientists, artists, philosophers, noblemen, church officials, orthodox conformists and nonconforming individualists. Ideas and the men professing them moved freely from one part of Europe to the other. René Descartes lived in Holland for twenty years, Voltaire and Montesquieu were strongly influenced by their study of and visits to England, while Englishmen and Scotsmen such as Locke, Hobbes, and David Hume spent extended periods of time on the continent. Moreover, there was an awesome catholicity about these intellectuals, a breadth of learning and interest that allowed them to escape the limits of narrow specialization and to participate in a variety of pursuits. Bacon was Lord Chancellor of England, the essayist Montaigne was mayor of Bordeaux, Gottfried von Leibniz interested himself in a multitude of scientific, political, and religious projects and left 15,000 letters full of comments on every conceivable subject, and Galileo in 1588 combined science and literature to present two lectures on the form, position, and size of Dante's *Inferno*. Perhaps the greatest example of this intellectual diversity was Leonardo da Vinci who engaged in the study of anatomy, the mechanics of flying and artillery, painting, and many other activities.

There was in all this intellectual activity a belief that man towered over his surroundings and was capable of giving them whatever form he desired. Bacon had explained that the proper end of scientific inquiry was to "endow human life with new discoveries and new powers," and da Vinci is reported to have summed up his attitude with the words "I know . . . I can . . . I will." There was an unwillingness to accept any limitations to the search for new secrets, and Galileo condemned "closing the road to free investigation concerning the things of the world and of nature, as though they had already been discovered and made known with certainty."

In the minds of many, intellectual curiosity did not threaten the political, social, or religious foundations of Europe. Everything was done in the name of established belief, and hardly an important philosopher, scientist, or political writer failed to claim that he was working toward the glory of God and the well-being of his ruler and his society. Descartes' search for mathematical certainty was an attempt to protect man against "doubt, illusions, and temptations," and many Europeans did not believe that his famous *cogito, ergo sum* (I think, therefore I am) was in opposition to a religious interpretation such as Martin Luther's *credo, ergo sum* (I believe, therefore I am).

Yet Europe exhibited an uneasiness about this free intellectualism, and political writers and scientists suffered imprisonment, exile, and even death for their opinions. Suppression was carried out by both the state and the church. The Italian philosopher Giordano Bruno was imprisoned for seven years and then burned at the stake in Rome in 1600 as a heretic against the Catholic religion. Nineteen years later the great legal scholar Johann of Oldenbarneveldt was executed by the Protestant Calvinists in the Netherlands for his heretical views. Hugo Grotius, the Dutch jurist, who is usually regarded as the father of international law, was sentenced to life imprisonment at the same time. He escaped after two years and fled to Paris where he published his famous *The Law of War and Peace* in 1625. Galileo could find a publisher for his study of mechanics only in Holland, and in 1633, as an old man of seventy, was forced to recant his theory that the earth moved about the sun. Pierre Bayle, who in 1697 published his *Historical and Critical Dictionary*, had to leave France and then was deprived of his professorship in Rotterdam because of his dangerous ideas. Descartes' *Discourse on Method* could be published only in Leyden, Fénelon was condemned by the Pope and disgraced by the French king, and Denis Diderot, the great French encyclopedist, was imprisoned because of his first important political writing. The list of indignities, and worse, suffered by outspoken intellectuals was long, and the right to speak, write, and investigate freely was never secure. But the men of new ideas, of new interpretations, kept coming on in ever-increasing numbers and became an important part of the European scene.

The European

To speak of a typical European is impossible. Edmund Burke argued that the European was distinguished by two things: "the spirit of a gentleman and the spirit of religion." Many of his contemporaries would have agreed. But a cynic contended that "to love God and own a carriage" was the mark of a good European, and undoubtedly a large number would have openly or secretly accepted such a definition. Some students of European history have maintained that the spirit of Europe was best expressed by the hereditary nobility, the great somebodies with their titles, their castles, and their aristocratic style of life. These nobles, complete with their rich clothing, their military paraphernalia, and their reminders of past glories, look down upon us from hundreds of paintings. They claimed precedence over all others in society and regarded with unabashed scorn any who dared to infringe upon their prerogatives. They often regarded themselves and were regarded by others as the embodiment of chivalry, men devoted to what has been called "arts and arms." Yet members of the nobility were often uneducated, arrogant, brutal, greedy, and dissolute men who had little but their titles to recommend them. Over the years even the titles had become somewhat shoddy. "Power decreases but titles increase," wrote the Duchess Sofie of Hanover in 1680, and hard-pressed monarchs had found it expedient to sell titles in order to replenish the state treasury. In many cases the nobles had been jostled aside by those who had no claim save talent and allegiance to the ruler and state they served. French kings relied upon those who were not nobles to govern, and in England the truly influential members of the nobility had been transformed into servants of the state. But nobles remained a glittering part of the European scene. They owned great estates, they congregated at the centers of power, and they participated in the more brilliant and colorful activities of European official life.

But any list of significant Europeans would include the names of many who were not nobles. There were the country squires, painted so strikingly by Thomas Gainsborough, with their hunting dogs, their guns, and their sturdy independence. Often uncouth and provincial, they served as magistrates, church wardens, and unofficial setters of style and manners in countless villages and towns strung over the European landscape. There were also the members of the rising commercial classes who lived in what they thought of as a world of domestic virtue and solid respectability. Some of these people were ridiculous in their pretensions and their lack of taste. They hungered after titles and attempted to copy the nobility. We may smile even now at the Nuremberg merchant whose idea of true splendor was to have a bed built of ebony and alabaster, adorned with gables, niches, and corinthian columns, complete with figures of angels blowing trumpets, or at Molière's Monsieur Jourdain in *Le Bourgeois Gentilhomme* who bought expensive clothes, engaged dancing, fencing, and music instructors, and attempted the study of philosophy.

Other members of the commercial classes, however, were practical people, "little given to dreams, parsimonious, very busy." They were often grim-faced, plain, and prosaic, and we can see the reprehensible harshness that was so much a part of their character in Frans Hals' picture of *The Women Regents of the Old Men's Home at Haarlem*. They thought of themselves as the God-fearing, hard-working, level-headed part of the society, and they illustrated in their homes, their activities, and their attitudes a determination to insure a continuity of order and accomplishment. They had a strong sense of civil responsibility, and they were devoted to their property. For them, Europe was a solid, continuing way of life, firmly rooted in the reality of the here and now.

Then, too, there were the explorers, travellers, colonists. Since the sixteenth century such men had extended the influence and authority of Europe throughout the world. They had created New Plymouths and New Amsterdams and named rivers, capes, and expanses of land after European cities and monarchs. The age of exploration had turned the European spirit outward, and one of those truly monumental and basically inexplicable developments of human history — the fact that the Europeans were going to Asia, Africa, and the Americas rather than Asians, Africans, and Americans coming to Europe — was permanently to influence the European view of the world.

By the eighteenth century the European saw himself as the product of a long historical and cultural development that stretched back to the period of early Christianity and to the classical world. Europe had endured great divisive experiences — the Reformation, exhausting political conflicts, the scientific revolution of the seventeenth century. But the European had confidence in his ability to combine the past and the present into a workable and meaningful whole. He believed in the rightness of what he had created and in the near-permanence of his situation. As Edward Gibbon wrote in his *Decline and Fall of the Roman Empire* in the latter half of the century: "The balance of power will continue to fluctuate, and the prosperity of our own, or the neighboring kingdoms, may be alternately exalted or depressed; but these partial events cannot essentially injure our general state of happiness, the system of arts, and laws, and manners, which so advantageously distinguish, above the rest of mankind, the Europeans and their colonies." Europe, at least for some, was a place of elegance and grace, of cosmopolitanism and high manners. There was an ordered stateliness, the echo of which we hear in the music of Haydn and Mozart and the visual evidence of which we see at Versailles, at Schönbrunn in Vienna, and at Peterhof in Leningrad.

An important part of our politics, our religions, our languages, and our visions of life is rooted in this great European accomplishment. But we are separated from this idea of Europe by the overpowering history of the last two centuries. The Europe of those days seems a distant age of aristocratic charm and royal grandeur, the remains of which largely exist now only as architectural monuments or as historical curiosities, interesting to the scholar or to the tourist but with little apparent relationship to the work-a-day contemporary Western world. What we think of as modernity — industrialization, contemporary nationalism, the democratic revolution, modern war, the new science, and ever-increasing secularism — has destroyed or modified this idea of Europe. Even as Gibbon wrote of his belief that events could not "essentially injure our general state of happiness, the system of arts, and laws, and manners," the historical ground was beginning to shift, and the idea of Europe was beginning its transformation into what was to be our modern Western civilization.

Young Man Reading Aloud to Two Women by Candlelight, Henry Fuseli, 1778, Collection of the Kunsthaus, Musée des Beaux-Arts, Zürich.

2

The Enlightenment

1687   Newton's *Philosophiae naturalis principia mathematica* published. This was the "capstone" of Newtonian science, and provided a scientific interpretation of an ordered universe operating by natural laws.

1689   John Locke's *Letter Concerning Toleration*. "Nay, if we may openly speak the truth, and as becomes one man to another, neither Pagan nor Mahometan, nor Jew, ought to be excluded from the civil rights or the commonwealth because of his religion."

1690   Locke's *An Essay Concerning Human Understanding*. An attack upon innate ideas. "Our observation employed either about external sensible objects, or about the internal operations of our minds, perceived and reflected on by ourselves, is that which supplies our understandings with all the materials of thinking."

1690   Locke's *First and Second Treatises on Civil Government*. Set forth the idea of civil government being a contract between rulers and governed.

1693   Locke's *Some Thoughts Concerning Education*. "Of all the men we meet with, nine parts of ten are what they are, good or evil, useful or not, by their education."

1697   Pierre Bayle's *Historical and Critical Dictionary*. The first of the great Enlightenment dictionaries or encyclopedias. Bayle "devoted himself to the establishment of historical fact and the destruction of fable and legend."

1700   Establishment of the Berlin Academy, Germany's first scientific organization.

1704   Newton's *Opticks* published, which contained his "Queries" regarding heat, pneumatics, the nature of gravitation, the relation of the world of nature to God, and the proper manner for undertaking scientific investigation.

1717	Gabriel Fahrenheit proposed the Fahrenheit system of temperature measurement.
1725	John Flamsteed published his catalog of the positions of approximately 3,000 stars.
1734	Voltaire's *Letters on the English*. The "first bomb hurled against the Old Regime." Voltaire was impressed by three things present in England and lacking in France: Newtonian science, healthy trade and commerce, and individual liberty.
1739	David Hume's *Treatise of Human Nature*. A sceptical analysis of man's ability to know anything beyond his own impressions and ideas.
1743-1744	Establishment of the American Philosophical Society in Philadelphia. This was America's first scientific society, devoted to the "promotion of useful knowledge."
1748	Montesquieu's *The Spirit of Laws*. "Law, in general, is the human reason, in so far as it governs all the peoples of the earth; and the political and civil laws of each nation ought to be only particular cases of the application of this human reason."
1751-1754	Benjamin Franklin's *Experiments and Observations on Electricity*.
1751-1772	Publication of the great French *Encyclopedia*, edited by Denis Diderot and Jean d'Alembert. Twenty-eight volumes, followed by a six-volume supplement. "The aim of an encyclopedia is to assemble the knowledge scattered over the face of the earth, to expound its general system to the men with whom we live, and transmit it to the men who will come after us."
1753	British Museum founded.
1755	Samuel Johnson's *Dictionary of the English Language*.
1755	Rousseau's *The Origin and Foundation of Inequality among Men*. A plea for efforts "to guarantee the weak against oppression, to restrain the ambitious, and secure to everyone the possession of what belongs to him: let us set up rules of justice and peace."
1758	Carl Linnaeus in his *Systema naturae* cataloged flora and fauna and established the basis for modern taxonomy.

1759   Helvétius' *On the Mind*. Helvétius "encouraged men to believe that new laws and new governments could make a new world."

1762   Rousseau's *The Social Contract* and *Emile, or Treatise on Education*. Both publications were condemned as "reckless, scandalous, impious, tending to destroy the Christian religion and all governments." *The Social Contract* contains the famous sentence: "Man is born free; and everywhere he is in chains." Emile defined a "natural" system of education.

1764   Voltaire's *Philosophical Dictionary*. Banned is Switzerland, Holland, France, and by the Catholic Holy Office in Rome. Was not really a "dictionary" but a "polemical tract," perhaps "the most savage rubbish-cleaner of the age."

1764   Cesare Beccaria's *Essay on Crime and Punishment*. The first modern study of penology. "It is better to prevent crimes than to punish them. This is the fundamental principle of good legislation."

1770   Holbach's *System of Nature*. A utilitarian argument stressing that happiness results from the harmony of individual and environment.

1771   First edition of the *Encyclopedia Britannica*.

1772   Raynal's *History of Two Indies*. The century's outstanding attack upon the institution of human slavery.

1774-   Joseph Priestley announced the discovery in his *Experiments and*
1786   *Observations on Different Kinds of Air* of a number of gases, including ammonia, sulfur dioxide, and hydrogen chloride.

1776   Adam Smith's *An Inquiry into the Nature and Causes of the Wealth of Nations*. The most comprehensive and influential attempt to describe the nature of economics. Regarded, sometimes carelessly, as the great early statement of free enterprise, free trade, and free competition.

1776   Jeremy Bentham's *A Fragment on Government*. "It is the greatest happiness of the greatest number that is the measure of right and wrong."

1776-   Edward Gibbon's *The History of the Decline and Fall of the Roman*
1788   *Empire*. The greatest, and most popular, historical work of the time.

1779   Jan Ingenhousz announced the theory of photosynthesis of plants.

19

1781	William Herschel discovered the planet Uranus by telescopic observation.
1781	Immanuel Kant published his *Critique of Pure Reason*. "Our intellect does not draw its laws from nature, but imposes its laws on nature."
1784	Kant's essay "What Is Enlightenment?" "Dare to know! Have the courage to use your own understanding; this is the motto of the Enlightenment."
1784	Henry Cavendish published *Experiments on Air,* reporting, among other things, that two parts of hydrogen and one part of oxygen produce water.
1787	Antoine Lavoisier, with collaborators, published a treatise outlining the method of chemical nomenclature.
1789	Bentham's *The Introduction to the Principles of Morals and Legislation*. A plea for a utilitarian approach to politics and a statement of the identity of enlightened self-interest and the welfare of the community: "the interest of the community then is what? — the sum of the interests of the several members who compose it."

ON JUNE 24, 1826, ten days before his death, Thomas Jefferson wrote a letter expressing his regrets at his inability to attend the ceremonies in Washington in honor of the fiftieth anniversary of the American Declaration of Independence. Jefferson had outlived almost all the other important political thinkers, philosophers, historians, pamphleteers, and talkers who contributed to what we now call the eighteenth-century "Age of Enlightenment." He was one of the last survivors of that group of men who had engaged in what he had once described as "an insurrection" of "science, talents, and courage, against rank and birth, which had fallen into contempt." Now, for the last time, he attacked "monkish ignorance and superstition," advocated "the unbounded exercise of reason and freedom of opinion," and declared his conviction that "the general spread of the light of science has already laid open to every view the palpable truth, that the mass of mankind has not been born with saddles on their backs, nor a favored few booted and spurred, ready to ride them legitimately, by the grace of God."

Jefferson's letter was a short summary of eighteenth-century revolutionary historical doctrine. It was radical in its condemnation of the past, it was optimistic in its view of human nature, and it was secular in its appeal to science as an authority on behalf of historical arguments. Many things have gone into the making of the modern Western world. But the revolutionary passion for change and improvement, the outspoken rejection of traditional authority, and the extreme secularization of society can be traced to the ideas and activities of the eighteenth century.

During the greater part of the century the majority of Europeans, in the historian Peter Gay's words, "believed in witches, applied spells, used home remedies long condemned by physicians, displayed a trust in authority long discarded by the educated, lived and died happily ignorant of the battles between Cartesians and Newtonians." Life was still largely rural. In the latter half of the century approximately 20,-000,000 of the estimated 24,000,000 Frenchmen were peasants, while Germany had only a fourth of its inhabitants living in concentrations of over 1,000 persons. Scattered throughout the West European countryside were those few places that could be called cities, conglomerations of people gathered about cathedrals, courts, and commercial centers. By the end of the century London, the largest city in the West, had a population of nearly 900,000. Paris had approximately 700,000 inhabitants while Amsterdam had 200,000 and Berlin 140,000. In the United States Philadelphia had a population of 80,000, New York 65,000, and Boston 25,000.

Life for most Europeans consisted of toil, frequent illness, and early death. In the 1780s a French minister estimated that of the whole French population one quarter died before the age of three, one quarter between three and twenty-five, and one quarter between twenty-five and fifty. A plague in the early years of the eighteenth century may have killed as much as a third of the population of Prussia, and an epidemic is estimated to have killed 80,000 in France in 1741. England had a death rate of forty-one per 1,000 people in the middle of the eighteenth century as compared with just under fourteen in the middle of the twentieth. In London the death rate was probably over fifty per 1,000 in 1700 and then fell to about thirty by 1800. Berlin's death rate appears to have been above forty per 1,000 at the beginning of the century and around thirty at the end.

Europe was a structured society along what we recognize as traditional lines. The organized Christian church, with the exception of dissenters such as the Society of Friends, was allied with the nobility in defending traditional values of place and deportment. George II had been the last British king to command an army in the field in 1743, but, to a great extent in England and even more so in France, commands in the armed forces, as well as ambassadorships and high preferment in the church, were largely reserved for those of noble or gentle birth. Serfdom had disappeared in England. But it existed throughout most of the century in parts of France, principally in several of the eastern provinces, and although King Louis XVI abolished serfdom on the royal estates in 1779, there were still serfs on noble lands in 1789. East of the Elbe River in Germany serfdom was widespread, and the symbols of a remaining feudalism ranged from the presence of the gibbet on the landlord's estate to the right of the Prussian noble to decide the marriage plans of the peasant girls who lived on his land.

The Intellectual Challenge

But in Western Europe and America new influences were growing. What has been called "a specific attitude of mind . . . gradually gained ascendancy among European intellectuals." The traditional structure was being challenged, and a new aristocracy of intelligence was threatening that of birth and station. Men such as Voltaire, Rousseau, Jefferson, and others were becoming the molders of opinion and the creators of manners and morals, and were potentially people of far greater power and importance than were many of those who possessed long-established claims to places of authority. There were also the new men of wealth who were mastering the techniques of industrial and commercial exploitation of nature. The energies, the talents, and the ambitions of men such as James Watt, James Hargreaves, Josiah Wedgwood, and Richard Arkwright were creating in the textile centers, the pottery works, and the coal fields the sources of new economic power. And with these new and thriving enterprises came a host of lawyers, managers, and assorted men with special commercial and industrial skills who drifted uneasily about the traditional social and political establishments.

The period of the Enlightenment, which extended from the latter half of the seventeenth century through the latter half of the eighteenth, was not one of dramatic political and religious upheaval. But it was a period of creative intellectual unrest. Such a condition was not new in Western Europe, and there was nothing unique in the intellectual concern of Europeans with the world about them and with the meaning of their history. What was different was that this pondering upon the human situation was translated into an activist philosophy that was to dominate modern Western civilization and was to spread into and permeate all areas of society. Put simply, in the eighteenth century Western man became dedicated to the application of intellectual ideas to social and political action, to the radical changing of the conditions of human life, and to the domination of human history. He developed a profound faith in his ability to manipulate his natural and historical environment and a hostility toward any institution that did not conform to his intellectual view of the world.

This faith in change and this confidence in the value of change were undoubtedly related to the eighteenth-century attitude toward science. As Alfred Cobban, in his *In Search of Humanity,* has written: "If we ask what was the most original, and in the long run the most influential new intellectual development of the early modern period in Europe, it is difficult, even considering the rival claims of new forces in religion, literature, and art, and allowing for medieval origins and anticipations, to deny that the answer must be the rise of modern science." The century was not unique for scientific advance, and did not compare in originality with the seventeenth; but it was an age more deeply affected by the scientific outlook. Europe had for centuries been the home of scientific thinking, but the results of that thinking had alleviated very little the pains of the body nor had they physically changed the face of the earth. There had been machines invented long before 1700, and there had been many ideas as to how these machines should be used. But it was the eighteenth century that showed the way for their large-scale applicability. Nothing seemed beyond the capabilities of man, armed with the new instruments of science. In 1768 Joseph Priestley, the discoverer of oxygen, wrote: "Whatever was the beginning of the world, the end will be glorious and paradisiacal beyond what our imaginations can now conceive. Extravagant as some people may suppose these views to be, I think I could show them to be fairly suggested by the true theory of human nature and to arise from the natural course of human affairs." Other ages had desired change and improvement; but the eighteenth introduced a moral passion for change that was deeper and broader than anything previously experienced in the Western world. Everything seemed on the move, and in 1776, the year of the signing of the American Declaration of Independence, the Englishman Jeremy Bentham wrote: "The age we live in is a busy age; in which knowledge is rapidly advancing towards perfection. In the natural world, in particular, everything teems with discovery and with improvement. The most distant and recondite regions of the earth traversed and explored — the all-vivifying and subtle element of the air recently analysed and made known to us, — are striking evidences, were all others wanting, of this pleasing truth."

The Age of Reason

Historians have long debated as to the principal elements of this intellectual revolution. Some of this argument has been valuable and warns us against foolish simplification; some has been pedantic and even trivial and has confused our view of the period. There were certain major characteristics or intellectual trends that can be easily identified and that give a clear idea of what the important eighteenth-century thinkers were attempting to do. First there were the philosophical, political, and historical implications of the word Enlightenment itself. The intellectual leaders of the eighteenth century believed that they had escaped from the oppressive darkness of the past into the bright world of the new day. Whether it was Enlightenment in English, *Éclaircissement* in French, or *Aufklärung* in German, the central meaning was clear. The German founder of the Order of the Illuminati, one of the numerous organizations of intellectuals that appeared in the century, stated that the "ideal of the Order is to diffuse light. We are fighters against darkness," and the German word *Aufklärung* was, in fact, derived from the frontispiece of one of Christian Wolff's books, which depicted the sun breaking through the clouds. Consistently throughout the century there was a call for light and expressions of confidence in the healing powers of the enlightened mind. "Enlighten the people," wrote Jefferson, "and tyranny and oppressions of body and mind will vanish like spirits at dawn of day," and the German philosopher Immanuel Kant pressed home the same point when he argued that "enlightenment is escape from self-inflicted immaturity." It was this rejection of a darkened past and claims put forward on behalf of a future of light that provided the stimulus for the idea of progress that dominated so much eighteenth-century thought.

To the question of how this enlightenment was to be achieved, the eighteenth century had a general answer. "Reason," John Locke had written, "must be our best judge and guide in all things," and the eighteenth century accepted the proposition that only the reasonable was both true and beneficial. Late in the seventeenth century Spinoza wrote that reason is "the light of the mind, and without her all things are dreams and phantoms," while in the latter part of the eighteenth Paul d'Holbach contended that "if error and ignorance have forged the chains of the people, if prejudice perpetuates them, science, reason, truth will one day break them." Man's most important attribute was his ability to think reasonably and then act upon the results of that thought. Ideas and institutions were not to be respected because they were based upon tradition, precedent, dogma, or authority, but only if they were reasonable. Was it reasonable that the ruler of one German state should be insane and that another should be a ridiculous philanderer? Was it reasonable that a prince should live in luxury while his people existed in misery? Was it reasonable, Rousseau wrote, "that a child should command an old man, a fool a wise man, and that a handful of individuals should gorge themselves with superfluities, while the starving multitudes are in want of the bare necessities?" Was an aristocracy of church and state that was based upon wealth and birth, not virtue and talent, reasonable? To all these questions the men of the Enlightenment gave a resounding No!

No traditional institution escaped this scrutiny of reason, and even the most venerable of the West's organizations, the Christian church, was criticized. In his *Encyclopedia* Diderot had written: "all things must be examined, all must be winnowed and sifted without exception and without sparing anyone's sensibilities." Locke had insisted that the irrational claims of the theologians must be set aside, while Sir Isaac Newton, in spite of his declared intention of supporting the truths of Christianity, had raised serious questions concerning the validity of some of the church doctrine. Few of the eighteenth-century intellectuals denied the existence of God; what they did was to treat his presence as irrelevant to man's problems. Science and history were divorced from theological interpretation, and there was a turning away from Christianity in the search for answers to questions such as: What can I know? What ought I to do? What may I hope?

Terrestrial happiness, not holiness or religious insight, was the overwhelming concern of the eighteenth century, and while it was argued that Christian morality might have something to contribute to this condition of earthly beatitude, theology had little to offer. A certain mocking of religious belief was a consistent occupation of the century. Edward Gibbon relegated religion to the position of "the best guide of youth and the best support of old age," but not suitable for a free, adult man. Voltaire wrote openly about the "sacred lies that fill the world." And Jefferson called upon men to "question with boldness even the existence of God; because, if there be one, he must more approve of the homage of reason, than that of blindfolded fear." Christianity must be cleansed of what were thought of as its cant, its illusions, and its hypocrisy. Only then could it play a significant role in a reasonable and just world.

The emphasis upon intellect meant that, in this world at least, the Word of Man should take precedence over the Word of God. The traditional Christian vocation was being lost, and in its place was erected the religion of man. In a truly revolutionary way man now claimed that he had inherited the earth. He was now his own judge and the creator of his own heaven and his own hell. The theologian Karl Barth argued that the eighteenth century gave birth to the idea of "absolute man," which he defines in these words:

> Man, who discovers his own power and ability, the potentiality dormant in his humanity, that is, his human being as such, and looks

upon it as the final, the real and absolute, I mean as something 'detached,' self-justifying, with its own authority and power, which he can therefore set in motion in all directions and without any restraint — this is absolute man.

The New Individualism

Here was an awesome and chilling doctrine. Not all the men of the Enlightenment were aware of the implications of this new individualism, and not all saw where the road from the eighteenth century led. One who was alert to the new direction of historical thinking was the philosopher Immanuel Kant. Kant realized that at the heart of eighteenth-century ideas was the belief that man was capable of mature, independent judgment. According to Kant, an immature man is one who "lacks the courage to use his own intelligence without another person's guidance. Men who remain permanently immature from laziness or cowardice make it easy for others to act as their guardians. How comfortable it is to be a minor!" But the mature man does not need a guardian. He trusts his own intelligence, and he demands the freedom necessary to follow where his intelligence leads. For Kant, there can be no traditional restraints upon the exercise of this freedom. "Enlightenment requires freedom, the possibility of applying one's own reason freely and publicly. But I hear voices calling from all sides: 'Don't argue!' The officer says: Don't argue — drill! The Clerk of the Treasury says: Don't argue — pay! The clergyman says: Don't argue — believe!" For those influenced by the doctrines of the eighteenth century such a situation was intolerable. There should be no drilling, no paying, and no believing unless such decisions sprang from the individual's own choice and resulted from his own deliberate judgment. Worthwhile actions cannot come from compulsion, and all binding obligations must be self-imposed.

Kant argued that man's freedom is not beholden to nature, society, or God. Man has absolute autonomy, even in relation to an omnipotent and just deity. True freedom is as hostile to slavish subservience to God as it is to subservience to society or nature. The only salvation available to man is that which he himself, by his own efforts, achieves. Man is the end of this world, not a means to something else, and he is responsible for deciding what that end will be. A man's vision of life is characteristic of his mind, and the forms by which we recognize experience are derived from the mind and not from God or nature. For Kant, the human mind is neither a degenerate offspring of the divine nor an accident of the cosmic order of nature. Rather it is creator of both the cosmos and the divine. It is man who gives order to the world. He projects values into it. And, because it is his world, and he is responsible for it, all appeals to external authority, secular or religious, are rejected. Neither nature nor God redeemed man. Rather man's task is to redeem nature, and even God. The final authority is what Kant calls the categorical imperative of the individual conscience, of the individual moralized will. There is nothing above this, and there can be no appeal from it.

Kant's speculations clearly showed the bitter reality that lay behind the theoretical ideas of the eighteenth century. Kant realized that man's traditional moorings were being cut away and that he was being left alone to face the storm of his life and his history. Man was now removed from the protection of any traditional shelter and freed from allegiance to any custom or law that violated his inner sense of duty and his moral reason. In the present-day sense of the word, Kant had described the alienated individual. Separated from his God, from his society if it did not satisfy the demands of his conscience, and from other men, each of whom was as free as he, modern man was divorced from his past and left to find his way into an unknown future.

The arguments posed by Kant and the other thinkers of the eighteenth century were so fundamental to any interpretation of life and history that they aroused the deepest emotions and subjected Western society to a shattering, centuries-long controversy. In 1765 the French Assembly of the Clergy issued its first condemnation of the literature of the Enlightenment, which it argued would, if not checked, undermine all religious, political, and social order. A contemporary of Voltaire's attacked the philosophers of the Enlightenment by pointing out that "their frightful ideas overturn and destroy every religious principle, there is no God or king, or faith or law." Since that time an important part of Western history has consisted of attempts to develop, modify, or abandon the ideas and institutions proposed by the eighteenth-century radicals.

Much of this historical quarreling concerned a few of the most important ideas of the Enlightenment. Was the eighteenth-century view of man simple and superficial? Was man basically an intelligent human being, capable of living largely by reason? The optimistic and secular bent of the century in great part ignored man's distinctly religious quest and failed, in the minds of many, to account for the problem of human evil. Could man, through education and conditioning, exorcise the turbulence in his soul and without the hope of heaven or the fear of hell become a member of a humane, tolerant society? Could he face the strains of his historical and personal existence without reference to a religious explanation?

The Legacy of the Enlightenment

It is easy to criticize the ideas of the eighteenth century. The recent experience of Western man has shown that a dedication to change can be an instrument of retrogression as well as of social and political advance. The consequences of revolution have been, in part at least, quite different from what had been expected. Kant, Jefferson, Voltaire, and others were convinced that the human mind could be liberated from the bondage of superstition, ignorance, and bigotry and that men could create a truly human community based upon the fusing of reason and morality, a community exhibiting a passion for humanity and decency and a hatred of fanaticism and stupidity. But the promise of a future where all men could actively participate in a culture of incomparable power and originality has in large part remained an illusion. In 1775 the last unfortunate old woman was burned as a witch in Western Europe. But since then Western man has shown an ability to commit crimes that make this episode a petty misdemeanor. The history of the West since the eighteenth century has been one of political triumph, material success and scientific accomplishment, and worldwide influence. It has also been one of intellectual dishonesty and cowardice, unimaginable criminality, and never-ending discontent. There has been painless surgery, vaccination and antitoxins, an extension of literacy, the franchise, and economic opportunity, and the abolition of human slavery and serfdom. There has also been squalor, rootlessness, hysteria, and a promiscuity of values.

But any attempt to arrive at an equal distribution of benefits and losses traceable to the eighteenth-century Enlightenment is a sterile undertaking. The liberal, reforming, scientific ideas of the century opened the door to what for most of us is a treasured part of our lives. Louis I. Bredvold, in *The Brave New World of the Enlightenment*, has had the courage to state a powerful historical fact: "the Enlightenment was the period when Europe really emerged from the Middle Ages and the Modern Mind was born." The important men of the century were engaged in a struggle for personal liberty, legal equality, and freedom of thought and expression. This struggle was so obvious, and so important, that we can have little patience with those who ignore these characteristics or dismiss them as of little consequence. Alfred Cobban has listed the ethical contributions of the Enlightenment, and his list is a good one:

> the principle of religious toleration came to be affirmed; torture, taken for granted from time immemorial as a necessary adjunct to civil and religious society, was discredited; war was no longer regarded as a necessary evil; slavery was denounced; utilitarianism proclaimed that

the object of government was the greatest happiness of the greatest number.

We have lived so long in a world where these principles have been reduced to cliches and to unexamined, rehearsed political responses that we forget how fantastically revolutionary they were — and, in some cases, still are. The noted French historian Marc Bloch wrote of what we call the Middle Ages: "Beneath all social life there was a soil of primitivism, of submission to ungovernable powers." This fated quality, this belief that some religious, environmental, or historical circumstance reduced man to a largely helpless and passive creature, has been true of the great civilizations of the past. Such an idea was anathema to the men of the Enlightenment. In 1734 Voltaire wrote: "I dare to take the side of humanity." What he meant by this statement was that the brutal and traditional restraints to which men had been subjected for so long were archaic and demeaning, that they no longer provided an acceptable interpretation of life. Voltaire and others were convinced that many of what we would call the historical controls exercised on men were fraudulent and had outlived their usefulness. They were contrary to the scientific and intellectual currents of the time and must be abandoned. In 1693 John Locke, in his essay "Some Thoughts Concerning Education," had written: "Men's happiness or misery is in most part of their own making." During the next one hundred years there was to be an ever-increasing demand that men be allowed to create their own happiness, and the Enlightenment "offered the first program in the history of mankind for the construction of a human community out of natural materials alone."

The Enlightenment was the result of a long development in European history. Its roots were in the restless, speculative, free European intelligence, and the ideas of the Enlightenment had been sheltered and nourished by the great European tradition of Christianity, classicism, and ordered liberty. But the Enlightenment threatened the traditional "idea of Europe," not only because of its concepts, but, more importantly, because of its dedication to translating thought into action. As Ernst Cassirer pointed out many years ago, eighteenth-century thought "consists not only in analyzing and dissecting, but in actually bringing about the order of things which it conceives as necessary." Peter Gay defines the philosophy of the Enlightenment as "the mobilization of sound thinking for the sake of right living." The famous opening paragraphs of the American Declaration of Independence contained little that had not been stated many times before. The difference was that the Americans were determined to implement these explosive ideas. Many Europeans, for many centuries, had asked the question posed by d'Holbach as to why the majority of people must "work without respite to satisfy the vanity, the luxury, the greed of a pack of useless and corrupt blood-suckers." But Holbach expected action to follow upon his statement, and the intellectual climate of the time supported him in this expectation. Science, the confidence in reason, and the faith in education were new weapons that were to break the limits of the established European civilization. Perhaps it is best to see the Enlightenment as part of traditional European history, as Friedrich Heer believes, "the last great flowering of the Christian political humanism of Western Europe." But it must also be seen as something else. And Heer goes on: "The millennium of the 'grand form' was coming to a close, and another world was rising."

One important result of the Enlightenment was that it contributed substantially to the fragmentation of Europe. After the eighteenth century it became more and more a fiction to argue that there was a general European consciousness or a European sense of identity. The Enlightenment dramatically severed one part of Europe from the rest. France, England, the Low Countries, some of the Swiss cantons, America, some of the British overseas colonies, to some extent Scandinavia, and parts of Germany participated in the Enlightenment and became the early geographical area of modern Western civilization. The ideas of the Enlightenment did attract attention in other parts of Europe, but they did not take root there, and borrowed ideas and institutions were warped and frustrated. It was the Enlightenment more than anything else that separated Spain, Italy, the Austrian Hapsburg Empire, Russia, and great parts of Germany from what we call the modern Western world. And throughout the greater part of what we call the modern period this was to remain true. As Alfred Cobban points out, the ideas of the Enlightenment "have survived in those nations of Western Europe, and their overseas extensions, where they first became influential." The Enlightenment thus set the geographical stage and provided the intellectual impetus for the modern Western historical adventure.

Many of the important aspects of the Enlightenment can be profitably studied by examinations of significant men of the period. Sir Isaac Newton was responsible for the new scientific interpretation that profoundly influenced the eighteenth century. Voltaire was the leading social and political critic of his time. Thomas Jefferson was most successful in translating what was regarded as right thought into right action.

Isaac Newton

On March 20, 1727, Sir Isaac Newton died. He was mourned in England as a national hero, and his body was buried in Westminster Abbey. The Lord High Chancellor of England, two dukes, and three earls acted as pallbearers, and the poet Alexander Pope wrote two lines that he intended as an epitaph for Newton's tomb:

> Nature and Nature's laws lay hid in night
> God said, *Let Newton Be!* and all was light

These expressions of admiration were genuine. Newton was regarded by many as the first man of his time. His countryman, the political philosopher John Locke, had called him "the incomparable Mr. Newton," and a famous French astronomer and mathematician was to describe Newton's scientific work as "pre-eminent above any other production of human genius." Voltaire reported that "Very few people read Newton, because it is necessary to be learned to understand him. But everybody talks about him." And Thomas Jefferson once remarked to John Adams and Alexander Hamilton that Newton was one of the three great geniuses of all time.

Newton's personal life was not particularly dramatic or colorful. Some fanciful and false stories have been associated with him, the best known that he became conscious of the law of gravity when an apple fell on his head. He was at times a quarrelsome man and at others kind and considerate. He was a university teacher and in 1699 was appointed the chief administrative officer of the British mint. He was president of the British Royal Society (The Royal Society of London for the Promotion of Natural Knowledge) from 1703 until his death and in 1705 was knighted. His writing style was dry and pedantic, although he was capable of occasional eloquence and could write sentences such as the following: "I do not know what I may appear to the world; but to myself I seem to have been only like a boy playing on the sea-shore and diverting myself in now and then finding a smoother pebble

31

or prettier shell than ordinary, whilst the great ocean of Truth lay all undiscovered before me."

The important thing, however, was that Newton was the outstanding scientific figure of his age, and his authority, before his time and since, may have been equalled only by that of Aristotle in the late middle ages. Of course, he had predecessors — Copernicus, Kepler, Galileo, Descartes, and others — and Newton himself said: "If I have seen further, it is because I have stood upon the shoulders of giants." The eighteenth century produced many notable scientists: the physicists Coulomb and Lagrange, the chemists Black and Lavoisier, the naturalists Linnaeus and Buffon. Modern biology, modern medicine, and modern chemistry were born during the century and resulted from the efforts of a number of exceptional men. But Newton's position was unchallenged. He was both the culmination of the great scientific thought of the seventeenth century and the initiator of the new scientific age of the eighteenth.

Newton's important scientific contributions appeared in his *Philosophiae naturalis principia mathematica* (The Mathematical Principles of Natural Philosophy), published in 1687, and to a lesser extent in his *Opticks: or a Treatise on the Reflexions, Refractions, Inflexions, and Colours of Light*, published in 1704. In the *Principia* he set down his laws of motion and of mechanics and his observations on gravitation and planetary movement. He explained the patterns of the tides, the paths of comets, and the irregularities in the movement of the moon. He provided new definitions of terms like force and mass, and he described space, time, and motion in a way that became fundamental to an understanding of modern Western science.

The *Principia* is not easy reading. Newton's scientific proofs were designed for specialists. But it is not difficult to grasp his basic general arguments. He was really proposing a new approach to knowledge. He called this the "mathematical way," or the method of "analysis and composition." Analysis consists "in making Experiments and Observations, and drawing conclusions from them." Composition is the stating of the consequences of these "principles" or "laws." According to Newton, a true scientist observes and experiments. He then expresses the results of this observation and experimentation in mathematical terms, or axioms. The method is one of first inquiring "diligently into the properties of things, and establishing these properties by experiments and then to proceed more slowly to hypotheses for the explanation of them." The scientist uses experimental verification and mathematical proof to arrive at a valid interpretation of natural phenomena. But he cannot begin with a hypothesis. "I frame no hypotheses; for whatever is not deduced from the phenomena is to be called an hypothesis; and hypotheses, whether metaphysical or physical, whether of occult qualities or mechanical, have no place in experimental philosophy."

In the *Principia* Newton gives an excellent description of the way in which his method works:

> by the propositions mathematically demonstrated ... we then derive from the celestial phenomena the forces of gravity with which bodies tend to the sun and the several planets. Then from these forces, by other propositions which are also mathematical, we deduce the motions of the planets, the comets, the moon, and the sea. I wish we could derive the rest of the phenomena of nature by the same kind of reasoning from mechanical principles; for I am induced by many reasons to suspect that they may all depend upon certain forces by which the particles of bodies, by some causes hitherto unknown, are either mutually impelled towards each other, and cohere in regular figures, or are repelled and recede from each other; which forces being unknown, philosophers have hitherto attempted the search of nature in vain; but I hope the principles here laid down will afford some light either to that or some truer method of philosophy.

Scientific knowledge thus consists of laws stating the mathematical behavior of nature. Whatever cannot be stated by such laws is not science and can tell us very little about the workings of the physical world.

The *Principia* was well received, although a second edition did not appear until 1713, and the introduction of Newtonian science into university study was not immediate. Scottish universities were the first to adopt the new methodology, followed by English universities. Acceptance outside of Britain was slower, but by the second quarter of the eighteenth century Newton's work was regarded throughout Western Europe as "the most perfect treatise on mechanics that can be imagined." For almost a century after the publication of the *Principia* mathematics, astronomy, and optics were developed along the lines laid down by Newton. In fact, although there were rumblings and the system became increasingly unsatisfactory, it was not until the twentieth century that the Newtonian views of space, time, matter, and energy were drastically revised.

But Newton's reputation was not only related to his scientific accomplishments. The effects of what we call the Newtonian interpretation spread far beyond the scientific laboratory and the classroom. Political, philosophical, and religious attitudes were all influenced by Newton. We can say that the Western world was ready for him, and that he provided many of the things for which the men of the eighteenth century hungered. He stimulated confidence in the capability of the human intellect to understand and describe the world. He offered an ordered universe that operated by laws not by chance. He stressed the stability of nature and, by inference, man. He proposed a method whereby the claims of religion and science could be reconciled. The Newtonian system was described by an enthusiastic French disciple as "exact, profound, luminous, and new." Who could want anything more?

Newton destroyed the grip of magic on the Western world. For centuries men had doubted the rational stability of the earth, and the natural operations of the planet seemed obscure. Nature was regarded as demonic and arbitrary — comets heralded catastrophic events and the movements of the stars were threatening. The end of this fragile world seemed always at hand, and refuge was sought in astrology, alchemy, and witchcraft. Newton, however, pointed out that it was possible for man's intelligence to grasp even the motion of the heavens. His method was a wonderful instrument for the refutation of the obscure, the irrational, and the discouraging. He showed that the mind could measure the universe and that behind the planets and under the waves was no hostile and chaotic force but understandable movement.

This discovery of an ordered and orderly world released Western man from his traditional metaphysical anxiety. He was now assured that natural phenomena were governed not by occult and wayward impulses but by permanent, measurable, and recognizable forces, and that order and harmony were preserved by the laws of space, time, and mass. Nature, Newton pointed out, is "always consistent to itself," and her behavior is uniform and reasonable. Gravity holds the universe together, and the regular movement of the planetary bodies promises the continued existence of the world.

Newton's scientific method had important philosophical implications. In restricting scientific inquiry to what we can observe, measure, and then translate into mathematical axioms, he ignored that painful centuries-long attempt to comprehend the why of the world. According to Newton, we are not to search for an answer to the question: Why is there light? Rather, we are to concentrate upon the problem of how light travels and the pattern of its behavior. We are, in Voltaire's words, "to examine, weigh, calculate, and measure, but never conjecture." Newton "saw and he made people see; but he never put his fancies in place of truth." The American David Rittenhouse praised Newton's method "because it pretends not to be of Nature's privy council, or to have free access to her most inscrutable mysteries; but to attend carefully to her works, to discover the immediate causes of visible effects, to trace those causes to others more general and simple, advancing by slow and sure steps toward the great first cause of all things." This was the way of true knowledge. We must believe what we see and not lose ourselves in the useless attempt to find some answer unrelated to the phenomena themselves.

But this method of explaining our environment had unexpected results. By avoiding metaphysical questions and despiritualizing nature, Newton divested the world of supernatural and even religious meaning. This was not what he intended. He had expected that his scientific philosophy would reconcile God, man, and the world and that scientific inquiry would not detract from God's power but sustain Him in the unchallenged position of "Author and Governor of the universe." Newton was horrified when it appeared that his interpretation might be regarded as irreligious. Five years after the publication of the *Principia*, he stated in a letter to a friend: "When I wrote my treatise about our system, I had an eye upon such principles as might work with considering men for the belief of a Deity, and nothing can rejoice me more than to find it useful for that purpose." Twenty years later, in the second edition of the *Principia*, he included his well-known General Scholium (an added remark), which was designed to quiet any doubts about his attitudes toward religion. Here he wrote: "From his true dominion, it follows that the true God is a living, intelligent, and powerful Being; and from his other perfections, that he is supreme, or most perfect. He is eternal and infinite, omnipotent and omniscient; that is, his duration reaches from eternity to eternity; his presence from infinity to infinity; he governs all things, and knows all things that are or can be done. . . ."

In fact, Newton believed that he had provided the best possible argument for the existence of God. It was obvious to him that "the most beautiful system of sun, planets and comets could only proceed from the counsel and dominion of an intelligent Being." The harmony of nature provided evidence of God, and we may be secure in our knowledge that "The hand that made us is divine." The wonderful concepts of space and time surely show that an all-powerful and all-knowing being has been at work. The most valuable proof of God is thus found in "his most wise and excellent contrivance of things," and we "admire him for his perfections." But we do not speculate upon Him or attempt to define Him or His purposes. The more we learn about God's creation — the world — the closer we shall come to Him, but we cannot know Him directly, for He exists "in a manner not at all human, in a manner not at all corporeal, in a manner utterly unknown to us." All we can do is to examine His works and to be confident that He will not desert us. As an eighteenth-century commentator wrote of Newton's system: "We are, from His works, to seek to know God, and not to pretend to make out the scheme of His conduct from the very deficient ideas we are able to form of that great mysterious Being."

This was a comforting doctrine. But, in spite of his disclaimers, Newton had changed radically the relationship of God and the world. All that traditional European pondering and argument over the definition of God, salvation by grace or works, predestination, and revelation had no place in Newtonian science. Disputes about the way God acted in human affairs had been reduced by Newton to mathematics. Space had become only a matter of geometry, and time was a measurable continuity of number. The richly textured earth that had contained the spirits of the wind and the forests, the mystery of paradise and hell, the direct contact of God and man had been replaced by a world that was hard, cold, and colorless. Divinity had hidden itself behind nature, and for the passion of Christ and the close and immediate wrath and mercy of God, Newton had substituted the great watchmaker, who still had his eye on the fall of the sparrow but whose interest was impersonal and abstract. God was no longer the final cause but the first, and He was not at the end of the world but at its beginning. The German philosopher Gottfried von Leibniz, who carried on an extended controversy with Newton and his supporters, was certainly correct when he claimed that from the point of view of a deeply religious person Newton had "a very odd opinion of the work of God." A century after the publication of the *Principia*, the English poet William Blake, speaking to the same subject, dismissed Newton as one of "The Scoffers," whose intellectualized and desiccated interpretation had failed to account for man's religious nature and whose "particles of light" were only insignificant "sands upon the Red Sea shore."

But what Leibniz, Blake, and others saw as a reprehensible analysis, many accepted thankfully. By the beginning of the eighteenth century most European intellectuals had tired of the long and apparently fruitless search for an absolute knowledge of God. They were dissatisfied with attempts to discover transcendental reasons for natural events. They wished for some kind of explanation that would provide order and be reasonable. They hoped to retain their belief in and their reverence for God but to free themselves of what they regarded as the obscure and ambiguous nature of religious revelation. They desired a God strong enough to work miracles but not arbitrary or contradictory. They wanted a world they could understand and that provided them with the opportunity to exercise their intellect and their ambitions.

Newton's interpretation provided all these things. He separated science and theology without — at least in his own mind — setting them against each other. He argued that the proper task of man was to know the laws of nature, while that of God was to maintain them. Thus both had important responsibilities. Even morality had a place in the Newtonian system, for as we learn about God's creations, we come closer to Him and we are improved. Most important, perhaps, Newton's interpretation of an ordered world provided a stimulus to a new kind of politics, philosophy, and history. The earth was now largely turned over to those who inhabited it, and they were free to examine, describe, and even change it under the general protection of a most benign deity.

Voltaire

The years from 1725 to 1775 are often called the age of Voltaire. Yet it may appear difficult to justify such a description. As a philosopher Voltaire cannot equal David Hume or Immanuel Kant. His influence as a political thinker cannot match that of Jean-Jacques Rousseau or Thomas Jefferson. He was not a highly original man, and some have argued that he even lacked moral stature. Moreover, many of the accomplishments that made him famous in his day no longer seem significant. With the exception of his novel *Candide*, his literary work strikes us as dated and stale. His histories are largely unread. Much of his polemical writing scandalized Europe. But we are not offended. In fact, we remember him best as a wit, a man with the pithy remark, the sly phrase, the memorable epigram, and associate him with comments such as "If God did not exist, one would have to invent him" and "History is after all only a pack of tricks we play on the dead."

But Voltaire's contemporaries — his friends and his enemies — realized his importance, and in one area of eighteenth-century life his influence was unquestioned. At a time of intellectual agitation, he was the great agitator. He was the opinion-shaker of the century and has been called "the loudest bell-ringer and the noisiest publicity-seeker in all Europe." And his agitation was to the point. When one sets aside his foppishness, his posing, his egotism, his petty jealousies — all those human frailties that Voltaire possessed in extra measure — he remains a man committed to the major intellectual controversies of his day. More effectively than anyone else he questioned a host of traditional habits and customs. He sincerely hated injustice, cruelty, and what he regarded as "hocus-pocus," and he consistently recognized such things for what they were. What he did, he did better than anyone else. He has been accused of superficiality. But Diderot, an editor of the famous *Encyclopedia*, wrote: "What is it that particularly distinguishes Voltaire from all our young writers? Instruction. Voltaire knows a great deal, and our young poets are ignorant. The work of Voltaire is full of matter, their works are empty." Fifty years after Voltaire's death, Wolfgang von Goethe remarked to a friend: "You have no idea of the significance of Voltaire and his great contemporaries in my youth, and how they dominated the whole civilized world."

Voltaire was born in Paris in 1694. He was educated at a well-known and fashionable Jesuit school and achieved his initial literary success at the age of twenty-four when his first play ran for forty-two performances rather than for the usual five or six nights. At this time he abandoned his given and family name of François-Marie Arouet and adopted that of Voltaire.

From his early years until his death in 1778 Voltaire was on the go. He wrote numerous books, pamphlets, and articles on a variety of subjects. He carried on an extensive correspondence with a large number of people. He knew most of the leading intellectuals of the day, and he maintained a continual interest in the scientific, historical, and philosophical arguments of the century. At any one time he was usually engaged in some personal or ideological quarrel that gained him both admirers and opponents.

He was also constantly on the run. In 1716 he was ordered to leave Paris, and a year later spent eleven months in prison because of some slanderous and defamatory verses that he had written. In 1726 he was beaten by the lackeys of a nobleman with whom he had quarreled, and when Voltaire appeared set upon a duel with the man responsible for this indignity, he was again put into prison and released only upon his promise to leave France. It was on this occasion that a priest advised the French government to lock up Voltaire "within four walls for the rest of his life."

Voltaire now left for England, where he remained for over two years and where he acquired a lifelong admiration for English institutions and political habits. In 1729 he was back in Paris. By 1734 he was again in trouble. His *Philosophical Letters*, which contained his comparisons of England and France — to the detriment of the latter — and his arguments in support of political and religious freedom shocked

French officials. The publication was condemned as "scandalous, contrary to religion, good morals, and the respect due authority," and a copy was publicly burned by the Paris hangman. Voltaire, meanwhile, had prudently left Paris again. For the next fifteen years he lived with the best-known of his mistresses in a chateau in the French countryside. He continued, however, to have problems with the French authorities. At one time he was forced to flee to Holland to escape prosecution, and permission to publish his writings was continually being refused. In response, Voltaire published clandestinely, usually without his name appearing on the publication, and he continually denied that he was the author of works readily recognizable as his. As he remarked, "One is obliged to lie and then one is still persecuted for not having lied enough." From 1719 to 1748 every major writing with the exception of his dramas (although even the play *Mahomet* was withdrawn because it offended against religious proprieties) was illegally printed.

In 1749 his mistress died, and Voltaire returned to Paris. By the next year, however, he was in Prussia as the guest of Frederick the Great. Frederick admired Voltaire, and he himself claimed to be a poet, musician, and philosopher. The relationship between the two men began well enough, but soon soured. They quarreled (Frederick even had one of Voltaire's pamphlets publicly burned), and in 1753 Voltaire left Prussia. He and Frederick were never to see each other again, although after a time they entered into a correspondence that lasted until Voltaire's death.

Voltaire did not think it safe to return to Paris, and a contemporary noted that he "does not seem to know where to lay his head." He wandered from city to city and wrote to his niece: "It is hard to be such an old bird and to have no nest." Then in the late winter of 1754 he settled in Geneva. Here, too, he became involved in controversies over theology, free speech, and municipal politics. He decided to purchase the estate of Ferney just over the French border, so that he could move back and forth depending upon the direction from which any danger might come. Here after 1760 he was to remain (except for occasional visits to nearby localities) for all but the last few months of his life. He became the "Old Invalid of Ferney" — as he described himself — and he wrote some of his most important pieces of propaganda on behalf of freedom of conscience, on the necessity to reform the French judicial system, and on the need to abandon any form of religious fanaticism.

What were the significant and lasting results of this long and turbulent life? Voltaire's clever statements — especially when they are at the expense of a plodding and thick-headed opponent — are still a joy to read. His relationships with his contemporaries still arouse interest. His love affairs and his personal life are an excellent source for those studying the manners and morals of the eighteenth century. But two of his activities are particularly important. One of these was his effort to introduce a new interpretation of history. The other was his attack on organized Christianity.

The eighteenth century was rich in monumental histories, the most important of which were probably David Hume's *History of England*, William Robertson's *History of Scotland*, and Edward Gibbon's *Decline and Fall of the Roman Empire*. Voltaire, however, is usually regarded as the first important eighteenth-century historian. He wrote three major historical works — *The History of Charles XII* (1731), *The Age of Louis XIV* (1751), and the *Essay on the Manners and Spirit of Nations* (1756). In his writing he attempted to redefine history and to present an interpretation that exhibited his ethical bent and his faith in the intellectual capacity of men to understand the past and to relate it to the present.

Voltaire believed that earlier attempts to account for men's historical experience had largely failed and were really nothing but the repetitious recording of acts of cruelty, injustice, and bigotry. History had been restricted to a study of wars, kings, and boundary disputes, as if the "globe on which we live is one vast scene of carnage and destruction" and as if the human adventure consisted of nothing but the activities of "tigers" and "monkeys." Moreover, falsehoods had been incorporated into what passed for history in order to justify the so-called heroic deeds of largely mythical kings and conquerors. The result was a collection of fables, superstitions, and ridiculous tales that darkened the human mind and kept men from understanding who they were and what had happened to them. Most important, and destructive, was the fact that history had become associated with political and religious dogmas that attempted to bind men to some outlandish interpretation of themselves and their world. Most historians had been liars who were interested in supporting some erroneous dogma or some self-serving political authority. They had excused every conceivable cruelty in order to justify the subjugation of mankind. As a result "the human race has nothing to show for a hundred battles that have been waged," and the glorification of war and conquest had misled people into believing that those who have been only "the plunderers of the provinces" should be recognized as heroes.

In place of what he regarded as a collection of fables and errors, Voltaire proposed a new type of history. First, it must be factually correct. As he once wrote: "The majority of historians, instead of discussing facts with men, tell stories to children." In Voltaire's view, such "stories" were more than the misrepresentation of actual happenings.

They were replete with all sorts of improbabilities, supernatural occurrences, and mysterious explanations. Such things must be eliminated, and nothing contrary to our common sense can be accepted as historically correct. If a historian tells us that a Christian king killed 360,000 Moslems or that another ruler became insane when he stole the arm of a saint's statue, we need read no further, for he will have nothing of consequence to say. Obscure and improbable statements are no more acceptable in history than they would be in a scientific treatise.

Voltaire also criticized the sources commonly used by historians. All authorities who may have a special bias should be distrusted. In particular, those who were themselves involved in any activity are certain to be unreliable because of their tendency to disguise their own failings with extravagant accounts of their successes. Even eyewitnesses may be wrong, for most men see what they want to see or what they are told to see, and, as he writes, even the depositions of 12,000 men can only be accepted as a probability. What Voltaire called "monuments" and "festivals" should especially be distrusted. These are almost certain to be the results of human pride, arrogance, and deceit, and "in general, be sure that when you see an old festival, or an antique temple, that they are works of error."

But Voltaire's interpretation was more than a mere discourse upon the prevalence of factual error. He believed that a new approach to the writing of history was necessary. In place of a record of wars and princely doings, he proposed what we would call intellectual and social history. "Ideas," he argued, "have changed the world," and history is primarily the conflict of ideas and the continual expansion of human understanding through the triumph of reason and common sense. As he wrote, "My principal object is to know, so far as I can, the manners of peoples, and to study the human mind; I shall regard the order of succession of kings and chronology as my guides, but not as the object of my work." There was a progression to men's affairs, and this could be examined best by looking at the ideas that accounted for laws, forms of government, and changes in institutions, manners, and customs. But these important matters had slipped through the fingers of the antiquarian and the chronicler of heroic deeds. Therefore, a new approach must be taken. "I would like to discover what human society was like, how people lived in the intimacy of the family, and what arts were cultivated, rather than repeat the story of so many misfortunes and military combats — the dreary subject matter of history and the common currency of human perversity."

Voltaire's interpretation of history was an excellent example of the attitude of the men of the Enlightenment. His emphasis upon man's intellectual ability to understand his past and his present was basic to the thought of the century. His attack upon what he regarded as myth and upon religious obscurantism found a ready audience. During the century history became increasingly an intellectual exercise, and this practice was to remain a common characteristic of Western civilization. History was divorced from theology in a way that would have been incomprehensible to men of earlier centuries, and it did take as its subject matter much more than the lives of heroes and the recording of wars. The concept of history as a conflict of ideas became the accepted approach, and it became habitual for Western man to regard historical actions as primarily the expressions of ideological conflict.

Voltaire also exhibited the century's general belief in the possibility of improvement. He was no naive optimist — "If this is the best of all possible worlds, what are the others like?" is one of his memorable sentences. But he rejected any idea of history as an unending cycle of repetitious events, as he dismissed any belief that men were fated to live generation after generation as the victims of an unchanging historical environment. He continually stressed the miseries of the past and the possibility of happiness in the present and the future. His histories do have a moral: Men may escape the age-old round of brutality and crime if they will follow the dictates of common sense and compassion. Thus the important historical figures are those who have contributed to the progress of mankind. "I call great men all those who have excelled in creating what is useful or agreeable," writes Voltaire. History is primarily the study of man's efforts to improve himself and his circumstances, and anything that does not contribute to this end is historically unimportant. "Just as it is necessary to know the great actions of kings who have changed the face of the earth, and especially those who have improved the condition of their peoples, so also we ought to ignore the vulgar crowd of kings who would only serve to burden the memory." History was instruction, which showed the errors of the past in order that they might be avoided in the present. It illustrated the folly of military conquest, the stupidity of religious fanaticism, and the shame of injustice. And it pointed the way whereby men might achieve happiness — which Voltaire identified with peace, security, good laws, and material well-being.

His interpretation of history was closely connected to Voltaire's attack upon Christianity, and it was his attitude toward Christian theology and Christian institutions that aroused the anger of many people, in his day and since. He was condemned as a blasphemer, "a kind of monster in society, who feels no obligation toward its manners and morals, its proprieties, its politics, or its religion." Some well-meaning people have attempted to soften or even obscure his abundantly documented hostility. But the evidence is overwhelming. He did compose crude and clever blasphemies upon the Christian mass and the idea of the trinity. He did write that "every sensible man, every honorable man, must hold the Christian sect in horror." His reputation as the great opponent of organized Christianity was deserved, and for two decades he adopted the habit of ending his letters with the well-understood phrase "écrasez l'infâme" (crush the monster).

Voltaire regarded the various European churches (he attacked Catholics, Protestants, and Jews with equal fervor) as expressions of superstition and fanaticism. The Bible was the most improbable of books, nothing but a long and repetitious chronicle of stupidity and fear. Christian fanaticism had resulted in a history of crimes against mankind. Several times Voltaire attempted to draw up a list of the number of people who had been killed by those attempting to forward the Christian faith. He usually arrived at a figure in excess of nine million. And he argued that most of these victims of intolerance had lost their lives over theological differences that neither they nor their oppressors understood. In one of his writings he has a Chinese official (obviously representing himself) listen to a religious dispute among a Jesuit, a Quaker, an Anglican, a Lutheran, a Puritan, a Moslem, and a Jew. After hearing their incomprehensible arguments, the official has them all confined to an insane asylum. As Voltaire once wrote: "Theology amuses me; that's where we find the madness of the human spirit in all its plenitude."

Voltaire's own religious beliefs were based upon his conviction that the existence of the world demonstrated the presence of God, and he frequently expressed his admiration for the creator of what he saw about him. He was awed by what he described as "the everlasting regulation of stars, the perpetual miracle of generation." And he saw himself as a true believer. "I am not an atheist, nor a superstitious person. I stand for common sense and the golden mean. I believe in God — not the God of the mystics and the theologians, but the God of Nature, the great geometrician, the architect of the universe, the prime mover, unalterable, transcendental, everlasting." In 1774 a visitor accompanied Voltaire, then eighty years old, to a high hill to observe the sunrise. Voltaire is reported to have taken off his hat and to have said: "I believe, I believe in you! Powerful God, I believe!" Then he turned to his companion and remarked dryly: "As for Monsieur the Son and Madam His Mother, that's a different story."

Voltaire's opposition to what he thought of as Christian fanaticism was sincere. He believed that the influence of organized Christianity had a deleterious effect upon political, social, and intellectual life. Christianity was the enemy of progress, learning, reason, decency, and humanity, and any close connection of religion and politics was disastrous. Therefore, the church must be driven out of public life, and its influence in political affairs abolished. He saw much of the suffering of his times as a result of the attempt of Christianity to enforce its doctrine through the instruments of political control. Political foul play was closely associated with religious persecution, and the privileged orders of society — the nobility and the clergy — were united in maintaining an obsolete and cruel ideology that hindered any attempt to forward liberty and justice.

In the 1760's a series of famous legal cases brought Voltaire into a head-on conflict with organized Christianity that lasted until his death. In the most famous of these, the Calas case, a Huguenot father was accused of having killed his son rather than allow the boy to become a Catholic. There was no evidence to support such a charge. But the elder Calas was declared guilty, broken on the wheel, and then strangled by the executioner. Voltaire's cry of outrage at this combination of ritualistic superstition and legal mayhem made the Calas name famous throughout France. In another case, a nineteen-year-old man was accused of mutilating a wooden crucifix and of making blasphemous remarks. He was found guilty, tortured, and then beheaded. His body was publicly burned, and a copy of Voltaire's *Philosophical Dictionary* was thrown on the flames. So it went, year after year, case after case, and Voltaire was untiring in his efforts to break the power of the church in legal and political affairs.

Voltaire was no revolutionary in the sense that he wished to overthrow the political structure of the French state. In fact, he supported the strengthening of the authority of the king at the expense of the nobility. He had no taste for violent upheavals and relied upon gradual reform and general enlightenment. In 1775 he wrote: "We would have to overthrow the whole world to put it under the government of philosophy. Hence, the only recourse that remains is to prevent the fanatics from becoming too dangerous." Fanaticism was the real danger, and this fanaticism was based upon superstition. He once proposed what we could regard as a Voltairian law of history. "The fewer superstitions, the less fanaticism; and the less fanaticism, the fewer calamities."

The methods Voltaire proposed to control fanaticism were practical but important. In spite of all his comings and goings and his contradictions, his central ideas during his last twenty years were remarkably consistent. He advocated a legal system that would control men — not to forward their salvation or to punish them for their sinful thoughts but to secure public order. He pressed for freedom of speech, a humane legal code, and religious tolerance. Crimes of "heresy" must be abolished, and there must be no secrecy at trials. Torture must end for it cannot produce truth, and the common reliance upon "half-proofs" was ridiculous. "As there are half-proofs, that is to say, half-truths, it is clear that there are half-innocent and half-guilty persons. So we start by giving them a half-death, after which we go to lunch."

In February, 1778, Voltaire left Ferney for Paris. His reception after twenty-seven years' absence from the city so closely associated with him and the Enlightenment was overwhelming. He was acclaimed as "the man of Calas," a hero who had carried on a long struggle for law reform, religious tolerance, and free speech. Old friends and new greeted him. Benjamin Franklin, the representative in France of the rebelling American colonies, brought his grandson to see Voltaire, who blessed the boy with the words, "God and liberty." After what he called "thirty years of absence and sixty years of persecution," Voltaire sensed at least a measure of success. "At last men are enlightening themselves," he wrote. He may have been more optimistic than circumstances warranted. But a drastic intellectual change had taken place during his lifetime, and Voltaire had played an important part in bringing about that change. "By the bells he rang and the fireworks he set off, he rallied the minds of the century," writes a French historian in what must be an unquestionable summary of Voltaire's activities. In late May Voltaire, "wrapped up in eighty-four years and eighty-four maladies," as he described himself, became seriously ill. On May 30 he died.

Thomas Jefferson

We usually think of the men of the Enlightenment as "philosophers" or "philosophes" — men of ideas, speculation, and learning. But they were generally not cloistered thinkers who shunned the hubbub of public places. Rather they regarded themselves as men especially qualified to act, as well as to speak, on behalf of mankind.

Of all the important figures of the Enlightenment, Thomas Jefferson was most successful in achieving this unity of thought and action. Born in 1743 in Virginia, Jefferson drafted the American Declaration of Independence and was successively governor of Virginia, Secretary of State in George Washington's Cabinet, Vice-President, and third President of the United States. He was instrumental in securing the passage in 1786 of the Statute for Religious Freedom in Virginia and used his influence to force acceptance of the Bill of Rights (the first ten amendments to the Constitution). His purchase of the Louisiana Territory from Napoleon in 1803 determined, almost at one move, that the United States would span the continent, and his establishment of the University of Virginia in 1819 was the most important early American expression of the idea of publicly supported higher education. He lived the dream of many of his contemporaries and participated in the actual building of what was in many respects a new society.

Jefferson was not a uniquely creative man or even a profound thinker. He leaned heavily upon popular intellectual opinions, and his talent lay in the application of these opinions to particular circumstances. He has been called a sensitized mind that picked up and transmitted every novel vibration. He himself knew this, and in 1825 he wrote of the Declaration of Independence: "Neither aiming at originality of principles and sentiments, nor yet copied from any particular and previous writing, it was intended to be an expression of the American mind. All its authority rests then on the harmonizing sentiments of the day, whether expressed in conversation, in letters, printed essays, or the elementary books of public right, as Aristotle, Cicero, Locke, Sidney, etc."

Jefferson illustrated, in an exaggerated form, the intellectual curiosity that marked the Enlightenment. He was interested in almost everything and was called by a contemporary "the greatest rubber-off of dust that I ever met with." He was a scientist and an inventor, an architect, the owner of one of the largest private libraries of his time, and a progressive agriculturist. He was a student of meteorology, chemistry, archeology, vertebrate paleontology, applied mechanics, and the classics. He wrote an analysis of the fossil remains of the first giant sloth found in North America and the first detailed description of the pecan. His *Notes on Virginia*, published originally in Paris in 1786, was the first comprehensive study of a specific geographical section of the United States. He studied the making of Parmesan cheese, collected recipes for the use of macaroni, planted Italian orange trees, and introduced Merino sheep from Spain. He compiled vocabularies of the American Indian dialects, invented the mould board plow and the swivel chair, and designed a four-sided music stand for string quartets. In 1796 he was elected president of the American Philosophical Society and served in that office until 1815 (during eight of these years he was also President of the United States). His well-known instructions to Meriwether Lewis in 1803, when Lewis and Clark were preparing to begin their exploration of the recently acquired Louisiana Territory, indicate the scope of Jefferson's interests. Lewis was charged to study the commerce of the Indians as well as their languages, traditions, religions, and diseases. He was to compile information on the soil, the animals, and the minerals and to record the proportion of rainy, cloudy, and clear days and the time of appearance of birds, reptiles, and insects. Everything, in fact, that might bear upon the ways of mankind was to be noted.

This curiosity, this yearning to know, was an important part of the Jeffersonian vision. The world was a great treasurehouse provided for man in order that he might better live on this earth. There were no forbidden areas of learning, no inscrutable mysteries, no sacred secrets. As a young man Jefferson described himself as one "bold in the pursuit of knowledge, never fearing to follow truth and reason to whatever results they led," and many years later he dedicated the University of Virginia to the "illimitable freedom of the human mind to explore and expose every subject susceptible to its contemplation." Knowledge was the great instrument for unlocking the future, and much of what we think of as the Jeffersonian interpretation of history is closely related to his awesome faith in the power of the human mind to master circumstances. His attitude toward the past, his suspicion of religion, his attack upon political and social aristocracy, his faith in education, and his concept of America were all rooted solidly in his confidence in man's intellectual capacity and his belief that intellectual effort could remake the world.

It is possible both to exaggerate and to ignore Jefferson's antagonism toward the past and especially toward Europe. His admiration for classical literature — "this rich source of delight," as he described it — remained with him all his life. He was fascinated by Roman architecture, and claimed that "antiquity has left us the finest models for imitation." He acknowledged the importance of English libertarian thought and French philosophical speculation and often expressed his respect for the cultural and scientific achievements of Europe. During the five years he spent in France in the 1780's, Jefferson kept a steady shipment of books, pamphlets, and latest mechanical inventions (watches, telescopes, a portable copying machine, an umbrella, and phosphoric matches) — all those examples of the European genius — moving across the Atlantic to America. When searching for a faculty for the newly founded University of Virginia, he turned principally to

England because of his belief that in most areas of learning Americans had not reached "a level with those of Europe." Jefferson was too alert to the awesome things going on everywhere and too much a citizen of the world to engage in any wholesale repudiation of the accomplishments of earlier centuries or of the European experience.

Yet this regard for the past was modified significantly by Jefferson's hostility toward many traditional ideas and institutions. In 1941 the American writer John Dos Passos published an article devoted largely to Jefferson's famous home Monticello. It was entitled "A Portico Facing the Wilderness," and the title could be used to describe Jefferson's general attitude. Influenced by Europe, he looked away from the Old World without rejecting it. But he was oriented toward the wilderness of the future rather than the certainties of the past, and he warned against "the Gothic idea that we are to look backwards instead of forward for the improvement of the human mind." The past had its glories, and these should be respected. But part of that past consisted of outdated and erroneous ideas, persistent remains of oppressive historical patterns that condemned men to a fateful round of "oppression, rebellion, reformation, oppression. . . ." One of Jefferson's best-known sentences was "I like the dreams of the future better than the history of the past," and this was no bombastic rhetoric. In 1789 he wrote to a friend, "The earth belongs to the living generation," and in this simple explosive declaration he expressed the point of view that dominated his thinking and his activity.

That part of the past that was a burden and a threat to "the living generation" must be abandoned. What this meant in practice was that all political, social, and religious ideas and institutions that could be broadly described as aristocratic were declared obsolete by Jefferson. Almost all of the significant intellectual leaders of the Enlightenment had expressed serious doubts about the validity of aristocratic institutions, and a growing murmur of discontent over aristocratic pretensions characterized the eighteenth century. But few important European political thinkers had declared their intentions of eradicating "every fibre of ancient and future aristocracy." Jefferson, however, was the declared enemy of any "monarchical and aristocratic party." He was determined to prevent the creation of any land-owning and military-oriented European nobility in America. There was to be no king (Jefferson even feared that the office of the president might be used by some to introduce a monarchy into the United States), no royal trappings, no ecclesiastical officials, and no "artificial aristocracy founded upon wealth and birth." Practices such as entail (the system whereby landed estates were perpetuated no matter the inefficiency and extravagance of owners and the claims of creditors) and primogeniture (the method of passing estates from eldest son to eldest son without any possibility of equal partition among heirs), which might provide the basis for a future aristocracy, were not to be tolerated, and Jefferson succeeded in abolishing these customs in Virginia where a land-owning caste had developed.

There was one particular aspect of the past that Jefferson opposed consistently all his life. This was the traditional identification of religion and politics. The unity of altar and crown had been the common European pattern, and Christianity had become part of what we would call the political establishment. Jefferson believed that this arrangement must be terminated and that church and state must be separated. He was himself what could be described as a quiet Christian. He was baptized, married, and buried according to the rites of the Anglican Church, and he regarded Christianity as "a religion of all others most friendly to liberty, science, and the freest expansion of the human mind." But he had no confidence in the results of religious revelation, and he confined his personal beliefs to the acceptance of a single, perfect God, a future state of rewards and punishments, and an identity of the love of God and the love of man. Our religious duties were primarily moral ones, and "we may promote the happiness of those with whom He has placed us in society, by acting honestly toward all, benevolently to those who fall within our way, respecting sacredly their rights, bodily and mental, and cherishing especially their freedom of conscience, as we value our own."

This "freedom of conscience," however, meant that no political authority may make religious belief a condition of active citizenship any more than it may make any liberty dependent upon "our opinions in physics or geometry." Political power cannot be used to forward religious ideas, and "coercion is a departure from the plan of the holy author of our religion." Freedom of religion must mean the freedom of "the Jew and Gentile, the Christian and Mahometan, the Hindoo and Infidel of every denomination." Jefferson never wavered on this argument against state religion. The Statute for Religious Freedom in Virginia (which with the Declaration of Independence and the establishment of the University of Virginia Jefferson regarded as his most important historical contributions) stated plainly and without ambiguity the Jeffersonian attitude toward religious beliefs as a test for citizenship. "That no man shall be compelled to frequent or support any religious worship, place, or ministry whatsoever, nor shall be enforced, restrained, molested, or burdened in his body or goods, nor shall otherwise suffer on account of his religious opinions or belief; but that all men shall be free to profess, and by argument to maintain, their opinions in matters of religion, and that the same shall in no wise diminish, enlarge, or affect their civil capacities."

The significance of the Jeffersonian attack upon aristocracy and state religion is often lost on us, and we fail to realize how revolutionary it was. Europe since its early days (and this has been equally true of most other cultures of which we know) had been identified with the activities and attitudes of a secular and religious aristocracy. A royal line of kings, counts, nobles, and barons, united by marriage, ownership of land, and military exploits, had been accepted as a necessary and important part of society. And alongside the assorted royalty had stood the powerful ecclesiastical leaders who were responsible for the true faith and were the guardians of the spiritual values embodied in the society. This arrangement was now declared at an end.

Jefferson's animosity toward any traditional — or what he called unnatural — aristocracy was sincere, as was his belief that religious opinions were not the proper concern of civil authorities. But his political philosophy was also influenced by a suspicion of all institutionalized instruments designed to control men. He even toyed with the idea that the best condition for men might be without government at all, for in "every government on earth is some trace of human weakness, some germ of corruption and degeneracy, which cunning will discover, and wickedness insensibly open, cultivate and improve." Political organization was always oppressive, and those exercising political power would inevitably use that power to coerce, to threaten, and to suppress.

Jefferson realized that the abolition of government was impossible. So he proposed to hedge in those in positions of power and to hobble their activities. By nature all men holding power are predatory, and "our legislators," he wrote in 1816, "are not sufficiently apprised of the rightful limits of their powers." Thus Jefferson demanded that the Constitution contain a bill of rights that would restrict the power of political authority. Freedom of religion, freedom of the press, the right to trial by jury, protection against unlawful search and inhuman and cruel treatment, the right to refuse to testify against oneself — all these were obstacles to the exercise of authority at the expense of the citizens. He never doubted that "a bill of rights is what the people are entitled to against every government on earth, general and particular, and what no just government shall refuse, or rest on inference."

Jefferson also proposed other methods of controlling the activities of political leaders. One of these was his argument that men did not give up their rights when they entered into society and that citizens always reserved "to themselves personally the exercise of all rightful powers to which they are competent, and to delegate those to which they are not competent to deputies named, and removable for unfaithful conduct, by themselves immediately." By making government the business of the governed in a way that was really new in history, Jefferson hoped to make political authority so weak, so temporary, so apprehensive of the wrath of the governed, that its natural tendency to act the tyrant would be thwarted.

The strongest defense, however, against any encroachment upon the human conscience or upon human freedom was education. Jefferson had a truly remarkable faith in education, and it is difficult to find any other individual in history who believed as deeply in its values. He saw his political beliefs, his historical interpretations, and his democratic theories directly related to the success of his educational ideas. In 1799 in a letter to a student at William and Mary College he wrote: "I join you . . . in branding as cowardly the idea that the human mind is incapable of further advances. This is precisely the doctrine which the present despots of the earth are inculcating and their friends here re-echoing; and applying essentially to religion and politics. . . ." Education will make the people ready "to understand their rights, to maintain them, and to exercise with intelligence their parts in self-government." Jefferson's writings abound with schemes for education, and he was ultimately to look upon his educational efforts as the most important activity of his life. Society, he argued, had the responsibility to provide educational opportunities for all citizens, and he proposed a system of public education that stretched from the grammar schools to state universities. He even advocated — unsuccessfully — a national university. He believed that education should be secular, practical as well as speculative, and closely tied to the local communities. It should be free of coercion (Jefferson seems always to have had a horror of the brutal pedant), and it should be experimental, continually changing in response to new problems and new opportunities. He himself advocated new courses in Anglo-Saxon and political science and was responsible for establishing the first law professorship in America (the second in the modern Western world) at William and Mary College. Jefferson largely assumed that education and enlightenment must go hand in hand, as must also education and freedom, and education and democracy.

The dream of a new world was an important part of Enlightenment thinking, and Jefferson believed that he had participated in the realization of such a dream. Men had broken with their history and engaged in something new, and "before the establishment of the American States, nothing was known to history but the man of the old world, crowded within limits either small or overcharged, and steeped in the vices which that situation generates." Thus, the American Revolution was not a mere matter of separation from Great Britain but a new departure in the affairs of men. In 1801 he wrote to Joseph Priestley, the British scientist, "We can no longer say there is nothing new under the sun. For this whole chapter in the history of man is new." A new land had called forth new laws and institutions and even a new human mind. America was to be something unique, not a copy or an imitation. Moreover, it was itself to be a model for others, and Jefferson wrote as President: "We feel that we are acting under obligations not confined to the limits of our own society. It is impossible not to be sensible that we are acting for all mankind. . . ."

In all these attitudes Jefferson revealed the confidence and the idealism that characterized the Enlightenment. The twentieth-century philosopher George Santayana described Jefferson's Declaration of Independence as "a salad of illusions." Santayana was not being complimentary. But in an important way, he was correct. Much of the thinking of the Enlightenment was influenced by a vision of the future that had little relationship to the experience of the past. The belief that men could be largely released to their own cognizance without strict religious and political controls, the contention that they could select from the past what was useful and discard what was not, the argument that secular and practical education was the path of human progress, and the announcement that America illustrated the possibility of a departure from what men thought of as their history — these were illusions of monumental consequences that have been associated with Thomas Jefferson. Those who were attracted by the Jeffersonian vision were prepared to accept the advocate of that vision as among "the small number of those who by their intelligence and their works have merited well of humanity." Those who dismissed it thought of Jefferson as a man "of sublimated and paradoxical imagination, entertaining and propagating opinions inconsistent with dignified and orderly government."

SUGGESTIONS FOR FURTHER READING

There is a great deal of available and valuable reading on the Enlightenment. Anthologies that give the flavor of the period are The Age of the Enlightenment, *edited by Isaiah Berlin (1961),* Les Philosophes, *edited by Norman L. Torrey (1960), and* The Enlightenment: The Culture of the Eighteenth Century, *edited by Isidor Schneider (1965). James Boswell's* Life of Johnson *and his* Journals *provide an incomparable picture of the times. A clear understanding of many of the basic ideas of the Enlightenment may be gained by a careful reading of the American Declaration of Independence, especially in the form in which it appears in Jefferson's* Autobiography, *and those students who have the opportunity to browse through the illustrations appearing in the French* Encyclopedia *will gain an excellent insight into the way in which eighteenth-century intellectuals viewed their world.*

There are many secondary sources from which to choose. Good historical surveys of the eighteenth century are M. S. Anderson, Europe in the Eighteenth Century, 1713-1789 *(1961), and R. J. White,* Europe in the Eighteenth Century *(1965). Perhaps the most stimulating short study is Alfred Cobban's* In Search of Humanity: The Role of the Enlightenment in Modern History *(1960). George R. Havens'* The Age of Ideas *(1962) is good, as is Peter Gay's* The Party of Humanity: Essays in the French Enlightenment *(1964). Louis Bredvold's* The Brave New World of the Enlightenment *(1961) and Robert Anchor's* The Enlightenment Tradition *(1967) are well worth reading. A good example of a specialized study based upon the period is Arthur Hertzberg's* The French Enlightenment and the Jews *(1968).*

The most readable and rewarding summary of Newton and his influence is still to be found in E. A. Burtt's The Metaphysical Foundations of Modern Physical Science *(1932; reprinted 1951). A brief biography is E. N. da Andrade's* Sir Isaac Newton *(1954), while L. T. More's* Isaac Newton: A Biography *(1934) is the standard life. The* Leibniz-Clarke Correspondence, *edited by H. G. Alexander (1956), is a good source for some of the arguments aroused by Newton's interpretations.*

Peter Gay's Voltaire's Politics: The Poet as Realist *(1959) is the most exciting study of Voltaire. Although published in 1906, Gustave Lanson's* Voltaire *(English translation 1966) is still valuable. Voltaire's activities as a historian are skilfully discussed by J. H. Brumfitt,* Voltaire: Historian *(1958), and by J. B. Black,* The Art of History: A Study of Four Great Historians of the Eighteenth Century *(1926; reissued in 1965).*

There will never be an end to new and significant studies of Jefferson. A good beginning to an understanding of Jefferson could be made by consulting the following: Thomas Jefferson: A Profile, *edited by Merrill D. Peterson (1967); Adrienne Koch's* Jefferson and Madison: The Great Collaboration *(1950); David Hawke's* A Transaction of Free Men: The Birth and Course of the Declaration of Independence *(1964); Merrill D. Peterson's* The Jefferson Image in the American Mind *(1960); Leonard W. Levy,* Jefferson & Civil Liberties: The Darker Side *(1963); and Daniel J. Boorstin,* The Lost World of Thomas Jefferson *(1948).*

And There Is No Remedy, Francisco Goya, ca. 1810, Museo del Prado, Madrid.

3

The French Revolution

1789   MAY 5 Meeting of the Estates-General. This gathering "brought to the center of political action a vigorous and talented body of men, of whom the great majority, whether of noble or clerical or common rank, were ill-satisfied with things as they were."

JUNE 17 The Third Estate constituted itself the National Assembly and invited the other Estates (the nobility and the clergy) to join it. This has been called the "first revolutionary act."

JULY 14 Storming of the Bastille. The Bastille was a fortress in Paris that was regarded as the symbol of despotism, and the date of its capture by a largely unorganized crowd became the most famous anniversary of the Revolution.

AUGUST 4-5 Surrender by the nobles of their traditional privileges.

AUGUST 27 Declaration of the Rights of Man and the Citizen. This declaration has been called "a manifesto of the revolutionary bourgeoisie" and "sounded the death-knell of the old regime."

1790   Civil Constitution of the Clergy. Church lands had been nationalized in 1789. Now clergy became salaried servants of the state. In 1791 Pope Pius VI condemned the Civil Constitution.

1791   Jews in France admitted to full rights as citizens. "For the first time in the modern history of the West all the Jews within the borders of a European state were united with all of its other citizens as equals before the law."

1791   New constitution adopted. National Assembly dissolved and replaced by Legislative Assembly. Constitution created a limited monarchy. Representatives to Assembly to be elected by votes of those who paid a certain amount in taxes. Abolition of hereditary nobility and titles and dissolution of ecclesiastical orders save for those engaged in care of sick or education.

1792   War breaks out between France and Austrian-Prussian coalition. Although the French initially suffered military reverses, their victory at the Battle of Valmy on September 20 proved to be the first of a long series of triumphs.

1792   Increasing violence in Paris. In August the Tuileries palace, where the king was housed, was stormed by a mob. The king was suspended. In September mobs ransacked the prisons and massacred those suspected of anti-revolutionary activity.

1792   Legislative Assembly replaced by National Convention. Members to the Convention were elected by universal manhood suffrage. On September 21 the monarchy was abolished, and France declared a republic.

1792   Proclamation of fraternal assistance decree, whereby the French offered assistance to all peoples wishing to overthrow their rulers.

1793   Execution of King Louis XVI on January 21.

1793   Committee of Public Safety established on April 6. Designed to protect the Revolution and ultimately exercised dictatorial power.

1793-
1794   Reign of Terror.

1794   Fall of Robespierre on July 27, followed by end of the Terror.

1795   The constitution of 1795 brought about what was called the Directory. Executive power was vested in a directory of five persons, with a two-chamber legislature.

1796   General Napoleon Bonaparte began his Italian campaign and achieved his first great victories.

1799   Napoleon carried out a coup d'état and overthrew the Directory. The Consulate established, with Napoleon as First Consul and in effective control. In 1802 Napoleon became Consul for life with the right to appoint his successor. In 1804 he became emperor.

1804   Civil Code completed. In 1807 the Code was renamed Code Napoleon.

1805   Battle of Austerlitz. Perhaps Napoleon's greatest military victory, the battle was described in dramatic detail by Tolstoy in his *War and Peace*.

1806   Formation of the Confederation of the Rhine. Organized under French auspices, the Confederation brought a great part of Germany under Napoleon's control.

1806   Austrian emperor laid down the old imperial crown of the Holy Roman Empire. It was said that the Empire "was slain by the Revolution. It perished unwept, unhonored, and unsung."

1806   Battle of Jena, where Prussian armies were defeated by Napoleon. After the battle one German leader said: "One cause above all has raised France to this pinnacle of greatness. The Revolution awakened all her powers. . . . The Revolution has set the whole strength of a nation in motion, . . . and thereby upset the old relations of states and the old equilibrium."

1806   Napoleon declared the blockade of Britain and the closing of the continent to British trade.

1808   French armies invaded Spain and began long and costly war with Spanish and British.

1809   Papal states in Italy incorporated with France. Napoleon was excommunicated, whereupon Pope Pius VII was arrested.

1812   Napoleon invaded Russia with Grand Army of 600,000 men. Moscow was occupied, but then Napoleon was forced to retire. "Trophies, glory, all those things for which we sacrificed so much had become a burden. There was no longer any question of adorning or embellishing our lives, but merely of saving them."

1813-1814   Napoleon's Empire slowly collapsed as an alliance of European powers forced him back into France.

1814   On March 31 the Allies entered Paris. On April 11 Napoleon abdicated. He was awarded the Mediterranean island of Elba as an independent principality. Louis XVIII, brother of the executed king, was placed on the French throne.

1815   Napoleon returned from Elba and easily regained control of France. The period following is known as "The Hundred Days." On June 18 Napoleon was defeated in Battle of Waterloo by British and Prussian forces. He abdicated a second time and was exiled to the south Atlantic island of St. Helena, where he died in 1821. His body was returned to Paris in 1840.

R evolution is a common word in the vocabulary of contemporary Western man. We speak of an intellectual revolution, a social revolution, a scientific revolution, an industrial revolution, a technological revolution. In each case we mean a drastic change in our affairs, a turning away from what had existed toward something new. Such revolutions introduce new anxieties, new antagonisms, new dangers. They also create new hopes, new promises, and even new certainties. They define anew the circumstances of our lives and present new interpretations of the individual and his world.

The most dramatic and bruising of all revolutions is the political, and in the minds of many, revolution itself is associated with political upheaval. Whereas intellectual, scientific, and even industrial revolutions tend to take place over a period of time and are to most almost imperceptible, political revolution, although it may have been foreshadowed long before the actual event, bursts upon men and subjects them to extreme and immediate pressures. The day-to-day routine is ruptured, and the effects of political revolution cut deeply into all levels of activity. The ideas and actions of political leaders become a matter of crucial concern to everyone, and the urgency of events forces men to make decisions quickly and to commit themselves to a course of action. Political revolutions are emotionally packed, turbulent, and violent in a way true of no other type of revolution.

In the latter half of the eighteenth century the Western world experienced a series of political revolutions. R. R. Palmer, in his *The Age of the Democratic Revolution*, points out that this revolutionary movement "manifested itself in different ways and with varying success in different countries, yet in all of them showed similar objectives and principles." There was a movement against "the possession of government, or any public power, by any established, privileged, closed or self-recruiting groups of men." A revolutionary situation existed, which Palmer describes as "one in which confidence in the justice or reasonableness of existing authority is undermined; where old loyalties fade, obligations are felt as impositions, law seems arbitrary, and respect for superiors is felt as a form of humiliation; where existing sources of prestige seem undeserved, hitherto accepted forms of wealth and income seem ill-gained, and government is sensed as distant, apart from the governed and not really 'representing' them."

There were two important eighteenth-century political revolutions. One was the American, and the other was the French. There is some debate as to their relative significance. Hannah Arendt has argued that the Americans posed the problem not of the order of society and its aims but of the form of government, and she writes: "The sad truth of the matter is that the French Revolution, which ended in disaster, has made world history, while the American Revolution, so triumphantly successful, has remained an event of little more than local importance." This interpretation is unnecessarily narrow, and masks the long-term but persistent direction of the American Revolution, particularly in its twentieth-century manifestations, and ignores the subtle, slow, and inarticulated American revolutionary influences at work in the world.

Yet it is true that the French Revolution was the crucial revolutionary act of the late eighteenth century. It was geographically central to the Western world, while the American Revolution took place on the periphery of that world. For its opponents and its supporters, the French Revolution posed an immediate threat or promise, while, far across the ocean, America was only a theoretical enemy or friend. The French Revolution dominated the imagination of Westerners in a way that the American never could, and Western literature, philosophy, and history were stained by the memory of the events in France. The passions and controversies aroused by the French Revolution were far deeper and lasting than those stimulated by the American. Throughout the nineteenth and into the twentieth century the French Revolution remained the single most important political event in modern Western history. Until the occurrence of the Russian Revolution of the twentieth century, debate over the meaning of revolution, its benefits and its price, was primarily related to the events in France in the seventeen-nineties.

It is relatively easy to set down the significant results of the French Revolution. A great deal of property — particularly land — was transferred from one group of Frenchmen to another. The position, organization, and responsibilities of the church were altered. Changes in the army, the educational system, and the law were introduced. Old economic restrictions were ended. New definitions of citizenship, patriotism, and the nation appeared. New values changed the individual's interpretation of himself and his community. The losers were the nobility, the church, and those whose positions depended upon the old aristocratic structure. The winners were the business and professional members of what we think of as the middle class and those peasants who succeeded in transforming themselves into land-owning farmers.

Deep and lasting animosities were introduced into European life. For many, the Revolution was one of man's most noble undertakings, "the wish of elevated minds and free hearts" and "the inevitable tendency of the human race." For others, it was a "most damnable event," a sinister act of madness that unleashed upon the world "a formidable, destructive, and shapeless beast that cannot be curbed."

The Background to Revolution

In the years preceding the Revolution, the traditional European society gave the outward appearance of power and stability. But there were forces that threatened the political and social foundations upon which this society rested. The intellectual temper of the time became increasingly hostile to the unquestioned acceptance of customary authority. The ideas of the Enlightenment were basically opposed to privilege conferred by birth, while the growing belief in the plasticity of institutions showed an impatience with anything that stressed a settled or fated aspect of human affairs. Moreover, during the latter half of the eighteenth century, Europe was cursed with a form of political sterility. The energies of the people appeared to outgrow the political structures, and old political loyalties became increasingly a matter of form and not of content. By the latter part of the century the European political systems commanded little respect, and this lack of respect prompted doubt and opposition. Attacks upon authority became widespread. In 1786 Thomas Jefferson wrote from Paris to a friend in America: "If anybody thinks that kings, nobles, or priests are good conservators of the public happiness, send them here." And in 1790 the German writer Goethe commented: "It hardly occurred to anybody in my youth to envy the privileged class or grudge them their privileges. But knights, robbers, and an infamous nobility — such are the ingredients of our novels and plays during the last ten years."

It was in France that the historical collision between the old way of life and its opponents took place. During the eighteenth century France was intellectually, culturally, and politically the leading nation of the Western world. French was the accepted language of European politics and society, Paris was the intellectual center of Europe, and the French court was regarded as the model to be imitated by royalty everywhere. Yet this splendor, real as it was, masked a serious crisis in French life. French political leadership was mediocre. The wealth of the church stimulated animosity and cupidity, while the continual efforts of the nobility to protect and even better its privileged position aroused the anger of those representing professional and commercial interests. Hostility toward the clergy and the nobility ranged from irritation on the part of those who felt themselves humiliated by the arrogance and influence of the upper classes to bitter hatred by the peasants who looked upon traditional land arrangements and duties as instruments whereby they were robbed of the results of their labors. From the seventeen-seventies the French government had been beset by financial difficulties, and one attempt after another to escape the threat of bankruptcy had brought only temporary relief.

The Revolutionary Beginning

In July, 1788, King Louis XVI announced his intention of summoning the Estates-General, a consultative body of the nation that had not been called into session by a French king for a century and a half. Ten months later, on May 5, 1789, approximately 1,200 deputies gathered at Versailles near Paris. Opening the proceedings King Louis faced the nobles with their gold-embroidered cloaks and their plumed hats, the clergy with its episcopal robes, and the plainly dressed representatives of what was called the Third Estate. In his speech welcoming the deputies, the king asked for their best efforts to solve the problems of France and spoke of "a general state of unrest and an exaggerated desire for change, which might completely pervert public opinion, if they were not dealt with at once by a conference of wise and moderate men."

From its first days the Estates-General was dominated by the members of the Third Estate. Here were the writers of pamphlets, the forwarders of projects, the untiring orators with their turbulent flood of words. These were the men who were to destroy the traditional French society. But they were not the incompetents and the misfits. Only a handful of them had ever suffered economic distress. They paid taxes and were, in large part, property owners. Many of them were lawyers or had been members of the royal service, while others were businessmen, bankers, landowners, farmers, and men of independent means. The first presiding officer of the assembled deputies was a distinguished astronomer turned politician. The Third Estate consisted largely of what we would loosely call middle-class people, energetic, competent, and ambitious, described by an observer as "the innovators and the restive, already impatient of authority."

Prior to the meeting of the Estates-General there had been indications of what changes these Frenchmen hoped to bring about in French society. At the invitation of the government, Frenchmen from all parts of the country had forwarded thousands of suggestions for changing the social and political relationships of themselves with each other and with their rulers. These suggestions were both particular and general, but there was a large measure of agreement on the major issues. There were arguments presented for the abolition of administrative arrest and for freedom of the press. Barriers separating the nobility from the professional and business groups were condemned, and there were calls for freedom from economic restrictions, for greater equality of opportunity, and for a larger voice in governmental affairs. Privileges of birth were attacked, and it was argued that all should have the right to enjoy the ownership of all classes of property. Implicit in these suggestions was the idea that the traditional regime should be replaced by a society based upon the ideas of the Enlightenment. All doors should be open to talent, and merit should be substituted for birth. In the most famous of the numerous pamphlets published at this time, Emmanuel Joseph Sieyès argued the case for a new French society. In *What Is the Third Estate?* Sieyès pointed out that those without titles or position in the church were the most talented, the most energetic, the most valuable part of the nation. They were, in fact, everything. Yet heretofore they had counted for nothing in the national life of France. What do they demand? To be something.

Soon after the opening of the Estates-General the members of the Third Estate acted to create a society in which they would be something. They forced the nobles, the clergy, and a recalcitrant king to abandon one position after another. They claimed to speak as an assembly of the nation, and acting upon this authority they moved to correct the abuses that so offended them. On July 27, 1789, a document to be known as "The Declaration of the Rights of Man and the Citizen" was brought before the assembly. The last clause of the declaration was adopted a month later, on August 27. Article 1 read: "Men are born and remain free and equal in rights." The traditional duties and obligations of the old regime were declared abolished, and throughout the declaration the rights of the individual were stressed. These rights, common to all human beings, were older and more important than any existing society. Each individual has the right to possess property, to live safely, and to resist oppression. It is the obligation of any political association to defend these rights, and the society is only a community of citizens expressing their common will through the laws and institutions. No authority may infringe upon the liberty of the individual members of society, and the agents of any political power are accountable to the people for their actions.

Even before "The Declaration of the Rights of Man and the Citizen" was adopted, the assembly acted to rid France of many of the aristocratic privileges that had caused so much discontent. During the night of August 4 the remnants of feudalism were abolished. The privileges of the noble courts, the noble hunt, the noble's right to have the peasant maintain a pigeon-cote and a rabbit-warren disappeared. Tax exemptions and tax privileges were ended. Civil and military positions were declared open to all, and "all citizens, without distinction of birth, can be admitted to all positions and dignities, whether ecclesiastical, civil, or military, and no useful profession shall be considered derogatory." Justice was to be administered fairly and without charge.

Thus the old hierarchical society fell. A whole conception of the order of things was now declared false. The church and the nobility, the mainstays of the old regime, lost much of their day-to-day control of the lives of those who had been thought of as their inferiors. Every Frenchman, no matter what his status had been in the old, rejected society, was now declared a citizen (the word itself was new) equal in civil rights to all other Frenchmen.

The Developing Revolution

"The Declaration of the Rights of Man and the Citizen" and the abolition of feudalism not only swept away the institutional supports of an old society; they announced the creation of a new, the principal characteristics of which were to be equal taxation, equal opportunity, equal justice, and the drastic reform of civil and ecclesiastical bodies. The actual destruction of the traditional framework of French political authority had been accomplished quickly and without encountering a great deal of opposition. But the task remained of creating a new authority and a new political instrumentality. A multitude of questions called for answers. What was to be the position of the king? How were equal justice and equal opportunity to be secured? How was reform of the church to be accomplished? What type of constitution should be written? What measures should be taken against those who refused to accept the revolutionary ideas?

Consideration of these questions was complicated by a turbulence that became part of French political life. In July, 1789, a group of Parisians stormed the Bastille, an almost empty prison that was regarded as the symbol of oppression, and then paraded through the streets with the head of the prison governor attached to a pike. In the countryside there were peasant riots, and in October another group of citizens escorted the king from Versailles to Paris, thus making him virtually a prisoner. There was growing discontent with their representatives on the part of those who hoped for more and of those who had expected less. For some the Revolution was going too slowly, for others too fast. Bitter factional quarrels among the various claimants to political leadership and a growing radicalism that was impatient with any delay in adopting more extreme measures pushed the Revolution into a series of political crises. Those who had been thought of as radicals in 1789 were to be regarded as conservatives by 1791, while the radicals of

1791 became the conservatives of 1792 and the radicals of 1793 the conservatives of 1794. One political leader after another rose to prominence and then was overwhelmed by events he could not control. Some who believed in the monarchy were ultimately to vote for the execution of the king. Others who were thought to be saviors in one season were denounced as traitors in another. And some buried in the national shrine as heroes were later disinterred and dumped into common graves. Important legislative measures affecting the position of the king, the church, and the state administration were ultimately incorporated into a constitution. The Civil Constitution of the Clergy, adopted in July, 1790, made the church a national institution. The clergy became salaried state employees and took an oath of allegiance "to the nation, the law, and the king." The church's property was nationalized, and within a few years a great part of its land passed into the hands of farmers and investors. But the king's acceptance of his new position was insincere, while many who now saw the implications of the Revolution and felt themselves threatened became its implacable enemies.

International Implications

The course of the Revolution was also influenced by its international implications. European governments depended upon the support of aristocratic landlords and the subjugation of the peasantry. Official Europe was appalled at the arrogance of the Paris "nobodies" who had usurped positions reserved for their betters. Monarchs, nobles, and all those who were satisfied with traditional arrangements looked at the Revolution with hostility and rightly suspected that revolutionary ideas and activities would not be confined to one country but would spread throughout Europe. If one king suffered indignities, then all kings were in danger; if traditional rights and duties were abolished in France, the same could happen elsewhere.

The response of the rest of Europe to the French Revolution was initially halting and confused. It was difficult to know what was happening in Paris, and for some time the true nature of the Revolution was hidden by the apparent support given by Louis XVI and by some of the nobility and the clergy. But by 1791 it was obvious that the Revolution was more than a minor argument over a few grievances and that it was increasing in intensity and thus becoming more dangerous. Many nobles had fled from France and were attempting to persuade the continental monarchs to intervene on behalf of the old regime. In June, 1791, King Louis and his queen Marie Antoinette attempted to escape from the country. But they were apprehended before they reached the border and were brought back to Paris, where a sullen and silent crowd watched their carriage proceed under guard to the palace.

In 1792, war broke out between revolutionary France and the rest of Europe. It was to last, with short interruptions, for over twenty years and was to become an important instrumentality for the creation of a new Western Europe. It was to create a new kind of political loyalty, define a new type of patriot, and introduce a new and violent emotion into European affairs. The map of Europe was to be redrawn, and European societies were to become politically conscious in a way never before experienced. War became the ally of political ideas, the creator of new national communities that were held together by enthusiasm, by the hope of victory and the fear of defeat.

Having decided to put down the Revolution by force, Austria and Prussia entered into an alliance and declared their right to intervene in French affairs in order to curb the excesses of the Revolution. This First Coalition of European powers against the Revolution was to be followed by others, and during the next twenty years all the major and many of the minor European states were to be involved at one time or another in the continuing war. There were some changing of sides and some periods of neutrality. But generally and at critical times England, Russia, Austria, and Prussia — alone or as allies — were engaged in war against the French.

Initially the Prussian and Austrian military action was successful. But as the campaign continued, it became obvious that the Revolution, for all its confusion, had engendered new enthusiasm and loyalties. The struggle against the enemy became a national undertaking in a way new to the Western world. As late as 1776 the French National Academy had defined nationality in terms of the part of the country in which a man happened to be born. The Revolution provided a new meaning for "patriot" and identified the individual with the nation as a whole. To meet the threat of invasion, the leaders of the Revolution turned to the citizens of France and raised a large civilian army that made up for its lack of experience by its enthusiasm. The *Marseillaise*, the first modern national anthem, which was written in 1792, called upon "the children of France" to rise and defend the national honor and the national prestige against the enemy. The Revolution produced "the nation in arms," where the energies of the entire country were focused on the military struggle. During the campaigns a French army of almost 800,000 men was assembled, the largest military force the West had ever seen, and the great majority of these were citizens who had been put into uniform by what was called the *levée en masse*, a raising of an army without reference to class, previous occupation, or standing in the society.

The Revolution was also fortunate in that its military program benefited by the talents of the new officers who were called upon to replace the unreliable or discontented nobility. Lazare Carnot, forty years old in 1793, became known as "the architect of victory," and he opened the door to other men who needed only the opportunity to show their talents. Among those who received their chance was Napoleon Bonaparte, who became a general at twenty-four. In engagement after engagement the new military leaders of the Revolution showed that they were far superior to those who were sent against them.

The revolutionary forces succeeded in throwing back the invading armies and then proceeded to carry the war beyond the boundaries of France. The Revolution now became international, for the French armies brought with them the promises and ideas of the Revolution. The French government proclaimed a brotherly assistance decree that promised to aid any people wishing to overthrow their rulers, and French generals were instructed to carry the Revolution with them and to proclaim wherever they went the abolition of all existing tithes, taxes, and feudal charges. Ideas proclaimed in Paris were now scattered throughout Europe and ultimately the world.

Revolutionary Tensions

The expanding war added new tensions to the Revolution. The Legislative Assembly, which was established under the new constitution of 1791, consisted of members who advocated a constitutional monarchy, of those who could be described as moderates, and of a group of talented, energetic, and ambitious radicals who were becoming convinced that France and the Revolution could only be saved by extreme measures. This political division was, however, misleading. Moderates, and particularly those who wished to retain the monarchy, were placed on the defensive by the international situation and by popular fears that the king was not sincere in accepting the Revolution. The initiative was with the radicals, the most important of which were the so-called Jacobins, who took their name from the Dominican premises that had become the meeting place for a group of politically minded citizens. Ultimately the Jacobins became the single most powerful political group in the country and outmaneuvered their opponents in the struggle for political power.

By 1791 most of the demands of those who had gathered at Versailles in 1789 had been satisfied. The privileges of the old order had been abolished. The wealth and influence of the church had been drastically reduced. The arbitrary power of the king had been curtailed. A constitution had been adopted, and a representative legislature elected. A new sense of community was being defined. But such successes only seemed to bring about new problems. The new constitution of 1791 had left many Frenchmen without the vote, and there was a growing protest that those who had benefited by the Revolution were attempting to create an oligarchy of wealth and property to replace the aristocracy of birth. War fever, unrest in the countryside, periodic shortages of food in Paris, the suspected plotting of those sympathetic to the old order, and the continual shifting alignment of political leaders made the situation explosive and dangerous.

Additional developments also began to play increasingly important roles in the continuing Revolution. One of these was the Paris crowd, or as the opponents of the Revolution were to designate it, the mob. Since 1789 the basically unorganized Parisian citizens had often set the pace of events, and to a greater or lesser extent the governmental representatives themselves were at their mercy. During 1792 the crowd, partly spontaneously and partly stimulated by the slogans of those who claimed to be its leaders, and also influenced by inflammatory rumors, took part in several bloody and violent acts. Some members of this group were the dregs of Paris society, brutal and destructive people who found in street action an outlet for their hostilities. But also participating were irritated and frustrated citizens who believed that they had been betrayed by the Revolution. Different types of people took part in different activities. In some of these crowd actions the participants were craftsmen (locksmiths, cabinet-makers, shoemakers, tailors, stone-masons, hairdressers, and engravers) and shopkeepers. In others they were merchants, civil servants, and professional men. Several times distressed and angry women, infuriated by rapid increases in the price of bread, played important parts in the disorders.

Moreover, the Revolution had reached down into all levels of the population and had created a political consciousness that expressed itself in political activity. In addition to an animosity toward the aristocracy, there developed an antagonism between the economically hard-pressed Parisian laborers and small shopkeepers and the relatively well-to-do business and professional classes. There was not any well-developed social consciousness as we think of the term today. But there was a growing awareness of social and economic inequalities, and the complaints of those who had not benefited economically from the Revolution added a new dimension to the turmoil in Paris. Those who thought of themselves as "the poor and the virtuous" looked with anger, and some envy, upon "the bankers, the fat farmers, the rich merchants." The poor, "who are watering with their sweat the earth that nourishes us all," were being oppressed by "the leeches," the bankers, the financiers, the merchants, and lawyers. The theme of political equalitarianism was translated in the minds of many into a form of social and economic equality. The dark murmur of something very different from anything anticipated by the early leaders of the Revolution was expressed in an anonymous song of 1793:

> We must shorten the giants
> And make the small folk taller;
> Everything at its true height
> That is real happiness.

The course of the Revolution was also influenced by the appearance of an extreme radicalism. The early leaders of the Revolution, who had been influenced by the philosophical ideas of the Enlightenment and had been primarily interested in achieving practical but historically important changes, gave way to men who were stimulated by the moving ideals of an absolute justice, an absolute equality, and an absolute freedom. Such men were impatient of delay and opposition, more-or-less violent in their written pronouncements and speeches, and dedicated to making the Revolution much more than a change in government. They had a vision of a new world, a new form of human fraternity without the contradictions and antagonisms that they associated with all previous human societies. They were self-styled but, in their own view, sincere friends of the people, defenders of mankind, advocates of a new and shining liberty. Many of the best known of the revolutionary figures — Georges Jacques Danton, Jacques René Hébert, Jean Paul Marat, Antoine Louis de Saint-Just, Maximilien Robespierre — were members of this group.

These radicals did succeed in becoming the dominant political power in France. But they found themselves continually thwarted by old and new opponents, and were forced to press for increasingly drastic measures to resolve the revolutionary crisis. The monarchy was abolished in 1792, and France was declared a republic. King Louis XVI was executed as an enemy of the Revolution in January, 1793, and in October the queen was beheaded. Many of the radicals themselves were to become victims of their former political companions who felt that those who lagged in revolutionary fervor were traitors to the Revolution. "We must establish the despotism of liberty," cried Marat, "to crush the despotism of kings," and in April, 1793, he proposed in a printed circular: "Let us arrest all the enemies of the Revolution, and all suspected persons. Let us exterminate without pity every conspirator, unless we wish to be exterminated ourselves." Tribunals were established to try "enemies" of the Revolution, and local revolutionary leaders throughout France were authorized to form surveillance committees and ferret out opponents. By the summer of 1793 what could be called a revolutionary dictatorship had been established and had assumed responsibility for protecting and forwarding the Revolution.

The Terror

The Revolution now entered a phase known commonly as the Terror. This aspect of the Revolution is often identified with the revolutionary period as a whole, and any discussion of the French Revolution is certain to call up mental pictures of screaming mobs, tumbrils, and the guillotine. For many, then and later, the Terror was the Revolution, the true face of revolutionary hatred — wild, unrestrained violence that consumed innocent and guilty alike in a fit of indiscriminate slaughter. For others, the Terror was the culmination of the struggle, a superhuman attempt to save the Revolution.

What we call the Terror, or the Reign of Terror, lasted from the summer of 1793 to the summer of 1794. Throughout the country approximately 30,000 people were executed, while another 10,000 died in prison. The revolutionary tribunal in Paris sent over 2,600 people to their deaths. The victims of the Terror came from all classes of French society, and no category of citizens was spared. Princes, milkmaids, doctors, washerwomen, stable boys, and stevedores were executed. Seventy percent of the victims were from the lower classes, although in proportion to their numbers in the total French society, the nobles, the clergy, and the rich suffered far more than did representatives of the lower-middle and working classes.

Those responsible for the application of the Terror were known as the Committee of Public Safety, established in April, 1793. Originally consisting of nine members, the Committee was increased to fourteen and then reduced again to nine. In September the number was set at twelve, and the same twelve members were reelected monthly for the next ten months. All but one of these twelve came from the middle class, and none had ever labored with his hands. Only one, and he for a short time, had engaged in commercial activities, and all but one had received a substantial amount of formal schooling. Eight of the members were lawyers, two were army officers and engineers, one had studied theology, and one was an actor. The oldest was fifty when he joined the Committee, while the youngest was twenty-six. All twelve could claim, at least in some measure, to be intellectuals.

The Committee of Public Safety, largely under the influence of Maximilien Robespierre, became the instrument for separating the good from the bad, the right from the wrong. The members of the Committee looked upon themselves as the conscience of the Revolution, as incorruptible judges, and they attempted to protect the Revolution from those who because of greed, sloth, immorality, or irresponsibility would destroy it. Each day brought to light new enemies of society, and new instruments were designed to crush the opposition. Ultimately, in June, 1794, the Committee was authorized to act almost without restraint. The enemy had only to be identified, and the Revolution moved against him. No witnesses were needed to establish guilt, there were no written depositions, there was no opportunity for argument.

In late July, 1794, those political leaders who saw themselves threatened by Robespierre united against him. He and a handful of his followers were executed, and the Terror ended. A reaction against extreme revolutionary ideas set in. The war against the rest of Europe continued, and there was no attempt to return to prerevolutionary conditions. A form of constitutional government, known as the Directory, was adopted. The men in positions of power were not incompetent, and the Directory provided a system whereby many could enjoy the fruits of the revolutionary victory. But the Directory did not succeed in securing broadly based support, and its efforts too often seemed irresolute and unpredictable. Conspiracies and intrigues — although not to the extent that is sometimes thought — were common, and the Directory was unable to still the fears or gain the confidence of either moderates or revolutionaries. There was little sense of direction, there was no leader who could provide a new focus for the energies and aspirations released by the events since 1789, and the existence of the government appeared more and more dependent upon the army. In November, 1799, Napoleon Bonaparte overthrew the Directory and assumed the inheritance of the Revolution.

The period from 1789 to 1794 shook the Western world as no similar period would until the World War of 1914-1918. The French Revolution changed the political focus of Western history and is often regarded as the beginning of modern European politics. It produced many of what were to become common characteristics of political life — nationalistic appeals, feverish political debate, the popular demagogue, the street-corner agitator, terrorism, and mob action. Our political vocabulary was permanently influenced by the revolutionary rhetoric that came out of the seventeen-nineties. Some have interpreted the Revolution as the most important source of our ideas of democracy, socialism, and nationalism. Others have seen it as the stimulus for revolutionary and military dictatorship and even modern totalitarianism. Most significant, perhaps, it influenced the future with its vision of a new morality, a new justice, and a new equality. Many were to look upon this vision as a dangerous form of utopianism. Others were to regard it as a goal toward which the world was tending, and as a young German of the time wrote: "I see generations crushed in the struggle; I see perhaps centuries of war and desolation; but at last, on the remote horizon, I see the victory of liberty."

The importance of the Revolution and the questions raised by it can best be illustrated by an examination of the responses of individual men. Edmund Burke was the great philosophical opponent of the Revolution and set forth the arguments that were to be most frequently used in combating revolutionary ideas. Maximilien Robespierre is usually identified as the spokesman for the extreme revolutionary point of view and for a period of time was the leader of revolutionary France. Napoleon Bonaparte was the great organizer of the energies released by the Revolution, and by providing institutional direction he modified the revolutionary aims and reinterpreted them.

Edmund Burke

For large numbers of people the French Revolution is associated with a series of dramatic events. The storming of the Bastille, the execution of the king, Marat's murder in his bath, the mobs in the streets, the violent debates, and at the end the figure of Napoleon with his hat and his sword — these are the raw aspects of revolutionary action. But coincidentally with this hurly-burly of historical episodes the Revolution confronted Western man with the most profound political questions. Could man radically change his historical environment or were there time-tested historical traditions that could not be discarded? Did all men possess what were called natural political rights, or did such rights exist only in the empty daydreams of impractical philosophers? Were men equal, or were they willing and unwilling participants in a hierarchical society that had been sanctioned by history and religion? Was the urge to revolution, the determination to destroy the old and create the new, an activity sparked by the higher aspirations of men? Or was such a desire only the expression of an ugly and malevolent violence?

These were the basic political questions posed by the Revolution, and historical commentators of that time and since can be divided into those who gave one set of answers and those who gave another. On one side were those who believed in the equality of men, in a secular society, in the ability, and the right, of men to change their institutions, their laws, and their relations, one to another, whenever these were thought unsatisfactory. Here were those who, in the years following the Revolution, were to be known as liberals, progressives, believers in human betterment and the power of the human intellect. Opposing them were those who thought equality a mirage, who stressed the value of tradition, and who were pessimistic about man's capabilities. These were the conservatives, the traditionalists, those who argued that change, if absolutely necessary, must be slow and gradual.

The arguments for the Revolution had been developed by the philosophers of the Enlightenment and were passionately stated by the Parisian revolutionaries themselves. A consistent and meaningful antirevolutionary position did not appear until after the Revolution was underway, and it was the English statesman Edmund Burke who in the early seventeen-nineties presented a conservative point-of-view that was generally adopted by those who could not accept the Revolution. From 1790 until his death in 1797, Burke was the irreconcilable opponent of the Revolution, and in his opposition he enunciated a political theory and a historical interpretation that appealed to those who believed that the Revolution was a great historical mistake and that its influence must be combated.

Burke was a contradictory and controversial character. A brilliant and imaginative man, he was also violent and unrestrained, with little pleasing wit and little personal attractiveness. Those who subsequently accepted much of his argument have described him as a great speaker and writer. Yet his prose is flowery and overdone for modern tastes, and his extravagant rhetoric seems strained by present-day standards. Even in his own time he was both ridiculed and respected. A contemporary reports that when Burke addressed Parliament he often "foamed like Niagara," and Samuel Johnson, a close friend of Burke's, remarked that "if a man will appear extravagant as he does and cry, can he wonder that he is represented as mad?" Burke was something of a mystery to friend and foe alike, and Edward Gibbon caustically but with a great measure of truth wrote: "Poor Burke is the most eloquent and rational madman that I ever knew."

Nor can Burke's emotionalism, violence, and exaggerations be ignored or dismissed as idiosyncrasies. His frantic anxiety about the world was a reflection of his character. His belief that he was alone in the struggle against evil stimulated his passion and aroused his animosity toward his "enemies," those real or fancied assailants who were attempting "to ruin" him and his country. Lonely and embittered, he saw himself as the disregarded prophet of his time, and he spoke sincerely, if somewhat wildly, when he argued that "I fear I am the only person in France or England who is aware of the extent of the danger, with which we are threatened." His rage and anguish at the direction of the world, his fears, and his political and personal loneliness prompted his extreme behavior. During the last seven years of his life he had one great and abiding emotional commitment: hatred of the French Revolution. All his energies, his passion, and his talents were directed against this monster.

Because of his opposition to the Revolution, Burke has been regarded by some as an almost pathological opponent of all change. Yet prior to 1789 he had been a leading reform figure in England for over thirty years. He had been chiefly responsible for an economic reform bill in the early seventeen-eighties. As a member of the English Parliament, he had attempted to reform the administration of British India, and he had argued against the oppression of the Irish, against the slave trade, against the imprisonment of debtors, against the suppression of Catholics and Protestant dissenters. He had opposed the British government in its attempt to repress the rebellion of the American colonists, and he had even expressed his disgust at the brutal provisions of the law against homosexuals.

Throughout his adult life, however, he had been a conservative. In every case where he had acted the part of the reformer, he had done so in the belief that he was defending a traditional right against a contemporary wrong. To him, such questions were not theoretical speculations but matters of practical good and evil as they existed in the world. Thus he argued that the British were wrong during the American Revolution because they were attempting to solve the problem by reference to vague questions of rights rather than to the actual circumstances of the case. He believed in the redress of practical grievances, but he was not prepared, as a young or an old man, to support any theoretical program that could be used to change the foundations upon which society and its institutions rested.

Burke was a declared enemy of the eighteenth-century Enlightenment. He disputed almost all of its principles, and he developed his political ideas in opposition to what he believed were erroneous, and dangerous, speculations about human nature, the purposes of society, and the relationship of man to his historical surroundings. While the men of the Enlightenment looked to the future, Burke had a passion for the past. While Jefferson, Voltaire, and others, with some reservations, trusted in man's ability to use his reason, Burke had little faith in human intellectual capacities. As early as 1756, in his *The Vindication of Natural Society*, Burke had set himself against what he looked upon as a destructive rationalism. Here he expressed his fear that "a mind which has no restraint from a sense of its own weakness, of its subordinate rank in the creation, of the extreme danger of letting the imagination loose upon some subjects, may very plausibly attack everything the most excellent and venerable." Religion, government, and tradition were being undermined by rational inspection, and "what would become of the world, if the practice of all moral duties, and the foundations of society, rested upon having their reasons made clear and demonstrative to every individual?"

Prior to the French Revolution, Burke had the opportunity to examine, at least superficially, the ideas of the Enlightenment at first hand. He made four trips to France, the last in 1775. During his visit in 1773 he listened to conversation in intellectual French circles, and he was appalled. Within a month of his return to England, he rose in the House of Commons to warn his countrymen about the dangers on the continent and to claim that these "infidels are outlaws of the constitution; not of this country but of the human race. They are never, never to be supported, never to be tolerated." Burke was certain that what he called the "spirit of innovation" was dangerous and that any encouragement of drastic social or political change was an act of treason. Although soon thereafter he was to support the Americans during their rebellion, the political theorizing of the colonists alarmed him. "I am much against any further experiments," he wrote, "which tend to put to the proof any more of these allowed opinions, which contribute so much to public tranquillity."

Burke was suspicious of the French Revolution almost from its start. He made his earliest recorded comments on the activities in Paris three weeks after the storming of the Bastille in August, 1789. In a letter he wrote: "The spirit it is impossible not to admire, but the old Parisian ferocity has broken out in a startling manner. . . . Men must have a certain fund of natural moderation to qualify them for freedom, else it becomes noxious to themselves and a perfect nuisance to everybody else. . . . What will be the event, it is hard, I think, still to say."

Within a short time, however, his opinion had hardened, and any lingering doubt disappeared. On November 1, 1790, he published *Reflections on the Revolution in France*. The book sold 12,000 copies within a month of printing, and the French translation was an even greater success. This was Burke's best-known work, and it is perhaps the most important anti-revolutionary document ever published. But its theme was to be repeated again and again by Burke from 1790 until his death, both in other publications and in speech after speech. Henceforth he was a constant and violent enemy of the French Revolution, of what he called "that putrid carcass, the mother of all evil . . . that plague-spot in the history of mankind." He saw that the Revolution threatened all established institutions, and he was certain that the revolutionary ideas would spread from France throughout the world. The revolutionary leaders had created "a schism in the whole universe; and that schism extended to almost everything, great and small." In the *Reflections* and in his later works, *Thoughts on French Affairs*, *Remarks on the Policy of the Allies*, and *Letters on a Regicide Peace*, Burke undertook the task of analyzing the French Revolution and then exposing it as a world-wide menace. For him, revolutionary France posed a threat never before faced by Europeans, and he wrote of the war against France: "I cannot persuade myself that this war bears the least resemblance (other than that it is a war) to any that has ever existed in the world. I cannot persuade myself that any examples or any reasonings drawn from other wars and other politics are at all applicable to it; and I truly and sincerely think, that all other wars and all other politics have been the games of children, in comparison with it."

In almost every particular Burke opposed the revolutionaries. He denied that human society was created solely for the benefit of individuals and that it should be changed merely because men were unhappy. Instead, he argued, society was an organic process that had a life of its own and did not even depend upon the happiness or unhappiness, support or opposition, of its members. Thus he speaks of the "great primeval contract of eternal society, linking the lower with higher natures, connecting the visible and invisible worlds." There is an "ancient, permanent sense of mankind," which expresses itself in established traditions, prejudices, and institutions, and wisdom is to be found in "the general bank and capital of nations and of ages." What has been developed by man over a long period of time is the true and the valuable. The human community has been created by centuries of experience and is slowly being improved. But no revolutionary has the right to take it upon himself to destroy the old and established because he thinks that he can put an end to political and social inequities and to human suffering.

The revolutionary belief that old laws could be discarded and new adopted was also in error. For Burke, laws were not simple expedients designed for men's convenience but were sacred expressions of historical, religious, and social experience. We are all locked within legal arrangements that have been sanctioned by time, and "It would be hard to point out any error more truly subversive of all the order and beauty, of all the peace and happiness, of human society, than the position that any body of men has a right to make what laws they please."

Law evolved from generation to generation, and it was slowly modified to express the changing condition of the community. But it could not be changed suddenly or drastically without creating the very confusion and suffering that it was designed to protect against.

Burke believed that the revolutionaries' attitude toward the changeability of the law sprang from two false premises. One of these was the reliance upon reason as a criterion for social and political judgments. Burke had little faith in man's reason, which he regarded as only a "certain intemperance of the intellect," only a "disease of the time." Reason was an inferior instrument for understanding the ways of the world, and enthusiasm, by which Burke meant a certain positive, unexamined comprehension of life, was far superior as a guide to action. "God has been pleased to give Mankind an Enthusiasm," he argued, which is more trustworthy than intellectual speculation. Reason, or what he thought of as common sense, was useful "for common affairs — to buy and sell, to teach Grammar and the like; but is utterly unfit to meddle with Politics, Divinity, or Philosophy." An unchecked intelligence was a menace to society, for it was continually prying into questions that were better left unexamined. There was a mystery to human history, and "the foundations on which obedience to governments is founded are not to be constantly discussed." The important things in the life of a society — affection, allegiance, loyalty, patriotism, religion — did not lend themselves to reasonable explanation. "Wisdom without reflection" was the sure guide, and "I do not enter into these metaphysical distinctions. I hate the very sound of them."

The second error, according to Burke, was the revolutionary belief that a society could be established upon the basis of any so-called rights of man. Rights to liberty, equality, and fraternity were for Burke only abstractions, and men did not have equal rights to participate in or to control their societies. He was himself satisfied with "the inequality which grows out of the nature of things by time, custom, succession, accumulation, permutation, and improvement of property...." Social inequality, as well as political inequality, was natural and necessary, and it was the duty of everyone to accept his position in a political and social scheme that Burke believed had divine support. "We are all born in subjection, all born equally, high and low, governours and governed, in subjection to one great immutable, pre-existent law, prior to all our devices, and prior to all our contrivances, paramount to all our ideas, and all our sensations, antecedent to our very existence, by which we are knit and connected in the eternal frame of the Universe, out of which we cannot stir. This great law does not arise from our conventions, or compacts; on the contrary, it gives to our conventions and compacts all the force and sanction they have. . . ." There was in the world an eternal order, and this order had the sanction of divine authority. "The awful Author of our being is the Author of our place in the order of existence and . . . having disposed and marshalled us by a divine tactick, not according to our will, but according to His, He has, in and by that disposition, virtually subjected us to act the part which belongs to the place assigned us."

Through the years Burke's opposition to the French Revolution became ever more violent, and at times hysterical. An acquaintance reports that whenever politics was discussed, "his irritability is so terrible that it gives immediately to his face the expression of a man who is going to defend himself from murderers." All change became to him a usurpation by those who "deserve no refutations but those of the common hangman." He became the enemy of anyone who disagreed with him, and he argued in Parliament that any "free thinking" that threatened any established institution was "never to be tolerated." His admiration for the past, which he saw being destroyed by the revolution of the modern world, became extreme. He could argue in 1790 that the Middle Ages, which he had spoken of in the seventeen-seventies as "wholly barbarous," possessed "generosity and dignity of thinking." He could defend certain absurdities of the British electoral system as "perfectly adequate," and in 1794 could speak favorably of "that happy despotism" that had formerly characterized France. He insisted that any restoration of the monarchy in France must entail much more than the return of the king. Everything must be brought back: nobility, clergy, traditional land arrangements. In much the same way, he could seriously state that if some 35,000 landed gentry were "taken out of this country, it would leave hardly anything that I should call the people of England."

Yet, in spite of his unceasing and violent opposition to the French Revolution, Burke had little confidence that he could stem the revolutionary tide. The revolutionary doctrine spread everywhere, and in 1793 Burke wrote to a friend: "The world seems to me to reel and stagger." In 1794 Burke retired from Parliament. In that same year his only son, upon whom he doted, died. In his sorrow Burke withdrew from public life. He refused to look at newspapers for long periods of time, and he attempted to shut himself off from a world he now despised. Even his religious faith provided little consolation. God, acting in His mysterious way, had seen fit to give the victory to the Revolution. A few months before his death, Burke wrote to an acquaintance that "there is the hand of God in this business, and there is an end of the system of Europe, taking in laws, manners, religion and politics, in which I delighted so much." But Burke was determined that the Revolution should not achieve a final triumph over him. According to his orders, he was not buried under the stone that marked his resting place in Beaconsfield church yard. Nor was his body left in the original coffin. By his direction his remains were transferred from one coffin to another and then put in a different place. This was done so that at some future date the victorious revolutionaries would not be able to exhume and dishonor his corpse.

Edmund Burke is usually regarded as the outstanding advocate of conservatism in the Western world. He has been the favorite political philosopher of those who have looked with dismay upon Western revolutionary ideas. And there is justification for this position. Many of Burke's arguments possessed a measure of validity. The historical past does have a continuing meaning, while history during the past century and a half has shown clearly that it is easier to destroy old traditions than to create new ones. There is more to a society than a mere collection of individuals, and men are tied together by something more than simple common interest. There is a mysterious current to the affairs of men and society, and human nature is not a malleable material that may be formed and reformed according to any passing desire.

In all this Burke and his conservative followers have some claim to consideration. But, having said that much, it is obvious that there were some serious failings in the Burkean philosophy. In too many places it lacks intellectual integrity and substitutes the weakest type of unexamined emotionalism for any meaningful explanation of the human condition. Burke claimed that he hated generalizations. Yet he was extremely fond of his own generalizations. His contention that poverty, ignorance, and suffering are the acts of God is a highly abstract and general argument for which Burke scorns to provide any acceptable proof. In the same way he claimed that society necessarily provides a class of men who are properly qualified to rule. Yet such a claim is empty without some explanation of how this is done or, in fact, whether there is any real connection between the possession of authority and competence.

Burke also set the pattern for conservative thinking by defining his philosophy as an all-or-nothing doctrine. In arguing that everything must be conserved, he locked his followers in the position of indiscriminately defending the present against any suggested change. Thus the trivial was included with the essential, the extraneous trappings of society with its essence. Burke supported every privilege, no matter how insignificant, and in doing so earned the accusation of an opponent who claimed that Burke wept over the lost plumage but forgot the living bird. Burke said that there should be change, but that this change should come slowly. In reality, it was never the right time for change, and conservatism became willy-nilly the defender of the status quo, whatever the status quo might be.

In Burke's time, and since, conservatism has been defensive. Burke hated what he saw happening in Europe in the seventeen-nineties, and his conservative followers have not been at home in the West. As a result conservatism has not been a program for living in the Western world but rather an argument for opposing that world. This is why so much conservative doctrine has been irrelevant and so much of the conservative vocabulary outdated. The dilemma of the Western conservative is illustrated by the historical significance of Edmund Burke. Almost two hundred years after his attacks upon the French Revolution, he remains the major conservative philosopher of modern times. His principles, almost unchanged, are still the bedrock of serious conservatism. Seen in this light, he has triumphed over his opponents, all of whom have been superseded by followers who modified, and in some cases distorted, their beliefs. This is Burke's victory, and his disaster.

Robespierre

The French Revolution produced many interesting and colorful historical characters. There was the dissolute but brilliant Comte de Mirabeau, the chivalrous but ineffectual Marquis de Lafayette, the sensual lover of life and revolutionary rhetoric, Georges Jacques Danton, the feared Jean Paul Marat, the young "Angel of Death," Antoine Louis de Saint-Just.

But of all those who played important parts in the Revolution, none is perhaps better suited to illustrate the radical nature of the event than Maximilien Marie Isidore de Robespierre. He came to Paris in the spring of 1789 as a member of the Estates-General, and his execution in the summer of 1794 is usually regarded as the end of the great revolutionary period. He participated in almost all the important debates that troubled France during those five years, and he succeeded in translating many of his ideas into political actions that influenced both his and later times. He expressed a theory of revolutionary politics that became a permanent part of Western political thinking, and he portrayed the high idealism and the narrow intolerance, the love of mankind in general and the cruelty toward individuals, and a belief in the vision of a better world that were to become the characteristics of the dedicated revolutionary.

Robespierre was born in Arras in northwestern France in 1758. His father was a lawyer, and Maximilien was awarded a scholarship to study at the University of Paris. After completing his studies, he returned to Arras, and from 1781 to 1789 he practiced law in his home town. He joined a literary society, and he wrote and published at his own expense several essays on various subjects. He enjoyed some small fame when he successfully defended the right of a citizen to erect a lightning conductor on his house, no matter the complaints of the neighbors at this innovation. Then in 1789 he was selected by his fellow-townsmen to be a representative to the Estates-General and left for Paris.

From the beginning of his political career Robespierre was the constant servant of what he regarded as the revolutionary cause. One of the early revolutionary leaders had stated that people would ultimately judge the Revolution by the amount of money it put in their pockets. But this was not true of Robespierre. He looked upon the Revolution with a religious fervor, and he believed that its purpose should be the creation of what he called "the temple of liberty," resting upon "the foundations of justice and equality." He saw himself almost from the first day as one engaged upon a great historical undertaking. In the early summer of 1789 he noted that the "present Revolution has produced in a few days greater events than the whole previous history of mankind," and two years later he argued that the basic principles of the Revolution "are universal, unchangeable, applicable to all mankind." In 1791 an Englishman set down a description of Robespierre. "He is a stern man, rigid in his principles, plain, unaffected in his manners, no foppery in his dress, certainly above corruption, despising wealth." This is a fair picture, and it is one that remained true throughout Robespierre's life.

Robespierre was what we would call a revolutionary extremist. On almost every issue he was prepared to push the Revolution, no matter what the doubts of others, toward that new human community of virtue, justice, and happiness. He was, for example, consistently anti-clerical, and he achieved his first important recognition when, one month after the opening of the Estates-General, he attacked the rich clergy. "All that is necessary," he pointed out, "is that the bishops and dignitaries of the church should renounce that luxury which is an offense to Christian humility; that they should give up their coaches and give up their horses; if need be, that they should sell a quarter of the property of the church, and give it to the poor." Also, probably more than any other important revolutionary leader, he was socially conscious and identified himself with the poorer classes. He protested against the constitution of 1791, which restricted the right to vote to those who paid taxes equivalent to three days' wages, and contended that every Frenchman, including Jews, actors, and Protestants, should be admitted to the franchise.

In July, 1791, Robespierre published a pamphlet entitled *Address of Maximilien Robespierre to the French*. Here he stated his present position and indicated what his future course would be. Again he stressed the social dimension that he thought the Revolution should have. "I have always held that equality of rights belongs to all members of the state, that the nation includes the working class, and everyone, without distinction of rich or poor." In fact, he seemed to argue that the poor were by definition the virtuous, and "I can testify that this large and interesting class, hitherto called 'the people,' is the natural friend and indispensable champion of freedom." He also expressed the belief that the Revolution was in danger because too many were too weak or too selfish to carry on with the struggle. And he set himself against these opponents in a manner that was to become common during the next three years. "There is nothing that cannot be done by money, by slander, by intrigue, or by bayonets. All these weapons are in the hands of my enemies; whilst I — a simple, weak, isolated individual — have nothing on my side but my courage, the justice of my cause, and the prayers of all good patriots." He concluded the pamphlet with another theme that was to occur again and again in his political statements. "The soul of the republic is virtue — that is, the love of one's country, and a high-minded devotion that sinks all private interests in the interest of the whole community."

In 1792, Robespierre initiated a small newspaper which he used to forward his ideas and to attack his enemies. Much of what he published expressed his dismay at the faltering Revolution. As he wrote: "Reason and public interest started the Revolution; ambition and intrigue have stopped it." Although France was becoming involved in what was to be a bitter international struggle with the rest of Europe, Robespierre argued that "our most dangerous enemies are not those who have openly declared themselves," and he announced his determination to make war on injustice, aristocracy, treachery, and despotism within France as well as without.

All these activities and these pronouncements were in the manner of preparation for the part Robespierre was to play during the last year of his life. In July, 1793, he was elected a member of the Committee of Public Safety. Robespierre did not become a dictator, and other members of the Committee were responsible for initiating and carrying out many of the directives of the group. But Robespierre's influence was great, and he became the spokesman and defender of the revolutionary government. He was identified with the activities of the Committee and is associated historically with the Terror. He was in his own mind the historical instrument cast up by the times to save the Revolution.

Robespierre's vision of the Revolution, a vision that was to become part of every subsequent revolutionary movement in the Western world, was expressed in a speech he made in February, 1794:

> It is time to mark clearly the aim of the Revolution, . . . We desire an order of things in which all base and cruel passions are enchained, and all beneficent and generous passions are awakened by the laws, in which ambition may become the desire to merit glory and to serve the nation, in which there will be no distinctions save those that arise on the basis of equality. . . . We wish to substitute morality for egoism, the empire of reason for the tyranny of fashion, contempt for vice for contempt for misfortune, pride for insolence, large-mindedness for vanity. . . . We wish in a word to fulfill the course of nature, to accomplish the destiny of mankind, to make good the promises of philosophy, to absolve Providence from the long reign of tyranny and crime. . . . May France, once notorious for its slavery, now eclipse the glory of all the free peoples of history, and become the model of the nations, the terror of the oppressors, the consolation of the oppressed, the ornament of the universe. And may we, while we seal our work with our blood, see at least the first rays of the dawn of universal happiness. That is our ambition. That is our aim.

These are noble and moving words, and they express the ultra-radical doctrine of the Revolution. They also pose a dilemma for any revolutionary, such as Robespierre, who is determined to translate these ideas into political action. If one believed, as did Robespierre, that beyond the contradictions, the quarrels, and the confusion there was the fundamental, ultimate reality of the revolutionary goal, then all must strive to achieve this condition of beatitude no matter what the cost. All the suffering and pain and effort must result in a better human condition. If, in spite of everything, the same vice, hypocrisy, and selfishness that existed in the past were to continue into the future, then the blood, the glorious statements, and the promises would have been to no purpose.

In order to guarantee the success of the Revolution, Robespierre adopted the method that has been advocated by countless revolutionaries since his time. The salvation of man would be achieved if necessary by force. Evil influences would be rooted out, malefactors would be destroyed, and those opposed to the great work of saving mankind would be exterminated. Here was the true purpose of the Terror. It was not basically a drunken policy of cruelty, although it was cruel. It was a bloody instrument for man's salvation. For Robespierre the "people" or the "nation" is by definition good. Or, as he once said, "the soul of the Republic is virtue." All conflict and controversy is, then, between the people and those who are enemies of the people, between the nation and those who are aliens and anti-national. One who sincerely believes in his principles cannot allow error and evil to exist, and a phrase spoken by one of Robespierre's contemporaries as early as 1791 contains the bare-bone philosophy of the Terror: "the gangrened limb should be amputated in order to save the rest of the body." According to this argument, the people are the nucleus of the pure. Others, not being pure, have no rights and are, in fact, not even part of the people. The "enemies of mankind" have no claims against the righteous, and "the punishment of the people's enemies is death." One of Robespierre's friends expressed the idea very well. "There are only two kinds of citizens: the good and the bad. The Republic owes the good its protection. To the bad it owes only death."

Robespierre believed that he could separate the good from the bad, the right from the wrong, the beneficial from the harmful. After all, he was the conscience of the Revolution, one who possessed special insights into the motivations of men. Thus "republican severity" or "virtue by intimidation" was justified. Terror and virtue were not incompatible. In fact, they complemented each other. As Robespierre explained, "the basis of popular government in time of revolution is both virtue and terror: virtue without which terror is murderous, terror without which virtue is powerless." Acts against the opponents of virtue were justified for they protected the Revolution from those who because of greed, sloth, immorality, or irresponsibility would destroy it. "The people is sublime, but individuals are weak," and the weak must not be allowed to destroy the sublime. The function of the Terror was to protect the people and not the enemies of the people. Patriots had nothing to fear, while those who were not patriotic deserved no consideration.

In Robespierre's view the nation was an entity that must speak with one voice. As early as September, 1789, he had stated that "the nation only needs one will, and that is its own," and later in a speech he claimed that "I recognize no principles but those of the public interest." The nation was indivisible, and the purposes of the individual and his nation were identical. Anyone who doubted such a unity was unpatriotic. In March, 1794, Saint-Just, whose own attitude closely paralleled that of Robespierre on this subject, argued that the true patriot could never differ with his nation. Therefore, anyone opposing the will of the nation is a traitor. There can be no loyal opposition, for such opposition "is then criminal because it is a form of isolation from the people." There are only factions, which divide the citizens and neutralize the power of the nation. The Terror was thus not a criminal act. It forwarded the greatest of principles and was excused from judgment. It was something entirely different from acts motivated by no great ideals. In Robespierre's words, "it is useless to attempt to attach the idea of crime to the love of liberty, that most sublime of all virtues." The lover of liberty and the defender of the Revolution had a special warrant and acted in response to the demands of a higher historical law.

Of course, Robespierre believed that the Terror would be temporary. Since his days as a lawyer in Arras, he had opposed the death penalty, and he persuaded himself that there would be no more executions once the enemies of liberty were destroyed. He also was a consistent defender of freedom of the press, but not freedom for those "treacherous journalists, the most dangerous enemies of liberty." He was just as certain that one of the aims of the Revolution was "to maintain the freedom of religion." As he said, the Revolution "will not allow peaceable ministers of religion to be persecuted." But "it will punish them severely whenever they dare to use their functions for the deception of citizens or the arming of prejudices and royalism against the Republic." In a speech of June 8, 1794, he set forth his hopes for himself and for those who believed as he. "Let us be generous toward the good, compassionate toward the unfortunate, inexorable toward men of evil, just toward all."

But always there were enemies. No matter how severe the revolutionary government was, new traitors continued to appear as soon as the old were destroyed. There was always a new "criminal horde" that threatened to undo the work of the Revolution. The end of the Terror always appeared just beyond the horizon, and Robespierre hoped that one last great effort would bring complete victory. In early 1794 he assured his listeners that "victory lies within our grasp. There are only a few serpents left for us to crush." It is reported that from his audience came cries of "Crush them! Crush them!" One of the proclamations of the Committee of Public Safety to the army read: "In a few days tyrants will be no more, and the Republic will owe to you its happiness and glory." But the number of enemies increased, and from the ruins of old treason came new and ever more threatening dangers.

By the early summer of 1794 Robespierre had become almost pathological in his suspicions. He saw enemies and traitors everywhere. Indiscretions became crimes, and any opposition to Robespierre's activities was an indication of collusion with the forces of evil. "Either these monsters must be unmasked and exterminated, or I must perish," was his cry of anguish. In his last speech of late July, 1794, he pointed out that, more than ever before, the nation was endangered by intrigue and treason. All the efforts thus far had not resulted in success. He implied that very few could be trusted and that more arrests and more executions must be carried out. He did not name those whom he suspected, but the tone of his attack and the scope of his accusations alarmed large numbers of those who listened to him.

Fear of Robespierre had become widespread, and those who felt themselves threatened entered into an alliance to protect their lives. Even some members of the Committee of Public Safety were prepared to act against him. On July 27, 1794, amid general attacks and counter-attacks and wild confusion, Robespierre was accused of attempting to become a dictator and of various other crimes. He rose to speak in his own defense but was shouted down and arrested. He is reported to have said: "The Republic is lost, for brigands have won the day." His last words of defense, after five years of many speeches, were "It's a lie!" in response to the charge that he was planning a public rising against other political leaders. The next day, in company with a handful of supporters, he was executed. His body was thrown into an unmarked grave.

Robespierre was the "dark spirit" of the Revolution, and after his death he was commonly attacked as "the most ferocious cannibal, the most monstrous scoundrel." What was probably the earliest published life of Robespierre was entitled *The Life and Crime of Robespierre, Surnamed the Tyrant, from His Birth to His Death.* He has been described as an "insolent demagogue," a dictator, a tyrant, a hypocrite, and a bigot. Yet he has also been called "the Incorruptible," "the deputy of mankind," and "the tribune of the people." A contemporary regarded him as a "republican who was perhaps too austere, but whose one wish was that liberty should triumph." Many years after Robespierre's execution, one of his friends wrote: "No one knows better than I how sincere, disinterested, and absolute was his devotion to the Republic. He has become the scapegoat of the revolutionists, but he was the best man of them all. It is fifty years since he died. But I still treasure in my heart the memory of him, and the lively affection which he inspired." So, too, we have the testimony of Bertrand Barère, a member of the Committee of Public Safety who lived until 1841. Shortly before his death Barère spoke of Robespierre. "He was a man of purity and integrity, a true and sincere republican."

If one must settle upon a description of Robespierre, perhaps the most satisfactory is that he was "the frozen embodiment of principle." His love of mankind was sincere, and he could not be persuaded, bribed, or frightened from pursuing the course he thought correct. He had a great belief in the future of mankind, and he was indifferent to the weaknesses, the doubts, and the procrastinations of others. He was a devoted patriot, and he sensed that without a change of human character as well as a change in political institutions the great promise of the Revolution would be betrayed.

Yet there is something forbidding about Robespierre. He was so convinced of his own virtue that he became the deadly enemy of those poor human beings who could not keep to the narrow path of righteousness that he had pointed out. Obsessed by his great goal, he grew more and more indifferent to the fate of those who perished on the way. His continual preachments about virtue become tiresome, and one can sympathize with Danton, who once in exasperation replied that virtue was what he did with his wife every night. Robespierre, of course, was offended, as he became increasingly offended by all those who did not see the clear, bright outlines of the great life. As is true of so many dedicated moralists, Robespierre had little sympathy with the poor, weak material that is human nature. Because life could not satisfy the demands he set for it, Robespierre was prepared to take cruel revenge upon humanity.

Moreover, he carried the smell of death with him, and all his protestations to the contrary we are not convinced that he could ever have freed himself from dependence upon the ultimate deadly weapon of persuasion. Fear and intimidation were important parts of his activity, and his indiscriminate suspicions undercut his great program. There were traitors in France, as there were those who had tired of the Revolution. But when the prisons were opened after Robespierre's fall, they were found to contain few adventurers, few corrupt politicians, few plotters against the state. The great majority were common people who had grumbled over some regulation, had made some rash remark, or had been accused by some suspicious or vindictive neighbor. Now released, they picked up their small bundles of possessions and went home, as bewildered at their sudden freedom as they had been at their equally sudden arrest. Ironically, they had escaped death at the hands of their great champion only because he himself had been destroyed by those who loved them less. In 1832, Sieyès, who had written over forty years before the most famous pamphlet extolling the virtues of the Third Estate, and now ill and delirious, said to his valet: "If Robespierre calls, I am not at home." Sieyès was suffering from a hallucination. But the fear he expressed had been real. The revolutionary tradition in the West was to take from the French Revolution, and from Robespierre, a belief in the ultimate realization of liberty, equality, and justice. But also from the French Revolution, and from Robespierre, was to come a reliance, however reluctantly arrived at, upon violence as a means to a great end and a willingness to sacrifice those who because of weakness or perversity were not prepared to accept the revolutionary definition of the methods to be followed in realizing the great promise of the future.

Napoleon Bonaparte

In 1799 Napoleon Bonaparte, the most talented of the young French generals created by the revolutionary wars, overthrew the government by a military coup and assumed control of France. Born in 1769, Napoleon had in the seventeen-nineties distinguished himself as a military leader. He had directed a brilliant Italian campaign and had led his army on an invasion of Egypt and Syria. His career after 1799 is so well known as to be legendary. He won a series of spectacular battles — Marengo, Austerlitz, Jena — and his armies marched into most of the capitals of Europe. He made himself emperor, established his brothers as kings in Italy, Germany, Holland, and Spain, and attempted to organize the continent against his long-time enemy England. In 1812 he invaded Russia and reached Moscow. He was forced to undertake a disastrous retreat and after a series of defensive battles against the allied forces of Britain, Russia, Austria, and Prussia abdicated and was exiled to the island of Elba in the Mediterranean in 1814. In the spring of 1815 he returned to France and easily seized power from the hands of the restored Bourbon king. On June 18, however, he was defeated at Waterloo and soon thereafter surrendered to the English. He was now exiled to the island of St. Helena off the African Atlantic coast. Here he died in 1821. His body was returned to Paris in 1840.

Napoleon so dominated his time and aroused such violent emotions that it is even today difficult to view him clearly and without prejudice. The English poet Lord Byron called him the "Thunderer of the scene." The sister of the executed French queen Marie Antoinette considered him "that ferocious beast, that Corsican bastard, that dog." Thomas Jefferson described him as "the great oppressor of the rights and liberties of the world," and almost a hundred years later Émile Zola saw him as "a hammer blow that cracked the brains of his times." Napoleon was the little corporal, the great general, the ruthless tyrant, the brilliant legislator, the vulgar upstart. He was a historical colossus, as he was the stuff that historical myths are made of. World-famous at twenty-six, he was master of France at thirty, virtual ruler of Europe at forty, an exile at forty-five, and dead at fifty-one. He was a legendary figure, but his accomplishments were real. He was a military genius, a gifted and imaginative administrator, a man of political action who was also a man of political thought, and one who knew the secret of creating that enthusiastic unity of national purpose that ties a people to its leader.

To understand Napoleon it is important to realize that he inherited the French Revolution and that many of his activities, his successes, and his failures were directly related to his attempts to consolidate that inheritance. Napoleon understood the temper of his period, and he was in tune with his age. As he himself once stated: "Nothing has been simpler than my elevation. It was related to the peculiarity of the times. . . . I have always marched with the opinion of the great masses and with events." He grasped the basic meaning of the revolutionary upheavals of the seventeen-nineties, and he never abandoned his claims to be a revolutionary. He once described himself in dramatic but realistic terms. "I am a soldier, child of the Revolution, sprung from the bosom of the people. I shall not allow myself to be insulted like a king." He identified himself with the aspirations of the French people in such a way that he seemed to be an instrument expressing the intelligence, the wit, the ignorance, and the power of the age and the country. He commanded the allegiance of millions because they saw themselves in him. His strength lay in the conviction of the French people that he was their representative and that people and ruler were pursuing common great aims. In this sense he was the first practitioner of modern politics.

It is usually pointed out that Napoleon's great achievement was that he brought an end to the confusion of the Revolution. He brought order where there had been disorder, stability where there had been infirmity, and strength where there had been impotence. Under Napoleon the bureaucratic machinery operated efficiently, taxation was regulated, and the average Frenchman was offered steady prices, an end to land speculation, and good roads free of highwaymen. Napoleon guaranteed the transference of land to the small farmer, he damped the bitter religious controversies that had wracked revolutionary France, and he united the country through a judicious mixture of severity and moderation. In all these ways Napoleon conserved many of the ideas of the Revolution and fitted them into a new organizational pattern. He did not attempt to suppress the turbulence of the Revolution but rather to channel it and, as he said, "to give a direction to the public spirit." In essence he bent the basic ideas of the Enlightenment and the Revolution to create a new society, and a new national state.

Napoleon made the principle of opportunity for all, the career open to talents, the basis of his political, military, and legal activities. One of the driving ideas of the Revolution had been the attack upon privileges accorded to birth and station, and a great deal of the support for the Revolution had come from disgruntled professional men and discontented junior officers and noncommissioned officers of the armed forces who had felt themselves to be the victims of prejudice. Napoleon himself was the best example of a man who had made his way to the top through his own talents and his own energies. No one had started with less and had gone further, and his own career was a constant invitation to the gifted and the vigorous to push themselves ahead and to seize the rewards available to those with the energy, the intelligence, and the foresight to take advantage of the opportunity.

Napoleon's claim that every private soldier's knapsack contained a marshal's baton was, of course, not literally true. But it was true enough to bring to positions of command in the French army men who were far more talented than those in the armies that opposed them. During his years in power Napoleon created twenty-six marshals, and they came from all social and political backgrounds — the old aristocracy, the middle classes, and the miscellaneous trades and occupations. One was an innkeeper's son, one had been a peddler, one a smuggler and fruit-seller, one an apprentice dyer, one a cooper, and one a barber. Some of them were vulgarians, some were money-grubbers, some were ridiculous in their attempts to ape the manners of the aristocrats, and, as they grew older, some became more interested in preserving their fortunes than in risking their reputations. But in the early years of Napoleon's rule they were the most brilliant collection of gifted military leaders ever assembled under one command.

Napoleon is usually thought of as a military man, and this common opinion is to some extent at least justified. No general in ancient or modern history won so many victories in so short a time. During his period of rule he was at war with at least one opponent for all but fourteen months, and his armies marched into most of the famous cities of continental Europe — Vienna, Berlin, Warsaw, Venice, Madrid, Lisbon, Rome, and Moscow. He was a brilliant military strategist, and in one campaign after another he exhibited what has been called "his marvelous activity, his astonishing quickness of decision, his incredible memory for detail, the sureness of his practical judgment." He tied the French people to him with his military victories, and he made the army an expression of the national spirit. He made war an integral part of the nation's activities and used the "nation in arms" as an instrument of politics in a way that was new to the Western world.

But Napoleon was more than a mere military conqueror. He himself argued that the purpose of all his activity, military and otherwise, was to provide "a means whereby a lead may be given to political and moral conceptions." He attempted to plant the seeds of the French Revolution throughout Europe, and in doing this he brought about a new relationship of church and state, established a body of uniform laws, and stimulated a national system of education. He sensed that the old institutions governing men's relationship to each other and to their society were defunct and that new patterns of allegiance must be developed. "All that is good, all that is beautiful, is invariably the result of a simple and uniform system," he wrote, and Napoleon attempted to install just such a simple and uniform system.

In his attitude toward religion, Napoleon combined the rationalism of the eighteenth century with the dynamic nationalism of the nineteenth. He knew the value of pomp and emotional trappings. And he was a master at manipulating the emotions of the French people. The intangible if real pursuit of national and individual glory was a part of the Napoleonic system, and the rolling thunder of the cries of "long live the Emperor" that swept through the ranks of the assembled army had an emotional intensity far greater than ever before experienced in Europe. But this was a secularly inspired emotion, and Napoleon had few religious feelings and regarded the church as an organization that could serve his purposes and not its own. He continued the revolutionary thrust and reduced the influence of the church. He subjected religious schools to government control, and he made the church, like the army and the bureaucracy, an instrument supporting the aims of the secular state. Because he was uninterested in, and even indifferent to, religious questions, Napoleon did not attempt to enforce any religious doctrine in France or in Europe. As a result there was generally freedom of conscience, and the expression of opinion on religious matters was relatively unhindered. So long as such religious opinion did not interfere with the operation of the state, Napoleon paid little attention to it.

This was not the case with education. The system of national education drawn up during the Revolution had not taken root in France. But Napoleon organized the schools as a part of the national purpose and stressed the training of teachers who could act as advocates and supporters of the national goals. "There never will be a fixed political state of things in this country until we have a corps of teachers instructed in established principles. So long as the people are not taught from their earliest years whether they ought to be Republicans or Royalists, Christians or Infidels, the state cannot be properly called a nation, for it must then rest upon a foundation which is vague and uncertain and be forever exposed to disorders." As much as the army, the educational system in France became an active participant in the attempt to forward Napoleon's idea of citizenship in the new national state that he had created. The state assumed responsibility for the education of the young and in turn expected the schools to become strong supporters of the state. A network of schools was established throughout France, and Napoleon relied upon the teachers in these schools to direct their educational efforts toward providing the state with dedicated, intelligent, patriotic graduates who could contribute to the welfare of the nation. No ruler had previously paid as much attention to the schools as Napoleon, nor had any ruler so realized the possibility of education acting as a support of his policy.

In the legal field Napoleon also carried on the Revolution. Working with the best authorities he could find, he introduced into France and other parts of Europe what came to be called the Napoleonic Code. Actually there were a series of Codes — a Civil Code, a Code of Civil Procedure, and a Code of Criminal Procedure, with a Commercial Code to be added later. The idea of the Codes was to lay down clear, precise, general rules by which administrative officials, judges, and juries would determine how justice could be done. The Codes were to provide a new standard of administrative and legal procedure to take the place of the old, discredited traditional instruments that were so ambiguous and contradictory. Some parts of the Codes can be criticized. The position of women was low. A woman could not give, sell, or mortgage real estate, she could not act as a guardian of her children, and she could not inherit from her husband until the claims of the children had been satisfied. Also, the Codes contained no provision for habeas corpus and no real guarantees for freedom of speech, assembly, or the press.

Yet even these omissions cannot detract from the importance of Napoleon's Codes. For the first time in civil law all men were to be regarded as truly equal, the family was protected against the government, property was secure, and the procedure of the courts was swift. When they were applied to countries outside France, the Codes stimulated a radical change in social relationships and in the social structure. In 1806 the Napoleonic Code was introduced into northern Italy. The remains of feudal rights, including those of the church, were struck down. The principles of civil and legal equality were reinforced. The legality of civil marriage was confirmed. Division of estates among heirs was established, trials were made public, and the remaining judicial rights of the church were eliminated. Similarly, in 1807 the introduction of the Code into parts of Germany guaranteed equality before the law and religious liberty, abolished serfdom and feudal rights, put an end to the special prerogatives, privileges, and offices traditionally held by the nobility, and established a system of equal taxation.

Napoleon provided the French, and others, with a working legal system, the idea of a comprehensive system of national education, and an operating government that protected those who obeyed the laws and ruthlessly punished all who sought to infringe them. He introduced a system of weights and measures, he created a network of roads, and he rebuilt parts of Paris. And he gave those who followed him a heady taste for military glory. He identified the national feeling with military campaigning, and he channeled patriotism into support for war. A son of France became a soldier of France, and Napoleon made war the final arbiter of any international dispute.

There is no question of Napoleon's talent. He was a military genius and a creative administrator. And he possessed that personal magnetism without which no popular political leader can succeed. But he was in many ways the victim of his own accomplishments, and his career illustrates the dilemma of the man of power who finds that the political instruments he wields with such skill are ultimately the means of his destruction. Napoleon made history. But in doing this he created the conditions that brought him down.

Since the seventeen-nineties, when he had first shown evidence of his amazing military capabilities during the Italian campaign, Napoleon had based his career upon his ability to defeat his enemies in battle. But he was never able to escape from his dependence upon military triumphs, and he was never to free himself from the implications of a military policy that demanded almost continual warfare. His early victories had forwarded great social and political ideas and had created the conditions for the establishment of new and meaningful European institutions. But more and more his wars became military adventures that promised less and less to those who had to endure the suffering and disorder produced by the continual marching and counter-marching of armies across Europe. Military campaigns became increasingly difficult to justify, and Napoleon showed a certain irresponsibility regarding the costs of his wars. In the end the gains could not match the price, and war became a liability rather than an asset. The Spanish campaign and the invasion of Russia were military disasters that threatened the entire Napoleonic system. War, which had brought Napoleon to the heights, undermined him, and for many, Napoleon's benefits of legal equality and religious liberty were obscured by the burdens of taxation and conscription in support of apparently purposeless wars.

Napoleon's image as a great European liberator was also tarnished by his own limited view of what a Western society should be. He was basically a cynic, and he was indifferent to moral or ethical considerations. He had provided equality, opportunity, and government-directed "progress." But he had little belief in an expanded view of the potentialities of individuals. He was alert to the desire of the French people for civil and social equality, and this he championed. But he had little sympathy with that other great battlecry of the French Revolution — liberty. "What they want is glory and gratified vanity," he said of the French, "but as for liberty they do not understand what it means." At times Napoleon even appeared to believe that liberty was of little value and that Frenchmen had little attachment to it. "The French are indifferent to liberty," he argued. "They neither understand it nor like it. Vanity is their ruling passion, and political equality, which enables them to feel that any position is open to them, is the only political right they care about." Napoleon's intolerance of any political activity independent of his own made him incapable of ascribing any action to anything but self-interest and personal egoism, and he scorned the arguments of those who might plead a disinterested devotion to an ideological cause.

In the early stages of his career Napoleon had been seen by many as the protector and advocate of the great ideas of the Enlightenment and the Revolution. But many of his former supporters, particularly intellectuals, lost faith. The composer Beethoven had originally dedicated his third symphony to Napoleon as a historical manifestation of the human striving for freedom. But upon hearing that Napoleon had made himself an emperor, Beethoven changed the dedication. More and more Napoleon the great liberator became identified as Napoleon the tyrant, and many of those who earlier had welcomed the appearance of his armies now hated the "French vultures." In 1814 one of Napoleon's opponents argued the case that would have been accepted by many:

> If administration consists in numbers; if, in order to govern well, it is sufficient to know how much grain, wine, and oil a province produces, what is the last crown that can be levied, the last man that can be taken, most certainly Bonaparte was a great administrator; it is impossible to organize evil better, to place more order in disorder. But if the best administration is that which leaves a people in peace, which nourishes in them sentiments of justice and piety, which is sparing of the blood of men, which respects the rights of citizens, the estates of families, most certainly the government of Bonaparte was the worst of governments.

Napoleon ultimately lost his sense of historical direction. He relied more and more upon what the poet Shelley called his preference for "a frail and bloody pomp" and no longer acted as a son of the Revolution. His own family had stood in line to receive its meals at a public soup kitchen. Napoleon, after fighting his way to the top, could think of nothing better than to make himself an emperor. He had shown his superiority to all the traditional nobility of Europe. But then he created a new nobility that was as ridiculous as the old. Men who had, as Napoleon claimed, "won battles without artillery, crossed rivers without bridges, made forced marches without shoes and camps without bread" received historically ludicrous titles. Between 1806 and 1814 Napoleon made one of his famous marshals a king, three of them princes, thirteen of them dukes, and six of them counts. By the end of his period of rule he had created thirty-one dukes, 452 counts, 1,500 barons, and 1,474 chevaliers. The fruits of the Revolution became empty designations such as Prince of Neuchâtel, Grand Duke of Berg, Prince of Ponte Corvo, Duke of Valmy, Duke of Danzig, Duke of Montebello, Duke of Elchingen, Duke of Dalmatia. An imperial comic opera went on throughout Europe, and the real accomplishments of Napoleon were masked by the artificial trappings of a new and meaningless royalty. The mother of one of Napoleon's new nobility, a tough-minded old peasant woman, expressed herself well and truly when she said of her title-encrusted and superficially adorned son: "When you cannot see the jackass for his burden, the beast is overloaded."

In many of his activities Napoleon himself became almost a parody of his own genius. The man with "the hat, surmounted by a pick-up plume, his ill-cut coat, and a sword" divorced one wife and then married a princess in a grotesque fairy-tale dream adventure of the country clod. He, the great destroyer of the past, was determined to found a dynasty. The end of his historical enterprise became his effort to leave his son a crown. His sense of reality was blurred by his pretensions. In early December of 1812 he could, in a famous bulletin, announce the result of the disastrous invasion of Russia with an emphasis upon pomp and a personal egotism that is stunning in its emptiness. The army had endured frightful suffering and staggering losses. Yet Napoleon's announcement to the people of France could close with the sentence: "His Majesty's health has never been better." This statement has been defended as an attempt to reassure the French people. But it was a factual lie and a fatuous insult to those thousands who would never again see their homeland.

In 1815 Napoleon's imperial structure was swept away, and his defeat at Waterloo sent him into exile and brought a king back to the French throne. In some ways he had been a great failure. He had not been able to consolidate his victories or to escape from the mad merry-go-round of war. Europe needed time to adjust to the revolutionary upheaval. Napoleon failed to provide this time, and the task was left to lesser men. How different, and perhaps less tragic, the subsequent history of the Western world would have been had Napoleon avoided his later ruinous campaigns and succeeded in establishing a powerful, dynamic, and unified supranational state in Western Europe. He experienced little difficulty in bringing the areas now occupied by the nations of Italy, Belgium, The Netherlands, and West Germany into close union with France. Here the seeds of the new revolutionary ideas and institutions could have bloomed. Here the benefits of the Napoleonic system could have been consolidated and a stimulating climate could have provided for the development of the creative energies of the continental West Europeans.

This did not happen. Perhaps the task was too great even for a man of Napoleon's talents. His legacy included his Codes, which remained in partial effect through large parts of Western Europe, the idea of the nation, particularly the nation as a military entity, and his own legend. But he failed to provide even for France any kind of solution to the divisive forces that continued to plague the country. The problems of the meaning of the French Revolution and the future course that France should take remained and promoted a continual frustration and animosity in French life. Most important, perhaps, Napoleon's failure was the failure of France to succeed in providing a stable and enduring revolutionary political pattern for Western Europe. France had been the leading intellectual, political, and cultural state in the eighteenth century, and from the seventeen-nineties she had attempted to institutionalize her influence throughout the continent. After Napoleon's

defeat she was to remain a leader in European thought, and her influence was powerful and fruitful. But she was not to be the example, and
the ideas developed in France were to be modified, warped, and distorted by France herself and by other national groups in Europe. The
new Europe was not to be organized by France. Instead there was to be
a searching for different solutions to the political problems posed by
the modern Western world.

SUGGESTIONS FOR FURTHER READING

*Books and articles on the French Revolution constitute a substantial spe-
cialized library. Good surveys of the period are J. M. Thompson,* The
French Revolution *(1965) and George Rudé's* Revolutionary Europe: 1783-
1815 *(1964). Georges Lefebvre's* The Coming of the French Revolution *(1947)
and* The French Revolution, from Its Origins to 1793 *(1962) are rather tough
going but valuable. R. R. Palmer's* The Age of the Democratic Revolution
(1959-1964) is long but challenging. Bernard Fay's The Revolutionary Spirit
in France and America *(1966) and Jeffry Kaplow's* New Perspectives on the
French Revolution *(1965) are worth examining. Perhaps the most satisfactory single commentator on the Revolution, as he is certainly one of the
most readable, is Alfred Cobban. His* The Debate on the French Revolution
(1950), The Social Interpretation of the French Revolution *(1964), and*
Aspects of the French Revolution *(1968) may be recommended without hes-
itation.*

*There are also some excellent studies of specific aspects of the Revolu-
tion and of particular participants. J. M. Thompson's* Leaders of the French
Revolution *(1929) and* Robespierre *(1939) are still worth examining. R. R.
Palmer's* Twelve Who Ruled: The Committee of Public Safety during the
Terror *(1941) guides the reader through one of the most perplexing, confus-
ing, and contradictory periods of the Revolution. George Rudé's* The
Crowd in the French Revolution *(1959) and his* Robespierre *(1967) are
good, as is Leo Gershoy's* Bertrand Barère, a Reluctant Terrorist *(1961). T. W.
Copeland's* Our Eminent Friend Edmund Burke: Six Essays *(1949) and
Cobban's* Edmund Burke and the Revolt against the Eighteenth Century
(1929) provide an excellent introduction to the study of Burke.

*Books on Napoleon will never be in short supply. Three good studies
will introduce the reader to the subject: Pieter Geyl,* Napoleon: For and
Against *(1949); F. M. H. Markham,* Napoleon and the Awakening of Europe
(1954); and Bernard Schwartz, The Code Napoleon and the Common-Law
World *(1956). Fascinating insights into Napoleon's character are to be
found in Ernest J. Knapton's elegantly written and scholarly* Empress Jose-
phine *(1963).*

Moonrise Over the Sea detail, Caspar David Friedrich, 1823, Nationalgalerie, Berlin.

4

The New Nineteenth Century

1807	Britain abolished the slave trade in her colonies.
1808	African slave trade prohibited by the United States.
1814-1815	Congress of Vienna. Meeting of the victorious powers following the defeat of Napoleon.
1815	France abolished the slave trade.
1818	Institute of Civil Engineers, the first professional engineering society, founded in London.
1819-1837	Jacob Grimm's *German Grammar* established basis for development of modern philology.
1821-1822	Friedrich Schleiermacher's *The Christian Belief* emphasized the emotional side of Christianity and rejected both traditional dogmatism and rationalism.
1824-1826	First Anglo-Burmese War. The result was British acquisition of extensive Burmese territory.
1824-1827	First war of the British on the Gold Coast in Africa against the Ashanti. A second war took place in 1873-1874.
1828	Test Act repealed in Britain. Removed necessity of office holders accepting "the sacrament of the Lord's Supper according to the rites and usage of the Church of England."

1828	Karl von Baer founded modern comparative embryology with the publication of *The Developmental History of Animals*.
1829	Catholic Emancipation Act passed in Britain. Removed the restraints and disabilities that kept Roman Catholics from holding office and voting.
1829	Date by which in the United States the principle of universal white manhood suffrage was largely established.
1830	French expeditionary force occupied Algiers. By 1870 France had subjugated Algeria.
1830-1833	Charles Lyell published his *Principles of Geology*. Usually regarded as the most influential of the early statements of the new revolutionary geology.
1831	New electoral law in France following revolution of 1830 extended the franchise but still gave the vote to only about 3 per cent of the adult male population.
1831	Foundation of the British Association for the Advancement of Science. In 1848 the American Association for the Advancement of Science was founded.
1832	Parliamentary Reform Bill passed in Britain. Gave the vote to only one person out of thirty but did break the political power of the aristocracy in favor of that of the middle class.
1832	The papal encyclical *Mirari vos* condemned liberty of conscience, liberty of the press, and revolt of any kind against an established government.
1833	Abolition of slavery throughout the British colonies except in India where slavery was abolished in 1860.
1835	Thomas B. Macaulay's "Minute on Education," which prompted the decision to use English as a medium of education in India.
1835-1836	David Friedrich Strauss' *The Life of Jesus* introduced the new principles of biblical scholarship. The Gospels were not historical documents but "myths," Jesus was the personification of an idea, and the miraculous elements of the New Testament were declared fabrications.

1836	Emile Girardin founded the first modern, mass newspaper — *La Presse* — in Paris. Girardin's paper was described as "political but cheap, aimed at the accumulation of advertising revenue, and made attractive to its readers by gossip, serial novels, and various other stunts."
1839-1842	First Afghan War between Britain and Afghanistan.
1842	As a result of the so-called Opium War, China ceded Hong Kong to Britain and opened some ports to British trade.
1845-1848	First and Second Anglo-Sikh War. Result was annexation of some and at least partial British control of other areas of the Punjab.
1846	First public demonstration of ether as an anesthetic in surgery.
1848	First Women's Rights convention held at Seneca Falls, New York.
1853-1855	Joseph de Gobineau's *Essay on the Inequality of the Human Races*. The most famous of the efforts to use race as the explanatory principle in history. According to Gobineau, the white race was superior to the black and the yellow in intelligence, love of order, capacity for reflection, and allegiance to civilized values. The mixing of races is disastrous, for it results in degeneration, and democracy itself is the inevitable result of "mixed breeds."
1854	The American Commodore Matthew Perry negotiated a treaty with Japan and opened the country to commercial contacts.
1854	Dogma of the Immaculate Conception of the Virgin was made an article of faith for Roman Catholics.
1858	Rudolph Virchow described the cell as the basic element of the life process.
1859	Charles Darwin's *Origin of the Species*.
1864	Papal encyclical *Quanta cura*, with the appended *Syllabus errorum*. An attack upon nationalism, socialism, and various other ideas of the century. "It is an error to believe that the Roman Pontiff can and ought to reconcile himself to, and agree with, progress, liberalism, and contemporary civilization."
1865	Joseph Lister initiated the practice of antiseptic surgery.

1867   Parliamentary Reform Bill in Britain admitted a large part of the city working class to the franchise.

1869   Opening of the Suez Canal. In 1875 Britain purchased the controlling shares in the canal from Egypt.

1870   Vatican Council proclaimed the dogma of papal infallibility, which stated that the Pope, when speaking on matters of faith or morals, was infallible.

1872   Ballot made secret for the first time in Britain.

1876   Britain's Queen Victoria declared Empress of India. An act illustrating the pomp and the power of the Western world and the international prestige that had been achieved in the nineteenth century.

The defeat of Napoleon in 1815 ended the international turmoil that had characterized Europe for over twenty years. The Western world, and Western Europe in particular, entered upon a period of relative stability. For almost a century there was to be general peace in Europe. There were wars — the Crimean War of the middle 1850's, the Franco-Prussian War of 1870-1871, and the Spanish-American War of 1898. But these conflicts were limited and did not introduce catastrophic suffering and dislocation into Western society. The American Civil War was bloody and prolonged, but its effects were largely confined to the United States.

There were continual military skirmishes in other parts of the world as the Europeans pressed upon the peoples of Asia and Africa. Although the years from 1815 to 1855 were regarded by the British as a time of peace, during that period British soldiers fought in India and Burma, humbled China in the Opium War of 1839-1842, carried out campaigns against the Ashanti in Africa, and engaged in numerous battles with the Sikhs, Afghans, and Gurkhas. But these activities occurred in far-off places, involved only small numbers of professional military men, and did not set off shock waves in Europe.

The nineteenth century was the golden age of modern Europe. London and Paris became the first true world capitals, centers of world-wide commercial, political, and intellectual influence. With their military strength, their technology, and their organizational talents, Europeans dominated world history. The triumphs of industrialization, national power, science, and intellectual discovery made the century appear as a period unlike any other in man's experience. A belief in progress and continual improvement entered into the Western consciousness, and a speech made in 1847 by the American Daniel Webster in praise of the "brave new world" of the nineteenth century expressed a common attitude.

It is an extraordinary era in which we live. It is altogether new. The world has seen nothing like it before. I will not pretend, no one can pretend, to discern the end; but everybody knows that the age is remarkable for scientific research into the heavens, the earth, and what is beneath the earth; and perhaps more remarkable still for the application of this scientific research to the pursuits of life. The ancients saw nothing like it. The moderns have seen nothing like it till the present generation.... We see the ocean navigated and the solid land traversed by steam power, and intelligence communicated by electricity. Truly this is almost a miraculous era. What is before us no one can say, what is upon us no one can hardly believe. The progress of the age has almost outstripped human belief; the future is known only to Omniscience.

This confidence in progress and improvement was often stated in the most vulgar platitudes. But the solid evidence was clearly at hand. One could see the mill towns, the railroads, and the gas-lit city streets. One could even marvel at the numerous mechanical gadgets such as the flushing toilet and the pull-over beer tap. And the intellectual triumphs were equally obvious. In the first half of the century the German scholar David Strauss established a new type of biblical interpretation, Charles Lyell developed the science of geology, Justus von Liebig introduced the scientific study of soils, and Jacob and Wilhelm Grimm showed the way for the comparative study of language and literature. After 1850 the pace was even quicker. Charles Darwin provided new insights into the origins of man, and Jean Charcot used hypnosis in psychotherapy. Ether became a common anesthetic, and the machine gun, the motion picture film, and dynamite were invented.

The century could be described in terms of power. It was also a time of increasing individual freedom. "Freedom is a new religion, the religion of our age," wrote the German poet Heinrich Heine, and the nineteenth century did witness a movement toward the conditions necessary for human freedom. Restrictions upon religious beliefs were eased, and human slavery disappeared in the Western world. There did develop what was described as "an extreme, perhaps an excessive, sensibility towards human suffering," and the brutality that had been so much a part of the eighteenth and earlier centuries became less frequent. Public whipping for legal offenses was largely abandoned, as were the press gangs, whereby individuals could be arbitrarily seized and forced into the military services. The bloodthirsty criminal law, which in England, for example, provided for the death penalty for some two hundred crimes in 1800, was amended, and there was a gradual gentling of manners. Throughout the century the franchise was continually extended, the harshest aspects of inequality were softened, and educational opportunities increased so that by 1900 Western European countries were engaged with mixed results in the historically unique effort to send everyone to school.

Tensions and Conflict

Yet an important philosopher has called the nineteenth "the darkest of all the centuries of modern time," and throughout the one hundred years there was dissension, argument, and conflict. None of the important controversies that had been sparked in the seventeenth and eighteenth centuries — natural versus human law, collective versus individual rights, tradition versus innovation, imperfect man and human perfectibility — were resolved. The bright confidence of the century was matched by doubt, ugliness, and confusion. In his *Paris in 1831* the French novelist Honoré de Balzac noted that Paris was "a city of contrasts, homeland of mud, of dung and marvels, of merit and mediocrity, of opulence and misery, of charlatanism and celebrities, of luxury and destitution, of virtues and vices, of morality and depravity." In 1839 the Englishman Charles Greville made a similar observation:

> On the surface all is light and smooth enough; the country is powerful, peaceful and prosperous, and all the elements of wealth and power are increasing; but the mind of the mass is disturbed and discontented, and there is a continual ferment going on and separate and unconnected causes of agitation and disquiet which create great alarm but which there seems to exist no power of checking or subduing.

Some of these tensions in European society resulted from the religious and spiritual schisms that had been created by the powerful secular and intellectual thrust of the eighteenth century. Old quarrels did not disappear but only became more exacerbated. Even as the West became generally more secular and as intellectual effort remade the Western world, hostile counter-movements grew alongside. A great part of the Roman Catholic Church found it impossible to accept the increasing secularization, liberalism, the new nationalism, and what were called "the errors of the century." A famous Catholic commentator argued in the eighteen-twenties: "There is no peace for the intellect except when it is certain of possessing the truth, and there is no peace for the nations except when they are under the rule of order. Society is so agitated because everything is uncertain — religion, morality, and government. The world is the prey of opinions. Reestablish authority and order will reappear." In every European country many Catholics looked with distrust, astonishment, and bewilderment at what was happening about them. In 1832 the Pope delivered the first of a series of crushing rebukes to liberal thought. Liberty of conscience and worship was condemned, as were the ideas of freedom of the press, separation of church and state, and all the "other harmful errors of those who, possessed by an undue love of liberty, do their utmost to undermine authority." In education, in politics, and in general intellectual outlook the Catholic Church was an opponent of what it regarded as the corrosive effects of modernism.

New and appealing Protestant denominations also appeared that were protests against many of the prevalent tendencies of the century. The best-known leader of such a denomination was John Wesley, the founder of Methodism, who died in 1791 but whose followers increased steadily throughout the nineteenth century. Wesley was a revivalist, who experienced almost daily the interaction of God and the devil in his life, believed in witchcraft and magic, and dismissed human reason as presumptuous and unreliable. Similar groups abounded in the West, and the scientific and intellectual advances of the century were matched by a growth of religious sects that attracted those people who hungered after supernatural explanations to the conditions of their lives. These denominations often exhibited "heat without light," but their combination of a rather simple but heartfelt religiosity, a firm reliance upon a literal reading of the Bible, and a dedicated belief in a strict if somewhat cramping morality made them powerful political and social influences.

There were also Europeans who were not necessarily supporters of any religious interpretation but who could not accept the intellectual, political, and historical direction of the times. In the eighteenth century there had appeared what came to be called the Romantic movement, and the influence of this movement continued into the nineteenth. The Romantics largely rejected reason and stressed the value of subjective emotion and intuitive knowledge. Enthusiasm was praised, while rationalism was attacked as cold, mechanical, and inhuman. An emphasis was placed upon what could be called the "inner music" of the human soul rather than upon rational debate, upon a brooding over the dark recesses of the human experience rather than upon what was described as a superficial arithmetic analysis of the affairs of men. Spirituality was opposed to intellect, and unexamined belief was set against rational explanation.

Romanticism, especially as it developed in Germany, was a rich and dangerous doctrine. There was a glorification of the submerged, primitive urges of mankind, of the earth, the fire, the wind sweeping through the trees — all those things that spoke directly to man without the interference of the intellect. The robust, unthinking, pious peasant was set against the hair-splitting, confused professor, and the spirituality of the tribal unit was glorified at the expense of the dry-as-dust, logical ideas of the rationalists. What many thinkers of the Enlightenment had seen as ignorance, superstition, and fanaticism were extolled as the living, moral, and healthy elements of human nature. Throughout the century this antirational, intuitive point-of-view, this examination of man's condition with the poet's eye, kept pace with the general secularization and rationalization of Western society.

Tensions were also introduced into the Western world by the great scientific accomplishments of the century. Unquestionably scientific knowledge strengthened the belief that Western man was becoming more and more the master of his world. It was easy to convince oneself that the more knowledge gained, the more benefits that accrued to the human race. Science was regarded as the ally of progress, the best indicator that the way of the future led ever upward. What was perhaps the most influential scientific triumph of the century — Charles Darwin's theory of evolution — could be used to show that there was a direction to men's affairs that tended toward "higher" forms of life, and to support a belief in unlimited human potentialities. In its simple, and vulgar, form, the theory of evolution fitted well into the nineteenth-century idea of progress. It justified economic competition as a form of "survival of the fittest," it provided "proof" for the argument that change itself was part of a natural development, and it even explained the military superiority of Europeans over peoples in other parts of the world. Thus economists could speak of "root, hog, or die" as a scientific law of business life, and Darwin's own fellow-student of evolution A. R. Wallace could argue that "It is the same great law of 'the preservation of favoured races in the struggle for life,' which leads to the inevitable extinction of all those low and mentally undeveloped populations with which Europeans come in contact. . . ."

Yet on a more significant level Darwin's theory, as other manifestations of science, revealed an intellectual and spiritual chasm before Western man. Although he used the words "improve" and "improvement," Darwin himself wrote in 1854 that "I do not think zoologists agree in any definite ideas on this subject and my own ideas are not clearer than those of my brethren." The direction and purposes of the evolutionary process were not clearly discernible, and Darwin could not persuade himself that he saw any evolutionary goal.

> But I own that I cannot see as plainly as others do, and as I should wish to do, any evidence of design and beneficence on all sides of us. There seems to me too much misery in the world. I cannot persuade myself that a beneficent and omnipotent God would have designedly created the Ichneumonidae with the express intention of their feeding within the living bodies of Caterpillars, or that a cat should play with mice.

The Darwinian theory had implications that went far beyond arguments about man's relationship to monkeys or whether some creatures had become extinct because there was no room for them in Noah's Ark. It raised doubts about the religious plan of the world and called into question the presence of any guiding hand, anything that could be described as "Divine Government," "Creator and Governor of the Universe," "Great First Agent," "Supreme Being." The theory of evolution sent a tremor of unease through the stable, confident nineteenth century. Not only was biblical history being questioned and, in Darwin's words, "no more to be trusted than the sacred books of the Hindoos, or the beliefs of any barbarian," but the Christian transcendent purpose of life was obscured. The why of man's beginning was as masked from view as was the purpose of his end. "I cannot pretend to throw the least light on such abstruse problems," Darwin wrote. "The mystery of the beginning of all things is insoluble by us; and I for one must be content to remain an Agnostic." The scope of Darwin's theory was so great that it, like other significant scientific achievements, left Western man dumbfounded before questions that seemed beyond the power of his mind. As the young American Henry Adams wrote to his brother in 1862:

> You may think all this nonsense, but I tell you these are great times. Man has mounted science and is now run away with. I firmly believe that before many centuries more, science will be the master of man. The engines he will have invented will be beyond his strength to control. Some day science may have the existence of mankind in its power, and the human race commit suicide by blowing up the world.

The Political Settlement

The controversies over the religious and scientific nature of human experience were equalled by those over political arrangements. A continual argument among the various claimants to political authority became part of Western political history. In the early part of the century the French diplomat Talleyrand wrote that "Europe's most pressing need and greatest concern was to do away with the doctrine of usurpation and revive the principle of legitimacy, the only remedy for all the evils which beset her, and the only one which will prevent their recurrence." But what was legitimate and what not? Who had the right to rule and who not? Which was the proper authority and which was improper?

After the defeat of Napoleon, the initiative in political affairs rested with the victorious powers. At the Congress of Vienna, which met in 1814 and 1815, the representatives of those powers engaged in a coalition against France met to set the political direction of Europe. The leading figures at the Congress were the Austrian Prince Metternich, Lord Castlereagh of Great Britain, Tsar Alexander I of Russia, and Prince Karl Hardenberg of Prussia. They were shortly joined by the French Prince Talleyrand, a survivor of the Revolution and the Napoleonic period and now dedicated to bringing France into alliance with the other European countries.

These men hated what they regarded as the excesses and even the principles of the Revolution, and had it been possible, they would have restored Europe to its prerevolutionary condition. But this could not be done. They, therefore, did what they could to guarantee that there would be no revival of the revolutionary fury. They reshuffled frontiers, buttressed conservative regimes, and tried to organize governments into an international shield against any possible revolutionary outbreak.

The practical work of the Congress was quite successful. Much of the territory that Napoleon and his predecessors had conquered was taken away from France. But the peace settlement was remarkably lenient, and a defeated and, it was hoped, repentant France was accepted as a member of what was loosely called the Concert of Europe. In Germany the Holy Roman Empire was not restored, and no attempt was made to reestablish the ecclesiastical states. In place of the 1,789 independent and semi-independent sovereign powers that had existed in 1800, a new German confederation of thirty-nine states under the leadership of Austria and Prussia was created. Switzerland's independence and neutrality were guaranteed. In order to guard against any new French attack upon Europe, what is now Belgium was united with Holland as a territorial buffer, and Prussia was given important areas along the Rhine River as well as territory taken from other German states. The influence of Austria was strengthened in Germany and Italy, while Great Britain received clear title to several important overseas possessions, including Malta, Ceylon, and the Cape of Good Hope. With some minor changes, such as the declaration of

Belgian independence in the eighteen-thirties, these settlements of European real estate were to last for almost half a century, and during that time international arguments over territorial claims were to be relatively unimportant.

But those attending the Congress of Vienna were interested in more than the rearrangement of frontiers and the parceling out of territory. They were also engaged in a search for order, for a way, as Castlereagh said, to "bring back the world to peaceful habits." This meant that authority, as much as possible, was to be vested in those who had occupied positions of power prior to the Revolution, and that rulers and the aristocracy were to be returned to their thrones and their privileges. Many of the changes introduced by the Revolution could not be undone. But perhaps they could be controlled, diluted, and kept from assuming a dangerous form. "Events that cannot be opposed must be directed," said Metternich, and the doctrine of traditional legitimacy was to be a guardian against any excesses that might upset the balance of Europe. Thus the old Bourbon monarchies were restored in France, Spain, and southern Italy, and the temporal authority of the Pope over the Papal States of central Italy was reasserted. The royal House of Orange was established in the enlarged Netherlands, and the position of the German princes was strengthened.

The political history of every European country was influenced by this attempt to burn out the corruption of revolutionary ideas. In France the "Irreconcilables" attempted to restore the religious orientation of society and to return to the "natural order of things." Divorce was abolished, censorship was used "to preserve society from the contagion of false doctrines," and special courts were established to try those suspected of treason. Napoleon's educational system was attacked, as was the University of France, where students "become irreligious and debauched and contemptuous of all virtues." An extreme form of conservatism developed whose supporters were prepared to defend any form of suppression. In the eighteen-twenties a prominent Paris priest petitioned the government to put an end to all independent newspapers and to institute a single government-directed publication that would be edited by the Minister of Police. Exhibiting an even more extreme attitude, a French political writer excused all measures against recalcitrant Frenchmen. "All greatness, all power, all order," he argued, "depend upon the executioner. He is the tie that holds society together. Take away this force and at that very moment order is succeeded by chaos."

In Germany, too, suppression in the name of traditional prerogative and order was common. Many Germans had expected that the defeat of Napoleon would result in a progressive, politically enlightened Germany. But this did not happen. As one cynic remarked, "the liberation of the fatherland amounts to nothing more than reinstating the Prussian nobility in its old rights." In 1819 a political commentator pointed out that "the German princes called the people to arms against Napoleon as the instigator of all their sufferings. The enemy has been defeated, and the people are now in a worse condition than before." The German landowning aristocracy was in many ways stronger and more arrogant than before the French Revolution. Serfdom had been officially abolished. But the "putting down of the peasants" was a common practice in Prussia, while the Prussian officers elevated themselves to the position of a military caste, separated from the rest of the German people.

Throughout Germany defenses of all types were thrown up to protect against the influence of revolutionary ideas. Constitutions had been granted by some of the rulers of the smaller German states. But these were weak documents, and the established parliaments had no independent strength and were dissolved at the first sign of trouble. The best known of the anti-revolutionary measures came in 1819, when, following upon student disorders, representatives of the nine principal German states, including Austria and Prussia, met at Carlsbad. Here were adopted what came to be called the Carlsbad Decrees. All politically oriented student societies were ordered dissolved, and inspectors were appointed for the universities. Strict newspaper censorship was introduced, informers were placed in the universities and the churches, and it was agreed that no teacher who had lost his post through political reasons in one part of Germany would be employed in another. A commission was created to keep governments informed of any revolutionary movement, and the right of states to intervene in the affairs of their neighbors in order to combat revolutionary activity was accepted. Although the Decrees were not implemented with any regularity, their existence illustrated the temper of the times and had an inhibiting effect throughout Germany.

Even in Great Britain, the most politically stable of the European countries, conservative leaders felt themselves threatened by what was called "the present insubordination, which if not checked, will finally produce great disorder." There were demands for a widened franchise and for parliamentary reform, and economic troubles resulted in cries for some form of relief. The government responded with punitive actions against the "disturbers of the peace." In 1817 the Habeas Corpus Act was temporarily suspended, and what were called the "Gagging Bills" became law. These regulations forbad public meetings except when licensed by a magistrate, and penalties were established for treasonable or seditious speeches or written articles. Two years later the "Six Acts" were promulgated. These were measures designed to stifle any opposition to the authorities. One of the acts forbad the practice of military exercises by unauthorized persons. A second provided for speedy trials and drastic punishments for all offenders against public order. A third allowed magistrates to issue warrants for the search of private houses. A fourth established penalties for what were called seditious or blasphemous libels. A fifth restricted public meetings to those called by government officials and, in particular, all meetings called for the purpose of complaining against church and state. The sixth subjected publications below a certain size to a heavy stamp duty already levied on newspapers and thus made it economically prohibitive to print material designed for distribution to the poorer classes. Troops and police were used to put down any show of discontent and throttle any argument over the propriety of the present political and social arrangement.

The measures taken to insure order seemed justified to the authorities. There were conspiracies, revolutionary organizations, and popular risings. A French duke and a German poet suspected of being a police agent were assassinated, and there was a plot to murder members of the British government. There were revolts in Italy, Spain, Poland, and Russia. Economic hardships resulted in working-class protest movements that appeared to pose revolutionary threats. In 1830 there was a successful revolution in France, and a middle-class constitutional king replaced the Bourbon monarchy. In 1848 revolutions broke out in almost every European country. But, with the exception of France where a short-lived republic was established, the revolutionary movements failed to take power. Political discontent and radical ideas continued to exist, and predictions of an impending political disaster were continually made. Yet the feared cataclysm did not occur, and Europe developed a remarkable political stability.

This stability did not mean, however, that the principle of aristocratic legitimacy had triumphed. The European aristocracy and its supporters remained a potent force, and Europe was throughout the century a class-structured society, where family background, education, and even speech patterns set off one European from another. But the ordered links in the great chain of precedence had been irrevocably broken. As the years passed, it became increasingly obvious that if the members of the aristocracy were to contribute to political life, they must accommodate themselves, at least after a fashion, to ever-changing circumstances. Many did this, particularly those who were members of what could be called the middle or lower aristocracy. Men such as Bismarck in Germany and Palmerston in Great Britain understood the historical realities of the nineteenth century and contributed significantly to the political activities of the period. But in these cases, and others, talent, energy, and ambition were the characteristics responsible for success, and aristocrats who survived throughout the century as important historical figures were those who could persuade that their claims were based on qualities other than a mere name or an ancient coat of arms.

The Middle Class

The dominant tone of society was not aristocratic. In 1830 an English politician exclaimed: "We don't now live in the days of the barons, thank God!" The nineteenth has been called the century of the middle class, and it was this difficult-to-define collection of people that increasingly expressed the aspirations and the reality of the times and contributed substantially to political and social order. The actual term "middle class" had been introduced in the seventeen-nineties and entered into common usage in the second decade of the nineteenth century. In 1830 a French newspaper defined a member of the middle class as one who read newspapers and novels, was interested in political debates, commanded industry, and possessed property. Others spoke of the middle class as those with clean hands and white collars. It has been estimated that in 1851 of a British population of 21,000,000 approximately a million and a half could be described as middle class. But middle-class influence was far greater than mere numbers would indicate. Its members dominated the professions — medicine, law, education, controlled the increasingly important business activities, and manned the rapidly expanding national bureaucracies.

The middle class was not a cohesive unit, and it consisted of diverse elements. Some of its members were careful hoarders of possessions; some were the most careless financial gamblers. Some were prone to the concoction of the wildest speculations; some were the most pedestrian of thinkers. There were conservatives and radicals, free-thinkers and conformists, servants of mankind and servants of the pocketbook. Members of the middle class were at once the great supporters of political authority and its most troublesome opponents. In spite of these differences, however, there was a certain general attitude that was identified with the middle class by both its friends and its enemies.

In politics, the middle class was broadly liberal in that its members were impatient of traditional restrictions and argued that the individual must be free of the religious, economic, and social restraints that kept him from developing his talents and his fortune. In place of ancestry and historical claims to positions of status, the middle class set the gospel of work, seriousness, respectability, and self-help. Members of the middle class defended both liberty and order and were convinced that it was possible to combine security and change. They were basically constitutionalists and had an abiding faith in the written instruments of government. Great believers in the contractual arrangements of life, they tended to develop a rather narrow legal attitude toward business, government, and all relationships of man to man.

The middle class saw itself as consisting of the "solid citizens," the hard-working, God-worshipping, self-reliant people who were best prepared to contribute to the general welfare. Such people possessed a balanced intelligence that fit them to direct the affairs of the nation. As one of their French spokesmen put it: "The influence of the middle class is a fact. . . . The centuries have declared it; the Revolution has announced it. It is to this class that the new interests belong. Its security cannot be disturbed without imminent danger to the established order."

The ownership of property was an important part of the middle-class ethic and was looked upon as a sign of particular political grace. People with property had the ability to discern the "legitimate interests" of society, they had a "stake in the country," and intelligence and general political capacity were identified with the talent for acquiring wealth. Put vulgarly, there was a tendency to assume that the smart man should be the rich man, or, more bluntly, the rich man is the smart man. It was admitted that all men have certain rights, among which were liberty of conscience and other civil rights. But there are special rights based upon "the natural inequalities it pleases Providence to establish among men." Such a right is that of political participation. Through most of the nineteenth century many believed that the right to vote and to take part in government affairs should be restricted to those who showed a capacity to acquire property or "a certain degree of personal wealth." Only such men possess the talent needed to govern, for "intelligence finds its place and achieves fortune."

The middle class has been mocked and ridiculed. Hardly an important literary man of the nineteenth century failed to pick a quarrel with middle-class style and middle-class wisdom. The stuffy virtue, the cliché-ridden pronouncements, and the undue attention to the appearances of life were offensive to many, and there was a shocking narrowness of outlook in the assumption of many members of the middle class that everyone was motivated by the same ambitions, the same desires, the same moral commitments as they.

And the middle class deserved the complaints levelled against it. But such attacks obscured the real historical contributions it made. The emphasis upon legality and upon ordered contractual arrangements reduced the arbitrariness in society. Political authority was hemmed in, and arbitrary acts on the part of authorities against citizens were reduced appreciably during the nineteenth century. Such actions did not, of course, disappear, but one has only to compare the behavior of those in positions of authority in the eighteenth and the twentieth centuries to see what an island of legal sanity the nineteenth was. Middle-class opposition to strong government was ultimately to become anachronistic and an obstacle to the continued operation of society. But such opposition did stimulate in individual citizens a stubborn defiance of political authority and strengthened their belief that the right to oppose their rulers was proper and not treasonable. The middle class was patriotic, but it was also anti-militaristic. It loved parades, but it looked with suspicion upon any form of military caste. It regarded the status of civilian as the proper and natural condition of man in society, and this attitude gave the nineteenth century a uniquely civilian outlook. The middle class was also humanitarian, and while this characteristic could and did degenerate on occasions into sentimentality and empty self-satisfaction, it was responsible for the idea of a certain minimum regard that one human being should have for another.

The Popular Revolution

The nineteenth century also saw a substantial beginning of what we must call the popular revolution. John Stuart Mill, who was perhaps the leading spokesman for English middle-class liberalism, noted that "the most distinct feature" of the time was that "human beings are no longer born to their place in life . . . but are free to employ their faculties . . . to achieve the lot which may appear to them most desirable." And the demands to participate in Western society as full citizens spread from the middle class to the common people. As the English critic Matthew Arnold wrote, the populace, "raw and half-developed," was now "issuing from its hiding-place to assert an Englishman's heaven-born privilege of doing as he likes, and is beginning to perplex us by marching where it likes, meeting where it likes, bawling what it likes, breaking what it likes." In earlier centuries there had been a great deal of talk and writing about the people. But seldom had such a term meant the uneducated, culturally delinquent, historically mute masses.

Both the aristocracy and the middle class looked with apprehension and alarm at those who claimed recognition not because of traditional status or wealth or intelligence but as simple human beings. There was a great deal of talk about "the lower orders," "the vulgar masses," and "the irresponsible poor." Many saw their sane, safe world threatened by the demands of those intoxicated by the belief that happiness was the right of all men and that life, liberty, and equality were meant for all and not for a favored few. In 1851 an Englishman wrote: "Already we have a revolution, slumbering, but gathering power in all our cities, and still we pursue our way with intrepid stupidity, dreaming of Eden in the very midst of the reign of terror." Some might argue that the voice of the people was the voice of God. But others were convinced that the voice of the people was the voice of blockheads or even of those who were prepared to plunder society because of envy, hatred, or anger.

"We are the people, our business is with the people, and to transact it we must take it into our own hands." So said an English radical in 1830. This did not happen. Control of European affairs did not pass from the hands of the aristocracy and the middle class. But active citizenship for all who wished to participate was slowly extended. The franchise was broadened continually until by the end of the century universal manhood suffrage was established in Western Europe. Legal equality — at least in theory — became also a fact of European life. The possibility of education, the mass dissemination of printed materials, and the determination of the people to adopt many of the habits and attitudes of the middle class — all these tended to create new citizens out of those who had been only silent members of the society. Of course, overwhelming disabilities remained. Careful manipulation of electoral districts and discriminatory election laws reduced the value of the vote. Equality of the law was more theoretical than an actual practice. Common education was poorer, common newspapers and books were less valuable, and common opportunities for betterment much more restricted. But the century did succeed in containing the explosive, dynamic thrust of millions who had only recently left the now-shattered restrictive peasant world and incorporating them, more or less successfully, into the greater European society. Social snobbery, inequality, discrimination, and great cultural differences remained at the end of the century. But one has only to compare the situation in 1800 with that in 1900 to see the measure of the accomplishment.

The Great London Exhibition

By 1850 the direction of nineteenth-century European life had in large measure been set. The movement to the city was under way — Paris between 1800 and 1850 doubled in population, London increased from just under one million inhabitants to two and a half million, and Manchester quadrupled in size. The significant literary form of the century, the novel, had achieved its first great successes at the hands of Dickens and Balzac, and mass-circulation newspapers such as the Paris *Presse* and the London *News of the World* had been established. The international Rothschild banking house was flourishing, and the conditions for spectacular commercial and industrial undertakings had been created. Social problems that ranged from the famine of 1848 to extreme working-class radicalism and extensive poverty cast a shadow over Europe but had not brought about catastrophe. France was in the last quarter of the century to settle upon a republican form of government. But elsewhere in Western Europe monarchy, modified by more or less representative and more or less effective legislatures, was becoming the accepted political system.

England exhibited best the European accomplishments of the first half of the century. She led the way in industrialization and in the development of national power. Queen Victoria had completed her first decade as England's ruler by 1850 and was to give her name to the rest of the century — to a period that stressed stability, responsibility, the development of empire, and peaceful accomplishment. By 1850 48,000,000 passengers were travelling annually on British railroads, modern parliamentary traditions were being developed, and a beginning had been made on significant social legislation that was to blunt discontent. In 1848 Thomas Macaulay published his popular *History of England* where he wrote that the development of England was "eminently the history of physical, of moral, and of intellectual improvement."

England provided at mid-century a dramatic example of the growing military and political supremacy of Europe in relation to other parts of the world. In 1850 Don Pacifico, a British citizen, was the victim of mob action in Greece. He appealed to the British government for the recovery of damages. When complaints to the Greek authorities produced no results, Foreign Minister Palmerston ordered the British fleet to seize Greek ships in retaliation. The Greeks then acquiesced and restitution was made to Don Pacifico. There were protests in England against these strong-arm tactics, but Palmerston in a parliamentary speech defended his actions. He argued that the British government was "bound to afford protection to our fellow-subjects abroad," and "as the Roman in days of old held himself free from indignity when he could say 'Civis Romanus sum,' so also a British subject in whatever land he may be, shall feel confident that the watchful eye and strong arm of England will protect him from injustice and wrong." Palmerston's words indicated that English, and ultimately European, power was becoming world-wide and would be exercised wherever necessary to protect European interests. The flags, the military forces, and the authority of Europe were moving out into the world, and few places were to be free of European influence and European demands.

On May 1, 1851, the Great Exhibition in London opened with "trumpets, cannons, royal troops, cheers, waving hats, fountains, organs, seven hundred choristers, flags." This was the first of the exhibitions of the nineteenth century designed to show economic, technical, and historical progress. Arranged in four general categories — Raw Materials, Machinery and Mechanical Inventions, Manufactures, and Sculpture and Plastic Arts — the Exhibition attempted "to present a true test and a living picture of the point of development at which the whole of mankind has arrived ... and a new starting point, from which all nations will be able to direct their further exertions." Over six million visitors came to marvel at the ingenious devices, the mechanical wonders, and the examples of man's progress.

Popular response to the Exhibition was favorable. The Crystal Palace, built specifically for the Exhibition, did suggest to many "both fairy tale and success story." Some critics saw the Exhibition as vulgar and pretentious, and one described it as made up of "pedantic imitations of classical architecture, ridiculous travesties of Gothic buildings, and the utilitarian brick box with a slate roof." The Exhibition did lack aesthetic refinement and was something of a historical sideshow — loud, garish, and extravagant. It catered to the emotions of self-satisfaction and self-congratulation, and many of the important elements of nineteenth-century European history were not represented. But what was there seemed to many to be the significant achievements that indicated man's "triumph over the blind powers of nature," and as one observer noted, the entire Exhibition proved that "we live in the days when men are industrious and desire to be free."

Many of the major problems that were to mark the century appeared soon after 1815, and individual responses to and interpretations of particular problems illustrated the condition of Western man. The Austrian Metternich regarded many developments in the early nineteenth century as dangerous and opposed to the good order of society. The German philosopher Hegel believed that he could discern amidst the confusion the historical realities of the time. The Frenchman Stendhal found little but disappointment in the Western world of the first half of the nineteenth century.

Metternich

Throughout the first half of the nineteenth century European political leaders came and went. They rose to prominence, served for a period, and then were replaced. But there was one who from 1815 to 1848 remained in power. This was Clemens Lothar Wenzel von Metternich-Winneburg-Beilstein of Austria. A leading architect of the political settlement after the defeat of Napoleon, Metternich has been called "The Coachman of Europe," "The Evil Genius," "The Champion of Historical Order." Mocked by poets, ridiculed by journalists, hated by intellectuals, and distrusted by other political leaders who often thought of him as a crabbed, cold, and cynical political juggler, for almost forty years he stood against what he regarded as the destructive revolutionary flood, against "the tirelessly active party of the innovators," against the "monstrous brew" of revolutionary ideology that threatened to overwhelm Europe.

Metternich was born in 1773, in Coblenz in the Rhineland. He was four years younger than Napoleon and fifteen years younger than Robespierre. Although he is usually thought of as an Austrian, he was twenty-one years old before he saw Vienna and spent his early years in what was probably the most cosmopolitan part of Europe, the borderland between France and Germany. He attended the University of Strasbourg and the University of Mainz, and when the French revolutionary forces overran the Rhineland, he and his family fled. He entered the Austrian diplomatic service and became ambassador at Berlin and then at Paris. In 1809 he became Austrian minister of foreign affairs, a post he was to hold until 1848. While in this position, and later as state chancellor of Austria, he was instrumental in creating the coalition that defeated Napoleon, in effect presided at the Congress of Vienna, became the spokesman for what has been called the Concert of Europe, and dramatically influenced the political development of Germany and Italy and therefore of Europe.

Metternich is often described as the instigator of reaction, a man determined to force upon a youthful and vigorous Europe the stale preachments of an outdated political authority. But he regarded himself as a prosaic, practical politician, a hard-headed realist without historical illusions. When he was eighty-two years old he remarked: "I was born sober, and I have always remained sober. I beg of you, no romances." Others might become intoxicated, but not Metternich. He set himself the task of making political arrangements that would allow the people of Europe to live together without committing a form of continental suicide by embracing some destructive enthusiasm. He saw his policies as a defense against the passions, the ideologies, and the utopian schemes that had ripped Europe during the last decade of the eighteenth century and the first fifteen years of the nineteenth.

Metternich was an enemy of revolutionary ideas. As early as 1794 he separated himself from those "who consider the present war like any other and the Revolution in its commencement as mere child's play." The Revolution threatened "the dissolution of all social ties, the destruction of all principles, and the spoliation of all property." A hatred of what he regarded as revolutionary rhetoric, revolutionary falsehood, and revolutionary demagogues remained with Metternich all his life, and over half a century after his first experience with the French Revolution in the Rhineland, he wrote: "All revolutions are lies, or at least so thoroughly larded with this wretched quality, that it is not worth while to try to separate one from the other. Never has a revolution truthfully declared its point of departure, nor carried out its promises. They destroy but do not create."

After 1815 Metternich attempted to bring what he called "these aroused people" of Europe back to the sanity of order and stability. He regarded Europe as a homogeneous cultural unit but divided politically. One must, therefore, try for balance, which, in time, would eradicate or at least control those "dangerous" ideas that could only result in political chaos and cultural disintegration. He wished to create a European community of interest where a liberal England, a bureaucratic Prussia, an autocratic Russia, a still-revolutionary France, and a dynastic Austria could live together in peace. But there was no place in such a Europe for any revolutionary concept that would upset this precious balance. There could be no hope of peace and stability if governments were to undertake crusades for such dangerous abstractions as freedom, justice, or equality. To Metternich such undertakings were only "fads," the "sickness of the times," and must be combated if the "demagogic" forces were not to make European life unbearable.

Metternich believed that there were practical political arrangements that could be made to ensure the desired stability. European governments must organize themselves as a league against revolutionary factions within all states. A subversive group in one country was a threat to all, and political interference in order to thwart the aspirations of any revolutionary movement was to be an accepted fact of international life. No revolutionary organization should be allowed to take root in any country and then from there spread its influence throughout all Europe.

Public opinion should also be guided, and the revolutionary restlessness of Europe should be tamed by a combination of surveillance and education. Metternich realized that the ideas of the Revolution could not be combated by force alone. The young must be indoctrinated in order to recognize the errors of revolution and the virtues of an orderly society. Thus education and the press must be controlled, and, as one who agreed with Metternich said, false ideas "must be held in check until the coming of a new generation untainted by revolutionary disease." Metternich himself often argued that the people were good, "but their ignorance is great; therefore they must be led."

Most important, Europe must have peace. And this peace could be secured only if Europe was accepted as it existed and if all dangerous attempts to introduce new political and national arrangements were abandoned. Metternich opposed violent revolutionaries and violent reactionaries, for both groups threatened the delicate balance of European life. He opposed the unification of Germany and Italy, for he believed that there was no place in Europe, and particularly in central Europe, for dynamic, ambitious, new national powers that would threaten stability. He refused to accept any argument for Italian unity and contended that "Italy is a geographical concept," not a nation, while he was determined to keep the thirty-nine German states as a confederation, a union that provided mutual benefits to all members but had no real political or military power.

Metternich knew that he had set himself against the current of European life in the nineteenth century. In 1820 he prepared what was called a "profession of faith." Here he argued that there had once been a European order, a balance between the old and the new, the stable and the unstable. But this balance had been destroyed, and Europe now faced the consequences. Metternich listed several of the causes for this instability. The continually increasing use of printing facilitated the dissemination of erroneous ideas and had introduced popular vulgarization into European life. The invention of new instruments of war had resulted in the creation of a new military power that could not be controlled by political leaders. The discovery of America had brought about an influx of wealth that had destroyed the value of landed property, upon which political stability depended, and had stimulated in Europe an unhealthy spirit of adventure and a continual dissatisfaction with existing conditions. In that same year, in a letter, Metternich put down what he believed was the only way to defend oneself against these influences. "To deviate in no way from the established order, whatever may be its origin, and where alterations are absolutely necessary to make them only with entire freedom and well-considered resolution — this is the first duty of a government that desires to resist the evils of the age."

The dynamic forces of European history in the nineteenth century were liberalism, democracy, revolutionary ideas, nationalism, and the new industrialization. Metternich recognized all these as threats to his concept of European order. He looked with disgust upon the thrusting middle class, those he regarded as "the half-educated," who were busy undermining the necessary institutional supports for stability and peace. The new commercial and industrial leaders were only "wealthy men, securing their personal advantage at the expense of the order of things." Europe was also plagued by what Metternich spoke of as "the greatest of all evils, the excesses of the young intellectuals." The universities of Europe, which should be the mainstays of true knowledge and conduct, had become centers of subversion, the source of the wildest and most dangerous political and social daydreaming. German students, in particular, with their ideas of nationalism and idealism and their speculations about society, offended Metternich. He regarded them as "grotesque and repulsive figures, in dirty old German costumes, a veritable abomination to God and man, with books under their arms, going to garner the false wisdom of their infamous professors." A latter-day German historian was to write that nothing put Metternich in "such a state of feverish agitation as the sight of a single bearded student."

Even European rulers had no sense of the necessary prerequisites of European order. "If you knew what I think about the inhabitants of these lofty regions," he once wrote, "you would take me for an out-and-out Jacobin." Those who should have known better had fallen victim to "the poison of error, ignorance, servility, and flattery." The French remained victims of the revolutionary virus and were a constant threat to international order. Great Britain became an influence for disorder through her preaching of liberalism and her pursuit of policies, for example, in Italy, that threatened the peace and quiet of the continent. Russia, in Metternich's opinion, had shown that she was not a true European power by her aggressive and acquisitive policies, and much of his time was devoted to building defenses against Russian influence in central Europe. The German rulers were weak and vacillating. Even his own sovereign, the Austrian Emperor, was of little assistance. A dull, slow-witted, bureaucratic egoist, he could be expected to ruin any effective or fruitful policies that Metternich might advance.

Even as he worked for his concept of stability and order, Metternich realized that the future threatened him and his efforts. In 1828 he wrote: "My life coincides with an abominable period. I came into the world either too early or too late; at present I am good for nothing. . . . I am spending my life propping up mouldering buildings." His pessimism became an important part of his attitude. "The existing society," he remarked, "is on the decline. Nothing ever stands still . . . and this society has reached its zenith." He despaired of his ability to cleanse nationalism, that great threat to European security, of its empty proclamations and its inflammatory claims, as he doubted the effectiveness of most of the defenses against popular discontent. Metternich realized that a fundamental schism had appeared in Western society between the old and the new. He also knew that changes would come and that his own position would gradually be undermined.

But he did what he could. He fought with the instruments available to him. As he said near the end of his life: "For thirty-nine years I played the rock from which the waves recoil . . . until finally they succeeded in engulfing it." He continually warned against the "danger of the times," and he attempted to isolate what he thought of as the potentially destructive elements from the rest of European society. He convinced himself that every opposition movement sprang from secret societies and conspiracies, and he relied a great deal upon police control and suppression. Censorship and the police became the supports of his policy. He tended to define all opponents as extreme revolutionaries, and he became the defender of all existing institutions because of his belief that no matter how frail and useless they might be and no matter how he himself might despise them, their destruction would introduce something even more disastrous. Thus a historian could write: "Above all, however, the conviction that this struggle between the positive and negative principles was a fight to the death led this mild and personally enlightened man to harshness and means of coercion which not only suppressed unhealthy excrescences, but also buds and plants which were entitled to life."

Metternich's planned concert of powers dedicated to the preservation of order lasted only a short time. By the middle of the eighteen-twenties the unity of governments was shattered. Britain was not prepared to pledge herself to a program of continual interference in continental affairs and discovered that too often her own national interests ran counter to those of the European continental powers. Metternich's policy was not popular in England, and even those English political leaders who were conservative at home did not hesitate to criticize the "dark despotism" of Metternich's central Europe. The English attitude during the revolutionary uprisings in Greece, the unofficial, and Metternich suspected even official, support given various nationalistic groups in Italy, and recognition of the independence of the Latin American countries indicated the impossibility of relying upon England as an ally against revolution. France, too, could not be trusted, and events in that country showed that the French were much more likely to be a cause of European disorder than a factor for European stability.

In Western Europe Metternich's influence soon amounted to very little. During the last two decades of his period of power he became primarily a central European statesman. He maintained an uneasy relationship with Russia, which was a conservative force but whose presence posed a continual anxiety over the Slavic parts of the Austrian state. In Germany Metternich succeeded in holding off the movement toward unity and in containing any tendency toward political liberalism.

Early in 1848, revolutionary uprisings took place in various parts of Europe, and Metternich resigned and fled Austria, taking refuge in England. His system, which he had always argued was based upon "the dictates of right reason," was in ruins. Order had been overwhelmed by the very forces Metternich had attempted to check. Revolutionary ideas, nationalism, and liberalism had taken their revenge on their great opponent. After the disorders were suppressed, Metternich returned to Austria, but as a man without important influence or power.

In some ways Metternich saw better than did many of his contemporaries the direction of events. He knew that liberalism was a divisive force, undermining certainty and lending support to factionalism. The middle classes were aggressive, ambitious, indifferent to the virtues of traditional political arrangements, and, by Metternich's standards, half-educated. Members of the middle classes tended to be enthusiasts over abstract principles, and such people, whether "Bible-reading Methodists" or radical journalists and teachers, threatened social and political equilibrium.

Metternich's attitude toward nationalism was also based upon a subtle understanding of European realities. From a narrow point of view, Metternich's responsibility was to defend the interests of Austria. A state held together by skilful diplomacy, a hard-working if often ridiculed bureaucracy, and a dynasty that claimed its right to rule by reference to historical factors other than national determination, Austria could not accept the claims of nationalism without inviting her own destruction as a European power.

But Metternich's view of nationalism was more than a case of special pleading for Austria. He looked upon himself as a European, a man of all lands, at home in Austria, in France, in Italy, or in Germany. He had nothing but disdain for those he thought of as boorish vulgarians who were prepared to sacrifice cosmopolitan Europe to the cause of narrow national ambitions. His attitude toward German nationalism and German unity was consistent. He did not think that European society could survive a united, nationalistically inclined Germany. The presence of such a powerful state would destroy the European system. Metternich toiled all his public life to keep any one national power from dominating the continent. He attempted to isolate a defeated but still dangerous France, to repulse the efforts of Russia to further her interests in central Europe, and to blunt English activities in Italy and the eastern Mediterranean. But he sensed that all this would be in vain if a powerful union of the German-speaking states was created. The influence of such a strong, unified Germany would create new tensions throughout Europe and ultimately threaten the uneasy stability so necessary for the European way of life.

Here, as elsewhere, Metternich's insights were to the point. Nationalism, and particularly German nationalism, was a threat to European peace. Yet Metternich's own policy was hardly an acceptable alternative. He was intelligent, and he possessed diplomatic talents. But there was about him the flavor of the past. His attitudes were deeply rooted in prerevolutionary Europe, and he was uncomfortable in the turbulent, dynamic world of the nineteenth century. He tended to see history and historical problems from the perspective of the eighteenth-century salon, and he too often identified political power and political reality with officials, embassies, and all those surface manifestations of international politics.

Metternich's policy also played a part in separating central Europe from Western Europe. His opposition to liberalism, nationalism, and industrialization made Western influence in central Europe tenuous and in many cases superficial. The Slavic peoples became second-class citizens of the general European community and were given little opportunity to contribute to and participate in European life. West European influence did reach central Europe but often in contorted and exaggerated forms that proved to be dangerous to the very order that Metternich treasured.

Perhaps Metternich's greatest failing was that he had little faith in the creative capacities of the European peoples. He could see very well what was being destroyed. But amidst the ruins he could discern nothing new blooming. Unquestionably great confusion and even suffering have been caused by overheated enthusiasts and by wild-eyed revolutionaries. But, equally, consistent cynicism about the value and necessity of change has led to disaster. Metternich isolated himself from the vital intellectual currents of his day. Thus he contributed little to a new vision of Western man. Ultimately, he was always forced to rely upon sterile political instruments — the police, censorship, surveillance, and desperate manipulation.

In May of 1859 an acquaintance called upon Metternich and recorded the visit. "Our conversation was lively and stimulating. On my leaving him he said to me again and again with emphasis, 'I was a Rock of Order.' I had already closed the door behind me when I opened it again softly to take one more look at the great statesman. There he sat at his writing desk, pen in hand, glancing upward contemplatively, erect, cold, proud, distinguished, just as I had formerly often seen him in the Chancellery when in the full glow of his power. . . . After a time he noticed me at the door, fixed upon me a long look of profound benevolence, turned away and said half-aloud, half to himself, 'A Rock of Order.'" It was a good enough epitaph. Less than three weeks later Metternich died.

Hegel

On October 13, 1806, a thirty-six-year-old lecturer at the German University of Jena wrote a letter to a friend in which he described Napoleon's visit to the city prior to his victory over the Prussian army. "I saw the Emperor, that World-soul," wrote Georg Wilhelm Friedrich Hegel, "riding through the city to reconnoitre. It is a strange feeling to see such a man before one, who, as he rides his horse, is reaching from here over the world and remaking it." Hegel and Napoleon were approximately the same age, one a French man of action and the other a German academic intellectual. As Napoleon was to capture the imagination of the French and remain a haunting memory long after his defeat, so Hegel was to be the most influential of German philosophers, whose ideas, modified and developed, were to spread beyond Germany throughout the world.

Hegel was born in Stuttgart in 1770, the son of a German civil servant, and was educated at Tübingen University. After leaving the university, he supported himself for several years as a private tutor and in 1801 joined the faculty at the University of Jena. When the university was closed in 1808, Hegel became editor of a newspaper and then an official in a school in Nuremberg. In 1816 he returned to university life, accepting a position at Heidelberg University, and then moving to the University of Berlin in 1818. Here he remained as a professor until his death in 1831. In his writings and in his lectures he developed what came to be known as the Hegelian philosophy, a dynamic and powerful interpretation of Western history and Western civilization that was to be praised and cursed in his day and since.

Any examination of Hegel is best begun with the Enlightenment and the French Revolution. Hegel was nineteen when the French Revolution began, and he was an ardent supporter during its first few years. The extremism of the revolutionary Terror and the implications of the revolutionary doctrine destroyed his earlier faith, but he realized that Europe could not return to the prerevolutionary period. The events of the seventeen-nineties had reduced traditional values and ceremonies to empty masquerades, and the ecclesiastical and imperial trappings that had been so important in European history for a millennium were now only archaic historical oddities. The Enlightenment and the Revolution had introduced new historical forces — new ideals, new passions, new power, and new fancies, delusions, and dreams. Hegel attempted to provide an explanation of these forces and to relate them to an overall interpretation of man's historical experience.

Hegel's historical interpretation was at least partially developed as an effort to combat what he regarded as the errors of the Enlightenment and the revolutionaries. The principles of the Enlightenment and the Revolution had been historically important; they had also been historically destructive. All sense of human community had been destroyed, and the bonds that should unite men had been loosened. The individual had been separated from general mankind, power had been divorced from morality, and abstract ideas had been substituted for the reality of life. French "liberalism" had ended in French "libertarian madness," and the arbitrary individual will had been substituted for the understanding of and allegiance to man's great historical purposes.

Hegel believed that his life's work was to illustrate the errors of what he regarded as these false doctrines. He was determined to eliminate any trace of destructive arbitrariness from history and to remove the discord between the individual and the world in which he lived. He was convinced that there was no genuine conflict between the individual and his society and that man could be reconciled with his political, cultural, and historical surroundings. "The aim of knowledge," he wrote, "is to divest the objective world that stands opposed to us of its strangeness and, as the phrase is, to find ourselves at home in it." The problem of divided allegiance and duality in the world was, for Hegel, only a problem of misunderstanding. And his was a great and powerful search for certainty, for a method by which the world could be understood, for a grasping of the underlying spirit that guides the affairs of men.

In many ways this search for certainty was a religious quest. Hegel had, in his youth, been a student of theology, and he was always to remain a God-seeker, one who was convinced that history reflected the purposes of God. He argued that "God governs the world," and that "the actual working of His government — the carrying out of His plan — is the history of the world." But for Hegel this was no hypothetical theological argument. God's purpose manifested itself in the actual world, and concrete historical events reflected the religious aims of the Creator. Hegel believed that the "secular is capable of being the embodiment of truth." In fact, the secular is the truth. There is a religious purpose to history, what could be called a religious "necessity." But, opposed to many religious thinkers, Hegel believed that the purpose and direction of history were understandable to men. He had no sympathy with those religious thinkers who argued that God directed man's activities but then took refuge in obscurantism or naive pietism in explaining how this direction was accomplished. God's plan, for Hegel, was a rational one, and "reason is the substance of the universe." What will happen is what must happen, and what must happen can be known to men. It is in this sense that Hegel's famous phrase "the real is the rational" must be understood. The world and its history are real, in the sense that there is a permanent core of meaning to history, no matter how it may be masked by superficial events. And this reality is proved not by intuition or inspiration but by the use of man's reason.

Thus the real is part of what one sees and is. Men understand themselves by examining themselves as they are, in history and in time. There are real and unreal things, as there are important and unimportant things. But one must look at things as they are, not as one might hope they would be. That man understands history who finds an identity between what is and what he believes is. Wholeness is thus achieved, and destructive duality, which renders man a stranger to his world and his history, is banished. There is a movement to history that is both necessary and rational. This movement Hegel called the dialectic. Every historical tendency creates or finds its opposite, and out of the straining between a position and its opposite comes a reconciling synthesis, which in turn becomes a new position. There is thus a moving equilibrium that constantly calls change into place and provides both continuity and direction to this change.

In his writings and, most importantly, in his lectures at the University of Berlin, Hegel sought to provide a definition for man and to solve the problem of authentic authority. He attempted to reunite the individual with his community and to show how reason, tradition, and even revolution could be constructive forces that would provide guidance and meaning to man. He did this by emphasizing what he regarded as the most important thing that any particular group of men have in common, and this was their nationality. Hegel saw that while the Enlightenment and the French Revolution had destroyed the old social and political arrangements, they had helped to create new ones. The old idea of a united, Christian Europe was gone. But there was a new center about which men could rally, and this was the concept of nationality. Here was a new unifying force, a new identity that would restore significance to individual men.

Hegel is usually regarded as the great philosopher of the national state. He believed that it was the state, expressing itself through political and historical activities, that formed the significant human unit and that it was the state that acted as the true creator of laws, arts, and morals. He argued that the history of the world was not of individuals, but of "peoples — totalities that are states." The state is not only an expression of physical power but also of the inner moral fiber of its citizens. It is the state that combines what Hegel called "the universal, essential will" with the aspirations of the individual. An individual can only fulfill himself as a member of a state, only when he acts in terms of the "laws and customs of the nation." The national state represents a natural family superior to the individuals that compose it. The people, considered only as individuals, are merely a formless mass, but as members of a state they exhibit a moral unity and thus participate in the earthly embodiment of the eternal spirit.

Even personal freedom is dependent upon the state, and such freedom must strengthen the state's authority, take a form compatible with it, and submit to its direction. The state is "that form of reality in which the individual has and enjoys his freedom; but on the condition of his recognizing, believing in, and willing that which is common to the whole." The state does limit the individual, "but this is a limitation of the mere brute emotions and rude instincts," "of the capricious and passionate self-will." The realization of freedom is beyond the capabilities of individuals and must be achieved in the state organized as "an individual totality." Anyone who broke with his society ran the risk of losing his individuality, and only an authority, accepted by all and acting in behalf of all, can protect individual and common rights.

Hegel's was a powerful and perceptive analysis of Western European society. His argument that Western men were divided into national groupings and that they were increasingly to look upon themselves as members of nations was irrefutable. Certain groups of men are tied to each other by a common geography, a common language, common religious and cultural conceptions, and common historical experiences. It is also true that an abstract freedom divorced from the requirements of living in society is an impossible dream, and that individuals find satisfaction and security only as members of a group that is, in some fashion or other, accepted by all, supported by all, and acts for all.

Yet Hegel's philosophy of nationalism has posed serious problems for the Western community. His argument was basically a revolt against the international ideas of the Enlightenment and against the theoretical cosmopolitanism that had been such an important part of eighteenth-century political thinking. He distrusted the critical and skeptical spirit of the Enlightenment, its striving for clarity and its opposition to any theological speculation. By stressing the uniqueness and indivisibility of the national states, he raised the question of whether the concept of a common human fate had any meaning. While he strengthened the individual's attachment to his own particular national group, he restricted Western man's horizons by emphasizing his particular, national characteristics.

Nor was it obvious how a mutually beneficial relationship between the individual's rational freedom and the demands of the state was to be established. By refusing to consider the possibility of the concept of freedom as an independent entity, and by arguing that there was no "real" conflict possible between liberty and authority, Hegel tightened the control of the society over its individual members. In his determination to reconcile everything, he subordinated the individual and led back to a new transcendental authority. He left no way for the individual to protest against those who happened to be in positions of authority and provided no guides for distinguishing between a proper and an improper authority. He had a low opinion of the press, he did not believe in any kind of a truly representative assembly, he claimed that the state had the right to require every citizen to belong to some church, and he regarded education as a process by which rebellious individuality is destroyed and students prepared for participation in the activities of the state.

By elevating the state Hegel also freed it from any moral restraint. It became a law unto itself and could not be called to account. According to Hegel, the rules of private morality did not apply between states. The state's highest duty is to preserve and strengthen itself. "A nation is moral when it is engaged in realizing its grand objectives and in defending its work against external violence," and the only criterion of judgment that can be applied to any activity is whether or not it advances the interests of the state. Each nation has its own unique laws and destiny, and each nation has the right to follow its own logic, to pursue its own interest. That this might result in conflict between national states was accepted by Hegel, and, in fact, he believed that the history of the world was a continuous struggle of great national states, which fulfilled their individual destinies through conflict. This international struggle was a sign of historical health and could not, and should not, be shunned. "Sentimental humanitarianism" was no substitute for pursuit of the power interests of the state, and Hegel spoke contemptuously of the "laurels of good intentions . . . dry leaves that had never been green."

In theory, Hegel's philosophy of nationalism could be applied to any nation. But, in reality, it was an interpretation designed for Germany and had a particular appeal for Germans. His early *Constitution of Germany*, published in 1802, was the argument of a patriotic man who wished the German state of the future to be the powerful expression of a people's fate. This was to be his theme throughout his life. He wished to provide a way whereby there would be a "gathering together" of the German people and a union created out of a geographic area. In his view the Germans were a unique people, and he believed that they were capable of creating a distinctive political and social order in tune with their natural characteristics. The archaic German disorder, which robbed each German of confidence in himself and in his society, would disappear and be replaced by a rational, and for Hegel divine, German nation that would overcome the contradictions of the modern world.

Anyone reading Hegel carefully is struck by the fact that, by a practice of exclusion, he stressed the unique quality of the Germans by discounting any but German claims to the position of a true nation. He argued that history passes from east to west. Thus Asia, for him, is the past or the beginning, and Europe is the present and the future. He went so far as to claim that "Europe is absolutely the end of history." He identified this "end of history," this culmination of man's historical efforts, with Christianity and contended that "the Christian world is the world of completion; the grand principle of being realized, consequently, the end of days to come." He even claimed that only the temperate zone could be the theater of history and thus largely confined his national philosophy to a European setting.

But he narrowed the application of his theory even more. If the Christian West was the end of history, some parts of that West were better prepared to play a historical role than were others. He dismissed the Slavs and the Americans as people who had not produced a religion and were thus outside history. And he had little to say about the English, who had what Hegel called a "whimsical originality," but did not even attempt to understand general philosophical principles.

His major concern, however, was to show that the German people were superior to the French and that it was the German state of the future that would be the carrier of a true national spirit. Hegel was convinced that the French were incapable of establishing a true national state. They lacked the necessary "totality of spirit." French thinking led to the idea of freedom as something "simple, homogeneous, and uniform," and French liberty is atomistic, setting one individual against another and prompting the refusal to give wholehearted support to the national principle. The French mistrust their own national authority, and the great crime of the French is that they "have maintained in the very depth of their soul — in their spiritual consciousness — the principle of disharmony." They are, Hegel suggests, "a product of the fusion of Roman and German blood, and still retain the resulting heterogeneity." In fact, this "heterogeneity" is a permanent stain in the French character, and Hegel contends that they have been subjected to "intermingled alien elements" that have diluted the original French quality and left them unable to create a meaningful national community. So, by an awesome show of exclusive definitions, only the Germans are left, and it is the Germans who are "predestined to be the bearers of the Christian principle and to carry out the idea of an absolutely rational aim."

In the last quarter-century there has been a great deal of debate regarding Hegel's influence on subsequent German history. Some aspects of this debate have been historically silly. It is ridiculous to attempt the establishment of a simple cause-and-effect relationship between Hegel and the German tragedy of the twentieth century. One may with certainty say that no German political leader ever read Hegel and then used the Hegelian system as a guideline for the activities of the German state. On the other hand, efforts to separate Hegel from the history of Germany are equally naive. Hegel was a German philosopher, and it is impossible to imagine his thought set against a French, English, or American historical background. What Hegel did was to express certain attitudes toward the Western world and Western history that were rooted in German thought and that posed some serious questions in his day and beyond. The importance of these questions and their implications are obvious in our contemporary world.

Hegel's philosophy exhibited what can only be called the German tendency to overstatement. Throughout the nineteenth and twentieth centuries one German thinker after another, each one brilliant and imaginative, proposed all-inclusive interpretations of man's existence. There was a German stress upon totality, upon a single answer for the total man, that would reconcile all contradictions and account for all human aspirations and activities. What came to be known as German idealistic philosophy was a search for the ultimate unifying principle of life. There was a German urge for a single answer and a determination to establish clear and uncontested boundaries between truth and falsehood. In a way foreign to other parts of the Western world, German philosophy, and particularly the philosophy of history, became a claim to certitude and demanded an exclusive allegiance to one theoretical explanation that accounted for the multifaceted experience of men. The result was that no matter how penetrating and stimulating any of these German philosophies were, they had about them the smell of intellectual tyranny. They required an unquestioned obedience in return for which they promised absolute understanding, absolute confidence, and absolute historical security.

A second characteristic of Hegel's philosophy was the emphasis he placed upon religion. In the eighteenth century there had been a general tendency to blur, or even to ignore, the religious arguments that had so plagued previous Western history. Important religious differences remained. But the fires of religious controversy had been damped, and while there was a continual reliance upon religious answers to life, particularly in the general population, serious thinkers regarded religious appeals as less and less appropriate in dealing with political, social, and intellectual problems.

Hegel, however, gave a strong theological twist to his historical interpretation. His emphasis upon the religious aspects of history, and specifically of German history, reintroduced the prickly question of religion in politics. Throughout his philosophy, and in his later years his religious views became more dogmatic and more extreme, runs the thread of doctrinal exclusiveness. German Lutheranism becomes increasingly the true religion, and God speaks, through history, to those who can only be described as a new chosen people — the German Lutherans. In fact, God's bias toward the Germans is an important element in Hegel's philosophy, and by fortifying his concept of nationality with religious justification, Hegel stimulated what was to become a dangerous German tendency toward claims to national and cultural superiority that were based as much upon a subjective sense of spiritual preeminence as upon actual material accomplishments. What came to be known as German *Kultur* had strong religious overtones that resulted in a tendency to regard non-Germans, particularly the Jews, the Slavs, and, at times, the French, as infidels, those who were less chosen, less clean, less capable of understanding and participating in history. There was the growth of a German religious self-righteousness that was to mar the genuine contributions that the Germans were to make to Western civilization.

By stressing national uniqueness, Hegel, as other German philosophers, promoted a certain German historical loneliness. Germany has been part of the modern Western community, yet its relationship to that community has been ambiguous. Large numbers of Germans were never to feel secure, or comfortable, in the company of the French or the English. They remained, in great part, an inward-looking people, searching for the world's approval and yet suspicious of those they hoped to impress. Prompted to assume a superiority over others, the Germans were uneasy that their claims and aspirations were always the object of ridicule. Important contributors to the general life of the Western world, they had recurring doubts as to the validity and even existence of that world. All national groups in the West have experienced difficulties in balancing parochial interests against participation in a broader cultural and historical movement. But in Germany this difficulty was exaggerated.

Hegel illustrated this problem by his belief in the natural opposition of German *Kultur* and French *civilisation*. This opposition was to be one of the most destructive elements in modern Western history. Obscured at times by the demands of practical international politics, German enmity toward France and French ideas was to be a continual thread in German thinking. Hardly an important German intellectual or political leader of the nineteenth and early twentieth centuries failed to express the belief that German and French ideas and German and French national aspirations were in conflict and that the success of one required the defeat of the other. And this was more than a mere argument over the practical problems that arose between two powerful and creative national groups, which found themselves at odds over boundaries, alliances, and material interests. Rather, it was also an ideological conflict, prompted on the part of the Germans by a strange combination of envy and feelings of superiority.

Hegel's philosophy was designed to answer what he regarded as the important questions of Western historical life in the nineteenth century. His analysis was profound, stimulating, and influential. Yet, in spite of all this, he often stated as a valid conclusion what was and is a mere rephrasing of a basic problem. For example, the following appears in one of his essays as an unchallengeable dictum of politics. "There may be various opinions and views respecting laws, constitution, and government, but there must be a disposition on the part of the citizens to regard all these opinions as subordinate to the substantial interests of the state; and to insist upon them no further than that interest will allow." To many in the West the truth or falsehood and the implications of such a statement were what politics was about. In this sense, Hegel had only restated the question and not, as he thought, provided the answer.

Stendhal

In November, 1799, the sixteen-year-old Henri Beyle was on the road from his native Grenoble to Paris to take his examinations for the polytechnic institute when he heard of Napoleon's seizure of power. Beyle never took the examinations. Instead he was caught up in the excitement of the Napoleonic period. He followed Napoleon through twelve campaigns and concluded his military career in 1812 with the disastrous retreat of the French army from Moscow. Three years later, while sitting in a cafe in Venice, he was told of Napoleon's defeat at Waterloo. "All is lost, even honor," was his comment at the news. He was thirty-two, an unemployed former member of the Sixth French Dragoons, the French military commissariat, and the Grand Army.

Throughout the rest of his life, Beyle, or as he is better known by one of his pseudonyms, Stendhal, remained an orphan of the French Revolution and Napoleon's Empire. He lived uneasily on the perimeter of post-Napoleonic society, in France and in Italy, a writer of books and an unofficial commentator on life. Two of his novels, *The Red and the Black* and *The Charterhouse of Parma*, are masterpieces of modern

Western literature. But he also wrote lesser-known and little-read books on musicians, painting, and love, a long essay on Shakespeare, a short study of Napoleon, two autobiographical fragments, and three unfinished novels. During his last ten years he was French Consul in the small Italian city of Civitavecchia. In 1842, while on leave from his consular post, he had a fatal apoplectic stroke as he walked down a Paris street. He was buried in a cemetery in Montmartre. His epitaph, describing him as a citizen of Milan, was written in Italian.

Stendhal's life was, in many respects, bizarre. In a period of twenty-five years he used approximately two hundred pseudonyms, and, although he had little property to bequeath, he drew up thirty-two different wills. His most serious attempt to participate in public affairs ended in humiliation when the Austrian government refused to accept him as the French Consul in Trieste. A sensualist, and extraordinarily fond of women, he was always haunted by the possibility of a sexual fiasco. A talented and imaginative writer, he received little recognition for his efforts, and he was never a member of any literary circle. A solitary figure, he regarded himself as a victim of what he called in his first novel "the malady of one's century."

But Stendhal was more than an interesting and talented crank. He occupied a crucial position in the cultural history of the modern Western world. He was the first important European man of literature who concerned himself with the problem of the alienated individual in Western society. Emotionally and intellectually a man of the eighteenth century, Stendhal in his youth had expected to see the realization of the ideas proposed by the philosophers and the revolutionaries. But after 1815 he became convinced that the pursuit of life, liberty, and happiness was to end in disappointment and despair. In all his important writing Stendhal portrayed the dilemma of the marginal and "homeless" man who can find nothing to which to give his allegiance, who once believed in the historical future and has then become disillusioned. Stendhal's distaste for his political and social surroundings was to be the recognizable mark of the modern European intellectual. His was the early voice in what has become during the past century and a half a deafening roar of protest against the stupidity, the materialism, the emptiness, and the hypocrisy of the Western world.

Stendhal's attitude toward the society in which he lived posed a problem that has troubled Europe since the first part of the nineteenth century. Modern Europe has provided its intellectuals with dramatic and new opportunities for expression, and members of the European community have enjoyed more freedom of speech, thought, action, and conscience than ever was previously experienced. Yet from Stendhal's time to the present intellectuals have been dissatisfied and frustrated by the very society that nurtured them. There has been a lack of faith in the stability and the value of European institutions and patterns of life. The majority of European intellectuals have been rebels, alienated men who were uncomfortable in and hostile to their social and political surroundings. In every country there appeared a gulf between the general society and a substantial number of that society's most perceptive and intelligent members. The result of this division was that a great deal of what we call Western culture during the nineteenth and twentieth centuries was developed by those who opposed the very society they were thought to represent.

Stendhal was an excellent example of this isolation. In the eighteen-twenties and eighteen-thirties he could find little that deserved his loyalty. Neither the old nor the new pleased him. He regarded the surviving members of the nobility as sullen and passionless men, obsessed by their fear of another social and political upheaval. Permanently scarred by their experiences, they had retreated into the empty world of snobbery and reaction. Nor were the old revolutionaries and the old Bonapartists much better. They had grown tame and self-seeking, most of them similar to Marshal Soult, who under Napoleon "was a great general, but under the Bourbons he has become a hypocritical and ardent worshipper before the power of the Jesuits." Yet even these were not the worst. Stendhal disliked the traditional conservatives, and he pitied the repentant revolutionaries. But he despised the smug, complacent middle class with its spiritual drabness, its political and financial intrigue, its insincerity, and its greed. He realized that the real heirs of the French Revolution had been the middle class, whose members constituted a new aristocracy of wealth and influence and who controlled the press, manipulated the stock market, and directed politics. In Stendhal's opinion this was the historical catastrophe of the post-Revolution period. Middle-class society was a conspiracy of wealth and power, where everything was for sale. The venal world of high finance and high politics had produced what he called "the age of charlatanism without talent." Everywhere conventional morality, sentimentalism, a deference before wealth, and an intellectual emptiness marked the victory of the middle class over Europe.

Stendhal's writings constitute a full-scale attack upon the early nineteenth-century bourgeoisie. But it is important to understand what he meant by the bourgeoisie. During the century there were two closely connected but distinctive definitions given to this term. One definition is usually associated with Karl Marx and considers the bourgeoisie as an economic class, a group engaged in the production and distribution of economic goods. The members of this class are the owners of property and those whose view of the world is almost entirely conditioned by the economic functions they perform. They are products of the capitalistic methods of production and distribution and, by economic necessity, are selfish, brutal, and politically reactionary.

Stendhal's definition of the bourgeoisie is more extensive, more subtle, and more damning than the Marxian. He knew that the bourgeoisie was economically activated and was distinguished by a narrow interest in business and property. But bourgeoisie is more than a mere economic classification; it is the description of a certain type of spirit, a certain frame of mind. For Stendhal the bourgeois was the man of no qualities. He had no deep feelings, only prejudices. He was intellectually mediocre and lacked originality. He measured the whole world by his own shadow and was apprehensive of anything that existed outside the small circle of his own experience. He was hard-hearted yet sentimental, cruel yet cowardly, culturally pretentious yet without any real understanding of culture. There was no spiritual tension in his life but only the simple stupidity and the narrow outlook proper to the shopkeeper and the peasant. He possessed no real understanding of the complexities and ambiguities of life but attempted to reduce everything to a set of conventional responses.

This sterile bourgeois society is the background for all of Stendhal's important novels. His leading characters, Julien Sorel in *The Red and the Black*, Fabrice del Dongo in *The Charterhouse of Parma*, and Lucien in *Lucien Leuwen*, are in their youth like Stendhal himself, ardent idealists without guile and bursting with enthusiasm. They believe that they can participate in the world in which they live. But they fail. Count Mosca in *The Charterhouse of Parma* points out that the secret of history in the nineteenth century is that "the vile Sancho Panzas always win out in the long run over the sublime Don Quixotes," and Stendhal's characters learn that the world is not divided, "as nincompoops believe," into good and bad men, heroes and villains, but "quite simply into dupes and knaves." The solid dullness of nineteenth-century France is too much for any idealistic aspiration. Thus, after having decided upon a military career, Lucien realizes that this is to be no glorious adventure. "I'll never make war on anything but cigars. I'll become the pillar of the military cafe in some dreary ill-paved little garrison town; my evening diversions will be billiards and beer, and sometimes in the morning we'll wage war with rotten cabbages on dirty workmen who are dying of hunger. . . . I'll be killed by a chamber-pot thrown by some toothless hag out of a fifth-story window! What glory!"

Stendhal's greatest novel, *The Red and the Black*, is primarily a eulogy over the lost generation that was consumed by the ideas of the

Revolution and the Empire but was forced to live under the Bourbon Restoration and the bourgeois monarchy of Louis-Philippe. In the novel Stendhal portrays the bitter hatred inspired in the heart of a gifted and energetic individual by his frustrations, and he indicts a civilization that he regarded as a vast and infamous conspiracy against truth. Julien Sorel is a spirited person caught in a ridiculous society, a man of feeling and ambition vainly attempting to maintain his integrity in the midst of overwhelming social and political corruption. Everywhere he is confronted by the prosaic, the intellectually loathsome, and the spiritually defunct. In the end he is broken by a hostile environment. In his prison cell awaiting execution, he sums up Stendhal's own interpretation of the sorry state of nineteenth-century Europe. "I have loved truth. . . . Where is it? . . . Everywhere there is hypocrisy or at least charlatanism, even among the most virtuous, even among the greatest. . . . No! Man cannot put his trust in man."

In *The Red and the Black*, *The Charterhouse of Parma*, and *Lucien Leuwen* Stendhal portrayed a world that had lost direction. War, revolution, and political reaction had brought about a dissolution of community life. Traditions were no longer direct, recognizable, and alive. The classic patterns of social, political, and intellectual life had been irreparably broken, but they had not been replaced by new and authentic expressions of historical experience. Europe had no dominant mood, and there was no decisive historical influence at work. The absence of any constructive principle had resulted in a historical inertia that exhibited itself in frivolity, snobbery, and vulgar stupidity. The old virtues had become ridiculous, while the new, in so far as Stendhal could see, were based upon a petty, boring, and hypocritical view of life.

In his writing Stendhal explored the reasons why individuals such as Julien Sorel could not find a place for themselves in the Europe of the first half of the nineteenth century. Stendhal did not search for solutions, for he believed that no solutions existed. He knew that neither Julien's death nor Fabrice's withdrawal to a monastery was a satisfactory answer. But he was convinced that there were reasons why Julien, Fabrice, and Lucien, and he himself, had failed, and in his search for these reasons Stendhal established a dialogue between the individual and society, a dialogue that explained the opposition of individual and society and introduced a new element into Western literature and Western cultural thinking that was to be both fruitful and destructive.

In Stendhal's view life was a conspiracy of the vulgar, the unintelligent, and the hypocritical against the sensitive, the idealistic, and the free-thinking. As a result, an intellectual must practice a systematic distrust of all slogans, all promises, all programs set forth by those in positions of power. It was his duty to expose plots, to impugn motives, to justify suspicions, and to believe the worst. "Look at life as though it were a masked ball," Stendhal wrote in his diary in 1814, and he freed his characters, and in so doing himself, from all allegiance save to their own integrity as individuals. A commentator has noted that Stendhal's "characters do not believe in anything. The religion of politics which might have given them a mystique has been vanquished. There remain only themselves." Julien Sorel, Fabrice del Dongo, and Lucien Leuwen ultimately become social, political, and historical agnostics, and Stendhal gives the impression that if you look deeply enough into life there is nothing there.

Yet Stendhal is not a nihilist. He does salvage something from the chaos about him. He places his wager upon the intellectual "outsider" who has the inner stamina to withstand all superficial historical change. The individual is real and important; the world of politics and society is not. The dream of what he called "the happy few" remained his only hope, and he invited his readers to join that small group of intellectuals who cultivate the rational knowledge of the human heart. The "Pursuit of Happiness" is an individual quest that each man undertakes for himself. In his novels and his incidental writing Stendhal shifted the focus of attention from the wide historical problems to man's enigmatic qualities, and he concentrated upon the sensitive individual. Thus he attempted to communicate an imaginative experience to his readers, and his characters are tormented individuals trying desperately to come to terms with themselves, trying to discover what kind of people they are.

Stendhal argued that society had no meaningful historical basis and that politics was an activity for fools and knaves. The intellectual's proper position was as a critic not a supporter, as a questioner not a participant, as a man who looked inside himself, not to the society as a whole, for his values. He was an uncommitted commentator who expected the worst of his fellowmen and was seldom disappointed. In this sense Stendhal was one of the first modern intellectuals, talented, idealistic, and cynical, a man of sensibility and perception who found himself out of step with his surroundings.

SUGGESTIONS FOR FURTHER READING

A rich harvest of readable and thought-provoking books has been devoted to the intellectual, political, and social history of the new Western world of the nineteenth century. Some of the best of the general works are

D. Thomson, Europe since Napoleon *(1957)*, *Hans Kohn*, A History of the European Century *(1965)*, *G. Kitson Clark*, The Making of Victorian England *(1962)*, *E. J. Hobsbawn*, The Age of Revolution, 1789-1848 *(1962)*, *A. Briggs*, The Age of Improvement, 1780-1867 *(1959)*, *W. L. Burn*, The Age of Equipoise: A Study of the Mid-Victorian Generation *(1965)*, *and Robert Leslie*, The Age of Transformation *(1964)*.

Intellectual histories of the century are particularly valuable. Benedetto Croce's History as the Story of Liberty *(1941) and E. Halévy's* The Growth of Philosophical Radicalism *(1938) are justly recognized as classics. G. P. Gooch's* History and Historians in the Nineteenth Century *(1952) is solid and enlightening, while Karl Löwith's* From Hegel to Nietzsche: The Revolution in Nineteenth-Century Thought *(1964) and Franklin Baumer's* Main Currents of Western Thought *(1964) are stimulating. The importance of science and scientific thought during the century has received increased attention in recent years. John C. Greene's* The Death of Adam: Evolution and Its Impact on Western Thought *(1959) and* Darwin and the Modern World View *(1961) are exciting studies of the subject, as is C. C. Gillispie's* Genesis and Geology *(1951). J. D. Bernal's* Science in History *(1954) is a good survey.*

A good introduction to Metternich is Henry F. Schwarz, ed., Metternich, the "Coachman of Europe": Statesman or Evil Genius *(1962). E. E. Kraehe's* Metternich's German Policy *(1963) is a specialized study of Metternich's most important area of political activity, while C. K. Webster's* The Congress of Vienna 1814-1815 *(1919) contains some excellent discussions of Metternich's policies. Unfortunately, most writing on Hegel tends to heaviness. But Geoffrey Mure's* The Philosophy of Hegel *(1965) and Hugh Reyburn's* The Ethical Theory of Hegel: A Study of the Philosophy of Right *(1967) are recent and worthwhile analyses as is that in Löwith's* From Hegel to Neitzsche. *The best understanding of Stendhal can be gained by reading* The Red and the Black *and* The Charterhouse of Parma. *Stendhal's notes for his intended study of Napoleon have been published as A* Life of Napoleon *(1956). Victor Brombert, ed.,* Stendhal: A Collection of Critical Essays *(1962), and Frederick Hemming's* Stendhal: A Study of His Novels *(1964) provide a great deal of information about the gifted and fascinating Frenchman.*

La Soupe, Honoré Daumier, ca. 1860, Cabinet des Dessins, Musée du Louvre, Paris.

5

The Industrial Society

1733 John Kay patented the flying shuttle. The shuttle has been described as "the first of a series of inventions which were to transform the manufacture of textiles, substitute the factory system for the older method of domestic production, introduce power-driven machinery into manufacturing processes, and mark the first steps in the Industrial Revolution."

1754 Society for the Encouragement of Arts, Manufactures and Commerce (later the Royal Society of Arts) established in Britain.

1763 First exhibition of industrial arts held in Paris.

1776 James Watt's steam engine was put to practical use. Watt's patent of 1781 enabled steam power to be applied directly and was thus "truly the beginning of the age of steam."

1793 Eli Whitney invented the cotton gin.

1794 Establishment of École polytechnique in France, an institution of higher technical education and devoted to mathematics and applied science.

1803 Jean-Baptiste Say's *Treatise on Political Economy*. Stressed the importance of the businessman in industrial development where he plays a creative role as the organizer of industrial power.

1807 Robert Fulton sailed his steamboat *Clermont* from New York to Albany. Although this was not the first steam-operated boat, it was the first commercial success.

1809- Albrecht Thaer's *Principles of Rational Agriculture*. This was perhaps

1812	the important early discussion of agriculture as a science and a business, involving animal breeding, deep ploughing, introduction of new crops, and agricultural bookkeeping.
1810	Founding of the famous Krupp works in Germany. In 1846 the firm employed 140 men. By 1912, 68,300 and had become the supplier to the German army.
1814	George Stephenson built his first railway locomotive.
1817	David Ricardo's *Principles of Political Economy and Taxation*. Ricardo's theory of rent, profit, and wages was a powerful statement used to justify the activities of the businessman.
1819	Simonde de Sismondi in his *New Principles of Political Economy* condemned the laissez faire doctrine and advocated state action to help the working classes.
1819	Steam (although augmented by sail) used for the first time to cross the Atlantic.
1824	Repeal of the British Combination Acts made organization of workers legal.
1825	Opening of the first successful railway system in England. In 1829 first operating railways opened in United States and France. The first German line opened in 1835.
1825	British law against joint stock companies repealed. Additional acts of 1837 and 1844 stimulated formation of companies.
1832	First mechanical generation of electricity. The first use of electricity to drive machinery was in 1873.
1833	Passage of the Factory Act in Britain. Act prohibited employment of children under nine, restricted labor of minors, and set down that children under thirteen were to spend two hours in school each day. A system of paid inspectors was established. The law was inadequate but did introduce the precedent of legislative action regarding working conditions.
1834	French law prohibited workingmen's associations of more than twenty persons if they had any connection with other such associations.
1834	Franz von Baader initiated use of word "proletariat."

1834	Cyrus McCormick invented his reaper. Technical inventions and improvements continued throughout the century. Some of the important were: steel plow, 1837; vulcanized rubber, 1839; steam hammer, 1839; sewing machine, 1846; dynamite, 1867; telephone, 1876; first practical gas engine, 1876; incandescent light bulb, 1879; diesel engine, 1892.
1845	Publication of Friedrich Engels' *Condition of the Working Class in England in 1844*. This has been called "a picture of the deepest poverty, taken from the dirtiest district of the dirtiest factory town in England, . . . beyond any question the best invective ever written against industrial society and its conditions, a partisan book like no other."
1846	Repeal of the Corn Laws in Britain and the introduction of the free trade era.
1848	Karl Marx and Friedrich Engels issued the *Communist Manifesto*. This was the most influential revolutionary document of the century. The conclusion: "Let the ruling classes tremble at a communist revolution. The proletarians have nothing to lose but their chains. They have a world to win. Workingmen of all countries unite."
1856	Henry Bessemer perfected the technique for converting pig iron into steel.
1860	Construction began on the London underground railway system. The Paris metro was begun in 1898 and the New York subway in 1900.
1863	First political organization of German working classes.
1866	First transatlantic cable laid.
1867	First volume of Marx's *Capital*, the best-known if seldom-read criticism of capitalism.
1874	Electrically powered streetcars began operating in New York City, replacing the horse-drawn cars. The cable streetcar had been put into operation in San Francisco in 1873.
1876	Opening of the Imperial Bank *(Reichsbank)* in Germany. A powerful financial influence in Germany's economic development.
1880	First employers' liability act in Britain granted compensation to workers who were injured while at work through no fault of their own.

1881   First of many important social legislative acts in Germany. Ultimately such laws included a sickness insurance act, an accident insurance law, and an old age and invalidity insurance law. Bismarck, the German Chancellor, justified the measures with the argument that the state "is not only an institution of necessity but also one of welfare."

1884   French law legalized trade unions.

1886   American Federation of Labor organized.

1891   Papal encyclical *Rerum novarum* expressed views on social questions and condemned the exploitation of workers. Won for Pope Leo XIII the title "the workingman's pope."

1895   The French Trade Union Congress organized the Conféderation Générale du Travail (C.G.T.) designed for direct action and the overthrowing of the capitalist system by means of a general strike.

1895   First automobile manufactured for sale in the United States. First motion picture showing in Paris. Wireless telegraph invented (first message sent across the Atlantic in 1901).

1901   Organization of United States Steel Corporation, the first billion-dollar corporation.

1903   Orville and Wilbur Wright made first flight in heavier-than-air flying machine.

1906   French law required employers to grant workers one day of rest in seven.

1914   Conveyor-belt mass production employed with greatest effect by Henry Ford in manufacturing his Model T.

W e associate our historical past with international disputes, political debates, and the careers of ambitious and talented national leaders. Wars, territorial controversies, political hatreds, the passing of laws, the rise and decline of nations — these are the things we recall first in contemplating our historical experience. We identify revolution as political change, and we have been conditioned to look at our situation through the eyes of politics and to define the character of Western man in terms of his political orientation.

This concentration upon politics and political revolution is natural. But it blurs our understanding and narrows our view of the complex nature of our situation. The political revolutions of the late eighteenth and nineteenth centuries were important and dramatic. But at the same time as this upheaval in politics was taking place, another revolution was underway. As the political revolutions of the modern Western world were pulling men loose from their traditional historical anchorage, what we call the industrial revolution was prying them away from their traditional social and economic foundations.

The industrial revolution, which began near the middle of the eighteenth century and had its first important impact early in the nineteenth, was a unique achievement of modern Western civilization. It was what economists call a "take-off." No other society had been able to break through the traditional restraints of "a pre-industrial social structure, defective science and technology, and consequently periodic breakdown, famine, and death imposed on production." Industrialization changed the physical environment and transformed the ecology of the planet. By substituting machine-power for human-power it delivered men from the age-old cycle of back-breaking toil and gave them mastery over raw materials. It brought about the factory system, a new type of human organization. It also created new values — new ways of looking at the human situation. In 1829, the year in which a Harvard professor appears to have coined the word "technology," the Englishman Thomas Carlyle in his essay "Signs of the Times" wrote that the nineteenth century could not be described as "a Heroical, Devotional, Philosophical, or Moral Age, but, above all else, the Mechanical Age. . . . It is the Age of Machinery."

By 1800 the basic technology for industrialization — the cloth-spinning machines, the steam engine, bone china, the screw-cutting lathe, the hydraulic press — had been developed. But the pace of industrialization was slower than one would believe from reading contemporary accounts. In the early nineteenth century the farmer still had his hoe, his spade, and his short scythe. Only gradually did metal ploughs replace wooden, as only slowly was the flail abandoned for the threshing machine. The old continued to appear beside the new, and the combination of the traditional and the revolutionary tended to obscure the dramatic effects of industrialization. It was the age of railroads. But it was also the age of the horse. The movement from the countryside to the city was slow in many places, and as late as 1846 less than 4 per cent of the cotton looms in Prussia were power-operated. In 1850 only a small part of the total tonnage of the British overseas merchant fleet was steam-driven, and the commercial world still thought in terms of wooden sailing ships such as the famous Yankee Clippers. Throughout much of the century, in a great part of the West, the green land, the woods, and the rivers remained close at hand.

But once underway, industrialization could not be stopped, and there was never any possibility of going back to an agrarian society. Moreover, the tempo continually increased. The output of English cotton goods rose from 40 million yards of cloth in 1785 to 2,025 million yards in 1830, by which time over a million and a half people were directly employed in or depended for their livelihood upon cotton production. In Belgium the number of steam engines increased from 700 in 1840 to over 2,000 in 1850. In 1830 there were a few hundred miles of railroad in the world. In 1840 there were over 4,500, and in 1850 over 23,000. By 1900 the lines stretched across Europe to Constantinople and Vladivostok and from New York to San Francisco. In the 1840's over 600 million tons of coal were wrenched from the earth, and by 1870 all the great river basins of Germany had been linked by canal. The population increased in the Western world at a truly staggering rate. In the area that was to make up the modern state of Germany the population in 1800 was slightly over 24,000,000. By 1914 it was 67,000,000, and this figure was reached although millions of Germans had left Europe for the United States. In 1850 only England had 20 per cent of her population living in cities of 100,000 or more. By 1910 this was also true of the United States, Germany, Belgium, and the Netherlands.

From its beginning the industrial revolution showed Western man's capacity for accomplishment and his tendency toward destruction. The Frenchman Alexis de Tocqueville, writing in 1835 of his visit to Manchester in England, spoke dramatically of this two-faced human experience:

> From this foul drain the greatest stream of human industry flows out to fertilize the whole world. From this filthy sewer pure gold flows. Here humanity attains its most complete development and its most brutish, here civilization works its miracles and civilized man is turned almost into a savage.

The industrial revolution produced wealth beyond imagination, and it presented new opportunities for the restless nature of Western man. But it also scarred the earth, promoted squalor and oppression, and, at least in some measure, as was claimed, "betrayed the spirit of man in the nineteenth century."

Complaints about the effects of industrialization have been with us since its beginning. Yet the Western temperament responded to mechanization, and Western man has carried on a long and true love affair with the machine. In 1795 the German poet Friedrich Schiller complained of "the monotonous sound of the perpetually revolving wheel." But this was a minority response, and the sounds of industrialization were music to many ears. In 1839 an Englishman wrote: "It is a proud feeling to be an Englishman and to know that the productions of the thousand busy hands and whirling wheels around him are destined to increase the comfort, refinement, or splendour of nations, spread far and wide over the globe." Newspapers, political speeches, and correspondence indicate the popular pride in industrialization. We may smile now at the extravagant prose used to describe the coming of the railroad, yet the following American attempt to combine poetry with machinery, complete with almost biblical overtones, expresses some of the stagestruck awe that was common in the nineteenth century:

> And the Iron Horse, the earth-shaker, the fire-breather, which tramples down the hills, which outruns the laggard winds, which leaps over the rivers, which grinds the rocks to powder and breaks down the gates of the mountains, he too shall build an empire and an epic. Shall not solitudes and waste places cry for gladness at his coming?

In March, 1776, James Boswell, the friend and biographer of Samuel Johnson, visited Matthew Boulton's Soho factory where some seven hundred workers were engaged in operating the great steam engines. "I sell here, Sir, what all the world desires to have — power," said Boulton to his visitor. Boswell himself was impressed by what he saw. "I wish that Johnson had been with us," he wrote. "The vastness and the contrivance of some of the machinery would have 'matched his mighty mind.'" And Boswell was correct. It took a "mighty mind" to grasp the monumental nature of industrialization. The phrase "annihilation of space and time" appears frequently in the nineteenth century to describe what was happening, and this was more than empty rhetoric. The railroad engine was "swifter than the greyhound, and powerful as a thousand horses." Moreover, "it runs and never tires." The first message sent across the telegraph lines — "What wonders God has wrought" — was both a pious platitude and an expression of reverent amazement at the fantastic new instruments now available for man's use.

The Western Businessman

All genuine revolutions cast up a new type of person, a man of the revolutionary times who expresses the reality of the revolutionary change. The industrial revolution created several new types. One of these was the Western businessman. Commerce had played an important part in the preindustrial period, but those engaged in commercial undertakings had possessed little political and social standing. In the nineteenth century there were still some who looked down with aristocratic haughtiness upon men engaged in commerce and industry. But the general attitude of society changed. Banks, insurance and utility companies, stock exchanges — all the institutions by which the commercial work of the world was carried on — came to be accepted as cherished symbols of Western society. Joint stock companies sprang up everywhere, and there was a growth of what was called "the investment habit." New methods of merchandising appeared, and foreign and domestic commerce swelled the fortunes of those who participated in these activities. Large amounts of capital were produced by the new industries that could be invested everywhere, and "all the going to and fro, the buying and selling, insuring and speculating, loading and unloading, warehousing and retailing, telegraphing and telephoning" became for an increasing number of people the way of life. The businessman was, in the minds of many, the typical Western man, dedicated to his own, and thus by necessity, to the public interest, convinced of his own intelligence and commonsense, and master of the most important activity undertaken by men.

The stimulus for the industrial revolution was profit, and the character of industrialization was influenced by its close relationship with those who had the knack of spinning money, of making investments, and of using the industrial machine as a mechanical goose to lay the most wonderful golden eggs. Revolutionary leaders are notoriously ruthless, and so were those who directed the industrial revolution. They had little sympathy with any who complained of their methods and accepted the fact that in the pursuit of wealth many might perish on the way. There was hostility to anything that stood in the path of maximizing profits or increasing efficiency. The idealized profit motive stimulated the energies of the businessman and sharpened his dedication to his enterprise. It also provided the spur that continually increased the speed of industrialization and forced it from one triumph to another.

The raw, rough world of the business entrepreneur was one of success and accomplishment. It also was one in which the drive for monetary reward took precedence over all other virtues. Centuries-old rules governing the quality of products were abandoned. A certain shoddy commercialism became a permanent part of Western life, and too often the arrogance of the businessman was only matched by his lack of taste and social consciousness. The greed, selfishness, and narrowness of the entrepreneur became proverbial in the West, and hardly a perceptive observer in the nineteenth century failed to comment upon these habits. The most popular novelist of the time, Charles Dickens, described the unattractive activities of the Dombeys, the Dedlocks, the Bounderleys, and the Gradgrinds, all those offspring of commercial success, and left us a dramatic picture of "the world of Podsnap, Boots, Brewer, and Veneering, the world of promoters, contractors, and company chairmen." Attacks upon the business community were unceasing and devastating, and a general suspicion of the businessman became endemic in Western society. Many were prepared to accept George Bernard Shaw's statement in the eighteen-eighties that the requirements of commercial success rendered "adulteration, dishonest dealing, and inhumanity compulsory."

The political history of every Western country illustrated the pressure of business and commercial demands. Laws were repealed and others enacted, the power of the state was used to forward the businessman's claims, and there was a close alliance, subtle in some cases and blatant in others, between politicians and bankers, investors, and managers. In 1830 the Englishman Samuel Taylor Coleridge wrote that "the stock-jobbing and moneyed interest is so strong in this country that it has more than once prevailed in our foreign councils over national honor and national justice." Religion and morality were bent to fit the prerequisites for business success, and then this new definition of propriety was pressed upon political leaders and the community as a whole. The hidden hand of God was assumed to be guiding economic development, and the fact that moral claims could be made for conflicting points of view was merely an indication of the mysterious ways of divinity. A German newspaper seriously suggested that "free trade is a consequence of the Christian religion," while many in France and elsewhere found evidence of the divine plan in the protection of local industries. And all were serious in their interpretation. The demand that the political climate be favorable to business was everywhere in the West, and hardly a government did not find itself in close partnership with the masters of the new machines, the new wealth, the new way of commercial success.

The Working Class

Many gained by the industrial revolution — gained in influence, status, and wealth. But many paid a terrible price. A historian has written: "In terms of economic productivity this social transformation was an immense success; in terms of human suffering, a tragedy." Large numbers of people were victimized. As the poet Goldsmith had remarked in the eighteenth century, "laws grind the poor, and rich men rule the law." Commercial expansion, industrialization, and urbanization "all took place within the shadows of the gallows." The exploitation of nature also became the exploitation of men. Great wealth was matched by great poverty, and while this poverty may not have been quantitatively greater than in earlier centuries, it was more offensive and, because of the large numbers of people involved, more destructive. It has been said that "twelve insanitary houses on a hillside may be a picturesque village, but twelve hundred are a grave nuisance, and twelve thousand a pest and a horror."

Tales of the suffering brought to millions by the industrial revolution are too well known to bear repeating. Well known, too, is the vulgar defense that was made of conditions whereby children worked long hours in mines for a pittance and women worked equally long hours in the factory for much less than a living wage. There was a terrifying lack of compassion on the part of those who benefited by industrialization, and a willingness to justify and excuse the consequent suffering. An English employer in the eighteen-thirties, and there were many who would second his words, could say that "it is to the interest of the worker himself that he should be constantly harassed by need, for then he will not set his children a bad example, and his poverty will be a guarantee of good behavior." Similarly, a French minister, in commenting upon a workers' revolt in Lyons, said: "The workers have to understand that there are no other remedies for them than patience and resignation." Traditions, habits, and practices that had in some way protected those who had nothing to offer but their physical strength and dexterity were, in some cases swiftly and in some slowly, pulverized.

The industrial revolution created a fetish of work. Work became the way by which a man filled his life and his only hope of establishing any contact with the world about him. Prior to the eighteenth century, and particularly in Catholic Europe, work had been only a part of man's existence. For example, in some parts of the continent there had been over a hundred holidays a year. But this pattern vanished, and "holidays," those periods when work was not done or was not available, became times of despair. Western man became in the nineteenth century a working man, in the sense that how he worked and what he did as a worker became his identifying mark. His occupation became more important in describing him than did his religion, his cultural background, or his intelligence. When the question was asked, "What do you do?" the expected answer was an occupational designation.

Yet the very process that made work so important robbed that work of significance. The product of the industrial process did not belong in any meaningful way to the worker, who was, in most cases, merely an appendage to the machine. He did not mark the product with his own personality, and few of the many occupations spawned by industrialization provided any opportunity for what could be called creative effort. The use of the term "hand" in describing the factory worker was indicative of the nature of so much of industrial labor, and those who were supposed to be engaged in what was termed God's great purpose had been themselves reduced to parts of the machinery.

As early as 1808 an observer noted that the factory system was producing "a new race of beings" and that there was occurring an "essential change in the general character of the mass of the people." Benjamin Disraeli, Friedrich Engels, and many others saw that industrialization was producing "two nations," those in command of things and those who were themselves "things" to be commanded. Beneath the veneer of progress and wealth there was the proletariat. Uneducated, brutalized, and dispossessed, the victims of laws and regulations designed to penalize any effort to improve their condition, large numbers of workingmen were scarcely distinguishable from the derelict, the wastrel, and the perennial scum of the slums. They spoke a different language, had different ideas and morals, and developed different loyalties. They had only the right to "toil, breed, suffer, and perish." In the industrial society, the workingman, employed or unemployed, was the bottom dog, and as the radical English journalist Robert Blatchford put it in picturesque language, "with nearly all the power, learning, and wealth of the world against him; with all the precedents of human history against him; with law, religion, custom, and public sentiment against him, the unfortunate victim's only hope is the justice of his case."

Thus as the industrial revolution created the Western businessman, it also created the factory working class, or the proletariat. And members of this class in large numbers became convinced that the way in which industrialization had been carried out was detrimental to their interests and that they had been robbed of the benefits that should have been rightfully theirs. They saw themselves increasingly as a separate part of society with special interests. Statements of this class consciousness were made throughout the century, and all expressed a hostility toward those held responsible for the condition of the workingman. As a 1864 manifesto drawn up by sixty Parisian workingmen stated:

> It has been repeated to the point of satiety that there are no longer any classes; that, since 1789, all Frenchmen are equal before the law. But we who have no other property than our hands, we who suffer every day from the legal or arbitrary conditions of capitalism, we who live under exceptional laws, which offend our interests at the same time as our dignity, find it very difficult to believe this affirmation.

Because industrialization was identified, at least in its reprehensible aspects, with capitalism, the workers' grievances against the results of the industrial society were expressed as attacks upon capitalism. These attacks were usually stated in moral terms, and an appeal was made from the present injustice to a more equitable society. According to William Morris, "It is enough political economy for me to know that the idle class is rich and the working class is poor, and that rich are rich because they rob the poor. That I know because I see it with my eyes. I need read no books to convince me of it." The evil of capitalism was taken for granted, and there was a widespread belief that capitalism could produce only inequality and an unfair distribution of wealth. Wrote Blatchford:

> We have seen that in this country the greatest share of the wealth goes to those who do nothing to produce it; that industrious men are generally poor, and rich men chiefly idle, that the best and the most useful men are not the best paid nor the best rewarded and that very often the greatest enemies of society reap the most benefits from society's labor.

Socialism

This hostility toward the results of industrialization was translated into programs for changing the order of things. Throughout Europe many workingmen and many intellectuals became socialists. There was a variety of socialist groups and socialist doctrines. But there were some general ideas held in common by those who called themselves socialists. Capitalism was condemned. Private property was attacked. The present political arrangements were regarded as allied with capitalism, and there was the demand for a new type of political authority. It was argued that large parts of the industrial sector should be publicly owned, and that what were called "the means of production" should be taken from private hands and placed under public control.

Many approaches were suggested for implementing the socialist programs. Some socialists were "moderates," in that they proposed using the political methods at hand to influence the society. They relied largely upon the organization of the workers into labor unions, upon gaining and then using the vote to elect representatives who would press for changes in the laws, and upon nationalization of basic industries, welfare measures, and legal regulation of industry to reduce or banish the harsh inequities of the industrial society. This was basically an "evolutionary" approach, whereby ultimately control of the political machinery of the state would bring about a cooperative commonwealth where justice would be secured and an equitable sharing of the wealth of industrialization would be achieved.

A second broad grouping of socialists, however, was more extreme. Members of this group did not believe that any compromise with the present political and industrial society was possible. They pledged themselves to a revolutionary overthrowing of the political authority and a seizing of the state, if necessary through violence. They believed reform of capitalism impossible and were convinced that the injustices of the present system could be ended only by radical means. Industrialization had divided society into classes, the exploiters and the exploited, the haves and the have-nots, and these classes were locked in an irreconcilable, to-the-death struggle. Participation in this class struggle was the way open for those who wished to change society, and the result of such a struggle must ultimately be the destruction of the present political and social arrangements.

Industrialization and Civilization

A common failing in examining industrialization is the tendency to regard it as solely an economic development. The industrial revolution, in its most relevant aspects, posed a problem in civilization, in the way in which Western man thought of himself and the values he adopted. Urbanization, the emphasis upon productivity, and the organization and development of industry were much more than economic matters. They cut to the heart of Western man's life and set off deep and abiding tensions. Also the effects of industrialization were complicated by the fact that the industrial revolution coincided with political revolution and the experience of modern nationalism. Thus the West faced the crisis of industrialization even while it struggled with the dilemma of politics and the problem of national identity. The Western individual was becoming an industrialized man at the same time as he was attempting to become a free man and a new type of citizen in a new type of nation.

The full implications of what it means to live in an industrial society are still not obvious to us two centuries after this revolution began. In fact, Western man has not entirely accepted the reality of industrialization. We have remained, in many ways, country boys, with a nagging memory of meadows and trees and the songs of wild birds. In an autobiographical poem, the twentieth-century German writer Bertolt Brecht expressed this strange dilemma: "My mother carried me, as in her womb I lay, into the cities. And the chill of the forests will stay within me to my dying day."

In his *The Machine in the Garden* Leo Marx has described the attempts of Americans to fit the industrial engine into their natural landscape and to retain the pleasures and the values of the "garden" while reaping the benefits of the "machine." There was what he calls an "ambivalent, look-both-ways kind of native progressivism," an attempt to reconcile "industrial progress and the older, chaste image of a green Republic." Many believed that this could be done. Marx describes the successful efforts in 1855 of the painter George Inness in his *The Lackawanna Valley* to show that "machine technology is a proper part of the landscape." In Marx's words:

> Inness's painting seems to say that "there is nothing inorganic." Instead of causing disharmony, the train is a unifying device. The hills in the background and the trees in the middle distance gently envelop the industrial buildings and artifacts. No sharp lines set off the man-made from the natural terrain. . . . It is noteworthy, too, that the animals in the pasture continue to graze or rest peacefully as the tidy, diminutive train approaches. . . . But, of course, it is the solitary figure reclining beneath the dominant vertical, the tree in the foreground, who finally establishes the quiet, relaxed mood. He holds no crook, but he contemplates the sight in the serene posture of the good shepherd looking out across Arcadia.

But the serene unity of engine and landscape was only temporary. The machine was too strong, and Marx uses Charles Sheeler's *American Landscape*, painted in 1930, to show what had happened in the latter stages of the industrial revolution. In Sheeler's picture "No trace of untouched nature remains. Not a tree or a blade of grass is in view. The water is enclosed in man-made banks, and the sky is full of smoke. . . . Technological power overwhelms the solitary man, but here the traditional figure acquires new meaning; in this mechanized environment he seems forlorn and powerless." Nature and man himself seem to have little place in the cold mechanization of power that has become our industrial society.

But the problem of Western man's adjustment to industrialization was more than nostalgic regret for a lost bucolic past. His political institutions and his intellectual frame of reference were rooted in the preindustrial era. The common view of man as a political and social animal came from a time long before the appearance of "the dark Satanic mills," long before the railroad, the steam engine, and the power loom. The sources of his religious experience were pastoral and tribal, while his political instruments — parliaments, ministers, congresses, councils — had all been fashioned without reference to the industrial experience. The vision of himself held by Western man was, to a large extent, preindustrial; he continued to see himself as a self-sufficient individualist, and he continued to use the speech patterns and the intellectual interpretations of a rapidly disappearing world. He became frustrated when his traditional institutions failed to respond to new circumstances. His education became somewhat archaic, and schools, churches, social groupings, and political organizations became less and less appropriate as expressions of an industrial age. It was difficult for him to realize that human nature was itself an ingredient of the industrial revolution and that while man was changing the world, he was being changed in turn by the world he had made.

In 1827 an Englishman wrote that the industrial revolution had increased the sum of human happiness by extending benefits to "those who before never would have hoped to share them. Nor are its effects confined to England alone; they extend over the whole civilized world; and the savage tribes of America, Asia and Africa, must ere long feel the benefits, remote or intermediate, of this all-powerful agent." His prediction was right, and none of us would wish to give up the wonders of industrialization. But we have become aware that the industrial revolution was much more than the building of machines that would produce an ever-increasing flow of wealth. In the twentieth century a scholar looked at a hundred years of industrialization and noted men's ignorance of the consequences of the industrial process:

> Accustomed for three generations to the spectacle of prosperity, pouring, as from an enchanted spring, from technical accomplishment, they are disposed to take it for granted that the problem which confronts them is the improvement of technique, without pausing to consider whether deficiencies of technique may not themselves be a symptom of more fundamental failings. Nurtured in the belief in the omnipotence of externals, they are apt to assume that their economic organization can be adjusted to the needs of an unforeseen situation, without being disturbed by the question whether the condition of readjustment may not be an alteration in their intellectual outlook, and the abandonment of certain of the cherished properties of their social relations.

There are many examples that could be used to illustrate the effects of industrialization in the Western world. The Manchester School was an early and influential expression of the aims and activities of the new class of industrial and commercial managers and businessmen. Pierre-Joseph Proudhon rebelled against many of the manifestations of industrialization and attacked what were often regarded as the virtues of the new society. Karl Marx saw industrialization as a great historical development and presented an interpretation that he believed was in tune with the realities of the industrial age.

The Manchester School

In 1957 the English historian A. J. P. Taylor published an article entitled "The World's Great Cities: Manchester." In his opening paragraph Taylor wrote that Manchester "is as distinctive in its way as Athens or Peking. It is the symbol of a civilisation which was, until recently, an ambition of mankind. . . ." Taylor was correct. If Athens, Peking, Rome, Paris, and other cities can claim to illustrate the aspirations and accomplishments of a particular group of men, motivated by a belief in a certain set of values, then Manchester too must be accorded the symbolical rank that Taylor proposes. It was the outstanding example of the new industrial city, the site of the new business and commercial activity that was such an important part of the industrial revolution. In 1844 the English statesman Benjamin Disraeli said that only a philosopher could understand the "grandeur of Manchester," and John Bright, whose name with that of Richard Cobden is permanently associated with the great days of the city, regarded Manchester as "the centre and heart of the greatest and most remarkable industry that the world has ever seen."

Manchester was the manifestation of new industrial, political, and social power. It had factories, fortunes, and commercial facilities. During the nineteenth century it developed its own distinctive institutions designed for life in the city. The Manchester Literary and Philosophical Society had been founded in 1781, and in the following years members of the Society included many of the scientific giants of the time, including John Dalton, James Joule, Arthur Schuster, and William Bragg, as well as men such as the engineer William Fairbairn and the socialist Robert Owen. Manchester had its own stock exchange. It had its own newspapers, one of which was the leading English liberal paper and another probably the outstanding workingmen's publication of its time. It was to have its own renowned symphony orchestra and by the end of the century its own great privately endowed research library. It had its own historical monuments, including St. Peter's Field where in 1819 troops had been used to suppress a meeting in support of universal manhood suffrage and the great Free Trade Hall. It had its own university, founded in 1851, where no teacher was required to avow a religious belief and where women were admitted equally with men. It also claimed to express a great historical purpose. "Every age," said Cobden, "every generation, has some distinguishing struggle that marked its history. In one century we had the contest for religious freedom — another century marks the era of political freedom — another century comes, and the great battle of commercial freedom has to be fought; and Manchester, and those free cotton districts around it . . . were pledged to take the lead in this great contest. . . ."

By the early part of the nineteenth century, Manchester was the second largest city in England, and was the "hub of the earliest industrialised area in the world." Incorporated as a municipally self-governing city only in 1838, it was a great cotton-manufacturing center on what could be called the frontier of the industrial revolution. Manchester and the surrounding Lancashire area of England consisted of a staggering complex of cotton mills, railroads, and engineering and chemical plants, where a million and a half people were employed. Manchester was the heart of the English export industry, as it was a center for radicalism, reform, and dissent. "Look up and all around this place you will see the huge palaces of industry," wrote an observer, and Thomas Carlyle found the noise of the Manchester mills starting in the morning at half-past five as "sublime as Niagara or more so."

Descriptions of Manchester abound. A large part of these stress the ugliness of the city. A visitor in 1808 found the place "abominably filthy, the steam engines pestiferous, the dyehouses noisome and offensive, and the water of the river as black as ink." Alexis de Tocqueville noted that "a sort of black smoke covers the city. The sun seen through it is a disc without rays. Under this half daylight 300,000 human beings are ceaselessly at work." In 1858 the American Henry Adams took a trip into the Manchester industrial district, which he later described as "a plunge into darkness lurid with flames." He had a "sense of unknown horror in . . . the weird gloom which then existed nowhere else, and never had existed before, except in volcanic craters." In its noise, its rapid growth, its contrasts of rich and poor, Manchester was a thrusting, bustling conglomeration of men and machines, the pattern for numerous industrial cities that were to stretch around the world.

The inhabitants of Manchester were also indicative of the industrial age. Churchmen, aristocrats, and military men played little part in the history of the city. In the main two groups of people dominated Manchester life. One consisted of the new men of industry and commerce, those who were busy making, buying, and selling. Driven by fierce competition and the fear of bankruptcy, Manchester merchants were hard-working, dedicated men whose lives were consumed by their business interests. Financial success was the singular mark of achievement, and as Cobden once remarked, in Manchester there was but "one opinion of a man's ability — the making of money." Preoccupied with their business activities, many Manchester merchants regarded themselves as men apart from other people and looked with indifference or even hostility upon those who were not engaged in industrial or commercial pursuits. A. J. P. Taylor writes of his own father, a Manchester man: "My father had been in Egypt and India; he knew Russia and most countries in Western Europe. He spent exactly three days in London, and hated them. . . . He felt that London was the enemy; it represented everything he disapproved of. . . ." The Manchester businessman was known for his commonsense, his energy, and his determination to pursue his own interests. A Londoner once wrote to Cobden that London people "differ very widely from you at Manchester. You . . . at Manchester resolve that something should be done and then you . . . set to work and see it done. . . ."

The other important group of Manchester citizens consisted of the workers, those who were described as "a vile gathering of haggard, anxious, dangerous faces." Workingmen and their families from all over England, as well as by 1841 over 34,000 destitute Irish, were jammed into Manchester, where they suffered from overcrowding, a lack of housing and sanitation, at times horrendous working conditions, and the continual threat of unemployment. Workers had few defenses against misfortune or the conditions of their employment. Some mill owners were humanitarian and did what they could to make working conditions as pleasant as possible. Others were not and were indifferent to the plight of their employees. But everywhere women and children worked for long hours, and a standard of living that was barely human was common.

Statistical measurements of the condition of the working class of Manchester are plentiful, as are their interpretations. In 1860 a survey showed that a man, his wife, and three children could be housed, clothed, and fed for 30 shillings a week. At that time a pattern-maker in the mills earned 32 shillings and an iron-founder 34. Bricklayers received 21 shillings for a fifty-five-and-a-half-hour week in the six "summer months" and 18 shillings for a fifty-hour week during the remainder of the year. A scholar has commented upon these findings. "If two children out of a family of three were also working and bringing home something like 15 shillings a week between them, such a family would enjoy a standard of living, in the material sense, as that of any comparable family in Europe." One may make of this comment what he will. Another survey four years later of 12.2 acres of the working-class district of Manchester found a population density of 231,147 to the square mile, with over 28 per cent of the families living in a single room. The needs of the inhabitants were served by thirty-one saloons and twenty-two brothels. Approximately one-fifth of the children of school age were in attendance.

But there was more to Manchester than booming industry and the problems of workers. There was also what Disraeli, in coining the phrase in 1846, called "the School of Manchester," which had brought forth "new principles expressed in peculiar language." The Manchester School became identified with a certain attitude toward the relationship of business and government. This attitude has commonly, and somewhat erroneously, been equated with laissez faire economics — the belief that there should be no regulation of business by government and that the benefits of industry and trade can be best passed on to society if the businessman is unhindered by any hobbling restrictions. Actually the important leaders of the Manchester School did not claim the right to an unrestricted economic freedom, nor did they advocate any well-developed theory of economics. They believed that they were practical men motivated entirely by the facts of the situation and were attempting to present a realistic plan for solving certain problems of business and trade. The Manchester School came into being in 1838 with the establishment of the National Anti-Corn Law League, which was dominated by Manchester men and whose spokesmen represented the Manchester point of view. In fact, the great activity with which the Manchester School is associated was the agitation to repeal the corn laws and to introduce free trade into England.

The English corn laws (it should be remembered that what the English call corn is in America called wheat) had been in existence for more than one hundred and fifty years when they came under attack by the Manchester School. The purpose of the laws was to insure an adequate supply of grain and to stabilize the price. They fixed import duties on grain and thus protected the agricultural interests from foreign competition. The arguments against the corn laws were many, and often contradictory and confusing. Put simply, these arguments were as follows. The Manchester businessmen believed that their wage costs were higher than need be because of the high price of grain which influenced what they had to pay their workers in order for them to purchase bread. Also, by forcing the English consumer to pay more for bread, the domestic market for textiles and other products was being reduced. It was argued too that nations that could not export grain to England would retaliate by setting import duties on English manufactured goods and thus restrict the exports of the fruits of English industry. Whatever the argument used, members of the Manchester School were convinced that the corn laws damaged British industry.

The controversy over the corn laws was more than a battle of economic interests. It was more, in Cobden's words, than "a mere contest for a few more pigs, a few more sheep, or a little more corn." It was an attack upon the privileges of the aristocracy, the great landowning families of England. And it was a bitter fight for political power. The free-trade movement was described as a struggle between "30,000 landowners and 26,000,000 of men," and it was claimed that "the owner of ten thousand spindles" should be the political equal of "the lord of ten thousand acres." The leaders of the Anti-Corn Law League mounted a great public campaign against the "special interests," and aroused even the working class to protest the favored treatment given one section of the population. Huge public rallies were held, thousands of speeches were made, countless pamphlets and articles were published, and year after year pressure was applied to force the government to abolish the corn laws. The opponents fought back against what they called "Manchester rubbish," but the political pressure exerted by the Manchester men was continual and effective. A London newspaper announced with chagrin the effects of a Cobden speech in Parliament: "Melancholy was it to witness, on Monday, the landowners of England, the representatives by blood of the Norman chivalry . . . shrinking under the blows aimed at them by a Manchester money-grubber."

Manchester was successful. In 1846 the corn laws were repealed. A Manchester newspaper announced "the victorious conflict with the spirit of feudalism. . . . The great dynasty of idleness is shaken to its foundations — the men who make the country, and keep it, have effectively vindicated their right to rule it." The repeal of the corn laws and the abolition of the Navigation Acts in 1854 brought England to a policy of nearly complete freedom of foreign trade. The actual results of the repeal of the laws are a matter of argument. The textile industry did expand, but so did other industries. Free trade may have been one of the reasons for this expansion. But there were probably other factors as well. The world's supply of gold increased markedly following the discoveries in America, and there was a general increase in productivity, commercial trade, and investment throughout the world.

But, in the minds of its leaders, the repeal of the corn laws was only the first step. Free trade was "a world's revolution and nothing else," designed "to promote the enduring interests of mankind." In 1846, at the moment of triumph, Cobden spoke of the ultimate goals of the free traders:

> I believe that the physical gain will be the smallest gain to humanity from the success of this principle. I look farther; I see in the free-

trade principle that which shall act on the moral world as the principle of gravitation in the universe — drawing men together, thrusting aside the antagonism of race, and creed, and language, and uniting us in the bonds of eternal peace. I have looked even further.... I have speculated on what the effect of this principle may be. I believe that the effect will be to change the face of the world, so as to introduce a system of government entirely distinct from that which now prevails. I believe that the desire and the motive for large and mighty empires, for gigantic armies and navies, for those materials which are used for the destruction of life and the desolation of the rewards of labour, will die away.... I believe that the speculative philosophy of a thousand years hence will date the greatest revolution that ever happened from the triumph of the principle which we have met here to advocate.

Cobden's claims may strike us as naive. But there were many who identified commercial freedom and the progress of humanity. In 1849 John Bright said that "industry, free and inviolate, is the only sure foundation on which can be reared the enduring edifice of union and of peace," and there was a belief in an almost automatic movement from free trade to the solution of all other political and social problems. The abolition of privilege, a just government, moderate and equitable taxation, expanded educational opportunities, and an independent and self-reliant citizenry were all expected to follow upon the freeing of the business community. "I believed Free Trade would have the tendency to unite mankind in the bonds of peace," said Cobden, and it was an article of faith among free traders that international controversy and war would end if only all others would follow the example of Manchester.

The industrial revolution had given an impetus to individual initiative, and Cobden and Bright believed that there was something natural and beneficial in each man standing by himself, without hindrance or assistance. They were convinced that direction and motivation should come from the individual and not from something outside him. Alexis de Tocqueville had noticed that this attitude was illustrated by Manchester itself. "Everything in the exterior appearance of the city attests to the individual powers of man," he wrote, "nothing the directing power of society. At every turn human liberty shows its capricious creative force." Cobden once wrote to a French friend who was discouraged at the prospects of his business: "Well, what must be done? Why, help yourself and God will help you."

It was this belief in the value of individual effort and the virtues of the free operation of the economy that was responsible for the position taken by Cobden and Bright on many of what we would call the social questions of the day. They were not simple economically motivated brutes, and in fact were regarded by many of their contemporaries as enlightened, humane, and generous men. They opposed slavery, advocated prison and parliamentary reform, supported the extension of education, and played important parts in the repeal of the "taxes on knowledge," a system of stamp duties that hindered the dissemination of printed material. But they did believe, on the whole, in an unregulated and undirected economy. They were convinced that attempts to regulate economic activities were "socialistic doctrines" and "mere sentimentalities" and thought that what was required in such matters was "a little head as well as heart." Thus they opposed acts that would have subjected factories to sanitary inspection or would set the hours and conditions of labor. They argued that the worker should be free to "work for whomever he pleased and on whatever agreement he liked as to the hours of his labour," and that "every man was the best and fittest judge of that manner in which his time should be employed, and of the object to which it should be applied." As Cobden put it in 1846: "You cannot do better than leave industry to its own instincts. If you attempt by legislation to give any direction to trade and industry, it is a thousand to one that you are doing wrong." It was only reluctantly and when faced with irrefutable and ugly facts that Bright supported laws regulating the labor of children, although he opposed those regulating that of men and women, while Cobden ultimately voted in Parliament to prohibit child labor and to limit the working hours of women in the mines.

In the same way, and for the same reasons, the two men opposed all efforts of laborers to organize themselves into trade unions. Cobden once expressed this opposition in what could be called a classic form of the Manchester philosophy. "Mine is the masculine species of charity," he said, "which would lead me to inculcate in the minds of the labouring classes the love of independence, the privilege of self-respect, the disdain of being patronised or petted, the desire to accumulate and the ambition to rise." But any efforts to control wages and working conditions by organization were certain to fail, for workingmen "might as well attempt to regulate the tides by force, or change the course of the seasons, or subvert any of the other laws of nature, for the wages of labour depend upon laws as unerring."

Many of the economic and social attitudes of the Manchester School were accepted by large numbers of businessmen, particularly in England and the United States. Certain principles, often jerked out of context, were translated into the concepts of "rugged individualism," the "free market," and "private initiative," and these selected phrases became a part of the vocabulary of business leaders. A hostility toward any government interference in business activities was characteristic of the members of the business community, as was the belief that the businessman was engaged in carrying out an almost transcendental plan. The annual report of the Manchester Chamber of Commerce, published at the height of the anti-corn law movement, had stated: "Whatever law interferes with the arrangement of Divine Providence to supply the necessary food of man is an infringement at once of natural and divine right." The identity of the divine purpose and the free market system, as well as the identity of economic and political freedom, was accepted as beyond question by most representatives of the Western business world.

The members of the Manchester School showed an important understanding of the industrial revolution. They sensed that it was something new, that it had a dynamic quality that could not be contained within traditional concepts of politics and economics, and that it was to play an ever-increasing part in influencing the direction of society. They attempted to channel the tremendous energies released by industrialization into what they regarded as a beneficial path. Yet the Manchester spirit, especially as interpreted by Cobden and Bright, failed to achieve its high purposes. To their disgust, once the corn laws were repealed, a large part of the merchant class lost interest in the wider problems of free trade, and after 1846 there was no longer what could be called a Manchester School. The struggle against aristocratic privilege was abandoned, and both Cobden and Bright were dismayed when Manchester Corporation adopted the scarlet gowns for officials and the "civic junketings" of the city of London. Eleven years after the repeal of the corn laws, in 1857, Cobden could write: "During my experience the Higher classes never stood so high in relative social and political rank, as compared with other classes, as at present. The middle class has been content with the very crumbs from their table. The more contempt a man like Palmerston (as intense an aristocrat at heart as any of them) heaped upon them the more they cheered him. . . ." After years of struggle for what he thought of as Manchester's interests, John Bright complained that "never did any unfortunate village by the moor ends require enlightening more pitiably than this Northern metropolis."

Nor did free trade lead to the goals Cobden had dreamed of. It did not become the pattern of world commerce, and it did not result in international peace. Not all went as far as an American who dismissed free trade as "a system devised by England to enable her to plunder the world." But protectionism, nationalism, and militarism, not free trade and pacifism, became the dominant characteristics of the Western world in the latter half of the nineteenth century. Moreover, in the minds of many, the men of Manchester failed to make an adequate response to what Matthew Arnold termed "pauperism and ignorance, and all the questions which are called social."

Perhaps the most unfortunate thing happening to the Manchester idea was that it became increasingly identified in the minds of large numbers of people as the expression of a narrow, cold-hearted justification of any and all business activities. A crude and brazen advocacy of laissez faire was ascribed to the free traders, and an opponent described the Manchester idea as "the system . . . of leaving men to practice for their own advancement all arts save actual violence." Such a description was erroneous, but here the important thing was what was believed and not what was true. Bright opposed what he regarded as damaging and dangerous restrictions upon business. But he was slandered as

> The Member for Manchester
> A Man who gave to misery all he had to give
> A sneer-

The fate of the Manchester School was somewhat indicative of that of the Western business community as a whole. An increasing number of people became involved in commercial enterprises, and for a large portion of the middle class business became a singular and consuming interest. Those engaged in commerce had wealth, power, and influence, and their efforts and talents brought comfort and security to many. But in spite of the important part that commerce has played in the West and the claims of business leaders, there is some question whether business activities, in Cobden's words, promoted "the enduring interests of mankind." The business ethic too often degenerated into a collection of clichés, and spokesmen for business interests tended to be inarticulate and dull. What could be described as a business philosophy was inevitably trite (an extreme example was the interpretation of Jesus Christ as a master salesman), and many were to agree with the American John Jay Chapman that a commercial civilization stimulates "a social life which is unintelligent and mediocre, made up of people afraid of each other, whose ideas are shopworn, whose manners are self-conscious." The emphasis upon commercial freedom as the most important, and at times the only, meaningful freedom reduced the scope of the Western concept of individual liberty. In fact, in many cases, commerce promoted a stifling conformity, what Herbert J. Muller in 1952 called the "acceptance of insincere, dishonest behavior that does pay — the routine hypocrisy in politics, advertising, publicity, commercialized sport, commercialized art, commercialized piety. . . ." Such an indictment is perhaps one-sided and unfair. But it expresses the ambiguous position of business and the businessman in modern Western civilization.

Pierre-Joseph Proudhon

"Do you happen to know, madam, what my father was? Well, he was just an honest brewer whom you could never persuade to make money by selling above cost price. Such gains, he thought, were immoral. 'My beer,' he would always remark, 'costs me so much, including my salary. I cannot sell it for more.' What was the result? My dear father always lived in poverty and died a poor man, leaving poor children behind him."

These sentences appear in a letter addressed to a female acquaintance by the Frenchman Pierre-Joseph Proudhon. They express the frustrations of the new industrial and commercial society as Proudhon saw it. Implicit also is his protest against what he regarded as the madness of the nineteenth century, "madder than all those that it claims to supersede." The century produced a great many protesters, men who looked with horror at what they saw happening in Western society and proposed alternative directions to that upon which their world seemed set. None of them mounted a more inclusive attack than did Proudhon, the anarchist, the mutualist, the enemy of government and commerce, that ever-busy "minority of one," who with justification was charged with "attacking property, inciting contempt for the government, and offending against religion and morals."

Proudhon was born in 1809 in the town of Besançon, in the Jura Mountain country in northeastern France near the Swiss border. "Rustic blood" ran rich in his veins, and he remained all his life something of a country boy, self-reliant, cantankerous, suspicious, opinionated, and brusque, contemptuous of finesse and polish. He wrote that he had been "born of a family of workers. . . . I don't know how many members of my family have been ruined, persecuted, killed, afflicted by all these slaveries, old and new." He became a printer and worked at his trade in various parts of the country before settling in

Paris in 1846. He was for a short period of time a representative to the French Assembly, a prisoner of the state, an exile in Belgium, and a continual irritant to those, and they were many, who found themselves the victims of his scorn. His brain was continually afire with "gigantic schemes," and he wrote a flood of articles, pamphlets, and books designed to forward the betterment of his fellow citizens. The most important of his writings included *What Is Property?*, *The System of Economic Contradictions or the Philosophy of Distress*, *The Confessions of a Revolutionary*, *War and Peace*, and *The Political Capabilities of the Working Classes*.

Proudhon's writings were an indictment of his times — of nationalism, of industrial organization, of urbanization, of parliamentarianism, of the many new political and social schemes produced by the century. His language was rough, emotion-laden, and extravagant. He usually wrote and spoke rhetorically, and his more extreme statements had a searing simplicity that made them both unforgettable and disturbing. He posed the question: "What Is Property?" He answered with the one word: "Theft." In one of his newspapers he printed the slogan: "What Is the Producer? Nothing. What Should He Be? Everything!" On another occasion, the slogan read: "What Is the Capitalist? Everything! What Should He Be? Nothing!" He wrote that "to indulge in politics is to wash one's hands in dung" and that "anarchy is suitable for an adult society just as hierarchy is for a primitive one." He described Karl Marx as "the tapeworm of socialism," and he dismissed his fellow radicals with the statement that "the majority of the revolutionaries, like the conservatives they are fighting, dream only of building prisons."

It is easy to look upon Proudhon as a buffoon, as a garrulous phrasemaker, as a crank who could not adjust to the new industrial world. He wrote extensively on economic problems but had little understanding of or real interest in what we would regard as economics. At times he posed as a philosopher and succeeded in losing himself in a mass of undigested speculations. He was a preacher of revolution yet in many things adopted conservative attitudes. He attacked the working class for its blindness and the middle class for its selfishness and yet wrote in all sincerity: "I have wept over the poor workman ... I have mourned over the bourgeois." His belief that women were fit only for domestic drudgery is offensive, and he can be accused of anti-semitism and a dangerous form of anti-intellectualism.

But Proudhon did raise some questions about the industrial society that were, and are, pertinent. He was not put off by easy answers. He recognized the hollowness of many so-called accomplishments of the times, and he realized that a price was to be paid for many of the triumphs of the century.

Proudhon believed that the two most powerful forces in Western society in the nineteenth century, nationalism and industrialization, were not blessings but disasters. Industrialization had resulted in the dangerous accumulation of capital. Nationalism had resulted in an unprincipled, all-powerful political authority. Both were fatal to any idea of justice and liberty. The organized national state had become a monster, "without intelligence, without passion, without morality." Industrialization had reduced the "people" to a "populace," demoralized, uprooted and alienated. The state and industrial capitalism despoiled the many for the benefit of the few, and political government and industrial exploitation were partners in a plot against the freedom of men. In his attacks upon these two great enemies, Proudhon was capable of what must pass as a rough eloquence. Of the results of industrial and commercial progress he could write: "I swear that my human dignity bristles with disgust. Ah, in such matters I have remained of the religion of Christ, which recommends detachment, preaches modesty, simplicity of spirit, and poverty of heart. Away with the old patrician, greedy and pitiless, away with the insolent baron, the grasping bourgeois, and the hard-hearted peasant. Such people are odious to me; I neither love nor see them." In the same tone he could write that to be governed by a powerful political authority means "to be kept in sight, spied upon, directed, law-driven, numbered, enrolled, taxed, indoctrinated, preached at, controlled, estimated, valued, censured, stamped, measured, forbidden, reformed, corrected, punished, repressed, fined, despised, harassed, tracked, abused, mocked, ridiculed, outraged, dishonored." This is a full bill of particulars that has a haunting ring. And Proudhon expressed the principle guiding his activity and his thought: "No more government of man by man, by means of the accumulation of power; no more exploitation of man by man by means of the accumulation of capital."

Proudhon made many attacks upon industrialization. The very virtues claimed for industrial capitalism were corruptions. The only purpose of work was to get rich, empty comfort was the aim of life, antagonisms were inflamed, and "the public conscience" had been "turned upside down." Acquisitiveness, as exemplified by "commerce and all its villainies," had perverted individuals and society, and capitalism was only industrial feudalism where France had been "given up to the monopoly of the companies." The good life had become erroneously identified as one wherein people were rich with possessions and stuffed with the goods of the earth. Society had become "intoxicated by its own good fortune" and "wished to hear of nothing but success, progress, and pleasure."

Moreover, industrial capitalism had undermined what Proudhon regarded as the true sense of property. His famous statement that property is theft has often obscured the fact that Proudhon was a strong believer in property and did not advocate its abolition. But he believed in property that was "intelligible, rational, and legitimate," and not "usurpatory and odious." Property, for him, was sacred if it was purged of injustice and "the sum of its abuses." He denounced property that was used to exploit others and that was distinguished by interest, usury, and rent. Property should be "possession in use," and when this condition was satisfied, property had a liberating influence upon men and was a safeguard against the commercial exploiter and against political authority.

But industrialization was hostile to this concept of property. The growing inequality of wealth and the power of concentrated capitalism were turning property from a liberating instrument into a device for exploitation. Property was no longer regarded as a source of security, as a means of expressing a man's work and his life, but as the instrument for creating a debilitating luxury and exercising unnatural power by some men at the expense of others. Property should be the expression of man's independence. But the crushing power of capital accumulation threatened the individual's independence and his sense of security. The misuse of property was resulting in excess wealth for a few and destitution for the many. Property had become the master instead of the servant of man, and a warped view of the real purposes of property had resulted in a baseness of behavior, a coarseness of morals, and a loss of conscience.

But the most important effect of industrialization was, for Proudhon, the destructive influence it had upon the working class. These were the people with whom Proudhon identified. In 1841 he expressed his intention of devoting himself to the improvement of the physical, moral, and intellectual condition of "the most numerous and the poorest class." And he never wavered from this commitment. In his books, in his actions, and even in his complaints, he devoted himself to the "cause of the poor, to the liberation of the lowly, to the instruction of the people."

The workingman was being destroyed as an individual by industrialization. Work was the basis of life. Yet men were being brutalized and exploited even as they pursued the thing that was most meaningful in their existence. Industrialization was making work a terror and a horror for men and was reducing them to anonymous pieces of human machinery. "A railroad, a mine, a factory, a ship, are to the workers who use them what a hive is to the bees, at once their tool and their home, their country, their territory, their property." Or, rather, that is what they should be. But they were not. The worker was being separated from what was rightfully his, the dignity of work, and was being transformed into a drifting, uprooted piece of human flotsam. His pride in his labor was being destroyed, and he was being turned into the helpless victim of overpowering and coercive forces. He was losing his status as a citizen and was being cast adrift, a lonely, demoralized, and dishonored individual. He was a stranger in the midst of a society that demanded his disgrace as a stipulation of its own development. Proudhon wrote of his youth: "In my father's house, we breakfasted on maize porridge; at midday we ate potatoes; in the evening bacon soup, and that every day of the week. We were fat and strong. Do you know why? Because we breathed the air of our fields and lived from the produce of our own cultivation." But the proletariat had no fields, and what he produced was not his.

The industrial society lacked justice, and it was this failure that most offended Proudhon. "A certain love of justice, helped by a lot of passion, has made me what I am," he wrote. Justice is the cement that holds the world together, and if it is absent then all other triumphs are nothing but empty marching to and fro. Justice is "the sentiment of our dignity in others, and, conversely, of the dignity of others in our own person." It is "a kind of respect spontaneously felt and reciprocally guaranteed to human dignity in any person and under all circumstances, even though the discharge of that feeling exposes us to some risk." Or, as Proudhon defined it at another time: "It constitutes the essence of society itself. It is the true form of the human spirit, a form which takes shape and grows toward perfection only by the relationship that every day gives birth to social life." Justice is expressed in equality and freedom from restraint and is the basic striving of the human consciousness.

How was justice to be introduced into life? Proudhon was convinced that this could not be done by any political reform or plan based upon what he called "false democracy" and "pseudo-democracy." And he scorned nationalism, parliamentarianism, and universal suffrage. They were "comedies," "humbugs," "lotteries," and "mystifications." He wrote, "I build no system. I ask an end to privilege, the abolition of slavery, equality of rights, and the reign of law. Justice, nothing else. That is the alpha and omega of my argument; I leave to others the business of governing the world." Proudhon believed that human life was full when it contained love, paternity, family, work, and justice, and these had nothing to do with politics. He attacked the ideas of the inevitability of the inequality of fortunes, the permanency of quarrels and war, the irremediability of poverty. He supported, in their place, the honorableness of work, the equality of fortunes, the identity of interests, and the end of antagonisms. Proudhon stressed the near-familial aspects of the human relationships. "Brothers, yes, and fathers, mothers, sons, uncles, aunts, nephews and nieces and cousins, and all those who are connected by all the spiritual, temporal, or carnal links that the heart conceives — that is the Republic!"

Proudhon did have a solution to the impasse that the workers had reached in the industrial society. But his solution was not so much a political plan of action as the pointing to a different way of life. The worker must depend upon himself, and "the proletariat must emancipate himself without the help of the government." Only then could he acquire the "respect for human dignity" that was the basis of justice. Men must associate together, but such association must be personal, individual, and without coercion. Anyone who grasped what this type of association meant had all the political judgment he needed. "To possess political capacity is to have the consciousness of oneself as a member of a collectivity, to affirm the idea that results from this consciousness, and to pursue its realization. Whoever unites these three conditions is capable."

This free union, this manifestation of the meaningful human community, Proudhon called "mutualism." Scorning any concrete political program, mutualism was a belief in the possibility of the working class uniting free of constraint or authoritarian direction. Only this freedom in unity would allow the individual "to worship God without priests, work without a master, borrow without usury, have possessions without mortgages, formulate his feelings without prejudice, participate in the government of his country without being represented by heroes or rogues."

There is something touching and almost pathetic about Proudhon's solution for Western industrial man. He recognized what was happening in Western society, and he strained to oppose the mechanized, sterile life that he saw as the result of the pressures engendered by the new organizations called into being in the nineteenth century. Yet he was caught in a series of contradictions. He argued that revolutions were "the successive manifestations of justice in humanity." But he believed that most revolutionary changes taking place had little to do with justice. He once wrote: "Equality! I had always thought that it was the natural fruit of liberty, which has no need of theory nor of constraint." But the dominant form of equality reduced all to exploited and rolled-out pieces of tattered humanity. He was a French patriot to the core, and he wrote "I glory in belonging to that proud race, inaccessible to dishonor." Yet in 1855 he complained to a friend: "I am sick at heart. I seem to see France entering upon an unending period of abasement, lying, and ridicule." He believed that a close attachment to nature was a necessary human habit. But he complained of the "desertion of the land" and noted with sorrow that "man no longer loved the land." He scoffed at those "people for whom traditions are nothing, who think you can change churches as you change underpants, who reshape people's morals and beliefs as, in their own rooms, they reshape the map of Europe." Yet men were being changed, rapidly and ruthlessly, and the human substance was becoming something different from what it had been.

Even the working class, the product of the industrial revolution, and Proudhon's own chosen people, at times failed him. In 1861 he wrote: "I am certainly working for them, but I know what they are and what they are worth, and I shall take good care not to lose their cause at the bar of reason and at the bar of history by defending them as they would like me to defend them." Workingmen were continually allowing themselves to become the victims of one hoax after another. They were attracted to the idea of universal suffrage, to the "antediluvian absurdity of communism," to the enticements of wealth. They too often lacked what Proudhon himself had — the instinct for freedom. He despaired of their behavior, although he never deserted them. "I have not the courage to kick the sufferer. Others can carry out that sorry task. By nature I fight against the strong; I do not crush the weak."

In January, 1865, Proudhon died. Many political journalists and middle-class liberals were in the large crowd that accompanied the body to the cemetery. But the great majority of the 6,000 members of the entourage were the anonymous working people of Paris. Near the end of his life Proudhon had written in what was surely a moment of true insight. "I have done my best. But I do not think that I rose to the level of my subject. Underneath it all there is something beyond all human thought." This was undoubtedly true. Anyone who claims that "liberty is the sum total of my system — liberty of conscience, freedom of the press, freedom of labor, of commerce, and of teaching, the free disposal of the products of labor and industry — liberty, infinite, absolute, everywhere and forever" is grasping for something that is almost beyond human comprehension.

But Proudhon cannot be called a failure. His criticism of industrialization and its effects was to the point. His argument that the new industrial society must be something more than a mere producer of wealth caught the ear of many workingmen, particularly in France. Proudhon expressed the antagonism that many were to feel toward industrialization and toward those who had benefited by this historical phenomenon. A strong and usually justified suspicion of political leaders and political plans and business leaders and business plans became part of the European working-class consciousness. And in an age where the instruments of power and control were beginning to threaten the very people for whose benefit they were supposed to be designed, Proudhon's warning was appropriate. "Whoever lays his hands on me to govern me is a usurper and a tyrant, and I declare him my enemy."

This was a simple sentence, but it said something important to a society that had become fascinated by its own material success and political triumphs and somewhat indifferent to the implications of its course.

Karl Marx

On March 17, 1883, Karl Marx was buried in Highgate cemetery in London. There was no religious ceremony. But Friedrich Engels, Marx's long-time friend and collaborator, made a short speech to the small group of people present. Engels had known Marx for forty years, and in his speech he attempted to set forth the important elements of Marx's philosophy of history. "Just as Darwin discovered the law of evolution in organic nature," Engels said, "so Marx discovered the law of evolution in human history; he discovered the simple fact, hitherto concealed by an overgrowth of ideology, that mankind must first of all eat and drink, have shelter and clothing, before it can pursue politics, science, religion, art; and that therefore the production of the immediate material means of subsistence and consequently the degree of economic development attained by a given people or during a given epoch, form the foundation upon which the state institutions, the legal conceptions, the art and even the religious ideas of the people concerned have been evolved, and in the light of which these things must therefore be explained, instead of vice versa as had hitherto been the case."

But, Engels went on, Marx did more. He "also discovered the special law of motion governing the present-day capitalist mode of production and the bourgeois society that this mode of production has created." And then Engels described what he thought of as Marx's principal characteristic. "Marx was before all else a revolutionary. His real mission in life was to contribute in one way or another to the overthrow of capitalist society and of the state institutions which it had brought into being, to contribute to the liberation of the present-day proletariat, which he was the first to make conscious of its own position and its needs, of the conditions under which it could win its emancipation."

Engels' tribute was approximately one thousand words in length. Since 1883 book after book, article after article, and speech after speech have interpreted Marx's ideas, and a vast library of Marxist literature burdens the bookshelves of the Western world. Yet the essence of Marxism, as an important historical argument, is present in Engels' speech. Here were stressed the principal points: the claim to scientific validity; the materialistic interpretation of life; the concept of class struggle as the stimulant to historical events; the uniqueness of the industrial society as human experience; the critique of capitalism; and the doctrine of the irreconcilable revolutionary.

Karl Marx was born in 1818 in Trier in the German Rhineland. He attended the universities at Bonn and Berlin and was awarded the doctor of philosophy degree by the University of Jena. In the eighteen-forties he became a radical journalist and an active participant in the intellectual life of the period. He was at various times expelled from Paris, from Brussels, and from Cologne. In 1849 he settled as an exile in London and, with the exception of a few short trips to the continent, remained there during the rest of his life.

In Marx's philosophy there is a staggering consistency. He was a man who relatively early in his life discovered what seemed to him to be the underlying principles governing the affairs of men, and his later writings are, in great part, only a development and an expansion of his early thinking. Many have argued that he had literary talent. This claim is nonsense. Much of his prose is turgid, heavy, vague when it should be explicit, and contorted. But he did catch the heart of his thought in sweeping, emotionally charged and historically dynamic statements that have worked themselves into the common speech of Western man. "The history of all hitherto existing society is the history of class struggle," "The proletarians have nothing to lose but their chains," "Workers of the world unite," "the expropriators are expropriated" — these, and many more, are easily grasped and explosive sentences that distill Marx's ideas into cries for action. As George Bernard Shaw wrote in 1887, four years after Marx's death: "Whatever may be the ultimate verdict as to Marx, it must be borne in mind that the extraordinary impression he makes does not depend on the soundness of his views, but on their magnificent scope and on his own imperturbable conviction of their validity."

Marx believed that his philosophy was particularly appropriate to the industrial age. It was pertinent, he felt, to the conditions governing the life of Western man in the nineteenth century. It fit the facts of the situation, while other interpretations did not, but were obsolete remnants of an earlier, preindustrial time. In Marx's view, the industrial society was a new phenomenon to which none of the old definitions of man and his world were applicable. Western man was basically industrial man, and his values, his way of life, and his insights into his condition were all governed by his existence in the industrial society. The philosophy that was attuned to the circumstances of the industrial age could claim to be scientific, could claim to speak to the actuality of the times. Any interpretation that was not based on the awareness of these new conditions was certain to be utopian, idealistic, and erroneous. As Marx wrote: "the ultimate causes of all social changes and political revolutions are to be sought, not in the minds of men, in their increasing insight into eternal truth and justice, but in the mode of production and exchange; they are to be sought not in philosophy but in the economics of the epoch concerned." Here, in the words of a scholar, Marxism constituted "a total break with existing reality, and a vision of something like a new eon." Marx advanced "a new view of the human condition itself."

The first necessity, Marx believed, for understanding what had happened, what is happening, and what shall happen in the world was to accept the materialistic interpretation. Material is real, for Marx, while the spiritual is not. "I have been led to the conclusion that legal relations, as well as forms of state, could neither be understood by themselves nor explained by the so-called progress of the human mind, but that they are rooted in the material conditions of life." Again and again, Marx stressed his belief that "it is not the consciousness of men that determines their existence, but, on the contrary, it is their social existence that determines their consciousness." Everything ultimately springs from the material circumstances of life, and nothing has an independent history separate from the material that created it. All notions of right and wrong, justice and injustice, are merely symptoms of the material conditions of life and cannot claim any independent validity. "Morality, religion, metaphysics, all the rest of ideology and their corresponding forms of consciousness, thus no longer retain the semblance of independence. They have no history, no development." This interpretation, particularly in regard to religion, could be put bluntly by Marx: "it is not religion that makes men, but men who make their religion." Material circumstance thus governs the way in which men live, no matter how much they may be misled into thinking otherwise. Material conditions fashion their religion, determine their laws, control their politics.

The most important material influence upon men is their economic circumstance, the method by which they supply themselves with the material necessities of life. This concept can be put as "labor created man." The way a man works is what he is. This means that, contrary to the commonly accepted opinion in Western society, man is not created by God but by his own efforts and his humanity is the result of his own activity. The meaningful definition of man must thus be sought by an examination of that factor responsible for what he is and what he thinks.

This interpretation of reality leads to the Marxist view of the class structure of society. The nature of man and his relationship to other men are conditioned by his economic position. Thus Marx defines a class as a group of persons in a society whose lives are commonly influenced by a common economic status in that society. An individual has no real existence except as he represents the class to which he belongs. This is true of everyone. Class identity, class morality, class interests are the realities of life. No matter how activities may be masked, they ultimately express a class point of view.

It is the division of mankind into classes that provides the tension that creates history. In *The Communist Manifesto* Marx put this point very simply. "The history of all hitherto existing society is the history of class struggles." There is no important history apart from class conflict, and men play a part in history as the instruments of the classes they represent. In the opinion of Marx, it is not nationalism or religion or any idealistic political doctrine that lies at the heart of historical activity, but economic and class interest. He argued that if one looked beyond the superficial explanations that were given for any action, he would find the dynamic stimulant to the human enterprise — class struggle. In like manner, the unifying factor was not some vague idea of a common mankind or nationalism but class. Men find their sense of community as members of a class.

In the nineteenth century this class struggle expressed itself in the conflict between the property-holding middle class or the bourgeoisie, and the propertyless working class, the proletariat. The industrial society had created two irreconcilable antagonists. "Society as a whole is more and more splitting into two great hostile camps directly facing each other — bourgeoisie and proletariat," and the class struggle is certain to be carried on by political, economic, and social means. No compromise is possible, and no matter how the conflict may be disguised, the two classes are engaged in a war that can only end with the victory of one and the defeat of the other.

Marx was convinced as to the outcome of this struggle. The ancient world had been succeeded by the medieval, slavery by feudalism, feudalism by the industrial bourgeoisie. The bourgeoisie will fight to protect its position. But it will fail. "The productive forces at the disposal of society no longer tend to further the development of the conditions of bourgeois society. On the contrary, they have become too powerful for those conditions." It is the proletariat that represents historically the industrial society. According to Marx, the proletariat created this society with his labor, he has been its victim, and he will be its inheritor. "The proletariat alone is a really revolutionary class. The other classes decay and finally disappear in the face of modern industry; the proletariat is its special and essential product." History cannot be denied, and no effort by the bourgeoisie can save it. Any setback to the proletariat can be only temporary, and any truce will be short-lived. "But the battle must break out again and again in ever-growing dimensions, and there can be no doubt as to who will be the victor in the end — the appropriating few or the immense working majority."

This victory of the proletariat will mean the disappearance of bourgeois justice, bourgeois equality, bourgeois liberty, bourgeois property. It will also end the class struggle and the exploitation of man by man. There is no class beneath the proletariat. Therefore, by securing its own emancipation, the proletariat will emancipate all mankind. The state as an instrument of class oppression will disappear, and there will be a period of revolutionary transformation, during which time men, in the absence of class antagonisms, will become fully developed human beings. In this transition period political, economic, and social authority will be expressed through the dictatorship of the proletariat. In 1852 Marx pointed out that he had proved that "the class struggle necessarily leads to the dictatorship of the proletariat," and that "this dictatorship itself only constitutes the transition to the abolition of all classes and a classless society." Ultimately, then, the dictatorship of the proletariat will wither away, and the alienation of men from their work, their state, and each other will end. The communist commonwealth will be at hand where the fruits of the industrial society will be used for the service of all mankind and where all shall live by the new commandment: "From each according to his abilities, to each according to his needs."

Marxism is a truly revolutionary doctrine. It does not present itself as a program for the reform of the old society, but as a plan for its destruction. In Marx's view, there can be "neither peace nor truce" between the proletariat and the bourgeoisie, and it is impossible "to transfer the bureaucratic-military machine from one hand to another." Rather, it is necessary "to smash it, and this is essential for every real people's revolution." Nor does Marx expect any revolutionary change to occur without violence. In fact, violence is part of change, and the painful and drastic shift from one type of society to another cannot be accomplished without the deep antagonisms expressing themselves in the violence that Marx described as "the midwife of every old society pregnant with a new one."

Marxism is also a refutation of what we think of as the liberal radicalism of the West. Western liberals have usually argued in terms of those moral standards that they believed were obvious to all men. They criticized the present in terms of some ideal society, and they assumed that in spite of differences of opinion among themselves, all progressively minded men were basically allies in the struggle against social and political evil. Marx, however, despised liberals. They were not, in his view, true revolutionaries, but only reformers, and he dismissed them as "economists, philanthropists, humanitarians, improvers of the condition of the working class, organizers of charity, members of societies for the prevention of cruelty to animals, temperance fanatics, hole-and-corner reformers of every imaginable kind." Marx cut himself off from the rest of the radical tradition of the West, and he demanded that those accepting his philosophy do the same.

The scholar Isaiah Berlin began his well-known book *Karl Marx. His Life and Environment* with the sentence: "No thinker in the nineteenth century has had so direct, deliberate and powerful an influence upon mankind as Karl Marx." The evidence in support of Professor Berlin's argument is overwhelming. Yet it is difficult for many to understand the appeal of Marx and Marxism. To even the casual observer Marxism appears to consist of many contradictions, lies, and false predictions. It has shown, in the words of Adam Ulam, a "hopeless lack of clarity. Fiction was piled upon fiction, paradox upon paradox." In 1925 the Englishman John Maynard Keynes undoubtedly spoke for many then and now when he wrote of Marxism: "How can I adopt a creed which preferring the mud to the fish, exalts the boorish proletariat above the bourgeois and the intelligentsia who, with whatever faults, are the quality of life and surely carry all the seeds of human advancement? Even if we need a religion, how can we find it in the turbid rubbish of the Red bookshops? It is hard for an educated, decent, intelligent son of Western Europe to find his ideals here, unless he has first suffered some strange and horrid process of conversion which has changed all his values."

Keynes may be correct. But his attack upon Marxism, as that of so many others, does not account for Marx's influence. Yet there are certain explanations for the success of Marx, and these explanations can tell us a great deal not only about Marxism but about certain characteristics of modern Western civilization. First, Marxism claims to be relevant to our society. Many may dispute this claim, but many have accepted it. Marx believed that his interpretation was "a necessary product of human development." In particular, he was convinced that it spoke to the realities of the new industrial age. He suspected that Western man was not going to be able to endure profound industrial and technological change without himself changing and becoming something very different from what he had been before. In the struggle with his new material environment, man's nature would be re-formed. He would no longer be the person he once was in the preindustrial world. His way of life, his values, his allegiances would all change. He would be a new man, created by his new environment and his new history.

In Marx's view industrialization had brought about a sharp break in Western history. Preindustrial political ideas, institutions, and vocabulary had suddenly become obsolete and had no relation to the world of the factory, the industrial city, or the proletariat. What did parliamentary debates, abstract statements about the rights of man, and references to life and liberty have to do with the reality of the way people were living? The hard facts of industrialization were being ignored, and the irrelevance of institutions and ideas was alienating Western man from the world he had created. Hannah Arendt has written that "our tradition of political thought had its definite beginning in the teachings of Plato and Aristotle. I believe it came to a no less definite end in the theories of Karl Marx." What caused this change was, in her words, Marx's belief that "philosophy and its truth are located not outside the affairs of men and their common world but precisely in them. . . ."

Marxism has also been a powerful intellectual instrument for understanding what was and is happening in the West and has attracted many of the West's most creative individuals. The French anthropologist Claude Lévi-Strauss has written: "It is a fact that when I was sixteen or seventeen years old, I was initiated . . . to the reading of Marx. That was for me a kind of revelation, and of course I've remained under this influence. . . ." For Lévi-Strauss Marx provided a method of "decoding" the mysteries of history and thus a guide that enabled one to see what was and is historically significant. Many others have agreed. For them Marxism is a standard by which one interprets what is going on about him. It provides a sense of intellectual certainty that is often missing in those who cling to a more liberal standard of values. A commitment to Marxism establishes a standard for discrimination, which provides answers to questions such as: What is the real meaning of my life? What are the forces changing the world? How may I relate myself to these forces? Marxism tells its adherents who is the enemy and who is the friend and supplies an insight into the direction in which the world is moving. It provides intellectual confidence that one can identify people, events, and ideas.

This intellectual certainty blends into what is called historicism, the belief that the direction of history is set and cannot be reversed. Much of the attraction of Marxism can be traced to the understandable desire many have to identify with the future and to be assured that they will be on the winning side of any historical encounter. Marx provided the strongest expression in the contemporary world of this form of historical authority. He argued that the modern world was upon a course from which there could be no escape. History, according to him, is governed by laws which, like the natural laws of science, cannot be altered by the efforts of individuals. In the long run, it will make no difference what opposition faces the Marxists. History has guaranteed the victory, and, as the Chinese Marxist Mao Tse-tung has said, "the east wind will prevail over the west wind." Isaiah Berlin has put the idea of Marxist historicism this way: "What history has condemned will be inevitably swept away: to say that it ought to be saved, even when that is not possible, is to deny the rational plan of the universe." Moral claims are immaterial (one might as well preach morality to a machine), and any vindication of actions must be sought in historical success not in moral judgments. Thus, as a student of Marx has pointed out, "the only sense in which it is possible to show that something is good or bad, right or wrong, is by demonstrating that it accords or does not accord with the historical process, assists it or thwarts it, will survive or will inevitably perish."

Marxism has also appealed to the deep urge for an absolute historical solution, for an end of all social problems, for a "leap into freedom" that many Westerners possess. Marx did provide a doctrine for those with revolutionary tendencies, for those who were certain that the world needed redoing. His revolutionary slogans and his catechism of easily learned responses caught the ear of the discontented, the alienated, and the insulted. Almost all the important revolutionary figures of the late nineteenth and twentieth centuries have been influenced by Marx and have used Marxism to justify their claim to power. It was not so much that they read Marx and then became revolutionaries, but that they were already revolutionaries who found in Marx something for which they were looking. Marx did offer in the minds of many a historical solution to the world of pain, injustice, and discrimination. As Alexander Gray, an opponent of Marxism, has admitted: "He saw visions — clear visions of the passing of all things, much more nebulous visions of how all things may be made new. And his visions, or some of them awoke a responsive chord in the hearts of many men."

SUGGESTIONS FOR FURTHER READING

One of the most exciting studies of the traumatic effect of industrialization and its implications is Leo Marx's The Machine in the Garden: Technology and the Pastoral Idea in America *(1964), which contains enough ideas to keep a student thinking for a long period of time. Also valuable is E. E. Morison's* Men, Machines and Modern Times *(1966). Good historical analyses of what happened during the industrial revolution are R. E. Cameron,* France and the Economic Development of Europe 1800-1914 *(1961), W. O. Henderson,* Britain and Industrial Europe 1750-1870 *(1954) and* The Industrial Revolution on the Continent *(1961), J. H. Clapham,* Economic Development of France and Germany, 1815-1914 *(1936), and E. J. Hobsbawm,* The Age of Revolution 1789-1848 *(1962).*

On the subject of Manchester, William D. Grampp's The Manchester School of Economics *(1960) is an excellent piece of scholarship, while Herman Ausubel's* John Bright: Victorian Reformer *(1966) and Donald Read's* Cobden and Bright: A Victorian Political Partnership *(1968) contain a great deal of interesting material on the intellectual and political life of Manchester. A. J. P. Taylor's article "The World's Cities: Manchester" is in* Encounter *(March, 1957). George Woodcock's* Pierre-Joseph Proudhon: A Biography *(1956) is good, as is the chapter on Proudhon in Alexander Gray's* The Socialist Tradition *(1947). Karl Marx, of course, has been the subject of numerous books, articles, and polemics. The best introductory study is still probably Isaiah Berlin's* Karl Marx: His Life and Environment *(published originally in 1939 but with later revised editions up to 1960). Gray's chapter on Marx in his* The Socialist Tradition *is excellent, while Franz Mehring's* Karl Marx: The Story of His Life *(1948) contains the basic biographical materials. The remarks on Marx in Hannah Arendt,* Between Past and Future *(1963 edition), and in Edmund Wilson,* To the Finland Station *(1940), are enlightening.*

Vivre Libre ou Mourir!, Gaillard, 1870, Bibliothèque Nationale, Paris.

6

The Nation States

1789-
1794
French revolutionary declarations contained statements that can be regarded as some of the first important expressions of modern nationalism.

"The source of all sovereignty resides essentially in the nation, no body and no individual can possess authority that does not clearly derive from it."

"Sovereignty is one, indivisible, inalienable and imprescriptible: it belongs to the nation."

1802
Hegel's *Constitution of Germany*. "Germany is no longer a state." Raises the question of how Germany may become a state and the historical meaning of German nationality.

1807-
1808
Johann G. Fichte's *Addresses to the German Nation*. Has been described as a celebration of "the German people as a people of salvation, speaking God's language and doing the deeds of God."

1810
Friedrich Jahn founded sports associations throughout Germany that combined physical education activities with blatant patriotism. Jahn's movement has been characterized as "a combination of moral idealism and crude and vulgar rowdyism, of folk populism and anti-semitism, of racialism and patriotism."

1814-
1815
Principle of universal military service introduced in Prussia.

1814-
1815
Louis XVIII becomes king of France following defeat of Napoleon.

1815	Formation of the first *Burschenschaft*, patriotic student organization at the University of Jena. Similar organizations spread throughout Germany until 1819. Slogan was "Honor, Liberty, and Fatherland."
1821-1831	Greek War of Independence.
1824-1830	Charles X in France attempted to bring back many features of pre-revolutionary France and introduced reactionary regime.
1830	Revolution in France brought Louis-Philippe to throne and initiated bourgeois monarchy.
1830-1839	Belgian independence gained from the Netherlands.
1831	Young Italy, a nationalistic, revolutionary group organized by Giuseppe Mazzini to bring about an independent Italian republic.
1841	Friedrich List's *National System of Political Economy* set forth the economic aspects of nationalism and the organization of economics and industry along national lines.
1847-1853	Jules Michelet's *History of the French Revolution*, the century's most rhapsodic praise of nationalism as an exalted undertaking.
1848	Revolutionary movements sweep Europe. In France Louis-Philippe was overthrown and the Second Republic was initiated. In Germany a great stimulus for the creation of a liberal, united nation. In Central Europe movements for the creation of national groupings. In Italy attempts to end foreign influences and create an Italian republic.
1848-1849	Meeting of National Assembly in Germany. A constitution written that called for a hereditary "Emperor of the Germans" and a national parliament. The King of Prussia was elected emperor but refused the offer, and the parliamentary movement dissolved. "The German people greeted its National Assembly of 1848 like a goddess of liberty — a year later it let it finish like a prostitute in a saloon."
1849	Johann Droysen's *Prussia and the Great Powers*. First of a series of German histories after 1848 that introduced the idea of the German power-state as a historical necessity. "The power or weakness of Germany determines the fate of Europe."

1851	Louis Napoleon overthrew the French Republic and later established the Second Empire.
1861	Kingdom of Italy proclaimed, which included much of present-day Italy. In 1866 the Venetian state was added, and in 1870, Rome, which had been part of the papal states, was annexed and made the capital of the country.
1864	Prussia and Austria wage war on Denmark over possession of the duchies of Schleswig and Holstein. This was followed by the 1866 war between Prussia and Austria, which resulted in the defeat of Austria and the end of her influence in German affairs.
1867	North German Confederation created. Included Prussia and the German states north of the Main River. The influence of Prussia was paramount.
1870-1871	Franco-Prussian War. Result was defeat of France and end of Second Empire.
1871	Creation of German Empire. South German states joined with those states already members of the North German Confederation. The King of Prussia was crowned German Emperor.
1875	Republican constitution adopted in France. The Third Republic.
1878	Congress of Berlin. Actions of the Great Powers guaranteed independence of Serbia, Rumania, and Montenegro and attempted to reconcile interests of England, Germany, France, and Russia with the nationalistic aspirations of the Balkan peoples.
1879-1894	Publication of Heinrich von Treitschke's *German History in the 19th Century*. Probably the most important German nationalistic history written in the nineteenth century.
1894-1906	The Dreyfus Affair in France threatened the republic.
1905	Union of Sweden and Norway dissolved, and Norway became independent. This action completed what could be called the formation of nations in Western Europe.
1919	Peace treaties following World War I extended the idea of nationalism into Central Europe. The states of Czechoslovakia, Yugoslavia, Poland, Hungary, Finland, Estonia, Latvia, and Lithuania established.

The eighteenth century has often been described as a cosmopolitan age. The common qualities of men were emphasized, and there was a general belief in universally accepted intellectual and moral values. There was a great deal of talking and writing about the rights of man and about the human community. Political leaders more or less looked upon themselves as "orators of the human race," and the famous documents of the period have a universality, an applicability to all who will bend their ears to hear the word. What the American Declaration of Independence speaks of as "the laws of nature and of nature's God" were "self-evident" general directives for everyone, and all men were regarded as largely motivated by the same desires and responsive to the same appeals.

In the nineteenth century, however, the history of Western man became uniquely the history of national states. What we recognize as nationalistic feelings had, of course, been present in Europe since the late middle ages. European monarchs had used such feelings in their controversies with the Catholic Church, and the centuries-old argument between secular and spiritual authorities had stimulated a form of unity among those who lived in certain areas and who were thought of as subjects of specific rulers. There had been a general "sorting out of the tribes" for several hundred years, as there had been a gathering-together of those united by geography, language, and general culture.

But modern nationalism with its intensity and its claim to express the distinctive and important attributes of men was a revolutionary statement of the human situation. In a way that was strikingly new men were identified in terms of their membership in national communities. History became basically national history — English history, French history, German history, American history — and the rights and duties of Englishmen, Frenchmen, Germans, and Americans superseded the rights and duties of man. The fate of the individual became involved as never before with that of his nation. If his nation prospered, he prospered, if it was defeated, he was defeated, if it was disgraced, he was disgraced. There was a common opinion that men could be understood only as creatures of their national history.

The German historian Golo Mann has pointed out that "the genius of Europe has given much to the world: things good and evil, generally things that are both good and evil — among them the state and the nation. Elsewhere, in Asia and Africa, nations and states did not exist in the past." It was in the Western world that the characteristics we associate with nationalism were developed. The modern state became a territorially united area with what were thought of as appropriate frontiers. The national government became a single sovereign and independent authority with one law and one expression of political and military power. Citizens were increasingly confined to a single allegiance, and each national grouping acquired a belief in its own historical individuality and its own historical destiny. Old provincial and even what we could call tribal loyalties were declared obsolete — although many of these proved to be more lasting than expected. A new human unit was created that not only provided a system of organization but transformed the spiritual and moral life of the people.

Definitions of Nationalism

The experience of nationalism confronted the West with a multitude of difficult questions. What was a nation? Was it basically the designation given a certain geographical area, a part of the map? Was it a group of people sharing a common language? What was the relationship of race and nationalism? Did nations represent spiritual principles or were they merely collections of individuals who had come together by chance and remained together only because of personal benefit? Could Catholics be patriotic citizens in a Protestant-oriented state and Protestants citizens in a state pledged to the forwarding of Catholic doctrine? Could Jews be members of a national community or were they to be only a more or less tolerated but alien minority? For what purposes was national power to be used and by whom? What did nationalism have to do with democracy and freedom? What were the signs of national vitality and national success?

The search for answers to such questions was complicated by the fact that although the nation state has been the common type of political, economic, and cultural organization in the modern Western world, and later elsewhere, it has been extremely difficult to define the very word *nation*. The Englishman John Stuart Mill in the mid-nineteenth century wrote that a "feeling of nationality" may come from various causes. "Sometimes it is the effect of identity of race and descent. Community of language and community of religion greatly contribute to it. Geographical limits are one of its causes. But the strongest of all is identity of political antecedents; the possession of a national history, and consequent community of recollections; collective pride and humiliation, pleasure and regret, connected with the same incidents in the past."

Every one of Mill's characteristics has been used to define nationalism and the nation. It is a common assumption, for example, that nations in some mysterious way correspond naturally to a geographical setting and that, as the German Johann G. Fichte claimed, "certain parts of the earth's surface, together with their inhabitants, are visibly destined by nature to form political entities." Rivers, seas, oceans, and mountains are thought to provide the dividing markers between national groupings, and it is argued that such providential boundaries must not be violated. Thus Germans have spoken of a Germany stretching naturally from "the North Sea to the Carpathians, from the Baltic to the Alps, from the Vistula to the Schelde," and Frenchmen have claimed the Rhine, the Alps, and the Pyrenees as "the ancient and natural boundaries of France." This interpretation has been described by K. R. Minogue in his book *Nationalism* as "a conception of the nation as a solid lump of territory," and is a favorite among those who visualize the world as a series of colored maps. But, in spite of all claims of destiny and naturalness of frontiers, geographical boundaries are usually much more run-of-the-mill affairs. They are accepted because nations are willing or are forced to recognize them, and the peoples of the world have been notoriously indifferent to rivers, mountains, and even oceans, and have crossed them with little regard to the fact that they were straying from their "natural" settings. Thus the Rio Grande marks the boundary between the United States and Mexico, not because it is "natural," but because the United States wished it that way and Mexico was forced to acquiesce. There is little "natural" about most of the boundary between Canada and the United States, and it is difficult to argue the naturalness of either the Oder or the Vistula river as the eastern border of Germany.

A second characteristic often used to distinguish a nation is race, and there is a general tendency to use loosely such a word in attempts to describe national groupings. German nationalists were fond of saying, "Blut will zu Blut" (men of the same blood long for each other), and there have been exhaustive efforts to prove that physical characteristics and certain racial qualities are embodied in nations. The common argument that the "typical" American is a WASP (white Anglo-Saxon Protestant) is, in two of three parts of this definition, based upon an appeal that could be described as racist and indicates that important American features are connected with people possessing certain characteristics springing from racial affinity. We have had a great deal of talk about the "decadent French race," "Semite blood," and "Alpines and Mediterraneans," all designed to show the identity of race and nation. And, because there is nothing that people will not believe, the whole problem of nationalism has been influenced by the attempt to identify race with nation and to use skin and hair coloring, head shape, and body size to distinguish one national group from another. Many well-meaning historians and others have rightly claimed that there is no "pure stock" among the human race and that racial purity is a ridiculous hypothesis. And from these indisputable facts the conclusion is drawn that race cannot be a characteristic of the nation. Yet the important thing is what people believed, and the history of Western nationalism has been influenced, and marred, by the attempt to bend national effort around the principle of race and to identify one nation with one race.

A more meaningful attribute of a nation is probably language. The German literary critic Friedrich Schlegel argued that "every literature must and should be national," and in the Western world a common language has tended to be a basic characteristic of the nation state. There was an almost continual organization of nations about language groupings in the nineteenth century, and if one compares a political map with a linguistic one, there is a slow but steady movement over time for the political borders roughly to match the linguistic. The two boundaries never corresponded exactly, and there was always some overlap and some oddities. Belgium has been a nation state for well over a hundred years, yet there is no Belgian language, while languages or dialects such as Provençal, Breton, Basque, Welsh, Frisian, and others have not become nuclei for new nations. Linguistic minorities have always existed, and will undoubtedly continue. But as Carlton J. H. Hayes said over forty years ago:

> It is readily comprehensible why language should be an important, probably the chief, factor in forming and sustaining a nationality. Uniformity of language tends to promote likemindedness, to provide an inclusive set of ideas as well as of words, and likeminded persons tend to develop group-consciousness, to experience a sense of common interest, to constitute a tribe or nationality. . . . Language, too, is the medium in which is expressed the memory of successful achievement or distressing hardship shared in common, and thereby it acquires cementing value for a nationality.

Yet probably as important as anything else, as Mill noted, in defining a nation is a belief in a historical identity, a set of historical memories, a faith in a unique historical tradition. The German Wilhelm von Humboldt called this feeling of nationalism "the memory of rights and liberties enjoyed in common, of glory won in battle and dangers shared together, the memory of close bonds which linked the fathers and which are now alive in the nostalgic longings of the grandchildren." To a greater or lesser extent, there has been what is called "the devouring flame of high patriotism," and in 1882 the Frenchman Ernest Renan wrote that it is essential for citizens "to have common glories in the past, a common will at present, to have achieved great things together, to intend to achieve more of them in the future." The members of a nation believe themselves to be a distinct group of men, with "a culture-pattern of its own, a distinctive complex of institutions, customs, and art." This past and these memories and even this claim to uniqueness may be partially true and partially invented. Minogue points out that "it is nationalists who have appropriated fairy tales from the nursery and brought them into politics. Further, each nation needs a legend, and these legends all have a fairy-tale character about them." National heroes, national aspirations, national traditions are the lifeblood of national states. As the Englishman John Maynard Keynes said: "Nations are real things." And because they are real, they define their own reality and transform the circumstances of their existence into tangible and deeply felt "truths" that are defended to the death by their citizens.

Beginnings of Modern Nationalism

Nationalism in its modern form springs from the French Revolution. It was the Revolution that shattered the old and traditional loyalties and substituted for them the national state and the national spirit. Religious groups were brought under the control of the state, and the state itself acquired many of the attributes of religion. The use of the national language was forwarded at the expense of local dialects, and a general scheme of national education, complete with an emphasis upon the concept of patriotic duty, was introduced. The national flag, the national anthem, and national holidays were adopted, and the national bureaucracy and the national army became instruments of the national purpose. The French showed how nationalism could be used to mold a society and to direct it upon a path of success and strength, and the lesson was not lost upon other Europeans. Throughout the nineteenth century there was a continual parade of new nations. In the 1820's the states of Greece and Serbia (now part of Yugoslavia) appeared. In the 1830's the Belgians separated themselves from the Dutch, and in the 1850's and 1860's Italy and Rumania became independent states. In early 1871 the various German states became the German Empire, while those peoples that did not succeed in establishing national states — the Poles, the Czechs, and the Slovaks — pressed their claims to nationhood and aroused sympathetic support in Western Europe.

During the nineteenth century nationalism was identified with both national independence and individual liberty. It was largely believed that only as a member of an independent nation could a man exercise his freedom, and that his liberty depended upon his nation being a sovereign authority. One important aspect of the century's revolutionary activity was that designed to promote independence for peoples who were thought to be oppressed by foreigners and thus denied both national and individual freedom. As the Italian revolutionary Giuseppe Mazzini argued, before men could be free, "they must have a national existence." Without a homeland, a fatherland, an anchor of patriotic affection in some specific part of the world, Western men were to feel incomplete, threatened, and without identity. One could give his life for liberty only if he had a fatherland worth living for. The claim to national independence by various peoples was blatant, rude, and at times almost simple-minded. "O, my brother, love your country," cried Mazzini. "Our country is our Home, a home God has given us, placing therein a numerous family that loves us, and whom we love; a family with whom we sympathize more readily and whom we understand more quickly than we do others; and which, from its being centered round a given spirit, and from the homogeneous nature of its elements, is adapted to a special branch of activity."

Because we are so accustomed to living in a world of national states, we often forget that the process of nation-building in the West was a soul-wrenching and painful undertaking. Yet there is evidence of this in our American history. The United States was undoubtedly the most fortunate of Western nations. It benefited in its formative years through gifted leadership, it enjoyed the unimaginable wealth of a virgin continent, it had no strong and aggressive neighbors, and there was what could be termed an almost naive but vigorous confidence in the future. But we know that the American nation was built at great cost. The bloodiest and most destructive war of the nineteenth century was the American Civil War, and the effects of that war were to twist American political life into grotesque shapes. Crimes were committed against the native Indians and the Negroes. There was social strife, human exploitation, glorious fortunes and criminal poverty, and both petty and great corruption. American institutions were the targets of vicious satire, and throughout the century many of the more perceptive Americans despaired of the republic and questioned, in Abraham Lincoln's words, whether the nation could "long endure."

In Western Europe the problem of nationalism was even more severe and produced new cultural and historical divisions. Of all the European national groupings the English were least scarred by the crisis of nationalism. They possessed traditional and time-tested institutions and a sense of national identity that allowed them to escape many of the divisive arguments that took place on the continent. Early in the nineteenth century a German remarked that England was the only real nation in Europe, the only thoroughly organized society. "Nothing in

Britain is isolated," he wrote. "Everything hangs together; everything affects everything else; all is united, combined, blended. It is the only nation at present that possesses a definite character, a civilization not fragmentary, like the others." The English succeeded in modifying their institutions while retaining a sense of continuity. There were strains in English society. But these did not provoke a crisis in national consciousness. The success of British industry, the growth of the British Empire overseas, and the general respect accorded the British everywhere indicated to Englishmen the proof of their national vigor and the correctness of their national purpose.

The French National Experience

In France the problem of nationalism was more complicated and tormenting. The Revolution had provided the vocabulary and the concept of French nationalism, but it had also produced the fissures that were to influence the national experience. Property had changed hands, many people had been elevated in the world and many had been cast down, deep-seated hatreds had developed, and a bitter argument about the nature of France itself had entered into the national life. Soon after 1815 and the departure of Napoleon an observer wrote, "We are on the top of a volcanoe," and France was to be subjected to a series of rendering political explosions.

In the search for institutions and ideas that could express their national identity, the French engaged in what could be thought of as a long civil war — complete with military combat, periods of truce, social disorder, and the overthrowing of governments — that went on throughout the nineteenth century. In 1815, after Napoleon's defeat, the old Bourbon monarchy was restored by the victorious powers, and the brother of the executed Louis XVI assumed the French throne as Louis XVIII. This monarchy, under Louis and his brother Charles X, lasted for fifteen years. In 1830 it was overthrown, and a "citizen king," Louis-Philippe, was crowned as "King of the French People." Eighteen years later, in 1848, another revolution sent Louis-Philippe into exile and established a republic. In December, 1851, Louis Napoleon, the nephew of the great Napoleon, overthrew the republic by a coup d'état and approximately a year later established the Second Empire, taking the title Napoleon III. In 1870 the empire disappeared as a result of defeat in the Franco-Prussian War, and ultimately another republic was established. This was itself a compromise and was accepted at the time largely because, as one political leader said, "it is the form of government that divides us least." The new republic was plagued with troubles and was subjected to almost impossible strains. It did survive, however, until 1940, perhaps because as much as anything there was no other feasible solution at hand and because many found themselves in the position of one Frenchman who said: "I am a republican, but only in sheer desperation."

These political upheavals were more than signs of institutional instability. They were also caused by continual disappointment by large numbers of Frenchmen in one political philosophy after another that was thought to express the national purpose, the spirit of France. Louis XVIII had adopted a policy of conciliation and had tried, as he said, to "heal the wounds of the Revolution." He had guaranteed equality before the law, equality of taxation, and the sanctity of private property. He had acknowledged freedom of worship, although Catholicism had been singled out as "the religion of the state," and he had accepted the revolutionary land settlement. Charles X, who came to the throne in 1824, abandoned the idea of reconciliation and attempted to return to what he called "the natural order of things." He identified himself with the extreme clerical and royalist factions and in July 1830, announced a series of laws that were aimed at the destruction of all opposition. He proposed to suspend the guarantees of freedom of the press, to dissolve the elected legislative chamber, and to reduce drastically the number of people allowed to vote for representatives.

The revolution of 1830 introduced what is called the bourgeois monarchy. Control of affairs was in the hands of the prospering property owners, and Louis-Philippe himself was described as one who "dressed in bourgeois style, speaking bourgeois wisdom, driving bourgeois bargains with his own government." The dominant tone of the government was set by the middle class, the property-owning, hard-working, self-reliant bourgeoisie. The regime was characterized in 1846 as "liberal by principle, selfish in habit, wishing and not wishing." Louis-Philippe's principal minister could claim that "all the great conquests are made, all the great interests are satisfied." But business scandals, petty corruption, a smug self-righteousness, and political blindness sapped the strength of the monarchy, and in February, 1848, discontented workers, disenchanted members of the middle class, and intellectuals took to the streets in Paris and toppled the government.

The new republic of 1848 was pledged to a construction of the "social and democratic" society. But it was a fiasco and served primarily to discredit the more radical among the French political leaders. The Second Empire did achieve a large measure of stability and was supported by a substantial number of Frenchmen. Louis Napoleon closed political clubs, censored newspapers, and silenced opponents. An extensive police system was developed, the legislature became little more than a body approving what the Emperor suggested, and critical teachers were dismissed. But Louis Napoleon attempted to make his government one representing all citizens. He financed workers' housing, hospitals, and orphanages. There was business prosperity, and a program of public works was initiated, the most remarkable being the renovation of Paris. Louis Napoleon also attempted to liberalize the government, and after 1859 he forwarded the idea of the liberal Empire. Amnesties were extended to opponents, concessions were made to the working class, and the cause of free, obligatory primary education was advanced. In 1868 a new press law allowed opposition papers to appear, and in 1870 a nationwide plebiscite indicated that the majority of the French people approved of the liberal Empire led by the man who was described by his enemies as "Napoleon the Little," or by a more sympathetic journalist as "Napoleon the Well-Meaning."

There was another side, of course, to the Second Empire. Corruption was widespread, and many of the economic benefits of Louis Napoleon's efforts settled into the pockets of the speculators. Working-class hostility did not abate, and Louis Napoleon's paternalistic projects did not gain the allegiance of the French working class. In foreign affairs he could not match his uncle's reputation. He did arrive at an understanding with England, and he did achieve some military glory in Italy and during the Crimean War with Russia. But he could not free himself of the Italian problem and the tangled knot of Catholic relations, and his adventure in Mexico in the eighteen-sixties was a disaster. He was distrusted by the businessmen who benefited from his policies, by the workers, and by the intellectuals. In July, 1870, he allowed himself to be trapped into a war with Prussia. In September, Louis Napoleon, at the head of the French army, was forced to surrender at Sedan, and the Second Empire disappeared.

So the French had tried in slightly over half a century a restoration of the old monarchy, a middle-class king, a republic, and another Bonaparte. One political convulsion had followed another, and each had produced more bloodshed, more hatred, more strain within the society. Political, social, and intellectual divisions appeared to deepen throughout the nineteenth century, and French national life was rocked by these animosities. Free-thinkers were set against the Catholic Church, Paris against the countryside, the most dedicated defenders of property against those who advocated the abolition of private property. Arguments over the schools, the churches, the army, and even the national flag and the national anthem alienated one Frenchman from another. To many observers France seemed continually on the verge of national disintegration. In the eighteen-fifties the Russian exile Alexander Herzen wrote: "The more revolutionary a country had been in the Western sense, the more impossible it had become for her to carry out any solution to her problems, and France, the victim of one false revolution after another, is now beyond repair. They have tried victories and violent exercises with her. They have set her marching to Egypt and Russia, they have tried parliamentarianism, a little republic and a little Napoleon — and has anything done any good?"

French national confidence was also shaken by a series of major and minor international humiliations. A cruel cartoon of 1815 had shown an eagle (Napoleon) leaving Paris and five geese (King Louis XVIII and his family) waddling in, and throughout the nineteenth century Frenchmen were haunted by the fear that France's greatness as a nation was behind her. One result of the postrevolutionary settlement in Europe after Napoleon's defeat was the isolation of France. Other governments still regarded France as a source of dangerous revolutionary ideas, and she was somewhat an outcast in the European community of nations. In international affairs France was both cautious and rash, and her foreign policy was condemned by one Frenchman as "without virtue or greatness." During the European scramble for colonial possessions, France was forced to withdraw claims because of British opposition, while the attempt of Louis Napoleon to force French rule upon Mexico was an exercise in futility.

The most damaging of all blows to French national pride, however, was her crushing defeat in the Franco-Prussian War of 1870. As a result of this disaster, France lost two of her northern provinces, most of her iron deposits, and great areas of forest and farm land. Over one and one-half million of her citizens were transferred to the newly created German Empire. The Prussian King was crowned as German Emperor in the Versailles Hall of Mirrors, and German troops paraded in Paris as conquerors. Only the gesture of protest against this humiliation was left to the French — the empty streets and the shuttered and still houses with which Paris greeted the victorious German soldiers.

But there was worse to come. Frustrated and embittered, the French engaged in their ugliest civil war before the eyes of their German conquerors. In March, 1871, a part of the Paris population, consisting of workingmen and radicals who saw themselves as defenders of the great revolutionary tradition, revolted against those who had taken charge after Louis Napoleon's defeat. A revolutionary government was established in Paris, and the authorities withdrew to Versailles. Here a new army was organized and invaded the city. Two months of deadly street fighting followed. But the struggle was an unequal one, and in late May the Parisians were overwhelmed. On May 27 the last battle was fought in the cemetery of Père Lachaise, where some two hundred last-ditch rebels were killed in an action that became legendary in working-class history. After the fighting ended, retribution was exacted from Paris. Nearly 20,000 men, women, and children were executed for their part or suspected part in the uprising, and thousands of bodies were dumped in mass graves. Over 40,000 were arrested, and of these, 13,000 were imprisoned or transported to New Caledonia or Guiana in South America. The horror and shame of France — the killing of Frenchmen by other Frenchmen — was witnessed by the victorious Germans, who looked upon the event as one more indication of the decay of a once-great nation.

During the nineteenth century France illustrated the agonizing dilemma of nationalism. What made a nation great? France was by most standards a shining part of Western civilization. French intellectual activity was stimulating and exciting, French artists led the world into a new era of color and design, and what was thought of as the French style of life was admired and envied. Paris, with its wide avenues, its bridges, and its tree-lined boulevards, was the showplace of the West. What other city could offer such wonders as the cancan, the Latin Quarter, the sidewalk cafes, the new and soon-to-be-famous department stores, and the great exhibitions? By the latter half of the century France, compared with most other places in the world, was a tolerant, humane, civilized nation, with a large number of creative and patriotic citizens.

Yet France was also something of a stalemate society. The problem of reconciling freedom with social organization struck many as insoluble, and a persistent strain of pessimism, cynicism, and discouragement entered into French life. "France will always exist," cried a political orator. But many Frenchmen were not so sure. The very virtues of the French people — strong family feelings, a searching intellectualism, the determination to preserve one's personal identity, a decided bent toward rationalism — appeared to keep France from becoming a disciplined and efficient nation state. French nationalism became defensive, and the focus of national purpose was blurred. The disappointments, the anxieties, and the frustrations of the past and the present raised apprehensions about the future. Émile Zola spoke of his fellow-novelist Gustave Flaubert: "When I used to declare my confidence in the twentieth century, when I used to say that our vast scientific and social movement must result in a broader development of mankind, he stared at me with his big blue eyes, and then shrugged his shoulders." Flaubert's response was, in many ways, distinctively French.

The German National Triumph

If the French found nationalism a horrifying dilemma, the Germans discovered in it a great instrument of historical purpose. The creation of the unified German state was the most important European political event of the nineteenth century. The German sense of historical reality, the German outlook on politics, the German definition of order, authority, and freedom were uniquely influenced by the way in which the German state was established and by the interpretation given German nationalism.

Until the second half of the nineteenth century there were Germans but no Germany. The settlement of the Napoleonic wars left a group of independent states in the area we think of as Germany. The most important of these were Prussia, Bavaria, Württemberg, Baden, Saxony, and Hanover. Each of these states had its own political institutions, ruler, and even cultural traditions. Some were Catholic, others Protestant. Some had close intellectual ties to France and England, others were part of that ill-defined area known as central Europe. But from the early years of the century there was a growing demand for a united German state. In 1808 Johann Fichte, in his famous *Addresses to the German Nation*, argued that the existence of a single, unified German state was a historical necessity if the Germans were to play an important part in world history. German universities became centers of agitation for unification, and slogans such as "Honor, Liberty, and Fatherland" became common throughout the German states.

It is probably true, as some have argued, that those supporting German unification were a minority of the German people. But they were a vociferous and influential group. Of course, there was the question of how Germany was to be united. There were Germans who believed in a form of liberal constitutionalism, as there were some who supported the idea of a federated state that would retain the various monarchies and particularistic institutions. There was also the possibility that Germany could be united by Prussia, the strongest of the states, and in 1813, Karl von Clausewitz, best known for his study on war, had pointed out that "Germany can achieve political unity in only one way, that is, through the sword, when one of its states will bring all the others under its sway."

In 1848 a series of revolutions swept through Europe, and there were many Germans who believed that the time had come to unite Germany as a liberal state. In March an assembly of 500 notables met in Frankfurt to call a general election that would establish a German National Assembly and thus decide the future of Germany. Elections were held, and in May the National Assembly met in Frankfurt. A Declaration of Fundamental Rights, modeled after the French Declaration of Rights of Man and the American Declaration of Independence, was adopted, and early in 1849 the Assembly completed work upon a constitution for a united Germany. This constitution called for a hereditary monarch, a parliament of two houses, with one house representing the various German states and the other consisting of representatives elected by secret, universal, and equal manhood suffrage. The constitution was submitted to the various German states for their approval, and the delegates at Frankfurt voted to offer the German crown to the King of Prussia. However, the Prussian King declined the offer and then ordered the Prussian members of the Assembly to withdraw from the body. Soon thereafter the Assembly was dissolved. There were some uprisings on behalf of the constitution, but these were easily suppressed by the armed forces of the various states. Rulers were quick to remove from their premises what the Prussian King called "the democratic filth," and liberalism in Germany acquired a reputation for weakness and failure that was to remain with it throughout the century.

Yet Germany was ultimately united. Through outright annexation of some of the smaller German states, through confederations that she could manipulate, through successful wars, and through coercion, Prussia extended her control over the rest of Germany. In January 1871 the King of Prussia was proclaimed German Emperor. A powerful and prosperous German nation now stretched from the west bank of the Rhine River eastward across the Elbe, the Spree, the Oder, the Vistula, to the Niemen. From Strasbourg, Metz, and Aachen in the west to Danzig, Koenigsberg, and Tilsit in the east the Germans could claim to be one nation and one people.

The German Empire has been called a combination of "the Prussian military monarchy, federation, and universal suffrage." The German states were allowed to retain many of the trappings of sovereignty, and the German constitution of 1871 gave the appearance of constitutional government. There was a parliament, the Reichstag, and there were political parties. But the position of Prussia was paramount. The executive leadership was vested in a hereditary emperor, who was also the King of Prussia. He represented Germany in all matters of foreign policy, he declared war and peace, he appointed all important officials, who were responsible to him and not to the Reichstag. The military oath was to him not to Germany as a nation, and there were no constitutional limits to his power. The German Empire was titularly a union of German states; but on matters of real consequence, Prussia was too strong, and this fact was to influence the operation of the German state and the concept of German nationalism.

The united German nation in the late nineteenth century was admired by many. It was militarily strong and industrially powerful, and it was socially and politically stable. Until 1890, under the direction of the chancellor Otto von Bismarck, Germany was a force for peace and balance in Europe. German influence was secure in central

Europe and the Balkans and growing in the Middle East, in Africa, and throughout the world.

But there had developed alongside the newly created German state a German nationalistic philosophy that was different than that found in other Western countries. It involved a worship of power, a justification of force, and a glorification of military success that was harsh and shrill. Arrogant boasting and contempt for any appeal save to "reasons of state" were common attributes of German political thinking and promoted a self-righteousness and an irrationality that stimulated the most extreme chauvinism. Hegel's theoretical glorification of the state was transformed into a chant of allegiance to the existing German Empire. The German Romantic tendency to engage in the wildest kind of dreaming — nature-dreaming, blood-dreaming, folk-dreaming, heart-land-dreaming, soul-dreaming, purity-of-race-dreaming, wind-in-the-trees and old-comrades-marching-dreaming — was combined with a devotion to the militarily mighty, highly organized German state. German culture was identified with German national success, the German spirit with German power, and there was a rejection of international values and cosmopolitan aspirations.

There were, of course, many Germans who did not accept this interpretation of German nationalism, and some saw clearly the "demonic character of power" and the implications of statements such as "there is neither law nor right except the right of the stronger" and "in the world of politics the law of force has the same validity as the law of gravity in the physical world." There were protests against the "idolization of the state" and against the argument that the German fatherland was to be found "where every Frenchman is called foe, and every German is called friend." But the belligerent nationalistic philosophy had so many supporters in German intellectual life, in the German business and military community, and among German politicians that it seemed the dominant interpretation of Germany's national purpose.

There was one aspect of this German nationalism that was difficult for non-Germans, and particularly Americans, to understand or even take seriously. This was the doctrine of the *Volk*. This German word does not lend itself to translation and has no exact counterpart in other Western European languages. The *Volk* is a unit of people, but it is much more than a collection of individuals who have come together by chance or choice. One belongs to the *Volk* through the accident of birth, and the *Volk* is primarily, when stripped of all its extraneous elements, an expression of the "merciless race struggle in history." The principal aim of the *Volk* is to keep what is German German. The *Volk* is based upon racial and cultural similarities and on a close association with the soil, on a community of language and tradition, on old customs and folkways. It is indestructible and imperishable, and it is the characteristic that sets one nation off from another and establishes a priority of value among nations. The German state was thus the instrument designed to forward this "essence" of the German people. In 1895 the famous sociologist Max Weber said: "We have not to bequeath to our descendants peace and human happiness, but the eternal struggle for the preservation and up-breeding of our national character."

This concept of the *Volk*, which worked its way into a great part of German historical thinking, was, in the last analysis, an argument for the supremacy of national states that embodied the principle of racial discrimination. Only a German could be a true member of the *Volk*, and from this simple fact it was a short step to the contention that the Germans, and their national state, were superior to other people. In almost every important German thinker there was at least a trace of the belief that only the Germans possessed the secret of the true society and the true nationality. And this belief in a national, and racial, superiority was often expressed in the most crass terms. The noted German historian Heinrich von Treitschke was a learned man. Yet he could lose himself in foolish, and dangerous, nationalistic speculations and reduce national differences to a series of insults. He called "the Polacks, Slovaks, and Walachians" the "proletarian" peoples, incapable of true national feelings, and he dismissed the Jews and the gypsies as "rabble." The English were cold and indifferent to the higher call of life, while the French were bigots and cynics, and they lacked a true sense of freedom. Moreover, they allowed themselves to be ruled by women and could not establish any meaningful relationship with nature. According to Treitschke, "in the forests" the Frenchman "lies on his stomach" and looks at the ground, while "we lie on our backs" and look at the sky. And, of course, in Treitschke's opinion, there was no hope for the United States. Here was a country of great wealth, but it was politically corrupt and intellectually mediocre. In addition, and this was important for Treitschke, it was "mongrelized."

This German nationalistic philosophy was a serious problem for the Western world. It stimulated a hatred of the foreigner, and made it difficult for anyone to be pro-German without being anti-French and anti-English. It easily lent itself to the organization of hatreds and resentments, and it justified arbitrary and irresponsible actions by the authorities if they were done in the name of the national purpose. The emphasis upon power allied with a sense of national distinctiveness stimulated extreme ideas, which ran deep in German society. A respected professor could say: "Let them hate us, as long as they fear us," and another intellectual could state that "if the worst comes to the worst, we shall let ourselves be buried beneath the ruins of European civilization." German nationalism had little to offer anyone but Germans, and the stressing of national superiority was certain to become not only an irritant but a danger.

Nationalism and Freedom

Unquestionably Westerners benefited by membership in a nation state. They were given a sense of community, a feeling of security, and a belief that they were participants in a great historical adventure. Nationalism did show a way whereby the great energies of the modern age could be organized and the power of the community brought to bear upon common problems. Strong nation states did promote order, reduce arbitrary violence, and provide a source of authority in resolving, or attempting to resolve, conflicting pressures within the society. So much that is valuable in Western life is dependent upon the nation that it is almost impossible to imagine our existence except as members of a national community.

But nationalism did demand a price, and if Western man became something more by being a member of a highly organized state, he also became something less. In 1967 K. R. Minogue began his book *Nationalism* with the sentence: "Nationalism, as the story is generally told, begins as Sleeping Beauty and ends as Frankenstein's monster." In theory nationalism was designed to forward the freedom of the individual. The German historian Heinrich von Sybel could argue convincingly that "the state is the realization of freedom through the power of the community." And throughout the nineteenth century individual liberty was expanded. But so was the power of the national state, and the two conceptions seemed to some to be on a collision course. In the eighteen-sixties the Englishman Lord Acton pointed out that nationalism, far from being the inevitable ally of individual freedom, could be its opponent, and in the early years of the twentieth century Max Weber noted that national power is "generally misused, and misused even more to the extent that it drapes itself in moral and legal considerations." The tender balance between authority and freedom was often upset by the demands of the state. The great power of the national states did threaten their individual citizens, and there was a continual conflict between what the German historian Friedrich Meinecke called "the inalienable rights of the individual" and "the inevitable egotistic and domineering nature of the state." The individual should "serve the state as a free man, as an individual and a man of culture," Meinecke went on. But nationalism too often "demands that the individual subordinate himself in a rigid and uniform manner to the needs of the state and the nation." The national state was a predatory instrument and leaned with increasing heaviness against the individual.

One particularly threatening aspect of modern nationalism was that it promoted what has been called "the fighting impulse," and there was a tendency to equate the value of a nation state with its ability to wage war. War has always been a threat to the life and the freedom of individual men. But as Clausewitz wrote: "The war of the present age is a war of all against all. No longer does a king fight a king, an army another army, but a people another people. . . ." In the modern age "every war will be regarded as a national concern." This identity of war and national vigor was a prominent characteristic of the age of nationalism. In 1809 Mme. de Staël wrote: "Let the bugle sound, let the national flag unfurl in the air, and you will see eyes normally so gentle, so ready to become gentle again at the sight of misfortune, suddenly animated by a sacred and terrible will." There were many in the West who believed that war was the thing that released the great moral energies stored in the nation and was the needed corrective to social selfishness and social atomization. Heinrich von Treitschke could write in all seriousness, and there were many who were to echo his thoughts if not his words:

> We are living in a battle zone: any moment the leader may call us back to arms. It is not for us to chase in blind greed after the thousands and thousands of glittering hopes for freedom that flit across this age of revolutions. It is for us to stand together in manly discipline and self-restraint, and to pass on the bulwark of our unity, the German kingdom, to our sons.

Nationalism was also a limiting doctrine in that it confined Western man to a single allegiance that claimed precedence over every other loyalty. The human being was reduced from a complex person with complex standards of judgment to a simple citizen with no destiny save that of his state. Liberty was often, by official and unofficial pressures, reduced to obedience, and healthy patriotism was turned into "blind respect, devoid of all ideas, for success and power." In the name of national success, the individual was called upon to endure indignities and to subordinate his judgment and his intelligence to ill-defined and questionable "higher purposes," for, as Golo Mann suggests, "nations have always managed to find some rational necessity, some ideological reason for murdering each other." In times of national stress, the pressures upon the citizen became extreme, and he was cut down, reduced, tailored, in a way that damaged his vision of his own life and the world in which he lived.

There were many men and events in the Western world of the nineteenth century that illustrated the effects of nationalism and the varied responses to this powerful influence. Otto von Bismarck towered above all other political leaders of his time and is identified with the appearance of the strong German state. John Stuart Mill was the spokesman for the English liberal interpretation of the state. The Dreyfus Affair subjected France to a horrifying experience of national division and illuminated some of the complex problems posed by Western nationalism.

Otto Von Bismarck

One man is usually associated with the creation of the great German state of the last half of the nineteenth century. And that is as it should be. Otto von Bismarck was, as much as any one man can be responsible for any historical event, the architect of the united Germany. "My highest ambition is to make the Germans a nation," he remarked on several occasions before 1871, and he succeeded. He was responsible for the political strategy that led to unification, and he guided the united Germany during its first twenty years. He stamped the new national German state with his own political principles, and he marked the character of the people within the state.

Bismarck was born at Schönhausen in Brandenburg in 1815, the year of Waterloo. Schönhausen was situated a short distance east of the Elbe, and Bismarck was a man who looked both to the German east and the German west. He knew the world of the Prussian Junker, the landowning military caste, that stretched eastward into Pomerania and Silesia. But Bismarck was not a Junker, nor a narrow provincial who knew nothing of or cared nothing for what lay beyond the confines of Prussia. He was a cosmopolitan, a man of the world, who had an understanding of European life.

Bismarck attended the University of Göttingen, and in 1835 he passed the examination that qualified him for entrance into the Prussian civil service. His career in the service was, however, short. Put simply, he could not get along with his superiors. He retired to his estate and spent the next eight years there. "I will play music the way I like or not at all," he is reported to have said, and this attitude was to be a permanent part of his personality. In the eighteen-forties he joined the Prussian foreign service and represented Prussia in several important capitals. In 1862 he was named chancellor of Prussia. He was then forty-seven years old, and he was to remain in this position for twenty-seven years. Until his retirement in 1890 he dominated European international politics, and he made German influence felt throughout the continent.

Bismarck was a man of overpowering personality — egotistical, intelligent, clever, dedicated, and ruthless. He was also a surprisingly solitary man who had no colleagues only subordinates. He had gargantuan appetites, for food, for drink, for conversation, for power. He could be a most pleasing, interesting companion, and he could be rude and coarse. He was, as he himself admitted, a man of contradictions. He once said: "Faust complains of having two souls in his breast. I have a whole squabbling crowd." He was known as the Iron Chancellor, yet when he was asked if this was an accurate description, he replied: "Far from it. I am all nerves, so much so that self-control has always been the greatest task of my life." He had contempt for most of mankind, and once his animosity was aroused he was vindictive and petty. An acquaintance who knew him well has left a description of this side of his character. "I have scarcely ever known anyone as joyless as Bismarck. One listened to the same stories over and over again. They were always stories in which Bismarck figured as the hero, while the other characters usually appeared in a ridiculous, and at times a despicable, light. The note of true gaiety was lacking, so that the laughter was always at someone's expense." He was the great realist, who prided himself on his ability to see to the heart of the matter. Yet he could, at times, indulge in silly superficialities. Thus, when speaking of the French and of the probability of another war with France, he stated that "our victory in that final war is probable, for in the history of the peoples the Germans play the part rather of a man, the Romance peoples that of a woman. A man often falls, but he can always pick himself up; a woman, once fallen, cannot recover."

In one of his first public appearances after being appointed chancellor, Bismarck said: "Germany does not look to Prussia's liberalism but to her strength." And then he made what was perhaps his most famous statement. "The great questions of the day will not be decided by speeches and resolutions of majorities, but by iron and blood." This was an oratorical masterpiece, and, as with any political simplification, not an exact description of Bismarck's policy. He used many methods of persuasion to achieve his objectives, and once Germany was united, he was basically a defender of order and peace on the continent. But what his statement did mean was that as the final arbiter, there was the fist, the military club, the state organized for war.

The steps that Bismarck took in the eighteen-sixties to create the united German state seem almost like the episodes in a film script designed to illustrate the way of political success. He achieved three quick and spectacular victories in war, and by using the strength of the Prussian army, the weakness of his opponents, and his own skill, he succeeded in turning the German dream into reality. The Danish War of 1864 and the Austro-Prussian War of 1866 drove Austria out of German affairs and left Prussia as the dominant German state. The North German Confederation, which consisted of twenty-two states and principalities in north and central Germany under the leadership of Prussia, was formed. The defeat of the French in the Franco-Prussian War of 1870-1871 created the circumstances that led to the unity of Germany. The southern German states now joined with the members of the Confederation, and the German Empire was established.

The empire was organized from the top down. The emperor, or Kaiser, was a hereditary leader who was responsible only to God and was the source of all executive power. His was a form of transcendental authority, and as a practical matter he expressed his leadership through a single minister, the Reich Chancellor. From 1871 to 1890 this was Bismarck. The German state was not a despotism, and the German citizen was not terrorized. The emperor voluntarily imposed upon himself certain restrictions in his relations with his subjects, and there was a widespread belief in Germany that emperor and citizens were united in pursuing common goals. The government was to provide security, order, and a direction in which Germany would move. The citizens were to use this security and this order to develop their talents. The government was "to ensure the unified integration of all social will and action with a view to preserving the social whole and all its essential parts." By such an arrangement, "the whole nation achieves unity and individuality." Bismarck himself, and there is no reason to doubt his sincerity, expressed the argument in these words: "I am convinced that it is the duty of any honest government always to strive for the greatest measure of popular and individual freedom which is compatible with the security and common welfare of the state."

Bismarck assumed, and so did many other Germans, that within the German Empire there could be no meaningful conflict between the rights of the citizen and the rights of the state. The aims of the individual and the state were the same, and any dispute was artificial. There was thus no need for any separation of powers within the state, each watching and checking on the other. There was no reason to distrust the state, for the emperor, the government, the bureaucracy, and the army marched with the people and expressed the aspirations and goals of the people themselves.

For Bismarck, the health and progress of the state, as he saw it, was the principal purpose of his policy. He was not a man who cared about causes or hypothetical principles. His concern was to make the instrument he controlled — first Prussia and then Germany — as strong as possible. In 1881, in a speech in the Reichstag, the German legislative assembly, he expressed very well his basic political program. "I have often acted hastily and without reflection, but when I had time to think I have always asked: What is useful, effective, right, for the fatherland. I have never been a doctrinaire. Liberal, reactionary, conservative — these, I confess, seem to me luxuries. Give me a strong German state, and then ask me whether it should have more or less liberal furnishings, and you'll find that I answer: Yes, I have no fixed opinions, make proposals. Many roads lead to Rome. Sometimes one may rule liberally, and sometimes dictatorially, there are no eternal rules. My only aim has been the creation and consolidation of Germany."

But Germany must exhibit a united will, and there must be agreement on the activities undertaken by the state on behalf of all. Bismarck once asked the rhetorical question: What kind of government would you have if it contained a Catholic, a socialist, and a conservative? At another time he wailed that "political parties will be the ruin of our constitution and our future." Authority must not be fragmented, and this emphasis upon unity forced Bismarck into the attempt to rid Germany of any influence strong enough to compete with him for the allegiance of Germans. He engaged in a long and ultimately fruitless attack upon the Catholic church because he believed that German Catholics could give only a fraction of their allegiance to the German state and must reserve some part of their loyalties to a non-German authority. He harassed Catholicism as a "state within a state" and in 1873 had laws enacted that reduced the disciplinary powers of the Catholic bishops, brought the education of the Catholic clergy under the supervision of the state, made it easy for congregations to secede from the Catholic church, and provided methods whereby there could be appeals made from ecclesiastical courts to secular courts of law. Church leaders who refused to acknowledge the new laws were imprisoned, including the Archbishop of Posen, the Archbishop of Cologne, and the Bishop of Treves. Within Prussia measures were even stricter. All religious orders except those concerned with caring for the sick were ordered dissolved, the state made appointments to vacant church positions, and civil marriage was made compulsory.

Catholics fought back, and instead of weakening the affection of German Catholics for their church, Bismarck's actions strengthened the Catholic community. Bismarck realized that the policy had been a failure, and he retreated. The election of a new Pope in 1878 provided an opportunity to end the struggle between church and state. The anti-Catholic laws were gradually abandoned, and by the latter half of the eighteen-eighties the last legal traces of the struggle had disappeared. But the attempt to suppress Catholic activity had an opposite effect from that desired by Bismarck. A strong Catholic political party became permanent in Germany, and Catholic political leaders were continual irritants to Bismarck. He never overcame his suspicions. In 1884, in a speech, he argued that the Catholic party "has this danger for me. One cannot cooperate with it without selling oneself. One is taken with it completely, and the moment always comes when the question arises: Will you fight now or will you continue to go along with me?" And then he stated the basic problem. One could not trust the Catholics, although many of them were "good honest Germans," because "the center of gravity" of much of Catholic life "lies outside the German Reich."

As Bismarck attempted to root out Catholic influence in Germany, so he moved for generally similar reasons against the socialists. In the eighteen-seventies the socialist party showed an amazing increase in electoral strength, and Bismarck, who saw socialism as another subversive movement designed to weaken the state, attempted to suppress it. He described the socialists as "robbers and thieves," and accused them of wishing to "turn everything in Germany upside down, above all the army and compulsory service, not caring if the Reich is left without defense." In 1878 an anti-socialist law was passed by the Reichstag. The provisions of the law gave the authorities great discretionary powers. Public meetings were banned, political organizations were ordered dissolved, books and other publications were suppressed. Bismarck is reported to have said at the time of the passage of the law: "Now for the pig-sticking," and the law was applied with severity. Leaders of the party were attacked, over 150 periodicals were suppressed, and over 1,500 persons were arrested. The anti-socialist law was renewed at its expiration and again every two years thereafter until 1890.

But, as with the struggle with the Catholics, Bismarck failed. The socialist party continued to grow, and in 1890 the anti-socialist law was allowed to lapse. By 1912 the socialists were the largest single political party in the Reichstag, supported 110 daily newspapers throughout Germany, and had created a nationwide system of fraternal organizations, youth groups, and assorted clubs in which members participated. And, as Bismarck had feared, the socialists did remain an alien group within the society. After Bismarck's death the socialists were still being attacked as "the party of hostility" and as "the deadly enemy of the national state." The socialists were, at least in their doctrine and in their official statements, opposed to Bismarck's Germany. In 1903, a socialist leader stated: "I want to remain the deadly enemy of this bourgeois society and this political order so as to undermine it and, if I can, to eliminate it."

By 1890 Bismarck's relations with the new German emperor William II had become strained. In March of that year he submitted his resignation as chancellor. It was accepted by the emperor, and Bismarck's career as leader of Germany was over. He retired to his estate, where he wrote his memoirs, engaged in a series of rather petty controversies with old and new enemies, and refought old battles for the benefit of the many who came to visit him. In 1898 he died.

In nineteenth-century European history only Napoleon can be compared with Bismarck as an influential and successful political personality. Bismarck gave political meaning to the idea of being German, and he created a prosperous and respected German state. In 1849 a German historian had written that "the power or weakness of Germany determines the fate of Europe." Bismarck's Germany was an important factor in the international stability that characterized Europe during the last quarter of the nineteenth century. Bismarck was not an adventurer, and after the unity of Germany was achieved, his efforts in international affairs were largely directed to maintaining the peace of Europe. He brought about a reconciliation of Germany and Austria, he established alliances with Russia and Italy, and he was always careful to avoid any action that would antagonize England. He knew that France remained embittered by the results of the war of 1870-1871, and he attempted to keep her isolated and without powerful allies. He ridiculed the idea of Germany becoming a colonial power, and he would have nothing to do with any suggestion that Germany enter into naval competition with England. He claimed that Germany was satisfied and had no territorial claims on anyone. When Bismarck retired as chancellor, Germany was the greatest military power in the world, her industrial progress was unmatched by any other country, she was a pioneer in social legislation, and her people were healthy, prosperous, and proud members of an orderly and largely admired nation.

Yet this Germany contained features that detracted from its accomplishments. Bismarck left Germany saddled with a Junker military aristocracy that was a violation of Bismarck's own principles — a state within a state, going its own way with few restraints exercised by the community as a whole. The claim of German military men that they were elevated to austere, dedicated service could not disguise their "hollow greatness," their brutality, and their intellectual barrenness. All Western countries faced the problem of civilian political control and military organization. But in Germany the freedom of the military from civilian direction was almost complete. Bismarck also left the country confronting the perils of political irresponsibility. The emperor was all-powerful, and Germany entered the twentieth century with an unrestrained aristocratic ruler who could threaten the welfare and even the existence of the nation through whim and lack of judgment. As a commentator has maintained "government by an irresponsible monarchy and an agrarian aristocracy was not enough. Bismarck's magnificently brilliant creation was a structure as ephemeral, as temporary, as the genius that created it. It was, indeed, only a puppet show after all, a magical construction that had no healthy life of its own, and that, once it had escaped from the control of its creator, was doomed to self-destruction." The bureaucracy and the army gave an illusion of order that concealed the strange, arbitrary quality of German leadership. In 1912 an Englishman noticed this feature of the German state and said: "When you mount to the peak of this highly organized people, you will find not only confusion, but chaos."

More important than the organizational problem, however, was Bismarck's legacy of state power and individual weakness. Bismarck did make Germany great and the German citizen small. The German state became a "far-seeing guardian of all the interests of the state and people," but individual Germans failed to develop what could be called civil courage, the courage of one's own convictions as a civilian. As a famous German historian wrote in 1899: "In my innermost being and with the best that is in me I have always been a political animal and have always desired to be a citizen. In our nation that is not possible, for with us the individual man, even the best among us, never rises above doing his duty in the ranks and above political fetishism."

Bismarck also left Germany with the dangerous belief in power and force. There appeared no limit to what Germany could do if she willed it. But there must be no "cowardly pacifist mooning" or "silly scruples over legality." Germany must always be the hammer and never the anvil, and she must avoid the "poison of sentimental humanitarianism." Thus he "left Germany with a taste for hero worship and with a tradition of political opportunism and of the unprincipled use of force." Germany became something of a European bully, and her leaders' habit of speaking in terms of force and power grated upon the nerves of other Europeans. As the novelist Joseph Conrad wrote: "The Germanic Tribes had told the whole world in all possible tones carrying conviction, the gently persuasive, the coldly logical; in tones Hegelian, Nietzschean, warlike, pious, cynical, inspired, what they were going to do to the inferior races of the earth, so full of sin and unworthiness." And, although he exaggerated, George Bernard Shaw expressed a common attitude when he wrote that Europe became "sore-headed and fed-up" with Germany. "We were rasped beyond endurance by Prussian militarism and its contempt for us and for human happiness and common sense; and we just rose up and went for it."

Bismarck must be held at least partially responsible for the German feeling of being unique and separate from the rest of Western society. He stimulated the idea that the German people and German culture must be safeguarded against pernicious influences from abroad. German nationalism turned inward, not out upon the world. As a scholar remarked, the Germans were not prepared to contribute to the "highest and most sacred values of mankind, the liberty, honor, right, and dignity of the individual," that great central purpose that drew "all the vital forces of Western civilization together."

Perhaps a fitting summary of Bismarck's career is contained in an article by Max Weber, the German sociologist, written in 1917. "As his political heritage, Bismarck left a nation without political education. . . . Above all, he left a nation without political will, accustomed to permit the great statesman at its head to care for its policy. Moreover, . . . he left a nation accustomed to submit, under the name of constitutional monarchy, to whatever was decided for it, without criticizing the political qualifications of those who now occupied Bismarck's place and who now took the reins of power in their hands."

John Stuart Mill

The nineteenth century was the period of English influence in the world. English territorial possessions stretched around the globe, and it could be said that the sun never set on the British Empire. English commercial success, English law, English clothes, the concept of the

English gentleman were all objects of admiration. The English way of life aimed at power without arrogance, intelligence without pedantry, and freedom without chaos. The English appeared to exhibit what the philosopher Santayana spoke of as "contentment in finitude, fair outward ways, manly perfection, and simplicity." England was also the great defender of political sanity. At the end of the century, when she was engaged in what must be called "a dirty little war" in South Africa, Mark Twain noted: "Every day I write (in my head) bitter articles about it, but I have to stop with that. For England must not fall; it would mean an inundation of Russian and German political degradations which would envelop the globe and steep it in a sort of Middle Age night and slavery which would last till Christ comes again. Even wrong — and she is wrong — England must be upheld. He is an enemy of the human race who speaks against her."

This sanity, this sense of balance, was embodied in the English idea of the liberal state. English liberalism emphasized rationality, tolerance, and a great measure of individual liberty. It was not a dogma to which human nature was to be bent, but rather an expression of the wishes of free men, who by joining together in a community did not abandon their claims as individuals. Definite opinions are reached by persuasion, free debate, and the exercise of reason. "The aims of liberalism have been to embody in life and thought the truth that while man is a social being, he does not exist merely for the social whole. . . . The main concern of liberal thought and policy was to provide protection against the bias of government to judge all human activities by their amenability to the sole purpose of social solidarity." The political instruments of liberalism were representative government, freedom of speech and conscience, and regard for the fair and reasonable law. The nation should attempt to be the expression of "human liberty and spontaneity," and liberal government was "government by consent — government by mutual compromise and compact."

It was John Stuart Mill who, in his writings and his activities, provided the best example of the nineteenth-century liberal thinker in action. Born in 1806 in London, Mill was the outstanding member of that group known as the Philosophic Radicals or the Utilitarians or the advanced liberal party. He wrote extensively on various subjects. In 1843 he published his *A System of Logic*. This volume was followed over the years by a series of books that expressed the liberal point of view. In 1848 he published *Principles of Political Economy*, in 1859 *On Liberty*, in 1860 *Considerations on Representative Government*, in 1863 *Utilitarianism*, and in 1869 *The Subjection of Women*. He was for a time editor of one of the leading liberal journals in England and served for two years as a member of the House of Commons in the British Parliament. After his death in 1873, his *Autobiography* was published.

Mill recognized the necessity and the danger of nationalism. He accepted the argument that it "is in general a necessary condition of free institutions, that the boundaries of government should coincide in the main with those of nationalities." Individual rights have little meaning outside of the organized national state, and "free institutions are next to impossible in a country made up of different nationalities." But nationalism "makes men indifferent to the rights and interests of any portion of the human species, save that which is called by the same name and speaks the same language." It also promotes false claims against the individual and attempts to change him into a pliant tool to be used for some obscure and ill-defined purpose. Nationalism usurps prerogatives that do not rightly belong to it and thus threatens the well-being of those it pretends to represent.

The nation was a useful and necessary form of human existence, but it always drew its power and its authority from those who constituted it. Mill realized that the relationship of the nation and the individual was not easily defined, but throughout his life he defended the proposition that the nation must, in some way, reflect the cumulative and practical interests of its citizens and must not acquire an independent life of its own. The purpose of the state was basically utilitarian and not the pursuit of its own glory or its own power or its own fate. Mill defined this utilitarianism as "the creed which accepts as the foundation of morals utility, or the greatest happiness principle, holds that actions are right in proportion as they tend to promote happiness, wrong as they tend to produce the reverse of happiness." For Mill the "general tendency" of men's activities is toward "a better and happier state," and any national government must accept as its basic and only purpose the forwarding of the happiness of its citizens.

In his discussion of the liberal state, Mill addressed himself to three principal questions: First, To what authority should people be subjected? Second, How are people to be persuaded to obey this authority? And third, How are abuses of this authority to be checked?

In 1831 Mill posed the question: "Where is the authority which commands confidence or deserves it?" He acknowledged that the old, traditional patterns of authority had been destroyed. "At all other periods there exists a large body of received doctrines covering nearly the whole field of the moral relationships of man and which no one thinks of questioning, backed as it is by the authority of all, or nearly all, persons supposed to possess knowledge enough to qualify them for giving an opinion on the subject. This state of things does not now exist in the civilised world. . . ."

Upon what basis then can any claim to authority be made? Mill denied that any political leader had an undisputed right to his prerogatives but must continually prove himself in order to exercise political power. Only those who had arrived at their ethical or political beliefs as a result of "articulate reflection" and "disinterested motivation" can claim authority. No one supporting what Mill and his friends called "sinister interests" could demand recognition as a proper authority, nor could such recognition be given to any who attempted to hold power "by platitude or mediocrity or ignorance or subservience to any popular delusion." Legitimate authority accepted limitations, abandoned claims to all-knowing wisdom, and presented itself as an instrument for the convenience and utilitarian well-being of the citizens of the nation.

The purpose of political organization was not to develop state power but to forward the welfare of individuals. Mill once wrote: "In England there has always been more liberty, but worse organization, while in other countries there is better organization, but less liberty." And he was prepared to accept this condition. There were actions the state should take. The law must be reformed, the "mouldering fabric of monopoly and tyranny" must be destroyed, and measures must be taken against "flagrant, social injustice." Mill was himself a radical reformer. He was for the extension of the franchise, he advocated the emancipation of women, he sympathized with the efforts of the working class to improve its condition, he was hostile to "landlordism," and he supported public and secular education. But these were practical tasks to be accomplished, and the results could be measured by the observable increase in the happiness and health of the people. Moreover, they were actions that allowed citizens better to engage in their own self-improvement and to handle their own affairs. They cleared the way for the development of the individual, and "modern nations will have to learn the lesson that the well-being of a people must exist by means of the justice and self-government of the individual citizen."

To the question of how the people of England will come to accept the necessary national authority, Mill had a general answer. Men must act "rationally," and "the prospect of the future depends on the degree to which they can be made rational beings." Active participation by all in the affairs of the country must be encouraged, and those in positions of authority must show that they are acting reasonably and not out of self-interest or on behalf of those who claim special favors. They must not allow themselves to become the tools of any special-interest group — the landlords, the commercial classes, the aristocracy. All political, social, and economic arrangements within a society are, for

Mill, relative, not absolute. They are "merely provisional," and government should not become the advocate of any political, social, or economic doctrine. In the past governments had become the slave to some ideology and had thus acted irrationally and harmfully. "They have not held the balance fairly between human beings, but have heaped impediments upon some, to give advantage to others; they have purposely fostered inequalities, and prevented all from starting fair in the race." Such governments could not expect to receive the allegiance of their citizens.

For their part individuals must prepare themselves for participation in national life. They must acquire "convictions as to what is right and wrong, useful and pernicious," and such convictions must be "deeply engraven on the feelings by early education" and maintained by efforts at continual and constant self-improvement. Responsibility for progress is always individual. In 1847 Mill wrote that "well-being cannot be secured by passive qualities alone" and "generally speaking, what is done for people benefits them only when it assists them in what they do for themselves." The state cannot act as a protective parent but must leave the individual free to pursue his own improvement. This was true of all classes of citizens. Even the "poor have come out of leading strings and cannot any longer be governed and treated like children. To their own qualities must now be commended the care of their destiny."

Mill's most important contribution to liberalism was his discussion of the restraints that must be placed upon authority. He continually made reference to this problem throughout his life, and in 1859 he published *On Liberty*, his classic statement defending the freedom of the individual. It was this publication that moved the American poet Walt Whitman to begin his *Democratic Vistas* with a tribute to Mill. Whitman recommended what he called "Mill's profound essay on Liberty" and agreed with Mill's argument that individual variety and the self-development of the many were the necessary conditions "for a truly grand nationality."

In his essay Mill stated that individual liberty consists of the following: the liberty of the inward domain of the conscience; absolute freedom of opinion on all subjects, practical or speculative, scientific, moral, or theological; liberty of tastes and pursuits; and liberty to unite with others for any purpose not involving harm to others. "No society in which these liberties are not, on the whole, respected, is free, whatever may be its form of government. The only freedom which deserves the name is that of pursuing our own good in our own way, so long as we do not attempt to deprive others of theirs, or impede their efforts to obtain it."

Mill knew that political authority would always attempt to impose its beliefs upon the citizens and that there was a tendency in any society to hustle its members toward some mythical goal, toward some consensus that would iron out differences. He knew, too, that this urge to unity is justified by the argument that it is for the benefit of those being subjected to the drive for unanimity. But for Mill this argument was fallacious. "The only purpose for which power can be rightfully exercised over any member of a civilized community, against his will, is to prevent harm to others. His own good, either physical or moral, is not sufficient warrant." There was no place in the liberal state for those who because of their own beliefs felt justified in demanding adherence to some code of belief or behavior. "The only part," Mill writes, "of the conduct of anyone, for which he is amenable to society, is that which concerns others. In the part which merely concerns himself, his independence is absolute. Over himself, over his own body and mind, the individual is sovereign."

In Mill's view the right to individual difference was so important that he was prepared to defend human eccentricity. "In this age the mere example of non-conformity, the mere refusal to bend the knee to custom, is itself a service. Precisely because the tyranny of opinion is such as to make eccentricity a reproach, it is desirable, in order to break through that tyranny, that people should be eccentric." In fact, Mill goes so far as to insist that eccentricity and extreme or uncommon opinions are directly related to the health of the society and to argue that "the amount of eccentricity in a society has generally been proportional to the amount of genius, mental vigour and moral courage which it contains." He admitted "a large tolerance for one-eyed men, provided their eye is a penetrating one: If they saw more, they probably would not see so keenly, nor so eagerly pursue one course of inquiry. Almost all rich veins of original and striking speculation have been opened by systematic half-thinkers." Only if diverse ideas and opinions are allowed can a nation possess that "rich diversity" that is the mark of a progressive, on-going community.

As expressed by John Stuart Mill, liberalism was not a method for drawing hard and fast rules of political behavior or for defining institutional patterns. In his *Autobiography* he stated that the problem of politics was not to set forth "model institutions, but principles from which the institutions suitable to any given circumstances might be deduced." This attitude became the mark of the liberal society. Thus, in the late eighteen-forties, an English statesman attempted to define the essence of the liberal approach. "It is by comparing opinions — by a collision of opinions — by rubbing one man's opinions against those of another and seeing which is the hardest and will bear the friction best — that men, in or out of office, can most justly arrive at the knowledge of what is most advantageous to the interests of the whole community." Here there is no attempt to state what the specific goals of good government should be. One is content to point out that they are truth and justice and that all we know is that the best way to reach them is by free inquiry.

In the minds of many in the nineteenth century, and even more in the twentieth, the liberal state was no state at all. It was only an atomistic collection of disparate elements that do not and cannot come together in any meaningful unity. Mill ended *On Liberty* with the words: "The worth of the state in the long run is the worth of the individuals composing it; and a state which dwarfs its men in order that they may be more docile instruments in its hands even for beneficial purposes — will find that with small men no great thing can be accomplished." This statement is far more a restriction than a charge to the state to undertake action in order to fulfill some historical purpose. It has none of the customary emotion-laden appeal expected of any nationalistic doctrine, and it points out no paths of glory whereby the citizens of any nation can march in steady ranks toward a promised destiny.

English liberalism was basically a program for small victories and many disappointments. This Mill knew. In summing up his life, he wrote: "In England, I had seen and continued to see many of the opinions of my youth obtain general recognition, and many of the reforms in institutions, for which I had through life contended, either effected or in the course of being so. But these changes had been attended with much less benefit to human well-being than I should formerly have anticipated, because they had produced very little improvement in that which all real amelioration in the lot of mankind depends on, their intellectual and moral state." A scholar of our own day has rightly said of Mill that he combined "an enthusiastic belief in democratic government with most pessimistic apprehensions as to what democracy is likely to do." As early as 1837, in a letter to a friend, Mill commented upon his disappointments and then expressed what could be called the natural conclusion of the liberal: "So we must linger on, each man doing for the present such good work as lies nearer his hand."

To "linger on" hardly seems a political slogan designed to rally men to any cause. Yet, contrary to what many have continually predicted, the idea of the liberal society and the liberal state persisted in the West, particularly in the English-speaking countries, and the liberal vocabulary became an important part of the speech pattern of politics. Political aims are usually expressed in liberal terms, even though the speaker may be insincere or may have twisted the meaning of the terms out of all recognition. It has been remarkably easy to scoff at the liberal belief in the reality of "human liberty and spontaneity," as it has been easy to mock what has been called "the bedrock decency of the human being." "Collective mediocrity" and "sinister interests" are as powerful, or perhaps even more powerful, than in the middle of the nineteenth century. But liberalism has shown amazing stamina and remains perhaps the only living political tradition in the West. Nor is this only because almost all Western nations have accepted some form of liberal institutions. The liberal attitude may at times appear anemic. But the moral outlook of liberalism has been lodged in the mind of what we can call the common citizen, and while he is not sure of the definition of liberalism, is often confused, and many times oversimplifies and warps the liberal principles, he senses that his own future is closely tied to that of the liberal outlook.

Over sixty years after Mill's death, another Englishman George Orwell described the face of one of Mill's contemporaries Charles Dickens. "It is the face of a man who is always fighting against something, but who fights in the open and is not frightened, the face of a man who is *generously* angry — in other words of a 19th-century liberal, a free intelligence, a type hated with equal hatred by all the smelly little orthodoxies which are now contending for our souls." Mill would have been happy to have accepted such a description of himself.

The Dreyfus Affair

On October 15, 1894, a French army officer named Alfred Dreyfus was arrested in Paris. He was charged with betraying French military secrets to the Germans. A court-martial of December 22 found him guilty of treason, and he was condemned to dishonorable discharge from the army, to deportation from France, and to exile for life in a prison colony. Early in 1895 Dreyfus was transported to Devil's Island off the coast of South America.

Thus began a historical drama that was to last for twelve years and was to subject French society to almost intolerable strains. The question of Dreyfus' guilt or innocence became a question of the nature and future of France herself. All the old controversies that had dogged France during the nineteenth century were sparked anew, and all the old wounds were ripped open. Advocates of the Revolution were set against those who one hundred years after the events of the seventeen-nineties would not accept the principles of the Revolution. The city was again set against the countryside, the clergy against the free-thinkers, the demands of the state against the rights of the individual. During the Dreyfus Affair long-time friendships were ruptured, the courts of the land became suspect, the excesses of anti-semitism, anti-clericalism, anti-intellectualism, and military arrogance appeared, political careers were ruined, and fear, violence, and hostility became a part of French national life.

The Dreyfus Affair occurred against a background of continuing political crisis in France. The humiliating defeat by Germany in 1870-1871 had been followed by a series of disasters, and in the eyes of many France seemed to be a society that was falling apart. There was little loyalty to political leaders, and the republican form of government seemed to be without supporters. In 1889 the republic was almost overthrown by an adventurer, General Georges Boulanger, who failed, in large part because of his own lack of nerve, or, perhaps, because as a French politician said of him, "he had the soul of a second lieutenant," and did not know how to take advantage of his opportunity. In 1892 the country was stunned by the latest and most revealing of a series of financial scandals in which important businessmen were implicated. The Dreyfus Affair was thus "a sore that broke out suddenly on a sick body."

Soon after Dreyfus was transported to Devil's Island, rumors of irregularities in the trial began circulating throughout France. Military and civil authorities regarded the case as closed; but others disagreed and demanded that Dreyfus be given a new trial. Politicians such as Georges Clemenceau, scholars such as Émile Duclaux, the Director of the Pasteur Institute, the labor leader and socialist Jean Jaurès, and writers such as Anatole France, Marcel Proust, and Charles Péguy claimed that the court-martial of Dreyfus had been a mockery and that the authorities were guilty of acting illegally. As Jaurès said: "Whether Dreyfus is guilty or innocent I do not care. But what I am concerned about is the tyranny of the sword. The military courts should not be allowed to seize without legal safeguards any citizen on any pretext. This is the question at stake, the real and only one."

Broadly speaking, two groups of Frenchmen found themselves opposing each other on the Dreyfus question. On one side were the anti-Dreyfusards, those who were opposed to any further consideration of the case. Here were believers in what was called the security of the state and who argued that an injustice against an individual, while reprehensible, must not be allowed to call into question the integrity of the constituted authorities. The welfare of the country and confidence in authority were much more important than righting a suspected wrong against an individual citizen. The anti-Dreyfusards also included many who saw in the attempts to question authority only another manifestation of their suspicions that traditional France was being undermined by socialism, secularism, and atheistic intellectualism. Extreme nationalists, conservative army officers and politicians, large numbers of the Catholic clergy, and anti-semites, who found an outlet for their prejudices due to the fact that Dreyfus was a Jew, believed that any reconsideration of the Dreyfus case was certain to weaken France.

The opposing group consisted of those who regarded themselves as the defenders of the great principles of the Revolution. Many anti-clerical intellectuals and supporters of rationalism, who were hostile to any form of national or religious mystique, pressed for a reconsideration of the case. Regarding themselves as defenders of individual liberty and the rule of law, a large number of teachers and university professors, students, and writers became known as Dreyfusards.

The controversy was carried on with extreme bitterness. Duels were fought. It is reported that a young man in proposing to a lady asked her to inform him as to her views on the case. Newspapers kept tempers aroused with reports of rumors and disclosures and with personal attacks. A well-known cartoon of the period is in two panels. The first pictures a pleasant gathering where a group of people are enjoying themselves at dinner. The caption reads: "They have not yet spoken of it." The second panel shows the room in disorder, with the former congenial companions trading insults and resorting to physical violence. The caption for the second panel reads: "They spoke of it."

The attacks upon the Dreyfusards were particularly vicious. Jews and Protestants were criticized as men who were not true patriots, and those who supported Dreyfus were denounced as traitors. One of those who was the target of such attacks complained that "heroism was needed even to utter the word justice. To protest against the violation of right was made into a crime, and to doubt the infallibility of a military court was considered treason." Intellectuals, in particular, were attacked by the anti-Dreyfusards. It was charged that the natural vigor of the nation was being destroyed by excessive intellectualism, and intellectuals were condemned as "enemies of the French soul." For many, intellectuals were opponents of a healthy national instinct, and they were denounced as "those presumptuous pedants who take themselves for the aristocrats of the mind." In a speech in February,

1898, the President of France ridiculed the pretensions of what he called "the intellectual elite," and another anti-Dreyfusard announced that "we must watch the university. It contributes to the destruction of French principles."

The Dreyfusards defended themselves by arguing that they were spokesmen of the real France, the France of liberty, equality, and fraternity, and that their opponents were obscurantists who wished to substitute the priest's cowl and the military sword for the Rights of Man and the Citizen. "France, poisoned with fear and hatred by a small group of men, was losing its honor. Innocent France was being murdered," remarked a Dreyfus sympathizer, and another Dreyfusard put forward the claim that "patriotism requires a fatherland which cannot exist without justice." The Catholic church was attacked for involving itself in politics, and the army was denounced as a group that had not accepted the republican principles that guided the political life of the country. Clemenceau probably expressed this idea most dramatically in one of his many speeches. "France is now a country with no security for the liberty, life, or honor of her citizens. A horde ganged up on us, a praetorian guard, a host of monks who have destroyed right, justice, and law and have savagely scorched all that forty centuries of human effort have accomplished. They denounce us as without a country. They speak more truly than they realize, for they have taken away our homeland."

What is usually regarded as the turning point of the Dreyfus Affair occurred in January, 1898. In Clemenceau's newspaper *Aurora*, the novelist Émile Zola published an open letter to the President of the republic. In his letter Zola made his points directly and brutally. He spoke of "a supreme slap at all truth, all justice," of "a malignant rabble of true culprits," of "the fearful miscarriage of justice," and of "the shocking denial of justice that renders all France ill." Briefly he reviewed the entire Dreyfus case, and he included in his letter a series of accusations against particular individuals who had been involved in the court-martial and subsequent actions. "I accuse Colonel du Paty de Clam . . . ," "I accuse General Mercier . . . ," "I accuse General Billot . . . ," "I accuse General Pellieux and Major Ravary . . . ," "I accuse the three handwriting experts . . . ," "I accuse the War Office . . . ," "I accuse the first court-martial. . . ." Zola realized that he would undoubtedly be arrested for publishing the letter, and he ended: "The action I take here is simply a revolutionary step designed to hasten the explosion of truth and justice. I have one passion only, for light, in the name of humanity which has borne so much and has a right to happiness. My burning protest is only the cry of my soul. Let them dare to carry me to the court of appeals, and let there be an inquest in the full light of day! I am waiting."

Zola's letter, which had been headed "I Accuse," had an electrifying effect. Over 300,000 copies of that issue of *Aurora* were sold, and over 30,000 letters and telegrams from inside and outside France were sent in response. Mark Twain wrote in the New York *Herald* of his "profound respect and admiration for Zola. Such cowards, hypocrits, and flatterers as the members of the military and ecclesiastical courts the world could produce by the million every year. But it takes five centuries to produce a Joan of Arc or a Zola." But there was also adverse reaction. One of the anti-Dreyfusards asked why Zola didn't "mind his own business? The letter *I Accuse* is a monument of stupidity, presumption, and incongruity. The interference of this novelist in a matter of military justice seems to me no less impertinent than, let us say, the intervention of a police captain in a problem of syntax or versification. . . ." Crowds throughout France burned Zola's article in public and hung him in effigy. In Paris the streets filled with mobs shouting "Death to Zola! Death to Dreyfus!"

The government could not let Zola go unanswered. He had attacked specific individuals and had accused the government itself of being involved in forgery, collusion, and the suppression of evidence. Zola was charged with criminal libel and was brought to trial. Clemenceau acted as one of his defense counsels, and in his speech to the court he set forth clearly the heart of the argument as the Dreyfusards saw it. He contended that the aims of civilian society and the military were different. "The principle of civilian society is liberty and justice, while that of the military is discipline, obedience, and order." Any conflict of these opposing principles must be resolved in favor of the civilian idea. "The army belongs to the people. It must embody the same principles as does the nation. If the civilian society in its anxiety over national defense fell into the slavery of the military, then the soil perhaps could be defended, but morally the nation would be lost. By forfeiting the principles of justice and liberty, we would give up what, to the entire world, has been the glory and honor of France. There is no civilian honor and no military honor. There is only honor for all." And he concluded: "Gentlemen, we represent the law, tolerance, the traditions of the French spirit."

In spite of Clemenceau's eloquence, Zola was found guilty, and in order to avoid imprisonment, he fled to England. The arguments for a re-examination of the Dreyfus case had become too strong to ignore, however. Much of the evidence used against Dreyfus at his court-martial was suspect, and an intelligence officer important to the case committed suicide under strange circumstances. The government reluctantly reopened the case, which was sent to the High Court of Appeals. A strange collection of secret documents was turned over to the court. Some documents that were thought to be of great importance in prov-

ing the treason of Dreyfus could not be found, while others did not provide the evidence that had been claimed for them. The High Court of
Appeals declared the court-martial of 1894 void and ordered that Dreyfus be brought back to the country and given a new trial.

The new court-martial was a farce. Those military men who had
committed themselves to a belief in the guilt of Dreyfus refused to
acknowledge any error in the case. Dreyfus was again found guilty of
high treason by a vote of five judges to two. But the court announced
that it had found what it called "extenuating circumstances," and
Dreyfus was condemned to a mere ten years in prison. The mystery of
how there could be a verdict of treason but with extenuating circumstances was too much. Such a judgment could not be let stand, and on
September 19, 1899, Dreyfus was pardoned. The Minister of War
issued an Order of the Day to the army which read: "The incident is
closed." On July 12, 1906, the High Court of France set aside the sentence of the court-martial and declared that the verdict of guilty had
been in error. Ten days later, on July 22, a military parade took place in
Paris. Dreyfus was given back his rank and restored to good standing
in the army. A crowd had gathered, and as Dreyfus left, a cry went up
of "Long live Dreyfus! Long live justice!" It is reported that Dreyfus
raised his hand in acknowledgment and then disappeared into historical obscurity. The Dreyfus Affair was over.

Alfred Dreyfus had been the victim of a miscarriage of justice. But
those who became involved in the Affair were convinced that the issue
was more than the innocence or guilt of one man. "France must find herself again," argued Clemenceau, and Dreyfusard and anti-Dreyfusard
agreed that the heart of the controversy was a dispute over what kind
of nation France was to become.

At the funeral of Émile Zola in 1902, Anatole France, a leading Dreyfusard, said: "France is the country of reason and of the pondering
spirit, the country of just judges and humane philosophers." No
doubt this was part of the truth. But the Dreyfus Affair clearly showed
that France was more than this. France consisted as well of anti-semitism, of chauvinism, of deep suspicions, and of a neurotic longing for
security. As important as anything, the Affair illustrated the terrifying
dilemma inherent in nineteenth-century Western nationalism. It posed
the questions of what was national strength and what were the attributes that were important to a national society.

This question of nationalism was at the heart of the Dreyfus Affair.
With some simplification, one could say that the serious anti-Dreyfusards, as separated from the simple Jew-baiters and the gutter hooli-
gans, were those who identified the strength of the nation with authority, order, and unity, even at the cost of individual liberty and justice.
Patriotism was a certain unquestioning loyalty that did not depend

upon intellectual conviction or the resolution of all doubts. The greatest threat to France, in this view, came not from a possible case of injustice but from divisions within the nation that weakened authority and confused the citizen. The army, the courts, the church, and all the institutions that provided security must not be undermined. The greatness of a nation was directly related to its military power, to the unexamined allegiance of its people, and to the unity of the society. As an anti-Dreyfusard expressed it: "When I speak of the necessity for a nation to arm itself with power I mean the material power that does not reason but imposes itself — the power of which the army is the most forceful argument of statesmen and nations." Anything that weakened such power, and thus the security of France, was treason.

The Dreyfusards, of course, had a different view of what constituted national strength. They saw that often those who claimed to speak for nationalism and patriotism possessed only a surface virtue. Marcel Proust wrote in 1906 that the "contrast that exists on the one hand between the culture, the intellectual distinction, and even the glitter of the uniforms of these people and their moral infamy on the other is frightening." The Dreyfusards claimed their victory as an indication of the true greatness of France, a country that did not need to sacrifice her great principles in her search for power and security. In his best rhetoric, Clemenceau put the meaning of the Dreyfus Affair in its clearest perspective. And, in doing so, he also posed what was a basic problem of Western nationalism. "A country which bases its honor on acquitting a criminal and attacking an innocent may call itself republic or monarchy, socialist or imperialist or democratic, may have a parliament, city councils, ministers, judges, hospitals, and theaters, all the external facades of civilization; it may construct railroads, conquer territories from defenseless Negroes, make use of electricity and the telephone, and beat the drums of exhibitions to book the hotels. All this will be but dust in the storms to come. Without firm foundations in thought, without the moral cement of right and justice, no society can prevail."

SUGGESTIONS FOR FURTHER READING

The usual method of approaching modern Western history is by way of political events, and the study of national states. For the student who desires to get his bearings on the subject, Carlton J. H. Hayes' Essays on Nationalism (1926; reprinted 1966) is still an excellent introduction. K. R. Minogue's Nationalism (1967) is a good short summary. Readable political surveys of national history are Paul A. Gagnon, France since 1789 *(1964) and Koppel S. Pinson,* Modern Germany: Its History and Civilization *(1966). Golo Mann's* The History of Germany since 1789 *(1968) is a fascinating study.*

A great deal of scholarship has been done on the problem of German nationalism. Excellent examples are Georg G. Iggers, The German Conception of History: The National Tradition of Historical Thought from Herder to the Present *(1968), Richard W. Sterling,* Ethics in a World of Power: The Political Ideas of Friedrich Meinecke *(1958), and Louis L. Snyder,* German Nationalism: The Tragedy of a People *(1952).*

Any good history of Germany will devote a substantial portion to Bismarck, and the works mentioned above may be consulted. A. J. P. Taylor's Bismarck *(1955) is a well-written, alive biography, while Otto Pflanze,* Bismarck and the Development of Germany *(1963), is a thorough, balanced study. Background material on Mill and English liberalism may be found in Crane Brinton,* English Political Thought in the Nineteenth Century *(1933), E. Halévy,* The Growth of Philosophic Radicalism *(1938), and Harold Laski,* The Rise of European Liberalism *(1936). Good specialized studies include Maurice Cowling,* Mill and Liberalism *(1963), and Joseph Hamburger,* Intellectuals in Politics: John Stuart Mill and the Philosophic Radicals *(1965). Nicholas Halasz,* Captain Dreyfus: The Story of a Mass Hysteria *(1955), is a fast-moving narrative account of the Dreyfus Affair. Three recently published books provide depth to the subject: Douglas Johnson,* France and the Dreyfus Affair *(1966), Harry Kedward,* The Dreyfus Affair: Catalyst for Tensions in French Society *(1965), and Betty Schechter,* The Dreyfus Affair: A National Scandal *(1965).*

The Battery, New York, 1855 detail, Samuel B. Waugh, Museum of the City of New York.

7

Europe, the United States, and Russia

1796   George Washington's Farewell Address. Traditionally, if somewhat erroneously, the address has been regarded as a repudiation of Europe.

1801-   Reign of Tsar Alexander I in Russia. Alexander was influenced
1825   in the early years of his reign by Western liberal ideas and initiated plans to modernize and liberalize the Russian state along Western lines. Most of these plans were abandoned.

1815   Holy Alliance proposed by Tsar Alexander I and ultimately agreed to by all important European powers except Britain. The basis of the Alliance was a declaration of Christian principles that were to guide rulers in relations with their subjects and with each other. The Alliance was never taken seriously by other European political leaders.

1816   Nicholas Karamzin's *History of the Russian State*. The first important historical argument that Russia and Western Europe were incompatible. Russia was established order and an expression of the true Christian faith, while West Europe was disorder, revolution, instability, and irreligion.

1823   Enunciation of the Monroe Doctrine by the United States. A statement that the American continents were no longer open to colonization or control by European powers.

1825-   Reign of Tsar Nicholas I. A repressive period often described as
1855   one of "orthodoxy, autocracy, and nationality."

1830-1831	Polish revolt against Russian rule. The revolt was crushed, and a policy of Russification was introduced into Poland.
1835	Alexis de Tocqueville's *Democracy in America*. The best known study of America by a European.
1836	Publication of Peter Chaadaev's "Philosophical Letters." A statement that Russia's past and present were largely meaningless and that she must become part of a greater European civilization. Insisted that Russia "has so far been a part of geography rather than history."
1837	Ralph Waldo Emerson's "The American Scholar." A famous argument that the United States should develop its own intellectual tradition and not rely upon Europe.
1843	Marquis de Custine's *Russia in 1839*. This report of a short stay in Russia set a common standard by which many Western Europeans regarded Russia as a despotic, barbarian society.
1846-1848	Oregon treaty with Great Britain and ceding of California by Mexico completed westward expansion of the United States.
1848-1849	Intervention of Russia in Hungary to put down revolutionary movement prompted a wave of anti-Russian feelings in Western Europe.
1853-1856	Crimean War. Britain and France thwarted Russia's attempt to increase her influence in the Near East.
1857	Formation of the Slavonic Society in Moscow. Marked the beginning of a movement to claim Russian leadership of the Slav peoples.
1864-1870	Period of reforms in Russia in areas of local government, the judiciary, and taxation.
1869	Nicholas Danilevskii published *Russia and Europe*. An attempt to show "the fatal consequences of this Westernization or Europeanization, and how far it is the origin of the disease from which Russia's social body suffers, a disease which is the source of all our social evils."
1877-1878	Russian war with Turkey and then the Congress of Berlin—dominated by Britain and Germany—stalled Russian attempts to penetrate Balkans and Near East.

1888   James Bryce's *The American Commonwealth*. The best known and most comprehensive nineteenth-century study of American politics and government by a European.

1893   Frederick Jackson Turner's "The Significance of the Frontier in American History." Probably the most influential and controversial exposition of the historical uniqueness of the American experience. According to Turner, European influences were minor compared with those of the frontier.

1894   Constance Garnett began her translations of nineteenth-century Russian literary masterpieces into English. The view most Englishmen and Americans have of Russian literature is derived from reading her translations.

1898   Spanish-American War "established the United States as a world power" and extended "the sphere of her personal interests and contacts."

1898   Formation of the *World of Art,* a periodical and also a movement that introduced Western artistic ideas into Russia. In the next two decades the Russians themselves became important contributors to the modernist movement.

1904-   Russian-Japanese War. Russian defeat is usually regarded as the
1905   first military setback to a European power by a non-European.

1905   As a result of disorders and strikes, the tsar granted a constitution that called for an elected legislature and guaranteed civil liberties.

1913   The International Exhibit of Modern Art, better known as the Armory Show, held in New York City. Introduced cubism, fauvism, and modernism to the United States. The exhibit aroused strong opposition but was instrumental in stimulating American artists to join the European modern art movement.

1915   Van Wyck Brooks' *America's Coming of Age*. A widely read plea for the United States to abandon its false and derivative facade and become an example of "a fresh democratic ideal."

Modern Western civilization has been largely a creation of European genius and European experience, and Western man was, and in important ways remains, European man. But in the nineteenth century Europe became increasingly involved with non-European societies, and this involvement raised questions about the scope and nature of European civilization. Could those who were not European, and specifically West European, become active participants in Western culture? Could European values and institutions be transferred to other parts of the world? Did non-European societies pose threats to the civilization developed by Europeans? These questions were particularly important as Europeans considered their relationships to the United States and Russia, countries which possessed ambiguous but significant connections with Europe, were influenced by it, and, in turn, exerted powerful influences upon Europe itself.

Since the late eighteenth century some Europeans had sensed that the future of Europe would be affected by the United States and Russia. Predictions of such a future were usually gloomy, and it was suggested that Europe would ultimately be ground "between two millstones," be destroyed by either "the American plague" or "the Russian cholera." As early as 1790 the German Melchior Grimm wrote: "Two empires will divide between them . . . all the advantages of civilization, power, genius, letters, arts, armaments and industry: Russia in the east, and America, which has become free in our own time, in the west. The rest of us, the peoples of the nucleus, will have become too degraded, too debased, to remember what we were, save for some vague and inexact traditions." This theme of a threatened Europe was to appear again and again. Napoleon, in exile on St. Helena, predicted that the world would soon be "the American Republic or the Russian universal monarchy." In 1840 the German poet Heinrich Heine stated his agreement with Napoleon and wrote: "What a discouraging prophecy! It opens up a terrible prospect. . . . What a future! The best we can hope for is to die of boredom as republicans!" The French literary critic Sainte-Beuve noted in 1847 that "there are only two peoples left. Russia is still barbarian, but large. . . . Old Europe will have to reckon with this youth. The other youth is America. . . . The future of the world is there, between these two powers."

These predictions of decline were usually voiced by those who had become discouraged by political events in Europe and wished to relate their personal disenchantment to a broader historical disaster.

Discontented aristocrats and frustrated conservatives and radicals found it convenient and satisfying to translate their own disappointment into prophecies of calamities. Actually, during the century neither Russia nor the United States posed any overt political or military threat to Europe. Both were largely involved in internal affairs, in what a Russian historian has called "the rough, preparatory toil of civilization." Neither had the inclination or the power to interfere significantly in European politics. But their potential strength and influence did require Europeans to consider them and did raise the wider question of the relationship of European civilization to the rest of the world.

The Promise and Threat of America

America had been settled by Europeans, and it was fairly easy to enumerate the habits and attitudes that had been carried to the New World. European political ideas, technology, standards of conduct, languages, religious interpretations, and cultural activities were securely rooted in American life. During the nineteenth century educated Americans read European literature, especially English literature, and philosophy, listened to European music, and carried on a continual dialogue with Europeans over questions of law, religion, and politics. Americans were well aware of their intellectual and cultural debt to Europe, and as Ralph Waldo Emerson wrote: "All American manners, language, and writings are derivative. It is a tax we pay for the splendid inheritance of English literature." There were matters of contention between the United States and the European powers. Quarrels with the British — over the boundary of the Oregon territory, the supplying of ships to the Confederate States during the American Civil War, and conflicting interests in Central and South America — continued throughout the century. But whatever the specific problem and the international irritation, Americans recognized a kinship with Europeans, and particularly with the British, that they did not have with inhabitants in other parts of the world.

This relationship was, however, influenced by the American belief that the United States should be a society different from those in the Old World. American independence was seen in significant respects to have been a rejection of Europe and a new departure in men's history. In his Farewell Address in 1796 George Washington stated that the United States had no interest in Europe's historical controversies and advised his countrymen to remain free of "the toils of European ambition, rivalship, interest, humor, or caprice," and to avoid "interweaving our destiny with that of any part of Europe." Washington's words were interpreted by many Americans as an invitation to reject Europe. "The true principle of American policy," declared the orator Edward Everett in 1824, "to which the whole spirit of our system, not less than the geographical features of our country invites us, is separation from Europe," and Americans did acquire the habit of regarding the United States as the new Jonathan as opposed to Europe the old Adam.

This sense of separation was strengthened throughout the century by the desires of millions of immigrants to cut their ties to the countries they had left and to change the conditions of their lives. For such people the United States was the "thirteen golden gates open to the victims of intolerance and despotism." Thomas Hulme, an English farmer who came to America in the early nineteenth century, announced that he had "bid an everlasting adieu to Boroughmongers, Sinecure placemen and placewomen, pensioned Lords and Ladies, Standing Armies in time of peace, and (rejoice, oh my children!) to a hireling, tithe-devouring Priesthood." A suspicion, and even hatred, of certain European institutions and political practices entered into American national life. Generations of Irish immigrants carried to America their animosity toward the British, while large numbers of Germans and Russians had rejected what they thought of as the bureaucratic-military political organizations of their native lands. The Jews and most of those coming from southern and southeast Europe had little to look back to, and while some — the Italians and the Greeks, for example — retained a sentimental attachment to their birthplaces and continued to speak their native languages and to retain some of their native customs, they expected to embark upon a new life in America.

Americans were also in search of a national identity and were anxious to stress the distinctive characteristics of their history and to ignore those that might detract from a sense of American individuality. Political leaders, businessmen, and intellectuals seized upon every opportunity to point out that the United States was a unique society and that her future and her fate were not bound to Europe. Almost every important American historian emphasized the differences between the Old World and the New. Early in the century George Bancroft argued that "Nothing came from Europe but a free people," who, "like Moses," had "escaped from Egyptian bondage to the wilderness, that God might there give them the pattern of the tabernacle." Near the century's end Frederick Jackson Turner presented his well-known interpretation where he contended that American democracy "was not carried in the *Susan Constant* to Virginia, nor in the *Mayflower* to Plymouth. It came out of the American forest. . . . Not the constitution, but free land and an abundance of natural resources open to a fit people, made the democratic type of society in America. . . ."

As Americans searched for ways in which to express their distinctive national experience, so Europeans attempted to put the United States into focus in terms of their own history. And they were not too successful. In 1783 the Academy in Lyons in France established a literary prize for the best essay contributed on the subject: "Has the discovery of America been useful or harmful to mankind? If benefits have resulted from it, by what means may they be preserved and augmented? If it has produced evils, by what means may they be remedied?" In the opinion of the judges no satisfactory essay was submitted, and the prize was never awarded. To some extent at least, the ambiguous result of this contest set the standard for European attempts to wrestle with the problem of America.

There was ample comment on America. But it tended to be contradictory, and much of it exhibited the prejudices of the commentator rather than describing America. A host of books and articles reporting on trips to the United States was published during the nineteenth century. Some of these, such as Charles Dickens' *American Notes*, were readable and interesting judgments. Others, such as Tocqueville's *Democracy in America* and James Bryce's *The American Commonwealth*, became scholarly classics. But many were ill-tempered and vicious slanders by those who made quick trips to the United States and then gained some reputation by reporting on the bad manners, the "barbarous dialect," and the grandiose ideas of the provincials across the ocean. As James Bryce noted: "European visitors who, generally belonging to the wealthier classes, are generally reactionary in politics, and glad to find occasions for disparaging popular government, eagerly catch up and repeat the stories they are told in New York or San Francisco." Such people seldom had anything of value to say about America, and perhaps Senator Thomas Hart Benton of Missouri described them best as "the riffraff of European writers who come here to pick up the gossip of the highways, to sell it in Europe for American history, and to requite with defamation the hospitalities of our houses."

Of course, there were Europeans who took America much more seriously. Many radicals, progressives, free-thinkers, opponents of the class structure of Europe were generally favorable toward the United States and adopted the Americans as models in their own struggle against European privilege, economic inequality, and political reaction. Until the last third of the nineteenth century the United States was the only important republic in the Western world, as it was the first national society to practice universal manhood suffrage. Copies of the Declaration of Independence were frequently displayed in the homes of European radicals, and Americans were described by a young German as "the most humane and happiest of all who have been chosen as contributors to the sublime work of inaugurating the Golden Age of Humanity." In the early part of the century the English radical journalist William Cobbett wrote that "this America, this scene of happiness under a free government, is the beam in the eye, the thorn in the side, the worm in the vitals of every despot upon the face of the earth."

There was something a little pathetic about the more extravagant of these claims on behalf of America. One European could announce that he was leaving the Old World in order "to realize the God-man" in his life on the American prairie, and another departed to establish "the religion of humanity" in Kansas. The Frenchman Benjamin Constant, in a letter to a female acquaintance, wrote: "America! America! America! If some day I leave Colombiers forever, if I see all liberty die out of Europe, there will still remain one refuge. . . . You may stay behind perhaps, but sad and embittered I shall go to Kentucky." Fortunately for him, Constant never was forced to make the long trip to Kentucky, and his threat to leave France was not meant to be taken seriously. But there was an undimmed belief in the United States as a land of opportunity and freedom. The twentieth-century English writer George Orwell expressed very well an interpretation that was undoubtedly accepted by many. "Nineteenth-century America was a rich, empty country which lay outside the mainstream of world events, and in which the twin nightmares that beset every modern man, the nightmare of unemployment and the nightmare of war, had hardly come into being. . . ." And Orwell continues that "for some decades, at least, life in America was much better fun than life in Europe — there was more happiness, more color, more variety, more opportunity."

Conservatives and traditionalists found offensive the very qualities praised by the radicals and democrats and regarded the United States as the natural antagonist of Europe. Politically, Americans were thought of as too raw, too young, too inexperienced. Moreover, they were "impatient of all authority and disdainful of all tradition," and thus unprepared to accept the restraints necessary for the maintenance of political order. The United States was described as a country "whose political principles are directly at variance with those of every other power," and an English historian could solemnly declare that "I cannot reckon Jefferson among the benefactors of mankind." In January, 1824, soon after the enunciation of the Monroe Doctrine, Metternich wrote to a Russian diplomat:

These United States of America which we have seen arise and grow, and which during their too short youth already meditated projects which they dared not then avow, have suddenly left a sphere too narrow for their ambition, and have astonished Europe by a new act of revolt, more unprovoked, fully as audacious, and no less dangerous than the former. . . . In their indecent declarations they have cast blame and scorn upon the institutions of Europe most worthy of respect, on the principles of its greatest sovereigns, on the whole of those measures which a sacred duty no less than an evident necessity has forced our governments to adopt to frustrate plans most criminal. In permitting themselves these unprovoked attacks, in fostering revolutions wherever they show themselves, in regretting those which have failed, in extending a helping hand to those which seem to prosper, they lend new strength to the apostles of sedition, and reanimate the courage of every conspirator. If this flood of evil doctrines and pernicious examples should extend over the whole of America, what would become of our religious and political institutions, of the moral force of our governments, and of that conservative system which has saved Europe from dissolution?

As Metternich's remarks indicate, it was the American example of a democratic society that alarmed European political leaders. Those responsible for the uneasy balance of conservatism, liberalism, and nationalism established after the defeat of Napoleon were apprehensive of any influence that might undermine political stability. American democracy, with its appeal to the discontented and its promise of wealth, was such an influence. Each American success appeared to indicate an alternative to the political structure and style of Europe. Conversely, each time the Americans experienced political difficulties — as during the Civil War — many European leaders were secretly or openly pleased at such indications of failure. A German traveller and aristocrat wrote in 1873: "Those among us who judge you from an exclusively European point of view see in you nothing but enemies of the fundamental principles of society. The more they appreciate your work, the more, in fact, they admire, the less they like you. I should add that they fear you."

America also posed a challenge to European cultural values. Throughout the century the European intellectual elite became increasingly concerned about the growth of aggressive mass movements that were undermining the positions of those who thought of themselves as guardians of the European spirit. The democratization of politics was accompanied by the democratization of culture, and the prerogatives of those who claimed to occupy the citadel of aesthetic, ethical, and philosophical values were being questioned or even ignored. Hardly an important European thinker failed to express his fears of a cultural leveling, a vulgarization, that was taking place, and distasteful European developments — middle-class philistinism, unruly democratic strivings, changing speech patterns — were ascribed to America and then criticized as evil and alien influences acting upon Europe.

The United States was used as an example of what the future held if Europe did not arrest her cultural decline. "Who among us imagines that in the United States of America there are thinkers, artists, or philosophers worthy of the name?" wrote a French author and literary critic. "Who concerns himself with American letters or thought?" America lacked cultural discrimination and seemed unfit to participate in the creative activities of Western civilization. As *The Edinburgh Review* pointed out: "America has done nothing, either to extend, diversify, or embellish the sphere of human knowledge. Though all she has written were obliterated from the records of learning there would (if we except the works of Franklin) be no positive diminution either of the useful or the agreeable." The United States might be materially rich and powerful, but according to Matthew Arnold, the Americans "have never been in contact with *Geist* (spirit), only with claptrap," and he voiced the complaint that was to be heard, with some variations, down to the present when he wrote, "what influence may help us to prevent the English people from becoming, with the growth of democracy, more Americanised?"

These arguments about the relative merits of Europe and America were all somewhat strained. They do indicate that the American had an exaggerated belief in his own innocence and virility, and that the European had a magnified view of his cultural vitality. The United States had her own national history, and certain aspects of that history — the availability of free land, a physical size that disturbed the European sense of order, and the relative absence of traditional class differentiation — were unique. There was also a persistent American drive to assert her own historical personality and to insist, as Emerson did in 1837, that "our day of dependence, our long apprenticeship to the learning of other lands, draws to a close." Traditional European cultural and political institutions were being threatened by the continual democratic revolution, and insofar as America expressed this revolution, she was a subversive influence.

Yet the nineteenth-century German historian Leopold von Ranke wrote: "We must be on guard against opposing Europe and America; what is found over there is but a development of our own blood and our own way of life." Ranke had never seen the United States, but he realized something that often escaped the notice of the most active traveller. In the essentials — industrialization, intellectual ideas, commercial organization, concepts of nationalism, and late in the century imperialism — the United States was a European society. She was in certain things much closer to specific European countries than such countries were to each other, and was much more a modern European nation than were many continental European societies. Most important, perhaps, the majority of Americans and West Europeans shared what a Russian commentator called those "ideas which take possession of the child in his cradle . . . which, in the form of various feelings, penetrate into the marrow of his bones with the air he breathes, and which shape his moral being."

The United States can best be seen as a national society complementary to those of Europe. With the possible exception of Great Britain, she was politically the most stable of Western nations. Yet she was also the most libertarian and thus encouraged Europeans in their struggle against both stifling traditional restraints and threatening mass ideologies. Emerson wrote that there was an American ideal, "but those who hold it are fanatics of a dream which I should hardly care to relate to your English ears, to which it might be only ridiculous." But many Europeans had the same dream, and Europe was also the home of equally "wild" ideas about the future progress of man. Proposals for change and improvement passed back and forth across the Atlantic. "We ain't what we want to be, and we ain't what we're goin' to be, but we ain't what we wuz," ran a Carolina proverb, and while many Europeans would have used different phraseology, the goal in mind was similar. Some Americans continued to speak of the European fondness for luxury, dissipation, and intrigue and to contrast American healthy masculinity with European lewdness and femininity. Some Europeans continued to describe America as a nation of "primitive people camouflaged behind the latest inventions." Political rhetoric kept old grievances alive, and even in the early twentieth century the mayor of a large American city promised his supporters that if the king of England ever came to the United States he would be greeted with "a punch in the nose." This was one American attitude toward Europe. Another was illustrated by the writer usually regarded as the most distinctive American personality, Mark Twain, who made at least a dozen trips to Europe and once lived there for nine successive years. Neither response could be called typical. Into the twentieth century the relationship of Europe and the United States remained ambiguous. America did not play an important part in European international affairs, and Europeans considered the United States as basically an interested observer and not an active participant in European history. But similar if not identical cultural and even political attitudes and close commercial, social, and intellectual relations had brought the Old and New Worlds much nearer each other than most Americans and Europeans realized.

Russia and the West

As the people of Western Europe were forced to accommodate themselves to the large and increasingly powerful United States on one side, so in the nineteenth century they found themselves confronted by the Russian giant on the other. To the east was that part of the Eurasian continent where, as it was said, "everything is on a larger scale, less detailed, less individual; and as the scale of land grows, so also does the scale of time. . . . One soul mingles with another like smoke." Here, in the popular European imagination, was the land of the Cossacks, of the bearded bomb-throwers, of the samovar and the icon, of ice and snow.

During the century Russia became a European political power. She participated in the coalition against Napoleon and played an important part in the post-Napoleonic settlement. She attended diplomatic conferences and entered into alliances with the nations of Western Europe. Her own particular national interests at times brought her into conflict with her European neighbors. Russian suppression of the Poles in 1830 and 1863 aroused the anger of European liberals. The Crimean War of 1853-1856 — in which Britain and France engaged in an inconclusive campaign against Russia, the Russian-Turkish war of 1877-1878, and British-Russian tensions along the northwest Indian frontier produced spasms of anti-Russian feeling. The autocratic behavior of the Russian tsar, rumors of the activities of the Russian political police, and stories of Russian prison camps in Siberia prompted popular suspicion of the Russian government. But in military and bureaucratic organization, in international commerce, in science and technology, Russia was an accepted member of the European community of nations.

There were some Europeans who felt themselves threatened by Russia and who visualized Western civilization being overrun by what were called "Asian hordes" or "those aggressive western Chinese." The Marquis de Custine, in his popular *Russia in 1839*, expressed his fear that Russia would "break into Europe" and "put an end" to European history. After Napoleon's defeat Metternich had raised the question: "What will happen to the balance of power, if, having rid Europe of the domination of Napoleon, we replace the western menace by an eastern menace, and establish Russian influence?" Years later, in 1841, he brought up the same point in a conversation with a British official: "It will be impossible to foresee or to limit the consequences. Hordes of Cossacks and barbarians, having seen the riches of more civilized countries, will be eager to return. They will overrun Europe, and some great changes will probably result from it, as has been the case in former times from the incursions of barbarians."

Men such as de Custine and Metternich might fret about the Russian danger. But there was a general lack of interest in Russia on the part of most Europeans. A political crisis in which Russia was involved did provide journalistic opportunities to bring the "barbarian threat" to public notice. But Russia remained largely a far-away land of confusion and mystery. Only a handful of educated Europeans had even the slightest knowledge of the Russian language, and there was little scholarly interest in Russia itself. Late in the nineteenth and early in the twentieth centuries translations of the Russian literary masterpieces appeared, and Russian music, art, and dance aroused enthusiasm. Most Europeans, however, if they thought of the matter at all, would probably have agreed with a British magazine, which, in 1847, pointed out that "Russian history, even in our day, is a sanguinary and cruel chronicle. Its brevity is its best excuse."

Russians, of course, were not so indifferent to their own history. Desperately patriotic and sensitive, Russian intellectuals throughout the nineteenth century engaged in endless discussions and at times acrimonious debates over such questions as: What was Russia and what was her role in the world? Toward what goal did she tend and how could she be true to herself? Ivan Turgenev, in one of his novels, undoubtedly exaggerated, but he showed the general tendency of the time when he had a character say:

> Suppose ten Englishmen meet, their conversation will at once be directed to cotton or the possibility of tanning the skins of mice, something positive and definite. Bring together ten Germans and the unity of Germany will at once naturally become the topic. Ten Frenchmen, in spite of every effort to avoid the subject, will inevitably come round to discussing the fair sex. But gather ten Russians together and immediately there arises the question of the worth and the future of Russia. They squeeze, they drain, they chew this unfortunate subject as children do with gum — and with the same result.

There was a unique aspect to this continual debate over Russia's future. Russian success or failure was almost inevitably seen in light of her relationship with the West. Those who admired Europe and those who despised it were alike forced to compare Russia with the West and to use their attitudes toward the West as a starting point for any discussion of their native country. As was said, "this world of the West impinges on us at every point," and ultimately, the problem of Russian historical identity could be brought into focus only by considering the question of whether or not Russia was a Western society.

Russian native culture — all those historical experiences, memories, and habits acquired over a long period of time — had developed in a way different from that of Western countries. Russia had experienced no crusades, no medieval scholasticism, no Renaissance or Reformation, no strong tradition of philosophical or scientific inquiry, no chivalry with its influence upon the conduct of one man toward another, no sustained spiritual challenge to the power of the secular authority. She had no history of strong, free, and independent intellectual movements that had meant so much in the West.

In the first quarter of the eighteenth century Tsar Peter the Great had attempted to impose Western techniques and Western institutions upon Russia. His effort has been described as similar to that of a powerful man who strikes an ox with his fist. The ox does not go down, but it knows that it has been hit. Western dress, Western institutions, and Western military and bureaucratic organizations were pressed upon Russia with incredible rapidity, intensity, and disregard for the desires of the Russians themselves. Amidst disorder, confusion, and waste, Peter, in the words of a Russian historian:

> introduced into Russia useful technical knowledge and skills lacked by the Russians. Russia had no regular army: he created one. It had no fleet: he built one. It had no convenient maritime commercial outlet: with his army and navy he took the eastern littoral of the Baltic. Mining was hardly developed, and manufacturing hardly existed, yet by Peter's death there were more than two hundred factories and workshops in the country. The establishment of industry depended on technical knowledge, so Peter founded a naval academy, and many schools of navigation, medicine, artillery and engineering, including some where Latin and mathematics were taught, as well as nearly fifty elementary schools.... There was no rationally organized administration capable of managing this new and complicated business, so foreign experts were called on to help to create a new central administration.

Westernization was carried on by Peter's successors, and Russia adopted many of the cultural and social patterns of the West. One historian has listed these importations as "fashionable dressing gowns, chocolates, cheap novels, and mistresses." But the influence of the West was much more significant than this listing would indicate. The diplomatic service, the army, the professions, and the educational system were modeled after Western institutions. Western ideas of all kinds found a welcome home in Russia, and German philosophers as well as French revolutionaries had numerous disciples among Russian intellectuals. Western literature, good and bad, found an audience in St. Petersburg and Moscow, while Russians in the professions and in politics established close relations with professional men and politicians in

Western countries. Some Russians were convinced that there were few important differences between their native country and Europe. Thus Turgenev wrote that "Russia is no Venus de Milo, kept in misery and bondage by a wicked stepmother. She is in fact the same kind of young woman as her elder sisters — except, I suppose, that she is a bit broader in the beam."

Yet in many ways Western influence was confined to a thin crust at the top of Russian society and did not succeed in penetrating deeply into the great peasant mass. St. Petersburg was a magnificent Western city, but in the countryside the turbulent peasant multitude remained largely unchanged. In the early years of the twentieth century a Russian states-man described his native land outside the great cities as "an icy desert and an abode of the Bad Man." A deep division appeared in Russian society, and those who participated in Western culture were separated by a continually widening gulf from those who were unaffected by Western ideas. In the eighteen-seventies a Russian wrote: "There are two layers of Russian people distinguished from each other not so much by privileges as by the fundamental difference that each represents a dif-ferent epoch of history — the upper the nineteenth century, the lower the ninth." European countries possessed internal social and cultural divisions, but in Russia these were so great as to produce guilt on the part of one group and suspicion and antagonism on the part of the other. The Russian peasant might be thought of as an unspoiled child of nature or as a brute in a dirty and lice-infested sheepskin. In either case, the Western-ized Russian found himself, to some extent at least, a stranger in his own land. A nineteenth-century Russian novelist has left us a descrip-tion of this cultural schism. "Were I a painter, this is the picture I would paint: a civilized Russian, standing before a peasant and bowing low, says: 'Cure me, little father! I am sick unto death!' while the peasant in his turn bows humbly before the civilized type and replies: 'Enlighten me, my lord, I am dying for want of light.' And neither offers to make the slightest advance."

Westernization did produce a certain intellectual demoralization and a persistent pessimism about Russian national and cultural potentiali-ties. Every borrowing from the West seemed another affront to Russia's own capacities, and hardly an important Russian writer during the nine-teenth century did not express his discouragement at what appeared to be Russia's cultural inferiority. In 1836 Peter Chaadaev published his famous "Philosophical Letters." Here he stressed the lack of creativity in Russia and the limbo of despair and loneliness in which Russians lived. "We belong to none of the great families of the human race, nei-ther Western nor Eastern, nor have we managed to incorporate any of their traditions. We stand segregated, as if condemned to banishment outside the passage of time, and the universal education of the human race has passed by without touching us." And he went on: "Alone in the world, we have given nothing to it, and have learned nothing from it. Whatever has reached us out of the progress of the human mind, we have disfigured and distorted." A little more bluntly and with even more exaggeration, Turgenev wrote: "The samovar and the bark shoes, these were not even invented by us. The old inventions came from the East, the new are borrowed from the West. If Russia happened to disappear from the world's surface, no one would notice the fact. The disappearance of the Sandwich Islands would cause more stir; the natives there have been the inventors of all sorts of spears and canoes."

This "wounded national feeling" was undoubtedly responsible for hostility toward the West and Western ideas on the part of some Russians. From the early years of the nineteenth century there were those who believed that Western influences were a danger to Russia, which had her own unique historical way. "We have become citizens of the world, and so have in many ways ceased being citizens of Russia — It is the fault of Peter," wrote the historian Nicholas Karamzin early in the century, and the opposition of Russia and the West was continually stressed. It was argued that Russia was a religiously oriented society while the West was characterized by an excessive emphasis upon rationality. The Russian was spiritually united while the life of the Westerner had been fragmented by his pursuit of various and contradictory goals. The political system of the West was based upon distrust and discord while the Russian state was the manifestation of a unified will. In the West legal arrangements were artificial and coldly logical while in Russia such arrangements were derived from the life of the people. Russia possessed an "inner truth" as opposed to the "outer truth" of the West.

Belief in Russia appeared to require a rejection of the West, and it was impossible to consider the history of Russia "without at once falling foul of the rottenness of the Western world." And this decay in the West meant that there was nothing of value to be gained there that could contribute to Russia's progress or future. A Russian historian wrote in 1838: "The time of the European nations is past, their strength runs out. They can produce nothing higher in religion, law, science, or art, nor have they carried mankind to its moral goal. Now the future belongs to the Slavs who will serve mankind." No matter how glorious the past of the West might have been, it had played its assigned part in the history of the world. Fyodor Dostoievsky, in his novel *The Brothers Karamazov*, puts the following words into the mouth of one of his characters: "I want to go to Europe. I know that I shall go only to a cemetery, but it will be the dearest of cemeteries. I know beforehand that I shall fall upon the earth and I shall kiss those stones and weep over them. But I shall be at the same time convinced in my heart that all this has already been a cemetery for a very long time and nothing else whatsoever."

It is difficult to separate reality from fantasy in these discussions of Russia and Europe. Western influences certainly often existed uneasily in Russia, and some became caricatures of their European models. Such, for example, was the case with Russian politics, which was neither creative nor stable. Russian political authority consisted largely of archaic autocratic appeals and repressive police measures. A Russian historian points out that early in the nineteenth century the Russian government adopted the theory "that it is not life that should give form and direction to institutions but institutions that should give direction to life" and began a century-long search for some light that "should illuminate without the risk of flame, lighten without the presence of light." The energies of the people strained against the government, which responded, when it could, with repression, and, when it could not do otherwise, with ill-humor and grudging acceptance of popular demands. A dreary mediocrity permeated Russian politics, and a well-known Russian minister could, in the early twentieth century, speak of "this insane regime, this tangle of cowardice, blindness, craftiness, and stupidity." The government from 1881 used emergency powers in its attempt to enforce docility and obedience, and the tsarist police were described as "an alien army of occupation." And, because the government utilized many of the Western political instrumentalities and was, sometimes justly and sometimes not, increasingly identified as Western and not truly Russian, the influence of Western political ideas and institutions was often looked upon as alien and harmful.

Yet the differences between Europe and Russia that existed in the nineteenth and early twentieth centuries can be exaggerated. Russia was becoming increasingly an important contributor to European life. Men such as the chemist Dmitri Mendeleyev, the physiologist Ivan Pavlov, the mathematician Nikolai Lobachevsky, the dramatist Anton Chekhov, the musician Igor Stravinsky, and numerous others played significant roles in European cultural and intellectual activities. Industrialization and technology were modernizing Russia, and there were even halting steps being made toward some form of constitutional government. The Russian educated classes were probably the most cosmopolitan in all Europe, and showed a remarkable creative talent. In the early eighteenth century Peter the Great is reputed to have said: "Europe is necessary to us for a few decades, and then we can turn our backs on her." This had not happened. Russia had retained many of her traditional customs and institutions, but she had incorporated many European influences into her national life and largely regarded herself and was regarded by others as a distinct but unquestioned member of the European society.

Europe and the World

The relationship of the United States and Russia to Europe illustrated some interesting characteristics of modern Western civilization. The history of the United States showed that European settlers could remove themselves geographically from Europe, create a new nation, undergo new experiences, and yet remain, in many essentials, European. It also showed that those who had not previously participated in or contributed to European civilization needed only the opportunity in order to do so. In Europe itself peasants were being transformed into citizens, and the United States indicated that while such a process would introduce strains, it would not be catastrophic.

The impact of Europe upon Russia revealed that Western science, technology, and political and cultural ideas could be adopted by already-established societies with different historical experiences. The process of adoption was traumatic and resulted in serious institutional and intellectual crises, and Russia illustrated the frustrations and ambiguities of a society being subjected to the effects of Westernization. The success of Western influences did arouse deep animosities. A Russian tsar in exasperation once exclaimed, "an Englishman is a *zhid!*" — thus illustrating in one short sentence his hatred of European liberalism and modernization and his anti-semitism.

But the appeal of European civilization was too great. European industrial and military power became the world standard, and the attraction of technology and organization was matched by the strength of European intellectual concepts and the idea of human freedom. European civilization also provided the opportunity for non-European peoples to participate in that civilization while retaining and developing their own unique characteristics. The Marquis de Custine had stated that the Russians had only the talent for "imitating other nations, and they imitate them in the manner of monkeys, making what they copy ridiculous." But both the Americans and the Russians were great givers as well as receivers and enriched European life as well as drawing sustenance from it.

Traditionally, many Europeans had been haunted by the fear of outside influence and outside force that would threaten their civilization. These fears in the nineteenth century and even in the twentieth were groundless. Any danger to Europe was to come from Europe itself, the result of European blindness, European stupidity, and the misuse of European power. During the American Civil War many European leaders were to sympathize with the South and were prepared to accept a strong slave-holding republic in order to weaken the national strength of the Yankee upstarts. In the early twentieth century, Russia was to become alienated from the West. But this was not the result of some mysterious historical current, some dialectical process, but rather of European war and European political failure. By the end of the nineteenth century Europe had become a world civilization, and this development was to expose her to new and unforeseen dangers. As Europe's influence and power grew so did her vulnerability, and her failures as well as her successes were to have drastic and unimagined effects upon Europeans and non-Europeans alike.

A large number of Americans, Europeans, and Russians have wrestled with the question of the relationship of America and Russia, and by inference non-European societies, to the Western "heartland." Alexis de Tocqueville is usually regarded as the most important European commentator upon America in the early nineteenth century. The Russian Alexander Herzen was fascinated by and attracted to the West but, after coming to Western Europe, rejected the civilization he had formerly admired. Henry James was probably the outstanding example of one who attempted to combine the American and European experience and to interpret the impact the two societies had on each other.

Alexis de Tocqueville

In January, 1835, a book entitled *Democracy in America* was printed in Paris. The author was a thirty-year-old Frenchman named Alexis de Tocqueville, and the book reported upon the impressions gained during a recent visit to the United States. It was an instant success. By 1840 seven editions had been published in France, and translations had appeared in Spain, Germany, England, and the United States. Throughout the nineteenth century *Democracy in America* was repeatedly reprinted in French and English, and additional editions appeared in Danish, Hungarian, Italian, Russian, Serbian, and Swedish.

Tocqueville was born in 1805, a member of a French noble family. His father and mother had been imprisoned during the Revolution and had been saved from the guillotine only by the end of the Terror in 1794. As Tocqueville himself wrote: "I came into the world at the end of a long revolution, which after destroying ancient institutions created none that could last. When I entered life, aristocracy was dead and democracy was yet unborn." He travelled widely — in Sicily, England, Ireland, Switzerland, and Algiers, as well as in America — and he was the close friend of many of the leading intellectual and political leaders of his time. He was a member of the French Chamber of Deputies from 1839 to 1848 and for a short period after the Revolution of 1848 was Minister of Foreign Affairs.

Democracy in America was written when Tocqueville was in the full flush of his young adult creative powers. The book has a remarkable style, contains striking insights, and abounds in quotable material on almost every subject of American life in the early nineteenth century. Tocqueville was himself the best of travellers, with a sure eye for the unique and the commonplace alike, good-humored and courteous, and able to relate what he saw to a general interpretation of politics and history. Tocqueville and his young friend Gustave de Beaumont arrived in New York on May 10, 1831. They were on an official mission for the French government to study the American penitentiary system. They travelled to Boston and then as far west as Green Bay, as far north as Sault Ste. Marie and Quebec, and as far south as New Orleans. In all they covered over 7,000 miles in a little over nine months and left America on February 20, 1832.

Tocqueville has been often described as a commentator upon revolution and upon the revolutionary movements that the Western world was experiencing. He saw that the old Europe had been destroyed and that it was impossible to return to a prerevolutionary condition. "Some good people have tried to rehabilitate the old regime," he wrote late in his life. "I judge it by the feelings it inspired in those who lived under it and abolished it. I see that all through the Revolution, cruel as it was, hate for the old regime outweighed all other hates, and that throughout the dangerous vicissitudes of the past sixty years the fear of its return has outweighed all other fears. That is enough for me." Tocqueville also realized that the Revolution had not ended in 1793, or in 1799, or in 1815. Rather, the West was enduring a continual revolution, "the same under all changes of fortune, of which our fathers saw the beginning, and of which we ourselves will in all probability not see the end."

No matter what outward form it might take, this continuing revolution had one abiding characteristic. It was what Tocqueville called democratic, which he defined as a movement hostile to any aristocratic institution or idea, any traditional claim that gave one person precedence over another. There was a "continuous, irresistible tendency" to modern history, and it appeared to Tocqueville that "some power superior to that of man" was hurrying the world toward democracy. In 1833 he wrote that "the immediate future of European society lies with democracy," and for him the question was not whether Europe would be democratic or aristocratic but rather what shape the coming democratic society would take.

Tocqueville made his trip to the United States and then published his thoughts upon the new republic across the Atlantic because of this belief that the promises and the threats of the prevailing historical movement, "its good and evil tendencies," could be seen best in the country that claimed to be the representative of democracy. As he wrote: "I confess that in America I sought more than America; I sought there the image of democracy itself, with its inclinations, its character, its prejudices, and its passions, in order to learn what we have to fear or to hope from its progress." As he put it in another way: "The question here discussed is interesting not only to the United States, but to the whole world; it concerns not a nation only but all mankind."

Tocqueville realized something that was often forgotten by other European travellers: America could not be judged by European standards. America was not a traditional society in the European sense of the word. The North American continent had been peopled by Europeans, and while the marks of the European origin were obvious, the Americans were separated from Europe by a new and different historical experience and by a rejection of much of the European past. In his first letter from America to a friend in France, Tocqueville wrote that he was confronting a society "possessing no roots, no memories, no prejudices, no routine, no common ideas, no national character...." Many of the basic principles of Europe were, in Tocqueville's opinion, even reversed in America. Thus, "In Europe we are want to look upon a restless disposition, an unbounded desire of riches, and an excessive love of independence as propensities very dangerous to society. Yet these are the very elements that ensure a long and peaceful future to the republics of America." The knowledge and the experience of Europeans were of little value in considering what was happening in the United States. "In that land the great experiment of the attempt to construct society upon a new basis was to be made by civilized man; and it was there, for the first time, that theories hitherto unknown, or deemed impracticable, were to exhibit a spectacle for which the world had not been prepared by the history of the past." The best that one could do was to try to discern some direction to American society, but it was impossible to predict the impact of this society upon the rest of the world. "The time will therefore come when one hundred and fifty million men will be living in North America, equal in condition, all belonging to one family, owing their origin to the same cause, and preserving the same civilization, the same language, the same religion, the same habits, the same manners, and imbued with the same opinions, propagated under the same forms. The rest is uncertain, but this is certain; and it is a fact new to the world, a fact that the imagination strives in vain to grasp."

Democracy in America has been called "a model of the spirit of fairness and justice," and the book is remarkably free of the carping pettiness that disfigures so many discussions of one country by a member of another. Tocqueville found much to admire in the United States. He responded to the free and easy relationships of the Americans, to their informality, and to their lack of aristocratic pretensions. He saw that the material prosperity of America, its unimaginable wealth of land and resources, had a favorable influence upon the institutions of the country. The Americans had "a happiness a hundred times greater than ours," and a confidence in the future that contrasted markedly with the more pessimistic attitude of the Europeans. "Every revolution," he wrote, "has more or less the effect of releasing men to their own conduct and of opening before the mind of each of them an almost limitless perspective." This had happened in America, and the Americans "have a lively faith in the perfectibility of man, they judge that the diffusion of knowledge must necessarily be advantageous, and the consequences of ignorance fatal; they all consider society as a body in a state of improvement, humanity as a changing scene, in which nothing is, or ought to be, permanent; and they admit that what appears to them today to be good, may be superseded by something better tomorrow."

Tocqueville's book contains many remarkable tributes to democracy. But perhaps the most interesting and quoted parts of his study are not given over to one-sided praise and commendation. As Tocqueville wrote, "because I am not an opponent of democracy I wished to speak of it with all sincerity," and as he stated again, "I am as little disposed to flatter my contemporaries as to malign them." He mentioned many specific things in America that offended him. He found that Americans showed a "troublesome" and "garrulous patriotism" that he thought both obnoxious and unnecessary. The vituperative nature of the American press startled him, and he believed that in America men "are often obliged to do things which they have imperfectly learned, to say things which they imperfectly understand, and to devote themselves to work for which they are unprepared." Many of his specific comments about local government, judicial powers, and the federal constitution are now outdated. But some of these remarks seem to us now almost prophetic. He thought that the rapidly growing American cities constituted a threat to the society. These cities "consist of freed blacks, in the first place, who are condemned by the laws and by public opinion to a hereditary state of misery and degradation. They also contain a multitude of Europeans who have been driven to the shores of the New World by their misfortunes or their misconduct; and they bring to the United States all our greatest vices, without any of those interests which counteract their baneful influence." Tocqueville was also alert to the most horrifying aspect of American life — the calamity of slavery. He thought that "the most formidable of all the ills that threaten the future of the Union arises from the presence of a black population upon its territory." The scars of slavery would not, in his opinion, heal, and he saw something that escaped the notice of many of his less perceptive and more optimistic contemporaries. He wrote that "among the moderns the abstract and transient fact of slavery is fatally united with the physical and permanent fact of color." He expressed his fears of the future with statements such as "the Negroes and the whites must either wholly part or wholly mingle," and "I do not believe that the white and black will ever live in any country upon an equal footing. But I believe the difficulty to be still greater in the United States than elsewhere."

The most important and influential aspects of Tocqueville's discussion of America, however, concern the "levelling" characteristics of American democracy and the problems posed by the American fondness for equality. To Tocqueville, there seemed almost a law of democratic vulgarity in operation in America. In his travel diaries of his trip he posed the question: "Why, when there are no lower classes, are there no upper classes either? Why, when understanding of government reaches the masses, is there a shortage of great spirits to take the lead in society? America clearly raises those questions. But who can answer them?" Democracy had many virtues, and Tocqueville never questioned them. But penalties were always extracted, in his opinion, for the benefits of a democratic society, and one of these was the absence of a sense of excellence, of taste, and of intellectual and aesthetic judgment. The roughness and low level of general culture that he saw in American life he believed a natural characteristic of a democracy. There were certain things that should not be expected of a democracy, and Tocqueville put this point clearly in *Democracy in America.*

> We must first understand what is wanted of society and its government. Do you wish to give a certain elevation to the human mind and teach it to regard the things of this world with generous feelings, to inspire men with a scorn of mere temporal advantages, to form and nour-

ish strong convictions and keep alive the spirit of honorable devoted-
ness? Is it your object to refine the habits, embellish the manners, and
cultivate the arts, to promote the love of poetry, beauty, and glory?
Would you constitute a people fitted to act powerfully upon all other
nations, and prepared for those high enterprises which, whatever be
their results, will leave a name forever famous in history? If you believe such to be the principal object of society, avoid the government
of the democracy, for it would not lead you with certainty to the goal.

But if you hold it expedient to divert the moral and intellectual
activity of man to the production of comfort and the promotion of
general well-being; if a clear understanding be more profitable to man
than genius; if your object is not to stimulate the virtues of heroism,
but the habits of peace; if you had rather witness vices than crimes,
and are content to meet with fewer noble deeds, provided offenses be
diminished in the same proportion; if, instead of living in the midst of
a brilliant society, you are contented to have prosperity around you;
if, in short, you are of the opinion that the principal object of a government is not to confer the greatest possible power and glory upon
the body of the nation, but to ensure the greatest enjoyment and to
avoid the most misery to each of the individuals who compose it — if
such be your desire, then equalize the conditions of men and establish
democratic institutions.

Tocqueville noticed that Americans spoke a great deal about freedom
and assumed that this was the principal characteristic of their society.
But Tocqueville believed that the American urge to freedom was conditioned by an overwhelming dedication to equality, and his comments
upon this urge to equality have probably attracted more attention than
any of his other remarks. "I think that democratic communities have a
natural taste for freedom; left to themselves, they will seek it, cherish it,
and view any privation of it with regret. But for equality their passion is
ardent, insatiable, incessant, invincible; they call for equality in freedom; and if they cannot obtain that, they still call for equality in slavery." The primary allegiance of the Americans was thus not to freedom
but to equality — equality of opinion, equality of justice, equality of condition. "Freedom cannot form the distinguishing characteristic of democratic ages. The peculiar and preponderant fact that marks those ages
as its own is the equality of condition; the ruling passion of men in those
periods is the love of equality."

There were no historical guides by which to judge the effects of this
urge toward equality, and there was no way of predicting whether social
and political equality would be beneficial or detrimental. "In the principle of equality, I very clearly discern two tendencies: one leading the
mind of every man to untried thoughts, the other prohibiting him from
thinking at all." Equality could liberate man, or it could enchain him in

the prison of common opinion. The Americans themselves frequently showed the latter results, and Tocqueville was not particularly impressed with much of what he saw. "It seems at first sight as if all the minds of the Americans were formed upon one model, so accurately do they follow the same route," and because of the pressures toward equality, all distinctions between men were being obliterated. The tyranny of the majority, the perhaps inevitable consequence of equality, was apparent everywhere in America, and "I know of no country in which there is so little independence of mind and real freedom of discussion as in America."

When Tocqueville returned to France and when he published *Democracy in America*, he believed that he had given his countrymen not only a fair picture of American political and social life but that he had, to some extent at least, shown them the possible future of the Western society. In spite of his awareness of the differences separating America and Europe, he suspected that the general direction of history on both sides of the Atlantic was basically the same. The nations of Europe could not stop the movement toward democracy, but this movement "is not yet so rapid that it cannot be guided. Their fate is still in their hands; but very soon they may lose control." The challenge facing the Western nations was the establishment of some form of democracy that would, while destroying privilege and introducing political equality, preserve individual liberty. He concluded *Democracy in America* with the words: "I am of the opinion that if we do not succeed in gradually introducing democratic institutions into our country, if we despair of imparting to all the citizens those ideas and sentiments which first prepare them for freedom and afterwards allow them to enjoy it, there will be no independence at all, either for the middle class or for the nobility, for the poor or for the rich, but an equal tyranny over all."

Tocqueville never again visited America. In 1840 he published two more volumes of his study of democracy in the New World. Thereafter, he largely concerned himself with his native France, and during the remainder of his life his writings were primarily a commentary upon his dwindling hopes and his growing fears. His faith in the spirit of democracy was replaced by a sense of unease, of frustration and disappointment, and the waning of belief in the possibility of Europe, and especially France, making a satisfactory transition to democracy. His *Memoirs* and *The Old Regime*, the latter a study of conditions leading to the French Revolution, and his correspondence are full of dark and brooding thoughts. Phrases such as "the democratic disease of envy," "a new and unknown virus," "a blind and rude effort" become increasingly common in his comments. The Revolution of 1848, the establishment of the short-lived Second Republic, and the creation of the Second Empire were events that colored Tocqueville's outlook. He became convinced that men had lost "the taste for freedom," and he wrote that "these seventy years of revolution have destroyed our courage, our hopefulness, our self-reliance, our passions, except the most vulgar and selfish ones, vanity and covetousness." It was difficult to read Tocqueville and not believe that he had abandoned any hope for democracy. He seemed to say that men were helpless to master their own fate and that the revolutionary movements of the late-eighteenth and nineteenth centuries had been largely destructive and had produced only confusion, discouragement, and terror.

Because of his later writings and some of the memorable passages in *Democracy in America*, Tocqueville in recent years has been described as a prophet of what is called the mass age. He is credited with having been one of the first to see that the tendency of modernity — democracy and industrialization — was toward a dull uniformity, a common mediocrity. The common mind, the common intelligence, the common aspirations had stimulated people to the search for "tranquillity and material comfort" but not for "manly virtues and great actions." Members of such a mass society have no real idea of liberty, morality, or individuality but combine personal irresponsibility with public conformity. As a result, according to Tocqueville, mass societies may be "rich, refined, ornate, even magnificent, powerful by the weight of their homogeneous mass. . . . But what will never be seen in such societies, I dare say, are great citizens and especially a great people. I am not afraid to state that in those societies the common level of heart and mind will never stop sinking as long as equality and despotism go hand in hand." Mass men are those who "want to be led, and they wish to remain free. As they cannot destroy either the one or the other of these contrary propensities, they strive to satisfy them both at once. They devise a sole, tutelary, and all-powerful form of government, but elected by the people. They combine the principle of centralization and that of popular sovereignty; this gives them respite: they console themselves for being in tutelage by the reflection that they have chosen their own guardians."

These pessimistic remarks were not directed to America. In fact, in the preface to the twelfth French edition of *Democracy in America*, published in 1848 at the time of the establishment of the Second French Republic, Tocqueville wrote of the United States as a model that deserved consideration.

> Where else could we find greater causes of hope, or more instructive lessons? Let us look to America, not in order to make a servile copy of the institutions that she has established, but to gain a clearer view of the polity that will be the best for us; let us look there less to find examples than instruction; let us borrow from her the principles,

rather than the details, of her laws. The laws of the French republic may be, and ought to be in many cases, different from those which govern the United States; but the principles on which the American constitution rests, those principles of order, of the balance of powers, of true liberty, of deep and sincere respect for right, are indispensable to all republics; they ought to be common to all; and it may be said beforehand that wherever they are not found, the republic will soon have ceased to exist.

Yet it was Tocqueville's doubts about America that caught the attention of educated Europeans. In spite of his warnings that the historical evidence on America was too limited to warrant judgment, Tocqueville's tentative statements about the low cultural level in America and the possibility of democracy degenerating into a tyranny of the mediocre were translated in his time and later into certainties by his countrymen and others. Few Europeans were prepared to look to America as a model or even as a source of hope. At best, America was an interesting but irrelevant society existing outside the mainstream of Western history. At worst, she was a threat, a place exhibiting the "tyranny of the herd," the home of conformity, low cultural standards, and blatant vulgarity. European supporters and opponents of democracy alike were prone to attack America — one for her failure as a democratic society and the other because she showed so well the deleterious results of democracy in action.

Alexander Herzen

In March, 1847, the thirty-five-year-old Alexander Herzen arrived in Paris. Two months earlier he had left Russia with his family, never to return, and he was to spend the remaining twenty-three years of his life in exile. In Russia he had been a leading member of that group known as

Westerners and had looked upon Western Europe as the home of liberty, constitutional democracy, and social progress. As he himself wrote, "our attitude toward Europe and Europeans is that of provincials toward dwellers in a capital," and he had associated himself with what he regarded as the noble and inspiring history of the West. Herzen viewed the recent revolutionary past of Western Europe, and particularly that of France, with almost romantic awe. "We had been accustomed to connect the word Paris with memories of the great events, the great masses, the great men of 1789 and 1793, memories of a colossal struggle for an idea, for rights, for human dignity. . . . The name of Paris was closely bound up with all the noblest enthusiasms of contemporary mankind. I entered Paris with reverence, as men used to enter Jerusalem and Rome."

Alexander Herzen was an outstanding example of the nineteenth-century Russian intellectual. As his countryman Fyodor Dostoievsky wrote: "He was an artist, a thinker, a brilliant writer, an extraordinarily well-read man, a wit, a wonderful conversationalist." He possessed a "solicitousness of truth" and a desire to participate in a community of humane, enlightened, free men. Deeply influenced by the powerful social and philosophical ideas that had come from France and Germany, and discouraged by the oppressive and stifling atmosphere in Russia, Herzen abandoned his native country for life in the "promised land" of the West.

In Russia during the eighteen-forties Herzen had been a minor novelist and cultural commentator, one of those talented but largely ineffectual and "superfluous" men who drifted uneasily on the edge of Russian society. After coming to Western Europe, however, he entered into a period of truly creative activity and became a figure of consequence in Russian intellectual history. His political books, *Letters from Italy and France* (1850), *From the Other Shore* (1850), *The Russian People and Socialism* (1851), and *The Development of Revolutionary Ideas in Russia* (1851), published during the early years of his stay in the West, are fascinating and stimulating commentaries upon Europe and Russia in the late eighteen-forties and eighteen-fifties and may still be read with profit. His autobiography, *Past and Thoughts*, written while in exile, is a masterpiece and has been correctly described as "among the noblest monuments of Russian literature." In 1852 Herzen moved to London, and a year later he inaugurated his Free Russian Press in the British capital. Here Herzen published pamphlets, books, and his famous periodicals, *The Polar Star* and *The Bell*. First published as a monthly and later as a fortnightly, *The Bell* was probably the most successful journal ever initiated by a political exile. Printed in editions of up to 2,500 copies, it was widely read inside Russia, and an observer noted that "the power of Herzen in Russia is unique. He is a true dictator of the new generation, and it is no exaggeration to say that his moral authority exerts influence upon the material authority of the government itself." Ultimately, Herzen was to lose his influence, but for over ten years he was the most important Russian political journalist of the time.

Yet this success was accompanied by a series of shattering experiences. Herzen was plagued by personal troubles — the infidelity and death of his wife, the drowning of his mother and his son, the death of two other children from smallpox, and bitter controversies with friends that led to estrangement. Most important, however, was his rapid disenchantment with the West. Within a short time of his arrival in France, Herzen roused himself from what he called "a fit of somnambulism" and looked more closely at his surroundings. "We know Europe from school, from literature," he wrote, "that is to say we do not know it, but we imagine it from textbooks and pictures." The vision of the West that Herzen had possessed in Moscow was very different from the reality he saw in Paris, and he was forced to reexamine his earlier beliefs about the value of the West as a historical model after which other people might pattern their societies.

As early as 1847 Herzen began to express his disappointment in the West, and these first complaints soon became sweeping condemnations. "At first sight," he wrote, "there is much that is still normal; things run smoothly, judges judge, the churches are open, the stock exchange hums with activity, armies maneuver, palaces blaze with light. But the soul of life has fled, everyone is uneasy at heart, death is at our elbow, and, in reality, nothing goes well." Herzen's early admiration for Western ideas and institutions was replaced by the conviction that the West was a stale society without clear direction or a sense of historical mission. Western Europe was not progressive and idealistic but old and tired, and Westerners had mistaken "the agonies of death for the pains of birth." In spite of all efforts to disguise it, senility was the basic fact of Western life. "Paris! How long has this name shone like a guiding star to the peoples? Who did not love her, who did not bow down before her? But her time has passed. Away with her. . . . Paris has grown old, and youthful dreams no longer become her." In 1850, in his *Letters from Italy and France*, Herzen included what can only be called a historical obituary on the West. "Europe is very old, and it does not have strength enough to enable it to soar to the height of its thought nor ability enough to realize its aspirations. Europe has, moreover, after its long career, the right to enter unashamedly into the great stream of history." In similar language, in *From the Other Shore*, he argued that "Europe will live out her miserable days in the twilight of imbecility, in sluggish feelings without conviction, without fine arts, without powerful poetry. Weak, sickly, foolish generations will somehow stretch on until the eruption, until some lava or other will encase them in stone and commit them to the oblivion of chronicles." The great days of Western Europe were in the past, and nothing could halt the inevitable decline. "Everything shrinks and withers in this exhausted soil: there is no talent, no creation, no strength of mind, no strength of will. This world has outlived the age of its glory." There were no vital reserves upon which the West could call, and "it is time to make an end to this stupid Europe, it is time to make room for a new world."

There were many things about the West that offended Herzen and influenced his changing evaluation. While in Russia, he had thought of Western Europe as a society propelled by a central historical drive that destroyed the old and the outmoded and created the new and the pertinent. He had assumed that there was a direction to Western history. But once in the West, he could find no such direction, no such drive. Instead, there was only confusion and a hideous conglomeration of the old and the new, the true and the false. The West was cluttered with a host of political and social institutions and intellectual habits which were without value but which Western man could not abandon. There was no clear focus to Western life, no steady surge that carried men toward some great goal. Rather, Western civilization consisted of "an obsolete, slavish, and spurious collection of ideas," of "absurd idols, which belong to another age and which linger on among us, a nuisance to some, a terror to others." The history of the past weighed heavily upon the West. The influence of "the Roman law, of feudal institutions, of Catholic priests and Protestant preachers, of a shop-keeper code" had resulted in one destructive compromise after another, and these compromises "reveal themselves in all their pathetic absurdity, in all their repulsive lunacy." Western men had erroneously assumed that they could build a satisfying civilization without resolving the contradictions in their lives. They had failed, and now they were lost in a jungle of opposing ideologies and institutions. The forms of Western life — political, social, and intellectual — were incompatible with the aroused desires of the individual, and the European art of compromise had gone as far as possible in the attempt to reconcile the demand for freedom and equality with archaic patterns of living. Western history was at an impasse. It could not go forward, and it could not retreat. The West was neither aristocratic nor democratic. Western man was not a slave, but he was not free. He thought in terms of the future, but he longed for the securities of the past.

Even Western revolutionaries, with all their great words and their noble slogans, had failed to transform Western society. Revolutionary movements had become exercises in futility, activities engaged in by those Herzen called "clowns of freedom." European revolutionaries were basically men who "at the same time undermine the old order and cling to it, light the fuse and try to stop the explosion." A series of half-victories and half-defeats had left nothing but revolutionary confusion and revolutionary daydreaming. Whatever they were called — democrats, radicals, socialists — Western revolutionaries had proved to be historical failures. Moreover, the influences of the society in which they lived had been too strong and had undermined their revolutionary resolve. "The French democrat is only an advanced bourgeois, and the German revolutionary is merely the German philistine in a different stage of development.... One abortive Western revolution is succeeded by another just as impotent." Revolution in the West had not been a creative experience, but almost entirely destructive. In Herzen's opinion, no radical reconstruction of the West was possible, and "the religious and political revolutions are petering out under the weight of their impotence.... They have stripped Throne and Altar of the prestige they once enjoyed, but they have not established the era of freedom. They have lit new desires in the hearts of men, but they have not provided ways of satisfying them."

The clearest indication of what had happened in the West, and for Herzen the most horrifying, was that Western society had been delivered into the hands of the money-chasing, comfort-seeking, narrow-minded bourgeoisie. Originality, intellectual stamina, and high purpose had disappeared, and "the habits of the bourgeoisie have become universal." Hatred of the bourgeoisie was one of Herzen's strongest emotions, and he was savage in his description of the effect of bourgeois thinking and living on the West Europeans. He even coined a Russian word, *meshchanstvo*, the bourgeois state of mind, which entered into the Russian vocabulary and carried the connotations of spiritual mediocrity, squalid self-indulgence, and hysterical fear of change. Because of this bourgeois influence, Western "conservatives and radicals are both rubbish — and mediocre rubbish at that." In a bourgeois society politicians were either "democrats who flatter the mob" or "aristocrats who slander the people." European life had been polluted by the ugly and stultifying attitudes of the bourgeoisie, and "the forms of life become less and less charming and graceful; people shrink into themselves, tremble and live like shop-keepers." Nothing in the West had been able to escape this debilitating influence. Western man had undergone a series of traumatic historical experiences. But "none has altered his ideas, while the natural historical process has left the slimy stratum of the petty bourgeoisie, under which the fossilized aristocratic classes are buried and the rising masses submerged." Everything had been poisoned by this "mean and squalid bourgeois atmosphere which covers the whole of France like a green scum." The brightness and the glory of Western life had disappeared, and Western man had become a mockery of the great aspirations he claimed to express. "I am truly horrified by modern man," wrote Herzen. "Such absence of feeling, such narrowness of outlook, such lack of passion and indignation, such feebleness of thought."

Thus the Russian who had come to Paris dedicated to the values of Western civilization became a critic of that civilization and denied that the West had anything to offer those who looked to her for guidance. What many thought of as the particular virtues of the West — her political institutions, her growing economic power, her developing sense of nationalism, her individualism, her ability to absorb and modify contradictory ideas — were for Alexander Herzen indications of decline. The "childish hopes, the youthful dreams," which had once been his, must be abandoned, and a new source of historical inspiration must be found.

In Herzen's case, this new inspiration was Russia. In 1858 he wrote that having begun his exile "with a shout of joy when crossing the frontier, I concluded it with a spiritual return to my own country. At the edge of perdition, I was saved by faith in Russia." According to Herzen, Russia was entering world history "full of strength and energy" at precisely the moment when the West was approaching a historical catastrophe. Russia carried within herself "the elements of a profound revolution," and she had no need to look to the West as an example. "I am convinced," wrote Herzen, "that Russia has entered upon a new era in her development, that she is leaving behind her the rocky road of her harsh upbringing and is entering now the broad channel of adult life. They do not know Russia who want to measure her in years and meters. Those standards which a study of Western civilization has set up in our minds can find neither room nor substitutes for the peculiar and individual properties of Russia's national life."

Herzen thus set his native Russia against the West. He had once written: "only the mighty thought of the West is able to fertilize the seeds slumbering in the patriarchal mode of life of the Slavs. Without the thought of the West our future cathedral will not rise above its foundations." But this attitude was abandoned, and "the more I lost all hope in Latin-German Europe, the more my belief in Russia revived." To a large extent, Herzen rejected his youthful years as a Westerner and admitted that his earlier interest in the West had been a mistake. The influence of the West upon Russian intellectuals had been disastrous, and such Russians had become ineffective and rootless individuals, "spoiled for Russia by European prejudices and for Europe by Russian habits." An over-developed interest in West Europe had robbed Russians of a knowledge of their own country, and "eternally looking toward Europe and attentive to struggles and questions beyond our frontiers, we were very little acquainted with our own Russian people."

Herzen conceded that Russia lacked the refinements of the West. She was, by comparison with Western Europe, crude and rough, and her history was full of suffering and oppression. But her cultural inexperience gave her a particular strength, and her mistakes were those of the energetic and spirited child not those of the clever and decadent adult, the spent bourgeois. The political and social arrangements of Western life were artificial and sterile, consisting of "phantoms, specters, empires, royalties, dynasties, dukes, princes, merchants, frontiers, alliances. . . . Wait a quarter of an hour: all this will not exist; it is but the outline of a dream." Russia, on the other hand, put no faith in such instrumentalities of political or social life. Rather, in Herzen's view, the future of Russia was not dependent upon the forms of community life but upon the mysterious strength of the Russian "people." Herzen was the first important advocate of what is called *narodnichestvo*, a belief that "among the people is preserved the secret of the true life, a secret concealed from the governing cultured classes." According to this interpretation, the true values of life are carried in the dark recesses of popular experience and are not expressed in political philosophies, social organizations, or cultural attitudes. Thus Herzen based his hopes on what he called "an infinite sense, embracing all the qualities of the Russian people, of the Russian way of life, of the Russian turn of mind."

Herzen believed that the world must be transformed in the light of men's new knowledge and their new aspirations. But the West was incapable of carrying out such a transformation, and any Western revolution was certain to be "poor in spiritual vigor and sickly in imaginative feeling." The West was able only to modify certain minor aspects of her condition, but a real revolution was beyond her capabilities. "Until these days the European world has undergone only reformations; the foundations of the modern states have remained intact; only some of their details have been changed. Such was Luther's Reformation, such the Revolution of 1789. The social revolution will not be like that."

Russia, however, had the capacity for true revolutionary activity, and she was uncontaminated by those experiences that had corrupted the West. The Russians did not have the confused thoughts, the superficial convictions, and the misdirected energies that characterized the European. A Russian revolution would not result in a "constitution made by the landlords." Nor would it bring to power "a pack of growling shopkeepers." It would be a "great social transformation," which would "pose the most vital questions." This revolution would be carried out "not by diplomatic intrigue, not by international degradation, not by chancellery stratagems, but by the open highway of freedom and progress." Not Europe but Russia possessed the characteristics necessary to move "toward a re-created society, toward a new and different form, toward a new organization of life."

Herzen retained this ultimate faith in Russia through all the ill fortune of his last years. His position as a political journalist was destroyed by his opposition to the Russian suppression of the Polish revolt of 1863 and by the belief that he was an accomplice of the violent revolutionary groups that appeared within Russia in the eighteen-sixties. The popularity of *The Bell* was forfeited, and in 1865 Herzen left London for Switzerland. Here he found himself involved in a series of controversies with a new group of Russian revolutionaries, both inside Russia and out, who were dedicated to the use of terror and assassination and conspiracy in order to carry out their revolutionary program.

Herzen was not impressed by these new men of violence, whom he once described as "the permanent tribunes of the clubs and cafes" and on another occasion as "the syphilis of our revolutionary lusts." To him, these Russians were only copies of the outdated Western revolutionary with their overheated imagination, their inapposite theorizing, and their excessive enthusiasm. In fact, they were, with their passion for destruction and their dependence upon violence, guilty of trying to introduce into Russia the defunct revolutionary ideas of the West. They believed that revolution could be spread "like an epidemic of smallpox, or suddenly injected into the brain like medicine forcibly poured down a horse's throat." Such an approach could only produce what it had already produced in the West — senseless spasms of destruction, useless fits of brutality, and, ultimately, sterile compromise. In his last writings — "Letters to an Old Comrade" and "The Physician, the Dying, and the Dead" — Herzen warned his countrymen against relying upon outdated and false revolutionary ideas. "Let every conscientious man ask himself this question: Is he ready? Is he so certain in his mind concerning the new organization toward which we are moving? Does he understand the process (apart from sheer destruction) that will accomplish the transformation of old forms into new? . . . Woe to the revolution that is poor in spiritual vigor and sickly in imaginative feeling. . . ." To introduce ill-suited revolutionary ideas into Russia would be fatal to the Russian spirit, and the result could be monstrous: "Ghenghis Khan with telegraphs, steamships, and railroads, with Carnot and Monge on the staff, their soldiers armed with Minié rifles and Congreve rockets, and led by Batu Khan."

Herzen's complaints had little effect upon those to whom they were directed. He was dismissed as one who "is not of the stuff of revolutionary leaders" and as "a confirmed skeptic." In January, 1870, he died in

Paris, the city of his early dreams and his great disappointment. It is, perhaps, a further irony that his son and namesake, to whom Herzen had dedicated one of his books as a pledge to the boy's revolutionary future, married an Italian girl whom his father described as "cold and calculating" and settled in Italy to become, of all things, a simple bourgeois.

Henry James

On July 26, 1915, the American writer Henry James became a naturalized British citizen. Shortly before the naturalization process was completed, James had written to his nephew to explain his decision. He stressed the sympathy he had for the British, presently engaged in the First World War, and his belief that he should through some act show his feelings of identity with them. "I have spent here all the best years of my life — they practically have been my life; about a twelvemonth hence I shall have been domiciled uninterruptedly in England for forty years, and there is not the least possibility at my age, and in my state of health, of my ever returning to the U.S., or taking up any relation with it as a country. . . . Regard my proceeding as a simple act and offering of allegiance and devotion, recognition and gratitude (for long years of innumerable relations that have meant so much to me), and it remains perfectly simple." The following February Henry James died. He was almost seventy-three years old, and he had been a British citizen for seven months.

James was born in 1843 in New York, a member of a family whose founder had come to America soon after the Revolutionary War. He and his brother William, who was to become one of America's most renowned philosophers, were educated in a variety of schools in America and Europe, and in 1862 Henry entered Harvard University. In the second half of the eighteen-sixties he began his career as a writer. He made several trips to Europe during the next few years, and in 1877 he settled permanently in London.

James had a long and productive life. He was the author of numerous short stories, plays, articles, and novels. His important writings include *The American, The Portrait of a Lady, The Bostonians, The Princess Casamassima, The Ambassadors, The Wings of the Dove,* and *The Golden Bowl.* He knew many of the leading literary men of his time, including the Americans Henry Adams, Stephen Crane, Hamlin Garland, William Dean Howells, and George Santayana, the Englishmen Rudyard Kipling, Robert Louis Stevenson, and H. G. Wells, the Frenchmen Gustave Flaubert and Émile Zola, and the Russian Ivan Turgenev. His career stretched from the American Civil War to the First World War — from Walt Whitman, whose *Drum Taps* he reviewed in 1865, to D. H. Lawrence, in whom he expressed an interest near the end of his life.

Probably no major writer has been attacked and defended with such vigor as Henry James. His prose style, his straining for effect, and his general outlook have offended many. Others have found these very attributes to be virtues of the highest order. He has been called "an effeminate old donkey," "the nicest old lady I ever met," "a literary gent," and various other uncomplimentary things by those who found him untalented and uninteresting. He has also been praised as the master craftsman, the most refined of writers. He has been condemned as an expatriate and lauded as a great cosmopolitan, subjected to scurrilous attacks as a racist, a prissy, and a secret sexual voyeur and extolled as a perceptive student of human nature.

One may argue about James' literary talent. But his importance as a cultural commentator, and particularly as a commentator upon the relationship of America to Europe, is unquestioned. He saw clearly the ambiguous connection of the New and the Old Worlds, and the best part of his fiction is concerned with the shock of recognition that took place when Americans and Europeans saw themselves as they really were and rid themselves of the illusions that handicapped their perception of their common reality. He saw the twisted, tormented course of reconciliation that must take place between America and Europe, and he attempted to set the position of the two areas in some kind of perspective that would make understandable the actions and the thoughts of both.

As a place to live and to work James chose Europe. He found European life much more attractive than life in America. The surroundings seemed to him more congenial, the society more pleasant, and the intellectual stimulus more intense. He was hypnotized by the "great lighted and decorated scene" of Europe, where, it seemed to him, action and thought were united in a cultural amalgamation that sustained the creative artist. Europe was old and traditional and, for James, culturally wise. It had the experience of countless centuries, and there was a ripeness and a subtlety that prompted a complex interplay of human affairs. London might be ugly, but it was "the biggest aggregation of human life — the most complete compendium of the world." James was interested in the question of morality, and what has been called "its relation to manners and to civilization." And he believed that it was in Europe that he could best study this question. Europeans seemed to him "more largely nourished, deeper, denser, stronger," and the continuity of human effort had made the human personality more complex and more complicated than anywhere else. As James once wrote, "It takes a great deal of history to make a little tradition, a great deal of tradition to make a little taste, and a great deal of taste to make a little art." Europe, for him, had the history, the tradition, the taste, and the art.

Yet Henry James remained, in spite of his liking for the amenities of Europe and its intellectual and cultural brilliance, an American observer abroad. He accepted the fact that it was "a complex fate being an American," and in 1878 he remarked that "I know what I am about, and I have always my eyes on my native land." His moral view had "an American bias," and Edmund Wilson has written that "James . . . is an American who . . . finally chooses to live in England; and he is imbued to a certain extent with the European point of view. The monuments of feudal and ancient Europe, the duchesses and princes and princesses who seem to carry on the feudal tradition, are still capable of making modern life look to him dull, undistinguished, and tame. But the American in the long run always insistently asserts himself."

One of James' principal themes may be briefly expressed in this way: What happens to an American when he confronts the old, established culture of Europe? As the American critic Randolph Bourne pointed out, James had a "wonderful sensitiveness to the spiritual differences between ourselves and the Older World" and "the subtle misunderstandings that follow our contact with it." In some of his early writings these misunderstandings centered about a conflict of manners. But in his later works the dramatic conflict in his fiction is grounded in differing conceptions of morality. Manners become less and less important in James' fiction. Rather, the serious problem is the way in which manners and conventions determine morals and morality.

In James' view, the usual contact of Americans with Europeans is superficial and false. In 1879 he wrote that Americans "are conscious of being the youngest of the great nations, of not being of the European family, of being placed on the circumference of the circle of civilisation rather than at the centre. . . . The sense of this relativity . . . replaces that quiet and comfortable sense of the absolute, as regards its own position in the world, which reigns supreme in the British and in the Gallic genius." Many of his Americans are adrift in Europe, the women shopping and buying, the men bored and indifferent. Such people have no understanding of European life and clutter the European landscape. For them, Europe is a grand and glorious fair where they may eat strange foods, look with rather vacant stares at art treasures, indulge themselves with guilty smirks in what they regard as immoralities, and attempt with money to fill the vacancy of the experience. They are "innocents abroad — wide-eyed, but boorish, culturally underprivileged." They have a "hankering after the externals of European culture," and are the victims of their delusions about Europe. They believe in "fables," and have a romantic view of country houses, castles, archaic sideshows that lead them further and further from any understanding of Europe. In 1869, before he had settled in Europe, James wrote of his impressions of the Americans abroad. "We seem a people of character, we seem to have energy, capacity, and intellectual stuff in ample measure." But "with culture quite left out. It's the absolute and incredible lack of culture that strikes you in common travelling Americans."

Many of James' portraits of Americans are devastating. He had a good eye for the ugly habit, the gawkish mistake, the vulgar blunder, the crass emptiness of the rich American who had come to Europe to spend his money or to debase himself before an aristocracy that was prepared to tolerate him because of his wealth. "Most of James' Americans produce obscure and vulgar 'things' which they sell in huge quantities, as a result of which they are able to travel to Europe to see and even to buy 'real' things." These are the cultural outsiders, those who sentimentally over-evaluate the very Europe that they look on with scorn. They see only the externals of their surroundings and never develop the inner eye that discerns what rests beneath the surface or behind the facade.

There was, in James' mind, little hope for such people. But there was another type of American who brought something of value to Europe and by combining his Americanism with the culture of Europe became a new man. In 1867 James wrote to a friend: ". . . we Americans are (without cant) men of the future. . . ." And he went on: ". . . I think that to be an American is an excellent preparation for culture. We have exquisite qualities as a race, and it seems to me that we are ahead of the European races in the fact that . . . we can deal freely with forms of civilization not our own, can pick and choose and assimilate and in short (aesthetically, etc.) claim our property wherever we find it." And then James spoke of the American quality that he was to discuss again and again in his writing. "We must of course have something our own — something distinctive and homogeneous — and I take it that we shall find it in our moral consciousness, our unprecedented spiritual lightness and vigor."

Americans with this quality wish to participate in the richness of European life without abandoning their American characteristics. They have a feeling for and an appreciation of European culture. As James wrote of his heroine Isabel Archer in *Portrait of a Lady*, "to live in such a place was, for Isabel, to hold to her head all day a shell of the sea of the past. This vague eternal rumour kept her imagination awake." Similarly in *The American*, Christopher Newman (the name itself is an indication of the singular position of the American — Christopher as the given name of the discoverer of America and a "New Man") says: "I have the instincts, if I haven't the forms of a high old civilisation."

In almost all of James' important fiction, he pits the spontaneous moral consciousness of the young American against the massed sanctions of European society, sets what must be called a sense of American righteousness against European social proprieties. His Americans are subjected to the ordeal of a European society that can find little place for the energies, the ambitions, and the aspirations of the newcomers from across the Atlantic. The Americans are inquisitive, self-reliant, and open-minded, and they expect these qualities to be accepted in place of the more traditional European attributes of taste and culture. Isabel Archer demands that Europe accept her for what she is — independent, intelligent, honest, and imaginative.

In this conflict of values, as James presents it, "innocence" is usually on the American side, "experience" and "knowledge" on the European. This American innocence is a source of American brightness and energy. It is also a measure of American ignorance, an indication of a superficial grasp of experience itself. Americans have little concept of evil or even of the complexities of life. They have basically a story-book view of existence, a simple morality, and have difficulty in separating the romantic and the real, the sentimental and the objective. Thus Christopher Newman in *The American* has this basic flaw in his conception of life. "The world, to his vision, was a great bazaar, where one might stroll about and purchase handsome things." So long as one sees life through such a haze of misconception, there can be little hope of understanding Europe or, for that matter, anything else.

The best of James' Americans are those who awaken from the empty dream of an enchanted Europe, of a Europe that does not exist. They are hurt and wronged by Europeans who see them as both naive and, because of their explosive energy, dangerous. They are tricked into scandalous marriages, disgraced socially, wronged by aristocrats "pretending to represent the highest possible civilisation and to be in every way superior." They are subjected to social, sexual, and cultural indignities, and their innocence and their "spontaneous moral sense" are marred.

And what is the result? One of Henry James' friends was the American Henry Adams, who wrote a book entitled *The Education of Henry Adams*. It is possible to argue that most of James' fiction could be put together under the single general title "The Education of an American." For James' Americans, or the best of them, do learn, and in this process of education Europe is the great school. It is both glorious and corrupt, beautiful and ugly, warmly humanistic and coldly cruel. In 1869 James published a short story "Gabrielle de Bergerac." Here he had a character remark while looking at an old castle: "The truth is, this old feudal fortress is a decidedly melancholy spot. It's haunted with the ghosts of the past. It smells of tragedies, sorrows, and cruelties . . . it's like that history of that abominable past of which it's a relic. At the first glance we see nothing but the great proportions, the show and the splendor; but when we come to explore it, we detect a vast underground world of iniquity and suffering. Only half of the castle is above the soil; the rest is dungeons and vaults and oubliettes." This description was appropriate to Europe itself, a combination of Western man's glories and crimes, his great accomplishments and his diseased past. In a similar way, a character in *The Princess Casamassima* remarks that Paris, "the most brilliant city in the world," is "also the most blood-stained."

So James' Americans learn that aesthetic refinement can often hide an emptiness of spirit and soul. They learn that innocence is only a limited virtue and that it ill becomes men to judge things by their appearances. They learn the truth of James' argument that "one of the responsibilities of being an American is fighting against a superstitious valuation of Europe." They learn that spontaneity must be combined with experience. As a character in *The Ambassadors* realizes, reality and even virtue cannot be measured by the cramped moral "notions with which he started from home." In the relationship of America and Europe, there could not be innocence on one side and experience and knowledge on the other. Instead, there must be a combination of these elements, a mingling of the strengths and weaknesses of the two great parts of the West. In one way, James' writing was one long sermon on the possibility of Americans becoming cosmopolitan members of Western society.

Henry James knew that this would be a difficult process. In spite of the fact that he lived in Europe the greater part of his adult life, he had a rather clear understanding of American realities. In 1904 he visited the United States. He was in New England and New York and then made a trip across the country to California. As he wrote: "I found my native land, after so many years, interesting, formidable, fearsome and fatiguing, and much more difficult to see and deal with" than "I had supposed." America was "an extraordinary world, an altogether huge 'proposition,' as they say there." It gave the "impression of material and political power; but almost cruelly charmless." Everything in America was bigger, louder, and stronger than in Europe. "The will to grow is everywhere written large, and to grow at no matter what or whose expense. . . ." There was in America "a question of scale and space and chance, margin and elbow-room, the quantity of floor and loudness of the dance-music; a question of the ambient air; above all, the permitting medium, which had at once, for the visitor's personal inhalation, a dry taste in the mouth. Thin and clear and colourless, what would it ever say 'No' to?"

Yet James did not reject America. In 1906, two years after his visit to the U.S., he remarked to a friend: "If I were to live my life again I would be American — steep myself in it — know no other. I would study its beautiful side. This mixture of Europe and America is disastrous. It makes a man neither one thing nor the other." But these words can be taken with some measure of skepticism. James' Americans do survive as Americans. They do awaken from their dreams, and they do bring to the European scene the strength and vigor of America. They show a remarkable capacity for learning, and James anticipates the impact of America upon the Western world in the twentieth century. He saw the shock that both America and Europe were to undergo as the power relationships and the influence within the West shifted. He visualized what could be described as a mutual fertilization process, whereby America and Europe would contribute to each other's own view of the world and thus become a strongly united cultural unit.

A critic has pointed out that James is primarily concerned with the question, "How may one take possession of the great house?" Here is a true insight into the problem James poses. The great house is that of Western civilization, and James sets forth the attempts of the Americans to realize what they regard as their inheritance. And he set down also the difficulties of this quest to possess, not merely to occupy or to own, this great house. In *The Ambassadors*, a character finds himself confronted by "the vast bright Babylon, like some huge iridescent object, a jewel brilliant and hard, in which the parts are not to be discriminated nor differences comfortably marked. It twinkled and trembled and melted together, and what seemed all surface one moment seemed all depth the next." This confrontation, in its most meaningful sense, is that of the American facing the dense, rich texture of European history and European experience and without vulgarization or arrogance comprehending its value and thus making himself in turn a contributing participant in the common life of America and Europe.

SUGGESTIONS FOR FURTHER READING

Particularly recommended as studies of the relationship of Europe and the United States are R. W. B. Lewis, The American Adam *(1955), Charles L. Sanford,* The Quest for Paradise: Europe and the American Moral Imagination *(1961), Seymour M. Lipset,* The First New Nation *(1963), and A. N. Kaul,* The American Vision *(1963). Henry S. Commager, ed.,* America in Perspective: The United States through Foreign Eyes *(1947), and Warren S. Tryon,* A Mirror for Americans: Life and Manners in the United States 1790-1870 as Recorded by American Travelers *(1952), contain interesting material, while Edward W. Chester's* Europe Views America *(1962) is a convenient summary of some of the important European commentators upon the United States in the twentieth century.*

The relationship of Europe and Russia has also received a great deal of attention. The following books may be profitably consulted: M. B. Petrovich, The Emergence of Russian Panslavism, 1856-1870 *(1956), Hans Kohn,* Pan-Slavism: Its History and Ideology *(1960), Edward C. Thaden,* Conservative Nationalism in Nineteenth-Century Russia *(1964), N. Riasanovsky,* Russia and the West in the Teaching of the Slavophils *(1952), and Robert E. MacMaster,* Danilevsky. A Russian Totalitarian Philosopher *(1967).*

The best source for Tocqueville is, of course, Democracy in America. *Tocqueville's* Memoirs *and much of his incidental writing are also available. Three recent studies discuss interesting aspects of this attractive and perceptive man: Jack Lively,* The Social and Political Thought of Alexis de Tocqueville *(1962), Marvin Zetterbaum,* Tocqueville and the Problem of Democracy *(1967), and Seymour Drescher,* Dilemmas of Democracy: Tocqueville and Modernization *(1968).*

Alexander Herzen's My Past and Thoughts *(reprinted in 1968) is a fascinating autobiography. His* From the Other Shore, *which contains many comments about the West and Russia, is also available in English translation. E. H. Carr's* The Romantic Exiles *(1933) contains many interesting and valuable comments on Herzen. An excellent introduction to Herzen and the Russian Westerners is Isaiah Berlin's "A Marvelous Decade," in* Encounter *(June, November, and December, 1955).*

There is so much material on Henry James that a student is in danger of drowning. A good start could be made with the following: Christof Wegelin, The Image of Europe in Henry James *(1958), Oscar Cargill,* The Novels of Henry James *(1961), Leon Edel, ed.,* Henry James: A Collection of Critical Essays *(1963), Douglas Jefferson,* Henry James and the Modern Reader *(1964), and Alan Holder,* Three Voyagers in Search of Europe: A Study of Henry James, Ezra Pound, and T. S. Eliot *(1966).*

Last Crumbs, Henri de Toulouse-Lautrec, 1891, Courtesy, Museum of Fine Arts, Boston.

8

Into the Twentieth Century

1882 Triple Alliance (Germany, Austria, and Italy) formed. The most important of the series of alliances and actions whereby Bismarck attempted to maintain the security of Germany and peace in Europe. Supplemented by the Three Emperors' League (Germany, Russia, and Austria), a policy of isolation of France, and friendship with England.

1882 Founding in France of League of Patriots. A belligerent, nationalistic organization designed to support the army and the power of the French state in order that the national "disgrace" might be revenged.

1882 British bombarded Alexandria, occupied Cairo, and British advisers took charge of Egyptian affairs.

1883 Beginning of German colonial empire with establishment of commercial interests in southwest Africa.

1885 Establishment of the Congo State with Belgium's King Leopold II as ruler and personal overlord. The Congo was administered and brutally and cruelly exploited as the personal property of Leopold. In 1908, following the revelation of scandals, the Congo was ceded to the Belgian nation by the king.

1889 Great Paris Exhibition, the first to be lighted by electricity and featuring the recently completed Eiffel Tower.

1889 British Naval Defense Act. Provided that the British fleet was to be as strong as the fleets of the next two strongest powers.

1889 Britain and France agreed on spheres of control on Ivory and Gold Coasts and Senegal and Gambia in Africa.

1890	Julius Langbehn's *Rembrandt as Educator.* An attack upon industrialization, democracy, and rational intellectualism as responsible for the decline of German culture.
1890	Pope Leo XIII adopted a policy of conciliation with the French republic. In the encyclical *Libertas* in 1888 the pope said that democracy and Catholicism were not incompatible.
1891	Pan-German League founded. An influential and sinister pressure group, the League included industrialists, military men, and intellectuals. The claim was made that historical necessity demanded a greatly expanded Germany and even world rule.
1893	French acquired a protectorate over Laos, following earlier control of Cambodia, Annam, Cochin China, and Tonkin in southeast Asia.
1893-1894	French-Russian agreement to support each other in case of an armed attack by Germany.
1895	Wilhelm Röntgen announced the discovery of x-rays.
1896	Madagascar proclaimed a French colony.
1897	Maurice Barrès' *The Uprooted.* A widely read attack upon intellectualism, science, and cosmopolitanism.
1898	Foundation of Action Française, an association dedicated to bringing about the destruction of the French republic. The beginning of a "forty-year vendetta against the Republic and the Jews, Protestants, democrats, immigrants, internationalists, and liberal Catholics."
1898	Passage of the first German Navy Bill and the beginning of German naval expansion.
1898-1899	Fashoda crisis involved France and Britain in conflict in the Nile region of Africa. France forced to retire.
1899	Baghdad railway concession granted to Germany by Turkish sultan.
1899	Nigeria made a British protectorate.
1899-1902	Britain put down the attempts of the South African Boers (descendants of Dutch settlers) to establish an independent republic.

1900	Boxer rising in China and the dispatch of European expeditionary force. Further concessions exacted from China.
1900	Sigmund Freud's *The Meaning of Dreams,* usually regarded as the beginning of psychoanalysis.
1902	John A. Hobson's *Imperialism,* the most important of the early critical studies of European imperialism.
1904	Conclusion of an alliance — the Entente Cordiale — between Britain and France.
1905	Albert Einstein announced his special theory of relativity. In 1915 this was supplemented by his general theory of relativity.
1905	Crisis in Morocco brought strain between Germany and France.
1905-1914	The "Liberal Era" in Britain. A period of reforms usually identified with David Lloyd George. Passage of new workingman's compensation act, an old age pension law, a national insurance act, a minimum wage bill, and the "People's Budget," which shifted the tax burden to wealthier classes by means of income and inheritance taxes, levies on unearned incomes, and taxes on unearned increments of land.
1906	Launching by Britain of the Dreadnought, the first all-big-gun battleship.
1906-1911	Strikes and labor troubles in France.
1906	Henri Bergson's *Creative Evolution* "asserted the primacy of spirit, sentiment, and individual instinct in arriving at truth and action."
1907	British-Russian entente. Largely concerned with conflicts in the Near and Far East, the agreement had wider implications.
1908	Georges Sorel's *Reflections on Violence.* Developed the "myth" of violence as a creative force in the solution of social and historical problems.
1909	First air flight across the English Channel.
1909	Robert E. Peary reached the North pole. In 1911 Roald Amundsen reached the South pole.

1911	Ernest Rutherford introduced the nuclear model of the atom.
1911	Thomas Morgan showed that certain traits are genetically linked on the chromosome and thus opened the way to the construction of genetic maps.
1911	Friedrich von Bernhardi's *Germany and the Next War.* "War is not only a necessary element in the life of people, but also an indispensable factor in culture, indeed the highest expression of the strength and life of truly cultured peoples."
1912	Sultan of Morocco forced to accept French protectorate.
1913	France increased military service from two to three years.
1914	Malaya brought under British control.

It was a confident and secure Western world that entered into the twentieth century. How numerous had been the accomplishments of the one hundred years since the French Revolution. The triumphs of industrialization, scientific investigation, and nationalism justified in the minds of most a belief in unending economic, social, and intellectual achievement. Freedom and power had been combined to create a political order that appeared to set a standard for the entire world. The symbols of Western success — the railroads, the military establishments, the factories, the intellectual excitement — were obvious for all to see. Each of the Western nations exhibited this sense of security and prosperity in its own way. Britain was solid, steady, responsible, the great arbiter of international disputes. She had the navy, she had the money, and she had the talent. She was at home in what seemed to many of her citizens to be the natural order of the world where "wider still and wider, shall thy bounds be set. God who made thee mighty, make thee mightier yet." In Germany the recently created state brought the Germans respect and even admiration. German science, German industry, and German power instilled in the German citizen a sense of security and of inevitable progress. In France this was the period of what was called "the sweet life," when the Germans, in a well-known phrase, spoke of being as "content as God in France." It was the time of "Degas and Renoir, of Lautrec and Monet, of bistros and the Moulin de la Gallette, of

Maxims and the Lapin Agile, of Verlaine and Rimbaud, of Zola and Sarah Bernhardt, of Debussy and Ravel." In the United States the western frontier was settled, a national identity had been established, and there was the common belief that the promise of the future lay with the Americans. Even that mysterious giant, Russia, appeared to be making her way, tortuously but surely, along what was regarded as the great Western road of progress.

European intellectual life was cosmopolitan, stimulating, and creative. In drama, music, art, and literature new and revolutionary forms of expression were providing new dimensions for the eye, the ear, and the mind. Men such as Sigmund Freud, Max Planck, and Albert Einstein were presenting new insights into the way men saw themselves and their surroundings. The wealthy enjoyed good food, large houses, and participation in the colorful world of the theater, international resorts, and social gatherings. In the more prosaic, day-to-day life of the West there was a poise and a sureness and even a form of grace, not flamboyant but subdued and disciplined. For the majority of the middle class it was an age of rather stiff manners and stiff dress. There was a belief in the value of hard work, in the necessity of solid and tangible possessions, and in a somewhat stuffy but sincerely held code of proper behavior. There was intellectual narrowness and a stifling moralism, but also a respect for knowledge, a sturdy commonsense, and a dedication to the principles at least of a tolerant and humane community.

In 1879 the German historian Leopold von Ranke had written that nothing could stop the progress of the West. "Irresistibly . . . armed with weapons and science, the spirit of the West subdues the world." And this had come to pass. The thrust of Western military power, economic penetration, and humanitarian zeal had shattered non-Western societies. British administrators and soldiers controlled the Indian subcontinent, China had been forced to make concessions to the European powers, and Africa had been parcelled out among those who coveted her. European flags flew everywhere, and "spheres of influence" had been established throughout the world. The West had taken up what was called "the white man's burden," and even those Asian and African societies that remained titularly independent were largely pawns in the hands of the Westerners who had the gunboats, the technical expertise, and the confidence to force their will upon the world. In 1903 the British political leader Sir Edward Grey remarked that "the independence of Persia is a phrase," and the statement applied to much more than Persia. A great part of the rest of the world lived at the political pleasure of the West, and the important decisions for Africans and Asians were made in London, Paris, Berlin, and St. Petersburg — and not in Delhi, Cairo, or Peking.

Life opened up to Europeans as a series of unending possibilities. Only Russia and Turkey required passports of foreigners, and the European was everywhere. He mapped unknown areas of the world, and he forced his way up forbidden rivers and through hostile jungles. As the representative of his government, he assumed fantastic powers over countless numbers of people, and he cataloged their philosophies, their languages, and their histories and created monuments of scholarship dealing with the varied ways of mankind. The opportunities for service, for thrilling adventure, and for participation in history beckoned the European to join in the most exciting enterprise. As one who lived through the period and who played a lusty and joyful part and accepted the challenge has written: "It was a glorious era."

Disappointments and Discontents

All this was true, and many of those who lived in these years were to remember them with nostalgic fondness. But there was another side to the history of the West as the nineteenth became the twentieth century. In London coaches drawn by beautifully matched horses paraded through Hyde Park, while footmen, in cocked hats, frockcoats, and white breeches, sat with folded arms alongside the drivers. But in 1900 one out of every three adult workers in the city died on public charity. In the faded photographs of the time the faces of men, women, and children — the workers in the sweatshops, the ruined farmers, the mute and suffering economic and intellectually disenfranchised — look out upon a world that had little glory and few rewards. In his famous Encyclical of 1891 Pope Leo XIII complained that "workingmen had been surrendered, isolated and helpless, to the hardheartedness of employers and the greed of unchecked competition."

There were big buildings, big factories, big battleships, big fortunes. There were also anxieties, frustrations, and political and social disorders. The brilliance of Western civilization, for many, was only the glitter of the fake and the heartless. The rising new aristocracy of industry and politics no longer opposed the old nobility but had come to terms with it. The snobbery of wealth reinforced the snobbery of birth, and both classes gained materially and both became spiritually bankrupt. There was irresponsibility on the part of the rich and the powerful that resulted in a host of subtle and not-so-subtle ethical and moral evasions. Success had bred vulgarity, and the German Jacob Burckhardt argued that the nineteenth century was an age "intoxicated with the false grandeur of mechanization, pleasurable comfort, superficial virtuosity, a mad lust for power and size, and a taste for cheap effects." Many were to agree with him.

This disappointment in the West was stated consistently throughout the last years of the nineteenth and early years of the twentieth centuries. A respected German publication in 1893 noted that "one sees the evil here, another sees it there: this one in the Jew, that one in the priests, this one in capital, that one in labor, this one in the lack of authority, that one in the lack of freedom — only one thing is certain: things are in a bad way. No one has the slightest praise for our era. It is bad, thoroughly bad, and getting constantly worse. We live in an evil time." And, in general agreement, a French writer stated in 1896: "Never has this French people of ours been so happy as it is today and never has it believed itself more to be pitied. Its grievances have grown with its comfort; and in proportion as its condition became better it deemed it worse. The mark of this century, favored among all the centuries, is to be dissatisfied with itself." These were signs of disenchantment, and in 1908 the French social critic Georges Sorel spoke of "unhappy Europe," which consisted of "ambitious Germans, Englishmen jealous of their authority, stingy Frenchmen, Italians clamoring for room to live, Balkan poachers, warlike Hungarians. What can you do with a basket of crabs that keep pinching each other?"

There were certain things in the West that prompted this sense of uneasiness. As always, generalizations must be regarded with suspicion. Yet it is difficult to deny that by the turn of the century a new and grating crudity had become part of the speech patterns and the actions of many Westerners. A swarm of gutter publications appeared in every part of the West, and there was a glorification of force and violence. There was bloody talk, particularly by many of the political leaders of Western nations, and there was bloody-mindedness. Intemperate, vulgar, and even depraved ideas made their way high and low through Europe and America. In 1900 a German lecturer in London spoke of a "lack of moderation in our public discussions," and in the speeches, the writings, and the activities of far too many people in high positions there was what must be called a corruption of moral and intellectual life. The German Emperor spoke openly of "idiotic civilians" who criticized the activities of the military establishment and wrote on the margins of state papers such words as "Rubbish! Tripe! Idiot! Son of a Bitch! Maniac! Scum!" An eminent legal scholar such as the Englishman Sir Henry Maine glorified force as a constructive element in men's affairs, and one of his countrymen dismissed complaints about the treatment of Asians and Africans with the words: "Whatever happens we have got the Maxim gun [the quick-firing automatic machine gun], and they have not." The American President Theodore Roosevelt suggested — perhaps facetiously — "taking ten or a dozen" of the American Populist leaders "out, standing . . . them against a wall, and shooting them dead," while the British political leader Granville remarked that "bombardment is a horrible thing, but it will clear the air and accelerate a solution of some sort or other." An American Attorney-General could argue that "the only true way of dealing" with troublesome workers "is by a force which is overwhelming." Brooks Adams, a member of one of America's oldest and most respected families, praised war as "the last and most crucial test of a nation's energy," and his countryman Alfred Mahan, whose writings on the uses of sea power were to influence the thinking of many statesmen, pointed out that the question of morality in international politics was "as little to the point as the morality of an earthquake."

Political Problems

By 1900 the Western world appeared to have achieved a large measure of political stability. Some form of representative government had been adopted in every important Western country, and what we could loosely call democracy — either in republics such as France and the United States or in more-or-less constitutional monarchies such as England, Italy, and Germany — had become a common pattern of political life. Western political arrangements seemed particularly appropriate to the times, and there was little popular support for drastic political change.

Yet there were indications that the Western talent for imaginative political activity had been blunted. The playwright Henrik Ibsen complained that "until now, we have been living on nothing but the crumbs from the revolutionary table of the last century, a food out of which all nutriment has been chewed." In too many cases, in place of creative thinking and an understanding of the historical situation of the West, there was jingoism, empty patriotism, and appeals to predatory and base instincts. Gustave Flaubert had pointed out earlier in the nineteenth century that "we live in the heyday of boorishness," and certainly the political life of the West exhibited few of the characteristics of elegance or intellectual refinement. "Barbarism lit by neon" was the later verdict of an Austrian writer on the Germany of the early twentieth century, and, to a greater or lesser extent, the same description was appropriate to other parts of the Western world. Politicians were often windbags who were enthusiastically applauded because they spoke of progress and victory and unending success. What have been called "coursing generalizations" became the habit of the times, and political expression was, on most occasions, nothing but mere garrulousness. Oratorical humbug and wild emotionalism became common, and a flabby showmanship replaced genuine political activity. Political leaders were awed by military parades, by wealth, and by their own empty rhetoric. It was said of one statesman that he had "learning without taste, eloquence without style, sweetness without light." And this description could have been applied to many others who claimed the right to occupy high political positions.

Every country in the West showed some signs of this political malaise. But it was most marked in France and Germany. By 1900 French cynicism toward politics had become widespread. Survival, not accomplishment, was the goal of most French politicians, and cleverness in political debate and a tenacity in hanging onto office were accepted as the signs of political success. Flaubert had remarked of nineteenth-century French leaders: "Most of the men present had served at least four governments; and they would have sold France, or the whole human race, to safeguard their fortunes, to spare themselves a moment's uneasiness or embarrassment, or else out of sheer servility, through their instinctive reverence for brute strength." The dilemma of French politics was illustrated by the career and character of the most brilliant, and perhaps the most hated, of French political personalities, Georges Clemenceau. A doctor by training, Clemenceau was a drama critic who praised Ibsen when others scoffed, and an intimate friend of Claude Monet, whose work, he wrote in 1895, was guiding man's visual sense "toward a more subtle and penetrating vision of the world." He commissioned Toulouse-Lautrec to illustrate one of his books and Gabriel Fauré to write the music for one of his plays. But his intelligence and cultural insight were matched by his vindictiveness, his brutality, and his cynicism. He was ruthless and possessed little or no faith in his countrymen to act in accordance with any ideal but the narrowest self-interest. He once summed up what must be regarded as the expression of a common French attitude toward politics. "Only the artists are on the right path," he wrote. "It may be that they can give this world some beauty, but to give it reason is impossible." It was said of Clemenceau that he avoided bad company by avoiding all company altogether.

Divided by bitter controversy over long-standing problems, shamed by her military defeat by Germany in 1870-1871, depressed by a feeling of isolation from other members of the Western community, and consumed by anxiety over her own identity, France at the turn of the century presented a picture of political despair. Democracy appeared to many to have become nothing but an attempt "to elevate the proletariat to the level of the stupidity of the bourgeoisie." French politics seemed a "pell-mell of compromise, of corruption, of charlatanism, and of absurdities." There was a growth of anarchist doctrines, of a belief in some great "pure" action that would free France and Frenchmen from the dilemma of political confusion. French intellectuals were demoralized and found it increasingly difficult to identify themselves with the political life of their own country, and Marcel Proust spoke for many of them when he remarked: "The question is not as for Hamlet, to be or not to be, but to belong or not to belong."

Germany, too, in spite of her prosperity and power, presented a picture of strain and tension in the early years of the twentieth century. German success seemed to indicate the value of German culture, and there was the dangerous tendency to equate material power with the power of the spirit, to harp upon the identity of German accomplishments and the Grace of God. A Swiss historian has remarked that the German concept of life "grew vulgar, narrow-minded, brutal, immoderate, aimless." The Emperor, William II, was erratic, arrogant, vain, and boastful, while his advisers ranged from sycophants to pedestrian bureaucrats. J. C. G. Rohl, in his *Germany without Bismarck*, has pointed out that many a German politician "held rather unusual beliefs about the proper relationship between his private interests and public obligations," and the Emperor appeared to prefer the company of a strange collection of intellectually defunct noblemen, panderers, know-nothings, and ambitious toadies. The very power of Germany acted as a stimulant to the wildest excesses of imagination and fantasy. A German wrote in 1900: "Even a courageous spirit like my own takes fright at the sight of such abysmal ignorance of the true facts, such unworldly thoughts, emotions, judgments, such illusions." What has been called "the Neanderthal temperament" appeared frequently in Germany, particularly in industrial, educational, and professional circles. Probably the best example of this type of activity was the founding of the All-German League in the late years of the nineteenth century. At the height of its influence, the League had only 18,000 members, but this membership included professors, military officers, and important civil servants. At one time thirty-eight of its members sat in the German parliament, and it had close ties with many newspapers and the German world of high finance. The League's chief aim was the establishment of a great Nordic state that would include not only the German-speaking Austrians and Swiss but also the Dutch, the Flemings, and the Scandinavians. In 1912 the League advocated the compulsory Germanization or expulsion of the Polish, Danish, and French minorities in Germany, the denial of voting rights for women, the establishment of an even stronger authoritarian structure in the state, and the withdrawal of citizenship from all Jews within Germany.

More than any other people in the West, the Germans expressed the darkest and most dangerous thoughts based upon the will to power and racial exclusiveness. Antisemitic literature flourished (Wilhelm Marr, who published *The Victory of Judaism over Germanism* in 1879, appears to have been responsible for the word antisemite), and Houston Stewart

Chamberlain's *The Foundations of the Nineteenth Century*, published in 1899, was only the most famous and influential of the many books stressing the racial basis of history and the value of being German. At times, many Germans seemed to anticipate some great catastrophe that would give them an opportunity to show how strong they were and to illustrate their superiority over the other nations of Europe. They spoke openly of "the empire of the human will," of the virtues of "powerful national action," and of "important national duties," and there was a great deal of wild talk about the glories of some final, world-shaking struggle between "Teutons" and the "Slavs and Gauls." Continual reference was made to the necessity of "advancing the national struggle" against the Poles, and one ethnic group or another was commonly described as "this inferior class of people." A German admiral wrote that "there is still a lot of room on this earth which is empty or could be made empty," and his failure to mention any specific area only made the statement more ominous.

Imperialism

The accomplishments and failures of Western civilization were indicated in a striking way by the relations of Westerners to the peoples of other parts of the world. What is called imperialism was in full flood at the turn of the century, and the control of a large part of the world by Westerners was accepted as a natural condition and one that illustrated the unique capabilities and character of the West. A French historian claimed that "colonies are to people as children are to families. A nation without a colony is a sterile power: all the praise and all the applause of history will go always to colonizing countries." The American liberal journalist William Allen White largely agreed and wrote: "It is the Anglo-Saxon's manifest destiny to go forth as a world conqueror. He will take possession of the islands of the sea. . . . This is what fate holds for the chosen people. It is so written. . . . It is to be."

Imperialism was a great historical adventure, and the conviction that there was something appropriate and inevitable about their presence and preeminence in every part of the world became an important part of the mental outlook of Western peoples. Even the costs of subduing and ruling the world did not seem too high a price to pay for such glory and triumph, although, as has been noted "two million graves of Scots, Irish, and English were scattered through India." In 1887 A. E. Housman, in his poetic tribute in honor of the fiftieth anniversary of Queen Victoria's reign, included a stanza marking the monuments to the success of empire:

> In dawns in Asia, tombstones show
> And Shropshire names are read;
> And the Nile spills his overflow
> Beside the Severn's dead.

But such things as these seemed paltry when set beside the presence of Western flags in every harbor and on every land.

Unquestionably, the West brought some valuable things to the rest of the world. It introduced Western medicine and technology, and it provided a measure of law, order, and security. Many Westerners sincerely sought the welfare and happiness of the peoples of Asia and Africa. Some Englishmen did devote themselves to India and "simply and silently laid down their lives, broken to pieces in the service of the poor and the suffering among the Indian people." In his farewell message, Viceroy Lord Curzon in 1905 set forth the high ideals of the imperialist undertaking in words addressed to those who remained behind. "To fight for the right, to abhor the imperfect, the unjust and the mean, to swerve neither to the right hand nor to the left, to care nothing for flattery or applause or odium or abuse . . . never let your enthusiasm be soured or your courage grow dim. . . ."

It is also true that those Asians, and to a lesser extent, Africans who were in a position to benefit from the Western presence were attracted to and influenced by Western ideas and institutions and themselves became Westernized. Western military and economic power and organizational ability fascinated the more alert Asians and Africans, and many were persuaded that they should borrow from the West the instruments whereby their own societies might be transformed. But Western success was associated with more than military might and economic wealth. There was an almost pathetic admiration for Western concepts of individual liberty. It is easy to scoff at this rather simple acceptance of Western libertarian ideas, and many non-Westerners were themselves to become disabused by their actual experience with their Western masters. But it was genuine. In 1878 a young Turkish diplomat visited an exhibition in Paris. In a letter commenting upon his experience in the French capital, he sat down a truly awesome — perhaps even embarrassing — description of what he regarded as the essence of the Western example. "In front of the central gate there is a statue of freedom; she has a staff in her hand and is seated on a chair. Her style and appearance convey this message: 'Oh worthy visitors! When you look upon this fascinating display of human progress, do not forget that all these achievements are the work of freedom. It is under the protection of freedom that peoples and nations attain happiness. Without freedom, there can be no security; without security, no endeavor; without endeavor, no prosperity; without prosperity, no happiness.' "

The going out of the Westerners into the world was often justified as a great civilizing mission, and there was a certain evangelistic fervor that animated those who went to far places. An English missionary could claim that "God has, in a strange way, given us India in trust for the accomplishment of His grand designs concerning it," or another that God had given India "to England for the benefit of its 180 million peoples so that you might communicate the light of the Bible and the knowledge of the true God to these My heathen creatures." Political leaders could argue that "the ultimate end of all our proceedings is to train the natives to self-government" and that Western nations were only acting as teachers to backward and childlike people who would some day become adults and take over their affairs.

These worthy purposes, however, were easily forgotten, and the civilizing mission of the West was often narrowly defined and often involved "little more than the establishment of law and order and the enforcement of contracts." In too many cases the great imperial adventure did nothing but provide "medals for the soldiers," "peerages for the generals," and "copy for the journalists." The Bible and the gun went together into the fabled places of the East and of Africa, and the combination was not a happy one. In the Belgian Congo, for example, there was a great importation of guns and ammunition and a vast export of ivory and rubber. In 1899 Herbert Spencer said that "the white savages of Europe are overrunning the dark savages everywhere . . . the European nations are vying with one another in political burglaries." Joseph Conrad, in his "Heart of Darkness," wrote: "The conquest of the earth, which mostly means taking it away from those who have a different complexion or slightly flatter noses than ourselves, is not a pretty thing when you look into it too much." And a historian of imperialism has remarked bluntly: "Every conquest and rule of one country by another has in it a stain of evil."

Imperialism did show the diseased backside of Western civilization. Even the Western missionaries, in spite of their medical and educational efforts, too often exhibited an offensive form of cultural superiority and seemed more concerned with changing the sexual habits of their parishioners and promoting observance of the sabbath than in matters of more substance. Viciousness and hypocrisy were present in most Western ventures. Many of those who carried the ideas of the West into Asia and Africa were examples of "a pig-headed mediocrity," or were vain and arrogant men who had a contempt for those they ruled that was only somewhat greater than their disdain for most of their own countrymen. Early in the twentieth century British administrators in India were described by an English political leader as "mediocre or even a trifle below that," and no matter the commendable laws that were passed, the hospitals and schools that were built, and the commerce that flourished, the Western presence in Asia and Africa was marred by its intellectual shoddiness, its crude racism, and its hypocrisy.

The argument that the colonies were being trained for self-govern-ment was a piece of political window-dressing and little else. The American philosopher William James described the claim to be "raising and educating inferior races" as "mere hollow pretext and unreality," and in 1902 wrote: "God damn the U.S. for its vile conduct in the Phi-lippine Islands." A scholar of African history pointed out that British control of Egyptian affairs meant "a top-heavy and exotic superstruc-ture, such as an enormous external debt, Western law courts, complete liberty of contract, and, in fact, all the paraphernalia of European civilisa-tion, with some of its worst and not many of its best features." Profit and power overwhelmed any more altruistic purpose, and Winston Church-ill in 1899 wrote of the "figures of the greedy trader, the inopportune missionary, the ambitious soldier, and the lying speculator, who disquiet the minds of the conquered and excite the sordid appetites of the con-querors."

An important part of the record of Westerners in their colonies was one of cruelty and destruction. Actions of Westerners often seemed based upon the slogan "exterminate the brutes." The South African Boers exterminated the Hottentot tribes, Leopold II of Belgium deci-mated the Congo population, and Carl Peters carried out a series of legal-ized murders in German Southeast Africa. The British General Kitchener advanced up the Nile and in the autumn of 1898 gave the Dervishes "a good dusting," as he described the slaughter of approximately 10,000 people. In 1900, at the time of the Boxer insurrection in China, when the Western powers dispatched troops to guarantee the subordination of Chinese interests to those of the West, the German Emperor issued a famous proclamation to his soldiers. "Just as the Huns, a thousand years ago, under the leadership of Attila, gained a reputation by virtue of which they still live in history, so may the German name become known in such a manner in China, that no Chinese will ever again dare to look askance at a German." An American pointed out that "barbarism has no rights which civilization is bound to respect," and there were many who believed that no one should "shrink from the open, uncompromising, straightforward assertion" of Western superiority, "seek to apologize" for it, or "refuse, from whatever cause, to uphold and support it."

Racism

At best, the great majority of Westerners treated Asians and Africans with a "stiffness and superiority." But there was worse. The destructive idea of racism was an important part of imperialism. Mahan and others spoke of a "natural selection" among peoples as if mankind were some type of stud establishment. The superiority of the whites was taken for granted, and the supposed racial inferiority of non-Western peoples meant that any action of the Western powers could be justified as the triumph of the better over the lesser breeds. An American Secretary of State sprinkled his correspondence with sly and not-so-sly references to "Chinks" and Latin American "Dagoes," and the German Emperor spoke of "miserable, decadent peoples." The worst excesses could be excused if practiced against "inferior" peoples. An English liberal admitted that "I, who could not bear to see a beast or bird in pain," could look "without blinking" at the tortures inflicted upon Indians or Africans. The "native mind" did not understand "anything but force," and even a humanitarian Englishman could spout such nonsense as "Asia is careless of human life, used to stern measures, respectful only of power."

The idea of racism was expressed in various ways. An English Viceroy regarded the Indians as nothing "but a set of unruly and ignorant and rather undisciplined school-boys." Others expressed the fear of sexual mingling and the debasing of the white race. But there was a large measure of agreement that non-Westerners were inferior beings and that the rule of the Westerner was in the natural order of things. Political domination was justified in terms of racial superiority, and a European socialist could point out that a nation was "kept up to a high pitch of external efficiency by contest, chiefly by way of war with inferior races." Conservatives, liberals, and radicals joined in the defense of the subjugation of the non-Western world and added their voices to the warning expressed in the following imperialistic stanza:

> Woe to the blinded statesman
> Who truckles to the base
> And sets above the nobler,
> The feebler falser race.

So the non-Western world was cut up and divided and despoiled. And in this great undertaking there was an ambiguity and confusion of purpose that were to haunt Western history and bedevil the relationship of the West and Asia and Africa throughout the twentieth century. India might be called the "brightest jewel" in the British Crown. But from a more realistic point of view British rule was a sterile enterprise, only "the control by some civil servants and the army of a predominately impoverished peasant population." The mixed picture that was imperialism was perhaps best illustrated in 1903. In that year what was called the Great Durbar was held in India in order to show the glory of empire and the strength of British rule. There was a ball, receptions, and a parade from the Red Fort to the Great Mosque. An Englishwoman who was present has left a description of the event.

First, mounted police, then five regiments of cavalry, then artillery, then the heralds, grand in yellow and gold, blowing a fanfare as they reached the mosque. After them, the Imperial cadets, a corps of young natives, sons of noblemen, all mounted on black chargers with leopard skins, and dressed in white uniforms and pale blue turbans. And then came the elephants, all decked and painted and bedizened with cloth of gold and dazzling frontlet pieces and great hanging ornaments over their ears, some wearing silver anklets which clashed and all having bells which sounded boom-boom tinkle-tinkle and made one think it really couldn't all be true, it was so lovely.

And so it was — all the glory and the power and the color of the conqueror. But there was something superficial about all the show, a certain artificiality that marked almost the entire imperialist era. Troops might march, and elephants might parade. But, as a long-time British official in India was to write: "There were three hundred million who no more raised their heads at that faint huzza than at the first the islanders had uttered when they first charged home on Indian soil."

In the eighteen-nineties the Catholic Pope Leo XIII, in an official statement commenting upon what he regarded as the important questions of the day, welcomed the coming century with both hope and apprehension. Many, perhaps a majority, could see only the hope and were prepared to accept the cry "Forward" as a magic and unfailing formula. But many of the more perceptive saw signs of an imminent intellectual and cultural crisis. The basically liberal and industrial society left many people unsatisfied, adrift with no guides save a certain banal romanticism about the inevitability of an ever-richer and ever-more-powerful future. Many men sensed an irreconcilable division between the life of the imagination, the flowering of the creative understanding, and the overwhelming power of science, nationalism, and industrialization. The great spirit of Western freedom had become identified with material wealth and with national power, and descriptions of the Western adventure too often had degenerated into sentimental religiosity and blustering patriotism. A certain resignation entered into Western life, as if men had lost their confidence in their ability to control their own destinies. It was in response to this feeling that a French historian argued that while the eighteenth century had been a historical movement toward freedom and individualism, the nineteenth, in spite of its accomplishments, had witnessed a movement toward fatalism.

There were many who believed that the spiritual and intellectual powers of the West had petered out. Democracy, industrialization, and nationalism were seen as narcotics that masked the absence of any profound response to the complexity of life. Christianity had "degenerated into a kind of festive decoration for weddings, funerals, and patriotic affairs. It was program music, and nothing more." The same was true of other spiritual or intellectual appeals, and the great concepts of truth, happiness, freedom, and fraternity were only part of what was described as "the small change of daily life." A certain phase of Western life seemed to be coming to an end, and there were many who longed for something that would sweep away the doubts, contradictions, superficialities, and sterility of an exhausted historical epoch. In the words of one French writer, Europe was only "an aging society, which believed itself to be at peace because it was tired."

There were many commentators upon the Western world, as there were many expressions of the condition of Western man, as the nineteenth century ended and the twentieth began. Friedrich Nietzsche, often regarded as the last of the great German classical philosophers, was an influential critic of the West and Western man and attempted to cut beneath the surface of Western life and to show what he believed were the false premises and inherent dangers of that life. Charles Maurras was a violent reactionary who in the early twentieth century stated again the arguments against the Western liberal society and attempted to return to a simpler, uncomplicated world. Thomas Mann, who began his career as a novelist as the old century ended, spent his long creative life in exploring the implications of the great changes that were taking place in the social and intellectual attitudes of the West.

Friedrich Nietzsche

On the morning of January 3, 1889, in Turin, Italy, Friedrich Nietzsche left his lodgings and stepped into the street. There he saw a cabman beating his horse. Nietzsche ran to the suffering animal and threw his arms about its neck. Then he fainted. He was carried back to his room, and after a short period he regained consciousness. But he had slipped over the line into madness. During the next few days he wrote a series of bewildering letters to acquaintances and various well-known personages, and his behavior frightened the neighbors and his landlord. A friend came to Turin and on January 9 left with Nietzsche for a clinic in Basle in Switzerland.

Nietzsche's condition was diagnosed as incurable insanity, undoubtedly caused by an earlier syphilis infection. After a short stay in the clinic, Nietzsche was placed in the care of his mother, who took him to Naumburg in Germany, where the family had lived since 1850. For eleven years, first with his mother and then after her death with his sister in Weimar, Nietzsche existed in the darkness of the mentally destroyed. Shortly before his death, the best-known drawing of him was made by a German artist. Here he can be seen propped up in bed, his hands resting on top of the comforter, his black mustache, his large, heavy head, and the vacant eyes looking sightlessly ahead of him. In 1900 Friedrich Nietzsche died and escaped from a world he despised.

Nietzsche was probably the most important European philosopher in the last half of the nineteenth century, as he was certainly that century's greatest and most searching critic. Born in 1844, he had attended universities at Bonn and Leipzig and was for ten years a professor at the university of Basle. In 1879 he retired from teaching because of illness and spent the next ten years of his life writing a truly amazing collection of works, the most important of which were *The Birth of Tragedy, Human, All-Too-Human, The Gay Science, Thus Spake Zarathustra,* and *Beyond Good and Evil.* During this time he wandered about Europe, spending short periods in Nice, in Sils-Maria, in Venice, in Turin, in Genoa, in Rome, in Lucerne. He lived in hotel rooms and boarding houses, with only his clothes and the paper upon which he wrote as possessions. He was all his life a solitary, quarrelsome, contradictory man, a genius and a crank, who found no peace and who appeared at times to speak from a far distance or from a great height. As one of his few friends said: "In your books I seem to hear the distant sound of falling water."

It is not an easy task to cope with Nietzsche. His arrogance is offensive, as is his tendency toward exaggeration. For many he is a blasphemer, a mad atheist, an empty thunderer whose philosophy is a dark doctrine of rage and destruction. He demands from his readers a dedication that we begrudge anyone, and he pulls us away from our day-to-day surroundings and invites us into an atmosphere where breathing is difficult. But most important, he scrapes our self-satisfaction and calls into question the premises of our lives. He mocks us, and for that we cannot forgive him. Nietzsche is not difficult to understand. In fact, he is probably the easiest of all philosophers to read, a most skilled and dramatic writer who presents his arguments clearly and forcefully. But he tells us what we do not want to know. And for that he is condemned as a dreamer, an insane man, one who is lost in a world of the most horrifying fantasies.

The best place to start with Nietzsche is with his vision of the Western world, particularly of Western Europe, and with what he saw as the condition of that world. Put bluntly, Nietzsche was disgusted by his age. In his view, Western civilization had become "plebeian" and "semibarbarian." A "levelling and vulgarization of man" was taking place, and at best the citizen of the West had become "a useful, industrious, variously serviceable, and clever gregarious creature." Mediocrity was everywhere, and only the unending search for some new and artificial stimulant spurred Western man on. Western life moved "restlessly, violently, tempestuously, like a mighty river desiring the end of its journey, without pausing to reflect, indeed fearful of reflection. . . . Where we live, soon nobody will be able to exist." Everything was "commonplace," and Western man was well on his way to becoming "the most intelligent slave animal, very industrious, basically very modest, excessively curious, spoiled, weak-willed." People were becoming very much the same, "all very equal, very small, very rotund, very amenable, very boring."

This was a truly horrifying indictment of what many regarded as a civilization of power and glory and satisfaction. But Nietzsche believed that he saw the symptoms of dissolution, of what he called "an absolutely fundamental convulsion" that would shake down the great house of the West. For one thing Nietzsche was convinced that what could be called Western culture had become exhausted. The shell was still there — the buildings, the institutions, the doctrines. But they were empty of content, and the modern mind had become "a kind of chaos," filled with odds and ends that meant very little. As Nietzsche put it in one of the aphorisms of which he was so fond: "Everything falls into the water, but nothing falls into deep wells." Superficiality and jaded attitudes were the marks of Western thinking. Western man was experiencing a "desolation of the mind," and he was attempting to live on a diet of "newspapers, politics, beer, and Wagnerian music." He had a knowledge of culture but no culture himself, and his life exhibited "an unspeakable poverty and exhaustion, despite the great variety borrowed from previous cultures." His goals were all small ones — domestic tranquility, the surface appearance of knowledge, military glory, empty trophies, commercial success. Genuine culture, for Nietzsche, was that which expressed the style of a people's way of life, a hard, clear, pure sense of values, an interpretation which instinctively gave life a meaning. But the West lacked style or, rather, attempted to make do with "a chaotic jumble of all styles." A living culture held life together. But this cohesive element was absent in the West, and "the ice that still supports us has become so thin; soon no one will be able to walk where we are now walking."

In an effort to escape their condition, Western men were engaged in the search for some ideal, some belief, that would disguise their cultural nakedness. Nietzsche saw the nineteenth century as "most inventive in producing intoxicants" that would blur the true outline of actual historical conditions. But these were what Nietzsche considered illusions, diseases, idiocies. Politics was basically "a facetious or a sham philosophy," nationalism was merely the creation of a "new idol," the "most unfeeling of all monsters," and racism, commercialism, and militarism were "morbid estrangements" of man from reality. The popular intellectual statements of the day, such as "the scientific spirit," "art for art's sake," and "pure knowledge," were only facades that attempted to disguise "skepticism and the paralysis of will." People hid "their dummy-heads behind the stalking-horse of an ideal," and the emptier the ideal the greater its attraction. Nietzsche found, for example, that his own people, the Germans, were excellent illustrations of what had happened to Western life. They had been the victims of one folly after another, "the anti-French folly, the antisemitic folly, the anti-Polish folly, the Christian-romantic folly, the Wagnerian folly, the Teutonic folly, the Prussian folly." In their stupidity, they had even accepted the idea that military strength was a proof of cultural vitality. Nietzsche saw this as nonsense, and he was satisfied that German military force did not prove the strength of German culture, but just the opposite. In fact, what could be called the "German spirit" had been defeated for the benefit of the "German Reich."

In Nietzsche's opinion, the most persistent and ridiculous of all illusions was that fostered by the Christian religion. In 1881 the phrase "God is dead" appears in Nietzsche's writings, and this realization influences the greater part of his interpretation of the world of the late-nineteenth century. It was Nietzsche's bald, straightforward statement that God had disappeared from Western man's life that accounted for much of the shocked response to his writings in his day and since. Modern Christianity was a fiction, and "belief in the Christian God has ceased to be believable." The Western world had no place for transcendental beliefs, for faith in any creator and guiding spirit, for any philosophy of Christian redemption. Western man had taken over his own world, and, no matter how he might attempt to disguise the fact, he had crowded God from the planet.

Nietzsche knew that this idea was offensive to many, and that Western men still regarded themselves as the children of God and still believed that, in some mysterious way, God ruled the world. For Nietzsche, however, such a belief was only the sign of cowardice. The evidence of the absence of God was irrefutable. The churches had become only "the tombs and sepulchres of God," and a religion dependent upon miracles and an undefined salvation had become meaningless. The modern world could not be understood if one clung to a Christian view, and Nietzsche argued that man must recognize "the falsity and mendacity of all Christian interpretations of the world." Contrary to their claims, Western men were not Christian, save in their pathetic allegiance to outmoded symbols and archaic institutions. "They have rid themselves of the Christian God and now cling all the more firmly to Christian morality." God, and even Christ, had little to say to the present situation of Western man, and, in Nietzsche's mind, this had been true for a very long time. As he wrote, "in reality there has been only one Christian, and he died on the Cross." Or, as he put it again, briefly and cruelly, "the gospel died on the Cross."

Many before Nietzsche, and large numbers of his contemporaries, had been haunted by the thought that the all-knowing, all-merciful, and all-protecting God had disappeared. But Nietzsche was the most extreme in stating what seemed an obvious fact and in drawing, again what seemed to him, the obvious conclusions. As Albert Camus was to write half a century after Nietzsche's death: "Nietzsche did not form a project to kill God. He found Him dead in the souls of his contemporaries. He was the first to understand the immense importance of the event. . . ." Nietzsche knew that the death of God was the most significant event in modern history, as well as the most terrifying and the most dangerous. He believed that he was facing the utter, destructive, awesome truth, and that this was his unique accomplishment. He once spoke of a friend and colleague as "that elderly, highly original man, given, not to distorting truth, but to passing it over in silence." This Nietzsche could not do. He "was determined to go to the very end of the positivist disillusionment, shed skin after skin of comforting beliefs, destroy every fortress manned by protective gods." As early as 1880 he had written: "Yet no pain has been able or shall be able to tempt me into giving false testimony about life as I recognize it."

Nietzsche felt the pain and the anguish of a lost belief. He once wrote: "How much truth can the human mind bear, how much truth does it dare to face?" He knew that the instant when man realized that God had withdrawn from him was the "most hopeless moment" in human history. The world had suddenly turned to dust and ashes, and the belief in some great redemption that would rescue mankind from "this transitory, seductive, illusory, paltry world," this "turmoil of delusion," was gone. Yet at the same time Nietzsche welcomed this knowledge.

Because God is dead, "the horizon appears free again to us, even though it is not bright." Man's divine origin had been regarded as his greatest attribute, the thing that would protect him against the ruin of time and death. But now any grandeur, any explanation, any triumph in the world must be sought in man himself and not in some religious explanation. Out of nothingness, man can create something — himself. That is his great task, the greatest that could be imagined. Now "there are only necessities: there is no one to command, no one to obey, no one to transgress." Men no longer need to "live concealed in the woods like timid deer," but can achieve an authentic condition and become the single, living reality in the world. They can achieve self-mastery, be themselves the reason and justification for existence. In this sense, Nietzsche's writing is a call to creativity, a demand that men remake themselves. But in doing this, they must not fall into the error of attempting to create another god and thus again humble themselves. As Nietzsche put it: "He who cannot endure the sentence, 'There is no redemption' ought to die out."

If Nietzsche angered many with his arguments that God was dead, he no less offended with his proposal of how men could live with this knowledge and, in fact, make new men of themselves. His statement "I teach you the Superman" has been attacked by many, in his day and since, and, because it was the type of statement that could be twisted and exaggerated, it has too often been dismissed as the raving of a madman. And Nietzsche himself was at least partially to blame for this interpretation. He pushed so hard and so consistently against the grain of propriety and his method of argumentation was so similar to a slap across the face that he could hardly have been surprised that the world did not thank him for his efforts. There are elements of Nietzsche's philosophy that revolt us and are amenable to an almost pathological distortion.

When the extravagances and the wildness are stripped away from Nietzsche, however, it is possible to see what he meant by his doctrine of the Superman. Nietzsche contrasts his Superman with what he called "the last man," the vulgar, matter-of-fact simpleton who does not understand that the world has changed or does not realize what it means to be alive in the last part of the nineteenth century. The Superman knows that "all things must be defined anew," and that the free man is one who "is determined in everything to depend upon himself and not upon some tradition." He accepts the fact that his life is "a dangerous crossing, a dangerous wayfaring, a dangerous looking-back, a dangerous trembling and halting." He sees that there are both "life-enhancing" and "life-denying" forces, and he makes a free choice of the former. He fixes his own goals and does not depend upon religion, nationalism, or any other "herd organization" to give meaning to his existence. He attempts to overcome himself, in the sense that he sheds his illusions, his tendency to copy other people, his habits of fear and frustration, and thus becomes a creative human being.

In achieving this condition, a new morality must be developed that will be appropriate to the new human situation. But this must not be any "relapse into old loves and narrow views." The Superman must not adjust to his environment, for such adjustment would mean that he would perish. Rather, he opposes his surroundings and separates himself from the accepted morality, which Nietzsche believed was the discipline of slaves, a conspiracy of the weak against the strong. For the Superman, life is not a struggle for existence; it is a struggle for power, the power to make something better of himself, to express himself as a new man. In this struggle the Superman must set the hardier human traits such as egotism, cruelty, and arrogance against the conventional virtues of sympathy, charity, and humility. He must combat the sickness of equality, mediocrity, and sentimental humanitarianism. He must, in other words, reject what Nietzsche regarded as the principal characteristics of the modern Western world.

Nietzsche believed that what he was doing was pointing out the possibility of a new kind of man who could maintain himself against an ever-increasing chaos. He thought that the situation in the West would become far worse before it improved. "Europe will grow increasingly dull, and European man will become increasingly insignificant." His sickness — the sickness of the morally weak, of the nationalistic, racially oriented, acquisitive, and militarily minded man of the nineteenth century — was certain to lead to disaster. Nietzsche foresaw "a succession of several martial centuries that have no equal in history," and there will be "wars such as have never yet been on earth." There is even the possibility that the human adventure will come to an end, move in some sort of reverse evolution whereby man will "turn into an ape, while nobody will take any interest in this astonishing end of the comedy."

Nietzsche is often described as a nihilist. And he did believe that the world, as it existed, was inexplicable in a way that Western man did not realize. Nihilism for him meant that "the goal is lacking; the answer to our why is lacking." If man could not grasp the reality of his life and if his life was robbed of transcendental meaning, then there were no morals, no restraints, no standards of judgment. Then one must accept the fact that "nothing is true, everything is permitted."

Yet, in spite of all this, Nietzsche thought that he was not contributing to the nihilism he saw about him but was rather struggling against it. He regarded himself as a lonely battler for that kind of moral order and moral conduct that was contingent upon man's condition in the late-nineteenth century. The world had changed, and changed primarily because of the activities of Western men. Yet people continued to act as if everything were the same, as if they could exist "on the mere pittance of inherited and decaying values." Men were advancing into the future with their eyes turned toward the past, and this behavior could only lead to disaster. They seemed afraid to face the conclusions of their own activities and thoughts. "The printing press, the machine, the railway, the telegraph are premises whose thousand-year conclusions no one has yet had the courage to draw." Nietzsche did not believe that the attempt to reconcile an old moral code with the conditions of modern life could succeed. Nor could simple ideas of good and evil be drawn from the long-dead past and propped up in the modern world as meaningful guides. In a period of unprincipled power and amoral organization, Western man had slipped his cultural anchor and was adrift. No one really believed in anything. As Nietzsche looked into modern life, he saw nothing there. And he was appalled at what seemed to him a violation of man's nature and a mutilation of his humanity. In this sense his writings were a continual call for Western man to abandon his suicidal course and to make something of himself.

Charles Maurras

In late January, 1945, shortly before the end of World War II, a seventy-seven-year-old man was brought to trial in Lyons and was charged with treasonable activities during the German occupation of France. For three days Charles Maurras defended himself at length, arguing that he, the great French patriot, could not be a traitor. In spite of his exhaustive defense, which in printed form was a hundred and ten pages long, the jury found him guilty, and he was sentenced to life imprisonment in isolation and to national degradation. When he was informed of the sentence, Maurras cried: "This is the revenge of Dreyfus."

There is no legal proof that Maurras was a traitor in the sense of having been pro-German or of having been a collaborator. All his adult life, however, he had been an enemy of what he called "the beast of democracy," one who was violent in his hatred of the France of the Revolution, of the republic, of liberalism. For half a century his had been a voice calling for the destruction of a political system that he believed was inimical to the true nature of France. He had played at least an ignoble role during the German occupation. In 1942 he had written that "our worst defeat has had the good result of ridding us of democracy." He had applauded the orders abolishing the state teachers' colleges, which he thought of as the sources of radical and atheistic thought, and he had approved of antisemitic laws. He had argued that those Frenchmen who fought for the Allies were traitors and that members of their families should be arrested as hostages and shot. As late as September, 1944, while in hiding from the French authorities, he had argued that the restoration of a democracy in France would be a disaster.

But these actions came at the end of a long life and were merely the last expressions of a political philosophy that had been consistently held since his early years. Maurras was born at Martiques, a small fishing village near Marseilles in 1868. In 1885 he came to Paris and there began that furious journalistic and political activity that was to last until his death in 1952. In numerous books and in approximately 20,000 articles, Maurras carried on a continual attack upon what he called "the evil of which we are dying." He threw himself into the struggle over the innocence or guilt of Dreyfus (he opposed any reopening of the case), and thereafter devoted his energies to the rescuing of the "true" France from her enemies. In 1898 with some friends he organized a League of the French Fatherland to oppose the liberal League for the Defense of the Rights of Man and from that time on acted as a tribune of those who fought doggedly against the "disease of the times." From his twenties until his seventies his views never changed. As a young man and as an old, he was a consistent and thorough reactionary, who believed that most of what had happened in France since the eighteenth century had been calamitous.

His most important organizational activity was the part he played in the creation and then the continuation of the League of Action Française. Officially founded in *1898*, Action Française proved a rallying point for those who believed that France was being threatened from within and without. A supporter of the Action Française remarked that Maurras and his friends "form an audacious avant-garde fighting against the scum who have corrupted everything they have touched."

The organization attracted many who supported the army and the authorities in the Dreyfus case, who were uncomfortable in a world where traditional beliefs were being eroded, who believed that civilization, and particularly French civilization, was being threatened by alien influences and by an emphasis upon sterile rationalism and liberal politics.

One of the major activities of Action Française was the publishing of a newspaper that carried the name of the organization. Established in 1899 as a fortnightly, in 1908 *Action Française* became a daily paper and provided an outlet for the writings of Maurras and those who were prepared to carry on a struggle with the "false" France. There was also a publishing house and weekly study groups. In 1908 a collection of young Frenchmen was organized under the name Camelots du Roi — Hawkers of the King. The organization consisted of young toughs who were enrolled to sell copies of *Action Française* and to engage in street fighting and other activities designed to show the opposition of true Frenchmen to those who were governing the country. The Camelots slapped politicians in public, broke up meetings, attacked professors, destroyed statues of "traitors," and took part in rowdy street demonstrations. Membership in the Action Française fluctuated, but between 1910 and 1926 stood between 30,000 and 40,000 members.

Action Française attracted a number of talented and influential Frenchmen, as well as many ruffians and hoodlums. But it was Charles Maurras who year after year put forward the basic ideas of the group and made himself its spokesman. It was he who, as he wrote, struggled in defense of "a menaced civilization" and declared that "all hopes float on the ship of the counter-revolution." He saw himself surrounded by what he described as Russian agents, "Scottish Jews," the "foreign thieves and villains." And he struck out at those he regarded as his enemies in coarse, brutal terms that were incitements to violence and to death. In 1936 he was sentenced to a term of imprisonment for having demanded the murder of more than a hundred members of the French Parliament, including the Premier, and his writings were a continual appeal to the French people to take matters into their own hands and to use any methods to rid themselves of those advocating the hated doctrines that had enslaved France and the French spirit.

Maurras himself did have a political philosophy, and he put into the strongest terms what many others were thinking. Basic to this philosophy was his rejection of what we commonly think of as democracy. Here was an evil that had been injected into the healthy body of France and had then spread, infecting thought and action. Democracy was a permanent conspiracy against the public welfare and meant a regime of profit and pleasure at the expense of any regard for the true values of society. For Maurras, there was no meaning to life without order, "heaven's first law," and democracy, with its characteristics of curiosity and tolerance, was fatal to any sense of ordered values. "Democracy upsets, menaces, torments, paralyzes, excites, and agitates." Moreover, democracy could not produce people of competence. Only a minority were fit to occupy positions of authority, and such people could not be found by any democratic process. Democracy produced division, and this inevitably led to decadence and decline. It stressed reason and the intellect while the true life force was found in unexamined impulses, the irrational, the intuitive, and the mystical. Finally, and perhaps as important as anything else, democracy was "foreign," a product of Protestant, Jewish, or German influences and thus unsuitable for France.

Maurras always identified this hated democracy with the French Revolution of the late eighteenth century. It was the Revolution that had introduced these fallacious doctrines into the country. In fact, according to him, the Revolution should not be called French at all, for it had been a foreign importation. It had been what he termed an Oriental, German-Judaic, individual, liberal, and destructive influence that was at variance with "traditional, classic, scientific, and social thought," with "Hellenic-Latin civilization, French order." It had substituted disorder for order, anarchy for authority, doubt for certainty, ugliness for beauty, and the false for the true.

Maurras attacked all of the important principles of the French Revolution and of the liberal nineteenth century. Liberty, as it was commonly thought of, was false and unrealistic. Such liberty prevented the submission of the citizen to the laws of the state and also to the laws of nature. Liberty led to nothing but disorganized thinking and set the individual free with nothing to restrain him from pursuing the wildest thoughts and actions. Religious liberty meant that anything could be challenged by the individual and that any truth could be put in peril because of individual doubt. The same was true of political liberty, which could only lead to disorder and confusion. True liberty, according to Maurras, required a generally accepted authority and was the product of certainty about the direction of the society and its aims. Those liberties that led to the unity and strength of a society should be supported; those that led to internal strife and disorganization should be abandoned.

Equality, too, was rejected as an erroneous doctrine. Men were not equal, and the "incompetent" should not be allowed to foster his ill-founded opinions upon others. Equality meant, for Maurras, the surrendering of power to the herd, to the lowest level of society, to the upstarts and those without any deep sense of what the nation or the national purpose might be. Maurras equated civilization with quality and democracy with quantity and equality, and an egalitarian society was "a government of numbers," and nothing else. He wished to see again those "protective and necessary inequalities," and he once expressed this desire in a good example of his explosive rhetoric: "Inequality or decadence! Inequality or anarchy! Inequality or death!"

Maurras believed that there were time-honored French traditions that must be accepted in their pure form if France were to avoid disaster. These were the traditions of hierarchy, authority, discipline, order, family, and property. He advocated what was called integral nationalism, which meant one religion, one national family, one unquestioned tradition, one safe harbor in which all true Frenchmen could gather. Expressing this nationalism and providing a center of loyalty was a royal family, and Maurras argued for a return of a French king. But such a nationalism could only be achieved if all hostile influences were rooted out of France. France must be returned to the true Frenchman, and there must be a purging of the polluting evil forces. There were, for Maurras, four groups within France that threatened the welfare of the country. These were the Masons, the Protestants, the Jews, and what he called the métèques. Maurras introduced the word métèque into the French language in 1894 and defined it as one who was a recently domiciled or naturalized citizen or his children. Such people could never be true Frenchmen. Maurras once supported a bill in Parliament to exclude from public office all those who did not have three generations of French ancestors who had lived continually in France.

The Jews, of course, must be expelled from French society. Maurras did not oppose them so much because of any racial or religious belief but because he looked upon the Jews as cosmopolitans, people who could never be truly French. In 1912, when Maurras in one of his frequent appearances in a French court found himself facing a Jewish tribunal, he refused to answer any questions and made the statement: "I am French, you are Jewish. It is impossible for me to reply to a Jewish judge."

Maurras found to his liking the order and hierarchy of the Roman Catholic Church. But he did not care for Christianity and, in fact, saw little merit in Christian ethics or Christian theology. He thought religious ideas in general of little value, and the internationalism of the Catholic Church offended him. He admired Catholic tradition and order and attempted to get along with the Church. He did go through his works and take out items disturbing to the Church, such as his famous contention that the Gospels were written "by four obscure Jews." But the violence of his statements and his general irreligious attitude proved too much for the Catholic Church, and in 1926 Action Française was condemned by the Pope. The newspaper and Maurras' writings were placed upon the Index of Prohibited Books. The ban on Action Française was lifted in 1939, but remained on some of Maurras' books.

It is easy to ridicule Charles Maurras. He was a somewhat pathetic figure with his wild words of violence, his almost comic attempts to restore the monarchy to France, and his childish rages. He lived too long, and when compared with the true masters of bloody action who played important historical roles in the second quarter of the twentieth century, he seems something of a ridiculous poseur. But he illustrated a frame of mind that was common in the West in the early years of this century. He was one of a large group of dissenters who found themselves strangers in the secular, liberal society of the West and opposed what they thought of as "a glib, utilitarian, mass civilization." What were usually looked upon as the accomplishments of the West were regarded by these men as moral, political, social, and religious decay. As a German contemporary of Maurras wrote: "Liberalism has undermined cultures. It has annihilated religions. It has destroyed nations. It is the dissolution of humanity."

An authority on Maurras and the Action Française has written: "In the early 20th century France as a democracy implied a way of life of a society which cherished values of tolerance rather than fanaticism, compromise rather than rigidity, persuasion rather than force, diversity rather than conformity, discussion rather than dogmatism." To many, these were the correct priorities. But not to men like Maurras. They could not tolerate such a conditional or tentative situation, and in their search for definitive answers and fixed standards, they engaged in "an open conspiracy" against the liberal society. Consumed by nostalgia for a time of certainty, they hoped "to destroy the despised present in order to recapture an idealized past in an imaginary future." To them, the secular community seemed no community at all, but only an incoherent human mass, without any ties of faith, common values, and spiritual identity. Basically, such people could not accept the Western idea of modernity, of a constantly changing and increasingly secularized life, and out of their resentment they created a new politics based upon what they thought of as a blood relationship, which would exclude the alien, upon the mystical unities of land, church, and family, and upon a rejection of democratic institutions and ideas and the principles of the revolutions of the eighteenth century.

We commonly assume that opposition to what we call liberal democracy is a development of the nineteen-twenties and nineteen-thirties. Certainly such opposition assumed a particularly virulent form at that time. But throughout the nineteenth century there had been a continual chorus of complaint, and in the early twentieth century dissent became sharper and more raucous. In an essay entitled "The French Dialogue," André Gide has written that throughout French literature, and he could have said throughout French life and the life of the West as well, we hear a perpetual argument: "Not between a political right and left, but — much more profound and vital — between the ancient tradition of submission to recognized authorities, and free thought, the spirit of doubt, of examination which works for the slow and progressive emancipation of the individual."

Thomas Mann

In 1930, the German writer Thomas Mann published a short autobiography entitled *A Sketch of My Life*. He began with the following two sentences. "I was born in Lübeck in the year 1875, the second son of Johann Heinrich Mann, merchant and Senator of the Free City, and of his wife, Julia Da Silva-Bruhns. My father, grandfather, and great-grandfather were citizens of Lübeck. . . ." By 1930, Mann had been a long time absent from Lübeck and from the Baltic, "a provincial body of water," as he called it. He had, apart from short interruptions, lived in Munich for over thirty years. In 1933 he was to leave Germany when Adolf Hitler came to power, never to return save as a visitor. He spent fourteen years in the United States, becoming an American citizen in 1944, and then settled in Switzerland, where he died in 1955.

Thomas Mann was a major figure in European literature of the twentieth century. He was an urbane, talented writer who in a series of monumental works contributed substantially to modern Western culture. But he always remained, to an important extent, a citizen of Lübeck, and his most significant writings are extended commentaries upon what had happened to his world and the world of the West in the years since the Mann family business in Lübeck, which had existed for over a hundred years, had disappeared. He once described himself as "a bourgeois gone astray," as "a bourgeois storyteller who all his life has actually told only one single story: the story of the burgher who sloughs off the burgher's skin. Not in order to become a capitalist or a Marxist but to become an artist; to achieve the irony and freedom of art, and art's capacity to flee and to fly." Mann believed that the history of the bourgeoisie was an important part of the history of the modern West and that the gradual decline of the bourgeoisie posed new and difficult problems for Western man. In 1922, he put forward the argument that "there is at hand the ending of an epoch: the bourgeois, humanistic, liberal epoch, which was born at the Renaissance and came to power with the French Revolution." Mann became the great chronicler of this now-disappeared bourgeois world and of the implications of that disappearance.

What we call, with some looseness of expression, the bourgeois, the burghers, the middle class, has been attacked by many. A persistent strain in modern Western thinking has been a suspicion of this middle class with its emphasis upon property, upon business, upon what were regarded as the proprieties of behavior. Middle-class life seemed to many a boring, sterile, empty way of existence, which had a stifling and reprehensible influence in the West. The business community had been a subject for ridicule by those who regarded the bourgeois as one who judged his life and his surroundings by their relationship to the making of money and whose exaggerated sense of respectability and property blinded him to the realities of what was going on in the world.

Mann was aware of the failings of the bourgeoisie. He recognized the emptiness of an overly fastidious belief in order and what passed, unfortunately, for elegance. He was well acquainted with the middle-class "willful love of mere largeness, its taste for the monumental and standard, the copious and grandiose." He knew, too, that there was a superficiality about the bourgeois response to politics, and that the bourgeois interpretation of the world was outdated. "Its attachment to liberal ideas of reason and progress seems to us laughable, its materialism all too crass, its monistic solution to the riddle of the universe full of shallow complacency."

Yet in spite of all this, Mann could not reject his middle-class heritage. He once posed for his readers the question: "Who am I, where do I come from, how is it that I am as I am and cannot do or wish any differently?" And he answered: "I am a townsman, a burgher, a child and great-grandchild of German middle-class culture." Mann had a deeply developed sense of the necessity of having roots, and he had what he called a "European sympathy for order and reason." He once wrote that "people ought to know where they belong. People ought to keep together," and he accepted the place and the tradition into which he had been born. "The German bourgeois," he once remarked, "was the prototype of German humanity." Responsibility and respectability suited Mann. They fortified him in his judgments and provided him with a sense of identity that he believed was so important. "After all," he once commented, "we are not gypsies living in a green wagon; we're respectable people." Or, in another place, "we are a people of the middle, of the world-bourgeoisie; there is a fittingness in our geographical position and in our mores."

Mann's attachment to the bourgeois way of life was partially based upon sentiment, upon a feeling that one must belong somewhere. Every individual required a sense of kinship with some other human beings who have "a sameness of vision." But it was more than this. Mann was attracted to the middle class by what has been called its "triumph of form," its allegiance to "a significantly ordered life." The bourgeois accepted the "reality of the commonplace" and was convinced that the world makes sense despite all indications and arguments to the contrary. The bourgeois was perhaps plodding and dull and ponderous. But he was in harmony with his surroundings and was endowed with an understanding of the "serious conduct of life." He had an "ethical bent," in Mann's words, which, "in contrast to the purely aesthetic impulse, to the pursuit of beauty and pleasure as well as to nihilism and the vagabond's flirtation with death," is a "perception for the duties of life, without which the impulse toward achievement, toward making a productive contribution to life and the development of humanity would be lacking." The "bourgeois spirit" might be inhibiting and even stifling. But it was also an inclination toward "world citizenship, world mean, world conscience, world prudence; it means the refusal to be carried away; it means the idea of humanity, of man and his culture, critically holding its own against all extremists of the Right and Left."

The literary form of Mann's argument about the bourgeois appeared first in 1901 with the publication of *Buddenbrooks*. This is the story of four generations of grain merchants in a Hanseatic city who have played important parts in the history and life of their community. The subtitle of the novel is "The Decline of a Family," and Mann clearly meant to show the dissolution of a social arrangement, the end of a period in European history that had been economically, politically, and culturally dominated by the well-established bourgeoisie. The four generations and the history of the family are represented by Johann Buddenbrook senior; his son Johann junior who is called the Consul, and Gotthold, the first black sheep of the family; the Consul's three children — Thomas, Christian, and Antonio; and finally, Thomas' only son called Hanno, a diminutive for Johann.

The story begins in the eighteen-thirties, when we see the family flourishing, gruffly sure of itself and confident of its place in society and in the world. The members of the family know who they are and where they belong. Time and again Mann presents us with carefully delineated descriptions of this bourgeois solidarity. We see the Buddenbrooks, for example, at a family gathering. "There they all sat," Mann writes, "on heavy, high-backed chairs, consuming good heavy food from good heavy silver plate, drinking full-bodied wines and expressing their views freely on all subjects." There is little truck with doubt or misgivings, and all rests on firm foundations. The family motto is: "Devote yourself heartily to your business but engage only in transactions that will let you sleep quietly at night." The well-grounded faith of the bourgeois here is incompatible with irony, skepticism, or any questioning as to the rightness of the world. Everything can be faced if one is honest, hard-working, and responsible. "Pull yourself together" is the answer to difficulties, and one is assured that if he does not let go he will inevitably make it through any temporary setback.

The Consul in the second generation is the first member of the family to suffer from doubt and misgivings. His sense of certainties slips somewhat, and there is a loss of the old vitality. With the death of the Consul, the family disintegration is hastened. One of his sons, Christian, is a man who has no energy left and who exhausts himself in the pursuit of sensations. He is determined to marry his mistress and to desert the business. As he on one occasion says of himself: "You see, I am quite exhausted and used up by the other things, the trifles. There is nothing left over for the serious stuff." The daughter, Antonio, called Toni, is a "silly goose," vain, impetuous, and spoiled. She is a woman of no character, the victim of unhappy marriages and her dread of not being respected and awarded the regard due her position.

Thomas Buddenbrook is left to carry on the business, and it is in his fate that Mann presents the clearest picture of the declining bourgeois. Thomas is conscientious, industrious, and competent. But he has lost his faith in the robustly unquestioning tradition. He continues to give the appearance of success in the face of the undeniable decline in the business and in his own energies. He is handicapped by his doubts as to the value of his undertakings, and he has even lost his sense of what is honest. He finds himself drawn into business speculations that are not quite proper and upon which his father and his grandfather would have frowned, and he fears that his passionate wife Gerda is betraying him. His only son Hanno is a sickly, musically inclined child, totally unfit for the business world. The decline of the business is matched by a decline in Thomas' hold on life. When he has a stroke and dies, the business is liquidated and the story of the Buddenbrooks ends.

This awareness of the "loss of bourgeois values, of bourgeois competence" remained with Mann throughout the rest of his life. Doubt, temptation, and flights of imagination that prompt irresponsibility and weaken any sense of duty are constant themes in his fiction. In 1903 he published *Tonio Kröger*. The protagonist, after whom the novel is named, is a young artist who has left the bourgeois world into which he was born. He is successful, but he retains the fondest memories of the world of certainty and solid virtues that he has left. He calls himself "a bourgeois who has strayed into art, a man of the Bohème with a nostalgic longing for his decent childhood home, an artist with a bad conscience." He stands, frustrated and at least partially paralyzed, between two worlds and is at home in neither. He is drawn to the "sea," "the whirl of shadows," a "world unborn and formless." But he is also attracted to the world of steady and prosaic routine, where one can act out of unexamined response and unthinking tradition. As Tonio writes: "My deepest and most secret love belongs to the blond and blue-eyed, the fair and living, the happy, lovely, and commonplace."

In what is usually regarded as Mann's greatest work, *The Magic Mountain*, bourgeois certitude has vanished, and we are left with an unstructured world where morality, conduct, and life itself are all ambivalent qualities that verge on the bizarre. The principal character, Hans Castorp, is an alienated merchant who has no defenses against intellectual anarchy, erotic temptation, or what Mann was to call "the blood-and beauty-mouthings" that were so common in what passed for the intellectual conversation of the day. Nothing remains but a cynicism, a frivolous superficiality that expresses itself in overheated emotions and empty activities. There is only the desire to escape from all authority, from any responsibility, to let oneself drift. Europe has become a sanatorium where progressive radicalism and reaction are alike divorced from any meaningful context and where knowledge has become the enemy of life, the ally of disease.

Mann was not searching for some dogma that would bind him to a rigid set of moral principles or unchanging social and political arrangements. He knew that the world in which he had grown up would have to change. But he knew also that something valuable had gone out of Western life with the decline of the bourgeoisie. The ethical business community of the traditional bourgeois had provided a balance-wheel for society that held the various demands of life in some sort of equilibrium. He believed that there was something in the old bourgeois way of life that still spoke to the condition of men in the Western world. As he wrote: "Our attitude toward the nineteenth century is that of sons toward a father: critical, as is only fair." In a book he published in 1918, and which was influenced by the shock of the First World War, he wrote that "we search in books, we search in the agony of these times for the remotest origins, the legitimate foundations, the oldest spiritual traditions of the hard-pressed self. We search for justification." We must, he believed, understand "by recognition" what we had lost by the destruction of the old bourgeoisie.

The decline of the bourgeois removed from Western society the organized order within which men could orient their thoughts and their actions. In 1926, in a speech entitled "Lübeck as a Way of Life and Thought," Mann said: "The middle class way of life, they tell us, is done for. It is hollowed out, finished, condemned to death, doomed, and destined to be devoured root and branch by a new world that has risen in the East. Certainly a tremendous wave of change is sweeping over Europe today — this we can all feel and experience. It is a wave of what is called the 'world revolution,' a fundamental upheaval of our whole view of life, sped by all the moral, scientific, economic, political, technical, and artistic devices at the command of the twentieth century." Many were to greet this decline of the middle class with joy and anticipation. But not Thomas Mann. In 1922 he wrote: "The question is put today whether this Mediterranean, classic, humanistic tradition is commensurate with humanity and thus coeval with it, or whether it is only the intellectual expression and apanage of the bourgeois liberal epoch and destined to perish with its passing." What this question asks is whether or not the liberal, humanitarian, balanced view of life that had been regarded as central to modern Western history is capable of being transferred to new intellectual, political, and social surroundings or whether it is so closely bound to the bourgeois point of view that it can live only if that bourgeois world lives and will disappear when the bourgeois world disappears.

Throughout his life Mann continued to press this question. In 1943, in a speech in Washington, D.C., he said that "middle-class" ideas are actually "nothing else than the liberal tradition." And he went on: "It is the complex of ideas of freedom and progress, of humanitarianism, of civilization — in short, the claim of reason to dominate the dynamics of nature, of instinct, of blood, the unconscious, the primitive spontaneity of life." There was, according to Mann, in bourgeois humanism a "contempt for all fanaticism," an opposition to "the irrational, the dark dynamics, the glorification of instinct, the worship of blood and impulse, will to power' and 'élan vital' and the justification of violence." The bourgeois world was not inimical to freedom of thought. It was, rather, the stimulant to free thought and free action, a balanced attitude that allowed a man to face "the passage of time, of change, of human inadequacy, of decadence and disintegration, of nonidentity, of the facetiousness of all permanence, and of all claims to truth, of the stupendous make-believe and fraud, of the pathetic and sad, the ridiculous and silly joke of it all."

Mann believed that the weakening of the bourgeois influence left the West exposed to new dangers. Minds now "flicker in the winds of time," and there has been a turning away from the bourgeois interpretation, "a beetle-browed about-face toward dictatorship and terror." There was the search in the West for the limitless, a search for a way to "dream apocalyptically," and there was a form of behavior that Mann called "romantic barbarism." In 1938, the French author and critic André Gide, in an essay on Mann, quoted from an address Mann had given earlier: "The present generation wants only to bid a lasting farewell to its own identity. What it craves, what it loves, is drunkenness. In a new war, it will achieve its final aim, and there our civilization will perish."

Thomas Mann was undoubtedly correct in his belief that something that had been important was going out of Western life in the early twentieth century. The traditional middle-class community — one of the supports of Western society — was being transformed. Not that the middle class itself was disappearing. But the old honesty, the old pride, the old security were gone. And new and meaningful standards of middle-class ethics were not being established by the business operators — the shallow go-getters, organizers, and promoters — who could only make money, not help to create a stable and fertile society. All traditional arrangements in the West were being shaken down, and the historical certainties were vanishing. But Mann believed that new and binding relationships must be found or Western man would perish. In a publication called *Last Essays*, Mann put forward the argument that "what we really need is a new order, new relationships, the recasting of society to meet the global demands of the hour. . . . The main thing is a transformation of the spiritual climate, a new feeling for the difficulty and nobility of being human, an all-pervasive fundamental disposition shared by everyone, and acknowledged by everyone within himself as the supreme judge." This was "not something that can be taught and created; it must be experienced and suffered." But unless the West could establish a new sense of historical security and a viable and accepted standard of conduct and belief, Western civilization would become only a collection of individuals and not a cultural grouping. A scholar has described this terrifying possibility in words with which Thomas Mann would certainly agree: "Man is a thing, life is an absurdity, nature is an aggregate of facts, society is a shell within which each man faces alone a crowd of strangers met by chance or statistical accident."

SUGGESTIONS FOR FURTHER READING

Gerhard Masur's Prophets of Yesterday: Studies in European Culture, 1890–1914 *(1961) may be safely recommended as an example of the best kind of cultural history, and H. Stuart Hughes'* Consciousness and Society: The

Reorientation of European Social Thought *(1958) is an excellent survey. Victor Brombert's* The Intellectual Hero: Studies in the French Novel (1960) *and Walter H. Sokel's* The Writer in Extremis: Expressionism in Twentieth-Century German Literature *(1959) contain interesting chapters on creative activity at the turn of the century.*

Two of the best political studies of the times are J. C. G. Rohl's Germany without Bismarck *(1967) and Eugen Weber's* The Nationalist Revival in France, 1905-1914 *(1959). More specialized books that contain valuable insights are Fritz Stern,* The Politics of Cultural Despair: A Study in the Rise of the German Ideology *(1961), Michael Curtis,* Three against the Third Republic: Sorel, Barrès, and Maurras *(1959), G. R. Ridge,* The Hero in French Decadent Literature *(1961), Walter Laqueur,* Young Germany: A History of the German Youth Movement *(1962), Koenraad W. Swart,* The Sense of Decadence in Nineteenth-Century France *(1964), and Paul Massing,* Rehearsal for Destruction: A Study of Political Anti-Semitism in Imperial Germany *(1949).*

The literature on imperialism is also extensive. A good beginning can be made with A. P. Thornton's many studies — The Imperial Idea and Its Enemies (1959), Doctrine of Imperialism (1965), The Habit of Authority (1966), and For the File on Empire: Essays and Reviews (1968). Other valuable works are Ronald Robinson, John Gallagher, and Alice Denny, Africa and the Victorians (1960), Margery Perham, The Colonial Reckoning (1962), and Stewart C. Easton, The Rise and Fall of Western Colonialism (1964).

Numerous attempts have been made to wrestle with Nietzsche and his thought. C. C. Brinton's Nietzsche *(1941) is a readable, straightforward biography. Walter Kaufmann,* Nietzsche: Philosopher Psychologist Antichrist *(1950), Arthur Danto,* Nietzsche as Philosopher *(1965), and Karl Jaspers,* Nietzsche: An Introduction to the Understanding of His Philosophical Activity *(1965), are full of fruitful comments. Ralph Harper, in* The Seventh Solitude *(1965), discusses Nietzsche in company with Kierkegaard and Dostoievsky, and Peter Heller, in* Dialectics and Nihilism *(1966), devotes himself to Nietzsche, Thomas Mann, and Franz Kafka. The chapters on Nietzsche in Erich Heller's* The Disinherited Mind *(1957) and Thomas Mann's illuminating commentary in his* Last Essays *(1959) are readily available and valuable.*

Further reading on Maurras can be found in the Curtis book cited above and in Edward Tannenbaum, The Action Française: Die-Hard Reactionaries in Twentieth-Century France *(1962), and Eugen Weber,* Action Française: Royalism and Reaction in Twentieth-Century France *(1962). Students interested in Mann should begin with* Buddenbrooks, The Magic Mountain, *and Mann's essays, which have appeared in several editions. Erich Heller's* The Ironic German: A Study of Thomas Mann *(1958) is somewhat contorted in presentation but worth the trouble. Henry Hatfield, ed.,* Thomas Mann: A Collection of Critical Essays *(1964), and Joseph Brennan's* Three Philosophical Novelists *(1964) can be profitably consulted, as can Peter Heller's book mentioned above.*

Wounded, Fall, 1916, Baupaume, Otto Dix, 1924, Museum of Modern Art, New York, Gift of Abby Aldrich Rockefeller.

9

The First World War

1914 JUNE 28 Assassination of the Austrian Archduke Francis Ferdinand. On July 28 Austria declared war on Serbia. This was followed by a mobilization of Russian forces and a German declaration of war on Russia. Germany also declared war on France, and after the German invasion of Belgium, Britain declared war on Germany.

AUGUST 3 Germany sent armies into Belgium. This tactic was designed to outflank the French army and win the war in the west before the Russians could mount an offensive in the east. The Germans pushed deep into France, but the advance was turned north of Paris in the Battle of the Marne in September. Both sides then extended their lines across France from the Alps to the English Channel. The Russians had advanced into east Germany, but in the Battle of Tannenberg and the Battle of the Masurian Lakes in August and September were thrown back with heavy losses.

1915 A great German offensive in the east. Russia lost Poland, Lithuania, and Courland and almost a million men. The German government announced a submarine blockade of England. In May the *Lusitania* was sunk with the loss of 1,198 lives, including 139 Americans. The beginning of strained relations between the United States and Germany.

1916 The bloody, great offensives of the war. The Battle of Verdun, the Battle of the Somme, and the Russian offensive in the east.

1917 German submarine campaign reached its high point. By October 8,000,000 tons of Allied shipping had been lost.

In March a revolution in Russia forced the tsar to abdicate, and a Provisional Government came to power. This government was overthrown in November by the Bolsheviks.

In April the United States declared war on Germany.

1918   On March 3 the Russians signed the Treaty of Brest-Litovsk, which marked Russian withdrawal from the war.

The last great German offensive in France in July and August. The effort failed, and the Allies went over to the attack.

In September the German generals stated that the war was lost. The abdication of the emperor was forced on November 9. Germany asked for peace.

NOVEMBER 11 Hostilities ceased on the Western Front.

1919   Treaty of Versailles. Germany gave up territory to France, Belgium, and Poland. She lost all her colonies. Her army was restricted to 100,000 men, her navy to six warships, and she was forbidden to possess military aircraft or submarines. She was forced to accept responsibility for the war and was to pay all civilian damage caused by the conflict.

1919   John Maynard Keynes' *The Economic Consequences of the Peace,* the best known of those analyses that pointed out the dangers of the peace settlement.

Adoption of the Weimar constitution in Germany provided for a president and elected legislature.

Communist rising in Berlin crushed by government with the help of the army. A soviet-type government was established in Bavaria, but was overthrown. Other risings of Communists were suppressed.

1920   League of Nations organized.

1920   Kapp Putsch in Germany. An attempt by a right-wing group to overthrow German government. Berlin was seized, but a general strike by the trade unions brought about the collapse of the Putsch.

1923   French and Belgian troops occupy the Ruhr district of Germany after Germany declared in default of indemnity deliveries. The Germans adopted a policy of passive resistance, and French attempted to establish a separate Rhineland state. Both attempts failed.

1923	Germany victimized by runaway inflation. The German mark, which had stood at 8.9 per dollar in 1919, fell to 4,200,000,000 per dollar in 1923. Currency was finally stabilized through drastic reform and foreign support of the new mark.
1925	Locarno treaties, which consisted of a series of mutual guarantees of frontiers by Germany, France, Belgium, Poland, and Czechoslovakia. The "spirit of Locarno" seemed to indicate that European problems could be solved by negotiation.
1926	Germany admitted to the League of Nations.
1926	Imperial Conference in London. The report of the conference stated that Great Britain and the Dominions (Canada, Australia, New Zealand, South Africa) "are autonomous communities within the British Empire, equal in status, in no way subordinate one to another in any aspect of their domestic or external affairs, though united by a common allegiance to the crown and freely associated as members of the British Commonwealth of Nations."
1926	General strike in Britain. The strike involved approximately 2,500,000 workers who struck in sympathy with the coal miners.
1926-1928	Financial crisis in France that resulted in decline in value of the franc and disguised repudiation of national debt.
1927	End of Allied commission's military control of Germany.
1930	Beginning of catastrophic economic depression that spread throughout Western world.
1933	Germany announced her withdrawal from the League of Nations and from any negotiations on disarmament.
1935	Germany denounced the clauses in the Treaty of Versailles concerning her disarmament and announced that she was immediately increasing the size of her army.
1936	Germany denounced the Locarno pacts and occupied the Rhineland.

There are catastrophic turning points in history, traumatic events that in a clearly identifiable and short period of time change the direction of societies and are readily recognized as crucial experiences. After such events things that did exist are no more and things that had never been thought of are commonplace. Something that was old and familiar goes out of life, and something that is new and strange enters. The way to the future that once seemed so clear and straight is now clouded and obscure. Old realities appear as anachronisms, and what was once the truth now is a lie. Political arrangements, social ideas, and intellectual interpretations are changed, and men are swept along down an unknown path toward an unknown future.

Such an event took place in the Western world in the first quarter of the twentieth century. A historian has written that for contemporary Western man, "the First World War was the decisive experience." It is commonly accepted that the war which lasted from 1914 until 1918 changed Western civilization in a permanent and basic way. The patterns of life, the language of culture and politics, and the relationships of one man to another were drastically altered. No statement as to the effect of the war seems too extreme. One commentator has written that "Since, under a July sun, bourgeois Europe entered into the century of total war, men have lost control of their history and have been dragged along by the contradictory promptings of techniques and passions." If one might paraphrase a French novelist, the war taught the West that, contrary to any philosophy and religion, men were born to moulder, to be cut to pieces by powerful engines of destruction. After the war to claim that man was a child of God seemed almost blasphemous, while to call him a reasonable creature was ludicrous.

In the years immediately preceding 1914, the leading European nations had prepared for war while political leaders expressed the hope that war would not come. Large conscript armies had been raised by most European countries, alliances had been made between nations, and extensive military plans had been drawn up. There had been a series of war scares during the early years of the century, and then in the summer of 1914 war came. An incident set fire to the continent. On June 28, 1914, Francis Ferdinand, the heir to the Austro-Hungarian throne, was assassinated in Sarajevo by Serbian nationalists. The Austrians, determined to put an end to their problems in the Balkans, pressed upon Serbia a set of humiliating conditions. The Austrian Emperor in a manifesto announced his determination "to put an end to Serbia's ceaseless provocations" and "to secure for my states calm at home and a lasting peace abroad." And the German Emperor, in support of his Austrian ally, stated that "the Serbs must be dealt with, and quickly." Serbia ultimately accepted most of the conditions and expressed her willingness to negotiate the remainder. But Austria stated that she was unsatisfied and decided upon war. Russia was prepared to support Serbia, while Germany stood by Austria. Through July the days passed, with declarations and counter-declarations, mobilizations, hesitations, and calls for action. For a month, the issue of war and peace seemed undecided. But early in August almost a century of peace in Europe ended. Germany and Austria were at war with Russia, France, and England. As a German political leader said in 1914: "All governments, including Russia's, and the great majority of their peoples, are peacefully inclined. But the direction has been lost, and the stone has started rolling."

Opposition to War

There were many in every European country who were opposed to war. Particularly among radicals and socialists there was a long-standing opposition to militarism. Again and again statements had been made that ways must be found for insuring that war did not come. The July 30, 1914, issue of the British *Labour Leader* carried a proclamation headed "The War Must Be Stopped. And We Must Stop It." In a similar vein, immediately after the declaration of war by Germany, a leading German newspaper declared: "Not a single drop of German blood must be shed in support of Austrian imperialism, not a single German soldier must take the field against the workers of other countries."

But all efforts to stop the war floundered upon the wild patriotism and the course of military events. In Germany, in France, and in Britain, those opposed to war found themselves faced with the impossible task of insisting upon peace while being unwilling to leave their countries defenseless against the enemy. The German socialists demanded peace and condemned a war of conquest but, at the same time, accepted what was called "the grim fact of war" and refused "to leave the fatherland in the lurch" in the face of a Russian invasion. "Before us stands the iron reality of war," said one of the socialist leaders in the Reichstag. "We have not to decide today for or against war, but over the question of supplies for the defense of the country." The war "forced us to make this choice: either we must take the side of militarism, or we must stand by and see our country overrun by the Russians. Prussianism is bad enough, but we prefer it to Russianism." With a few exceptions, there was everywhere a rallying to the various national causes. The Frenchman Jules Guesde, who had been a violent opponent of the French government, became a minister in the French cabinet, while Gustave Hervé, who had earlier advocated a general strike by French workers to stop any European war, became a belligerent defender of France and changed the name of his newspaper from *The Social War* to *Victory*. German pacifists became ardent supporters of the war, and long-time anarchists, radicals, and critics of the German state enrolled in the ranks with their countrymen in defense of the homeland.

In every country there was what in retrospect appeared to be a strange justification of the war as a great cleansing agent that would clear Europe of old hatreds, old tensions, and old weaknesses. The war was expected to promote the manly virtues of courage, fraternity, and sacrifice and to put an end to petty self-indulgence and the pursuit of private and selfish interests. In a speech of September, 1914, the British politician Lloyd George spoke of this hoped-for development. The war, he said, "is bringing a new outlook to all classes. The great flood of luxury and sloth which had submerged the land is receding, and a new Britain is appearing. We can see for the first time the fundamental things that matter in life, and that have been obscured by the tropical growth of prosperity." There was even the belief that the actual fact of war would forward the idea of peace. As a group of German politicians said in their statement supporting the voting of war credits: "We trust the hard school of war will awaken in new millions of people a horror of war, and win them over to the ideas of socialism and of peace on earth." This same view that peace was the ultimate goal was expressed by an editor of a London newspaper on the day war was declared by Britain. "We have to do our part in killing a creed of war. Then at last, after a rain of blood, there may be set the greater rainbow in the Heavens before the visions of the souls of men. And after Armageddon, war, indeed, may be no more."

The Military Campaigns

Every combatant nation entered the war under the impression that victory could be achieved quickly. No one had plans for a long struggle, nor for anything that approached what the war became. In November, 1914, the French general Joseph Joffre rejected the idea of issuing steel helmets to his army, declaring that "we shall not have time to make them, for I shall twist the Boche's neck before two months are up." The Germans, too, had only plans for immediate success, something analogous to the triumphs achieved in the nineteenth century by the Prussian army. When the early strategy failed, every nation fell back upon one expedient after another, in the hope that something would turn up. As a writer spoke of officials in the Austrian Foreign Office, but in words that could apply to all belligerents: "They have no plans. None of them has any idea as to where and under what conditions the war could be ended." Desperation replaced logic. Again, Crown Prince Rupprecht's comment about the German general Erich von Falkenhayn could apply to almost all military leaders. "General von Falkenhayn was himself not clear as to what he really wanted, and was waiting for a stroke of luck that would lead to a favorable solution."

The actual chronology of the war is well known. The German plan of battle called for a quick defeat of France before the Russians could threaten Germany from the east. In accordance with this strategy, the German armies swept through Belgium in the early days of August and struck deep into France. The French suffered a series of defeats and were forced to give up a great deal of territory. But the German line was ultimately turned north of Paris. Then both the Germans and the French and British extended their defense trenches across France, and the war on the Western Front entered into a long period of terrifying and barbarous trench warfare. On the east, the Russians broke through into Germany. The Germans, however, succeeded in throwing the Russian armies back, and here the struggle was a devastating movement to and fro that gained little but cost a great deal in men and morale.

Warfare of the kind practiced during the First World War was something new to Western man. In the mainstream of Western thinking war had always been regarded as an uncivilized activity that brought little but suffering. But the brutal, mechanized murder that was twentieth-century war was something beyond imagination. War became blind destruction, and almost every battlefield was what the French called "un terrain à catastrophe." Shells, guns and men were consumed at an inconceivable rate, and the price in human lives was unparalleled. The sixteen active belligerents in the war suffered total casualties — in military personnel alone — of 37,500,000, substantially more than half of the forces mobilized. More than 8,500,000 were killed or died of wounds or disease. In the French, British, German, Russian, Austrian, and Italian armies at least one man out of every ten mobilized was killed or died of causes attributable to the war. The Russian army alone suffered nearly 4,000,000 casualties in the first year of the war, and her total casualties were more than 9,000,000, 76 per cent of the total mobilized. On the British sector of the Western Front between January, 1915 and September, 1918 it was estimated that a soldier posted there had approximately five months of trench service in front of him and that the wound putting him out of action would, in one case out of four, be fatal.

The fair land of Europe was also ravished. Ancient towns were reduced to rubble, fertile fields were gouged and scarred by artillery fire, and forests, streams, and valleys became places where no living thing dwelled. Armies moved into the ground like hunted animals, and the trench "was the only haven in a desolate landscape, guarded by the wire, protected by the gun, and threatened by gas." Descriptions of this destruction were plentiful, and one must stand for a multitude. Ten years after the war ended, in 1928, a traveler wrote of a trip to Verdun and then to Rheims in northern France.

> A landscape that fills one with horror: mile after mile of military cemeteries; trees burned to charcoal still stretching their limbs to the sky; ruined farms and, in the distance, the bare white and grey shimmer of the chalk downs. The thickly packed little white crosses in the graveyards, thousands upon thousands, seem in the broad landscape almost unimportant.

And what was accomplished by this slaughter and destruction? The answer must be very little. One military campaign after another was a debacle. The battle of Verdun in 1916 cost the French 315,000 men, the Germans 280,000, and the Germans gained seven miles in four and one-half months. The first battle of the Somme was an unbelievable British disaster. Thirteen British divisions went "over the top" in regular waves and became human targets for the devastating German machine guns. Nineteen thousand were killed, and 57,000 casualties were sustained, in what has been called "the greatest loss in a single day ever suffered by a British army." In the summer and fall of 1917, the battle of Passchendaele accounted for some 400,000 casualties with no significant result. The third Ypres offensive cost the British and Germans half a million casualties, and the British advanced five miles. Mute evidence of the hopeless endeavor exists still at the Ypres memorial where there is a listing of the names of 45,000 British soldiers whose bodies could not be identified. These mutilated bodies and those of their comrades are buried in fifteen cemeteries.

No one seemed able to do anything about this endless killing. It is impossible to overstate the abysmal incompetence of the political and military leadership in every country. Those Europeans who claimed the right to positions of power showed themselves without resources or imagination in confronting the terror of twentieth-century war. The machine was running away, and no one could gain control. Civilian administration of the war was largely abandoned to the military, and here there was little but general lack of qualifications for command. Not a military leader during the whole four years could really be said to have understood the situation, and all that most could think of was to kill more men. It has been pointed out that the British general Haig and the French general Joffre were both very simple and very ignorant men. In Haig's case it has been argued that this was due to his inability to think clearly, while Joffre was said to have had nothing at all on his mind. The

British general Kitchener had not foreseen trench warfare, and when it came he could only complain: "I don't know what is to be done; this isn't war."

The military plans were hopeless. For example, Colonel de Grand-maison, Chief of the Operations Bureau of the French General Staff, had a mystical belief in the value of the dauntless attack. "In the offensive," he argued, "imprudence is the best assurance.... Let us go even to excess, and that perhaps will not be far enough." What this meant in practice was open frontal attacks by infantry against well-placed artillery and machine guns, and this doctrine cost France thousands of men with little gain to show for the sacrifice. Grandmaison was ultimately discredited and was to find death himself at the head of a brigade trying to establish the correctness of his theory. Other French leaders pursued a policy of what was called "Grignotage," or "nibbling away at the enemy." Such a practice has been rightfully described as trying "to bite through a steel door with badly fitting false teeth." Equally futile were German leaders' plans for victory. Massive offensives were attempted that broke themselves upon the enemy front and left the situation very much as it had been before.

In a way that is truly amazing, the common soldiers, on both sides, put up with the unending mutilations, the indignities, the repeated displays of incompetence, and the stink of death. In history books and old photographs, we can still see them — the farm boys, the schoolteachers and students, the owners of small shops, the clerks, the factory workers — with their uncomfortable uniforms, their patient faces, and their awesome courage. But there was a general revulsion and horror at what was happening. A noted German socialist wrote in 1916: "The present massacre, one whose like has never been seen, is reducing the adult working population to women, the aged, and the cripples." And a disgust at the bloodletting was to find expression in all the great literature produced by the war: Robert Graves' *Good-Bye to All That*, E. E. Cummings' *The Enormous Room*, Erich Remarque's *All Quiet on the Western Front*, John Dos Passos' *Three Soldiers*, and Ernest Hemingway's *A Farewell to Arms*. A French woman writer protested against the continual statements of "so and so many killed — abstractions with which the world juggled in figures" and at the reduction of everything to parts of an inhuman machine "moved by a deadly maniac hand." The Frenchman Henri Barbusse, in August, 1914, had written that he was prepared to fight against German militarism, German imperialism, and the German monarchy. By 1916, however, he was writing in his novel *The Fire*: "Shame on military glory, shame on the armies, shame on the profession of soldier that changes men step by step into stupid victims and ignoble executioners."

Effects of War

But the war did more than slaughter millions. It produced an emotional inflation that vulgarized and cheapened those very things for which men thought they were fighting. There was throughout the war an increasing indifference to words, and this indifference to words produced an indifference to what the words signified. Words such as freedom, country, liberty, democracy, justice, and patriotism came under a cloud and were tarnished in a way that was to create permanent strains in Western society. What was called "patriotic rubbish" was substituted for honest speech, and the lie, the half-lie, the coated and disguised truth were everywhere. Governments lied as a matter of course, and there is a great measure of truth in a British Prime Minister's ironic statement that the War Office kept three sets of figures: "one to mislead the public, one to mislead the Cabinet, and a third to mislead itself." Eminent scholars and intellectuals, whose lives had been devoted to the search for truth, busily produced uncritical polemics to influence their countrymen and prostituted their professions in order to participate in war propaganda. The Society of Medicine in Paris, for example, published a report on the discovery of "polychesia" (excessive defecation) and "bromidrosis" (body odor) in the German race and reported its findings that urinalysis could be used for the detection of German spies: German urine was found to contain 20 per cent non-uric nitrogen as against 15 per cent for other nationalities. Religion was enlisted in the struggle, and Christ became the Lord of War, pressing one group of Christians to kill another. The Word of God was reduced to a patriotic slogan and was transformed into a battlecry by ministers, politicians, and generals.

The physical horror and the arousing of violent passions introduced a new brutality and coarseness into Western life. In 1918 the German Emperor wrote on the margin of a report "the world war lacks in style." This was true, but there was more than a mere absence of grace and poise. Throughout the nineteenth century Western society had been largely and basically civilian where force was reduced to a minimum and certain, perhaps artificial, amenities were observed. The war infected Western society with the standards of the barracks room, and the habits of the military camp were transferred into civilian society. There was a callousness and a rudeness and an acceptance of violence. As the German Karl Kautsky remarked, the World War "brutalized almost every strata of the society" and "brought despair in the place of quiet thought and reflection." The brutality, the hatred, the violence that had always existed under the surface in Western society found expression in the war and became commonplace. Many men could be described in the words used by a member of his staff about the German general Erich von Ludendorff: "He was a man blind in spirit. He had never seen a flower bloom, never heard a bird sing, never watched the sun set." The idealistic expressions of the liberals, the socialists, and the radicals were obliterated by the war, and in their place appeared the crassest of materialism, the emptiest appeals to force, the language of the gangster.

The war affected every section of the population. The traditional upper classes — statesmen, financiers, generals, churchmen — who had been beneficiaries of the triumphs of Western civilization and had enjoyed the privileges of the best education and social position had failed in a time of crisis and forfeited their claims to speak for the West. Large numbers of the common citizens were demoralized and felt themselves betrayed and abandoned by those to whom they had looked for direction. But the effects of the war were most disastrous to the middle-class liberal group that had dominated the intellectual life of the West during the nineteenth century. The confidence and the healthy vigor that had characterized these groups in every nation were fatalities of the fighting. A disproportionate number of the most energetic, the most brilliant, and the most promising of the middle-class young did not return from the battlefields. The junior officer corps in every country, drawn largely from the middle class, suffered extensive casualties, while many of those who did survive nursed a grievance against the society that had been guilty of allowing such a catastrophe to take place. Something went out of the middle class in the years from 1914 to 1918. The certainties, the allegiances, and the dedication were weakened and, in many countries, destroyed. It is a literary and perhaps extreme description of the situation that appears in F. Scott Fitzgerald's *Tender Is the Night*, but Fitzgerald realized that something had happened during the war that had turned much of the middle-class world into a nostalgic memory.

> This Western-front business couldn't be done again, not for a long time. The young men think they could do it again, but they couldn't. . . . It took religion and years of plenty and tremendous sureties and the exact relation that existed between classes. . . . You had to have a whole-souled sentimental equipment going back further than you could remember. You had to remember Christmas, and postcards of the Crown Prince and his fiancée, and little cafés in Valence and beer gardens in Unter den Linden and weddings at the Mairie, and going to the Derby, and your grandfather's whiskers. . . . This was a love-battle — there was a century of middle-class love spent here. . . . All my beautiful lovely safe world blew itself up here with a great gust of high explosive love. . . .

In every country the internal spiritual balance of the society was shattered. Traditions were distorted, and the struggle opened old wounds
and created new ones. The political framework of Europe was
destroyed by the war. Three major countries — Germany, Austria, and
Russia — suffered defeat. Three empires — the Russian Romanov, the
German Hohenzollern, and the Austrian Hapsburg — disappeared. In
Russia, incompetence, weak leadership, and impossible-to-imagine suffering led to a revolution that drastically changed the relationship of that
country to the rest of Europe and the world. Some riots and a few days
of disorder in the capital, and the old regime fell, without supporters and
without regrets. After eight months of an unstable provisional government, the Bolsheviks, the most extreme Marxist group in Europe, seized
control of the country. The Bolshevik leaders rejected almost all the
basic ideas of Western society and mounted a revolutionary political,
social, and intellectual offensive against the West. After their victory in
a bloody and horrifying civil war, they remained a menacing and to a
large extent alien society on the outskirts of the Western world.

The destruction of the Austrian empire reduced a once-important
state to a frustrated fragment and brought about in central and eastern
Europe a group of small, proud, quarreling national societies that provided a stage for a series of political adventurers who ultimately were to
bring little hope or security to their peoples. But the effects of defeat
were most demoralizing in Germany. For the Germans defeat was unexpected, unprepared for, and unacceptable. The meaning of being
German had been so strongly identified with a successful German state
that the defeat of that state called into question the validity of the
German identity. A shocking intellectual and spiritual crisis was produced in German thinking. The Germans had had the best army, the
most organized state, the most energetic people — and yet they had been
defeated. Somehow history had cheated Germany, or, perhaps, the
results of the war had been a mistake that could be rectified at a future
date. The following description of the return of the German army to
Berlin a month after the war ended illustrated the bitterness, the emotion, and the refusal to accept the war's outcome:

> The first German troops from the front marched through the Bran-
> denburg Gate on December 10, 1918. These were the veteran troops
> of the Empire. The imperial black-white-red, the black-and-white of
> Prussia, the white-and-blue of Bavaria, the flags of the other states
> floated from the ranks of the veterans. Flowers decked their helmets.
> Women and children and old men trudged alongside, weeping, cheer-
> ing, laughing. The men marched with cadenced steps, the bands
> blared national songs as the long lines of field-grey troops filed
> through the great gate. They halted. A hush fell. The soldiers' hel-
> mets came off. A massed band played, and a chorus of school chil-
> dren sang an old German anthem.

The victors of the war were little better off than the defeated. For the British the war meant the end of their trade and naval supremacy, while their ability to act as a force for international stability was weakened. Even more important were the effects in France. The cold slaughter of the war filled the French with disgust and terror. Henri Lichtenberger wrote: "The French have always been considered a military people, and we acknowledge that the war of the eighteenth century or the heroic war of Napoleon did have a certain attraction for them. But the scientific war of the twentieth century, with its formidable machinery, systematic devastation, fearful reprisals, and its terrifying consequences for civil populations struck them as a hideous regression to barbarism. Their whole being revolted against it in absolute repulsion." The fact that little had been gained by the terrible victory also left them frustrated. As a scholar has written, "the French had lost that primitive *élan* which carries men into battle." The purpose of France and French history seemed to be lost, and "in the absence of a potent common purpose uniting the nation, social divisions, which during the preceding one hundred and fifty years had repeatedly resulted in civil war, became accentuated, inhibiting still further national action."

The war violated most of the basic premises of Western life. The political arrangements, of which Western man was so proud, had been strained by prolonged armed conflict. Political leadership had come a cropper when faced with a crisis. The words by which men lived had shown themselves to be hollow. As a result many Westerners became cynical about all appeals and thus became potential traitors and appeasers. Most important, perhaps, the war had called into question Western man's proud assumption that he could direct his affairs by using his intelligence. The war showed that events might be beyond man's intellectual control and thus suggested that he was not master of his destiny. In what may be the best, brief description of the effects of the war, Paul Valéry wrote: "The war has disturbed the economic structure, the policy of states, and the life of the individual. But worst of all these afflictions is what happened to the mind. The mind has been cruelly wounded. It now doubts itself." Doubt was perhaps the great legacy of the conflict. There was doubt about the validity of the philosophical principles of Western life, the political institutions, the intellectual capacity, and the very nature of man himself. Nationalism, industrialization and technological progress, and liberal democracy had shown themselves as enemies rather than benefactors of Western man. The entire Western civilizing enterprise had been called into question.

Many examples are at hand to illustrate the effect of the war upon the Western world. The war created a large number of cultural and historical orphans who could not find a place for themselves in the postwar society. Robbed of certainty and alienated, such people became a new form of the historically dispossessed. The war was also responsible for the popularity of certain philosophies that seemed to speak to the desperation and discouragement so prevalent in the years following the end of hostilities. Probably the best known of these interpretations was that by Oswald Spengler, and the title of his famous book *Decline of the West* became almost a cliche. Sigmund Freud was a famous psychologist who used his specialized insight to illuminate some of the hidden forces that were placing particular strain upon Western man and Western civilization.

The Dispossessed

Each of the serious shocks that Western society had experienced in the late eighteenth and nineteenth centuries had produced "homeless people," the uprooted, the disinherited, the historical drifters. The First World War was no exception to this pattern. But the crisis produced by this alienation appears to have been, perhaps because we are at least in part still victims of it, more extreme, more intense, than previously. For many people the war destroyed every sense of belonging to a stable and creative community, and, for them, as Paul Valéry wrote in 1919, "the illusion of a European culture had been lost." They were men who were described by George Bernard Shaw as "falling, falling, falling endlessly and hopelessly through a void in which they can find no footing." The Western world appeared as socially, economically, and politically absurd, and there was nothing in that world that could claim wholehearted allegiance. Such people looked upon themselves as the true dispossessed, those whose country, whose sense of certainty, and whose intellectual orientation had been stolen away.

Members of this group came from every social and economic stratum of society. Some were aristocrats who had lost wealth and status. Some were intellectuals who found it impossible to accept a world that appeared without purpose or reason. Some were the half-educated, the intellectually and culturally deprived, the new men from underground, bitter, hostile, and vicious. All had been spiritually maimed by the war, and all bore a grudge against a civilization that had betrayed them.

For those who felt themselves wounded by history, there was a rejection of the commonly accepted ideas and institutions of the West. Western political and economic life was regarded as "a permanent conspiracy of the rich and the ambitious, the great chiefs, parasites, and flatterers," while the cultural climate in Europe and America had become nothing but "a vacuum of historic twaddle, crushed education, bumptious political forgeries, and cheap sports." Everywhere they saw the "chaos and putrid decay of the times," the evidence of "church slime, bourgeois slime, military slime." The West seemed old and worn-out, "vile and ugly," and as André Malraux wrote in 1926 in his novel *The Temptation of the West*, there appeared a "hopeless contradiction . . . between man and what he has created." There was nothing left to which one could be loyal, and "there is no ideal to which we can sacrifice ourselves, for all we know is lies, and have no idea what the truth is."

This alienation from the West was particularly obvious in the area of politics. The war had shown a surprising absence of political talent, and there was little change in the postwar years. Western man seemed to have become politically dumb and to have lost his capacity for political activity. It is hard to overestimate the sterility of Western political life in the nineteen-twenties and, in most cases, in the nineteen-thirties. In a time of great need, the West failed politically. It seemed true as one commentator pointed out: "This is the day of the little man — each one looking like the others; you could exchange any of them for any other and nobody would notice."

In England, it was the age of Stanley Baldwin, who knew that the world was going mad but who said "I have no idea what is the matter with it," and who was described by George Orwell as "simply a hole in the air." The United States, the strongest power in the West and the one that might have provided the leadership needed, found its political expression in three presidents who reduced any political philosophy to a mere business practice and who were such cultural ciphers that one, Warren G. Harding, could be justifiably slandered by the poet E. E. Cummings as "the only man woman or child who ever wrote a simple declarative sentence with seven grammatical errors." Many British members of Parliament were rightly described as "a lot of hard-faced men who look as if they had done very well out of the war," while, with equal justification, a large number of corrupt and vacuous French politicians could be depicted as men who "live from hand to mouth, deal with the problems that they cannot elude, elude those that can still wait, restrain the drive of life with all their might, strive to stay put, to stay put at whatever price." A great many of the West's leading intellectuals were prepared to agree with a German writer's comment that "the whole system is a racket. Some are swindlers, others are swindled, but it is always the people who are the victims." The West became a political wasteland, and there seemed no possibility of change. In August, 1937, Albert Camus wrote: "Every time I hear a political speech or I read those of our leaders, I am horrified at having for years heard nothing which sounded human. It is always the same words telling the same lies. And the fact that men accept this, that the people's anger has not destroyed these hollow clowns, strikes me as proof that men attribute no importance to the way they are governed; that they gamble — yes, gamble — with a whole part of their life and their so-called 'vital interests.'"

This animosity toward Western politics was translated into an attack upon liberalism, parliamentarianism, and the entire middle-class system of political values. There was a strong belief that liberal, democratic ideas were now exhausted and that nothing further could be gained by pursuing this line of Western political development. The problems of politics seemed so great and to demand such drastic measures that the democratic process struck an increasing number of Western intellectuals as too weak and too faltering. The future required some new type of political arrangement that would not suffer from the handicaps of the old, and even such long-standing virtues as free speech, the absence of terror, and individualism were dismissed as outmoded and superfluous characteristics of life. There was a turning-away from traditional patterns of political behavior toward anything that promised to lead out of the cul-de-sac of one meaningless election after another, of an unending series of empty political debates. In fact, there was among Western intellectuals at least a partial rejection of politics altogether, in the sense in which they had been customarily practiced in the West, and political activity was often classed with "refrigerators, balance-sheets, and cross-word puzzles" as undertakings that had nothing but a peripheral interest and importance.

But the withdrawal from Western society was much more than a matter of refusal to accept Western politics. Irving Howe has written that "the twentieth century has been marked by a crisis of conduct and belief that is perhaps unprecedented in seriousness, depth, and extent," and this crisis struck at the very heart of Western civilization. The most precious attribute of contemporary Western man — his intelligence — was called into question. Many of those who were themselves intellectuals rejected their own heritage and were attracted to new philosophies of action and irrationalism. Convinced that there had been what was called "the overdevelopment of the intellect," they looked for something that would "cut through the verbiage of the illusion of knowledge to the achievement of a new reality." In 1927 a German scholar remarked that "in every sphere of life we see a revolution of the mind, seeking and finding a new form of expression, of the rhythm of life." There was an emphasis upon heroic vitalism and a repudiation of reason and intelligence. Many influential intellectual leaders, particularly in Germany but also in France and every other country in the West, abandoned the search for rational meaning in life and sought the secret of existence in movement and action. This was not a return to earlier traditionalism but an urge toward a new world of emotionalism and unexamined activity. Examples of this new irrationalism, of this revolt against the mind, could be given by the thousands. But a few of the important expressions of this attitude are enough. In 1929 the German philosopher Ludwig Klages published a book entitled *The Mind as the Adversary of the Soul,* where he argued that there was a continual and irreconcilable conflict between stale reason and instinctive vitality. Klages called for a general rebellion against any concept of an ordered universe, against science and humanitarianism, and spoke out in defense of an uninhibited, primitive way of life. In much the same way, the gifted German poet Gottfried Benn wrote of "Metropolis, industrialism, intellectualism, all those shadows which the age cast over my thoughts, all these powers of the century which I took issue with in my work — there are moments when this whole tortured life vanishes and nothing remains but the wide plains, the seasons, the earth, simple words."

A dramatic example of this attitude can be found in the writings of the German author Ernst Jünger. Born in 1895, Jünger, as a young man, fought in the First World War and also spent a period of time in Africa. In his literary work Jünger stressed "a direct plunge into adventure, into daring, into pure existence." War, as all action, was a creative not a destructive experience, wherein men struggled against that great enemy — "the eternal Utopia of peace, the pursuit of happiness, and perfection." For Jünger, the world was "a landscape of ice and fire," where men were swept along by powerful, unknown forces. "Blood, roses, and splendid tears" were the only realities, while all else was only smoke and fog, pale shadows of the real life. Systems of morality and a dependence upon reason merely crippled men, and blind, unseeing struggle was the only regenerative force. It was with men such as Jünger in mind that Thomas Mann complained that here was an emphasis upon "the impotence of spirit and reason ... while by contrast the power of the lower regions, the dynamic of passion, the irrational, the unconscious, is exhibited with bellicose piety."

In all of this emphasis upon action there was a worship of the strong, the passionate, even the brutal. Praises were sung in honor of those "who consume their whole life in a single hour and die happy," and there was a continual "hymn to life, youth, and ecstasy." The German poet Hanns Johst went so far as to say that "whenever I hear the word culture I cock my pistol," and, in a similar manner, the future Nazi leader Martin Bormann argued that "every educated man is a future enemy." There were many who were prepared to accept the claim of the French surrealists that "hysteria is not a pathological phenomenon and can be considered in every respect a supreme means of expression."

This glorification of the "blood" at the expense of the brain was not confined to poets and artists, or even to intellectuals. Many of the dispossessed were "fighters who could not become debrutalized," and "armed bohemians to whom war is home and civil war fatherland." The scum and near-scum of Europe responded to the call to irrational action, and many of the crack-brained and nit-witted were prepared to undertake any project that promised excitement and some form of reward. Sentimentality, a twisted eroticism, and a feeling of comradeship that could not be found elsewhere brought the toughs, the street-brawlers, the armed bullies and thugs together into paramilitary groups that engaged in political demonstrations and political acts of violence. The German Free Corps, the French Cross of Fire, and the British New Party attracted those who had no stake in contemporary Western civilization and felt no loyalty toward it. As Ernst von Salomon, a young German who was a member of the Free Corps and who wrote the best-known history of the movement, remarked: "We were cut off from the world of bourgeois norms. . . . The bonds were broken, and we were free. . . . What we wanted, we did not know. And what we knew we did not want."

This feeling of alienation from the past and the present entered into the lifestream of the West. It appeared in every country, but was particularly evident in Germany. There the violence released by the war remained a fact of political and cultural life. This violence was stimulated by the inflation of 1923, which undermined confidence in ordered economic arrangements and reduced large numbers of people to an unfamiliar and terrifying financial hardship, and there was a later catastrophic economic disintegration in 1929 and 1930. Germany also contained "a lost generation" of demobilized soldiers who had little to return to, and she possessed a discontented population of refugees from the east, the bitterest of displaced aristocrats and semi-aristocrats who had seen their lands and their possessions taken over by inferior nobodies. Loans made by German citizens to the government during the war were not repaid, there were heavy reparations demanded by the victorious Allies, and there was the loss of export markets. Military defeat marked the German mind, and as a German wrote, "our history has gone astray." The democratic government established after the war was regarded by many Germans as a betrayal of the national purpose, and there were many who agreed with the general who announced: "I am prepared to take part in any Putsch that has a fifty-one per cent probability of success."

Assassination was the method of dealing with political opponents, and from 1918 to 1922 no fewer than 376 political murders took place. There was a series of attempts to overthrow the government, and in the nineteen-twenties an Englishman could write that Germany was "a land of sheep without a shepherd, rushing hither and thither seeking a direction and a world view."

The feeling of isolation from Western history and from Western society prompted a movement toward new ideologies and a response to new charismatic appeals. What was called "a young, ardent, and irresistible collective belief against a civilization of fragmented and contradictory ideas" stimulated a drift toward those "heroic" doctrines that were dedicated to actions that would destroy the old, hated world. In 1927 Paul Valéry noted that "the image of dictatorship is the inevitable (and, as it were, instinctive) response of the mind when it no longer finds in the conduct of affairs the authority, continuity, and unity that indicate reflective will and the rule of organized knowledge." Various ideologies that were dedicated to the destruction of the West and which, in one degree or another, "represent the final, deepest degradation of reason" attracted many of the real and supposed dispossessed. Some yielded to the "irresistible attraction of Marxism," while others found in fascism an instrument whereby they might take revenge upon the civilization that had disappointed them.

Throughout the nineteen-twenties and nineteen-thirties the liberal Western civilization was in a more or less state of siege. Its enemies were everywhere. The straining flags, the sound of heavy boots upon the pavements, the screams of hatred were indications that a time of extreme danger was at hand. A new kind of world seemed in the making, and weakened by despair and a sense of hopelessness, Western civilization appeared to await its destruction. Even those who still believed in the virtues of Western society, and they were a majority, felt themselves terrorized, abandoned, and at a loss as to how to combat their enemies. There was a hopelessness, a suspicion that little could be done against the inevitable onslaught. In 1939 the English poet W. H. Auden caught the flavor of the general atmosphere of the time in one of his stanzas:

> Read on, ambassador, engrossed
> In your favorite Stendhal;
> The Outer Provinces are lost,
> Unshaven horsemen swill
> The great wines of the Chateaux
> Where you danced long ago.[1]

Oswald Spengler

In January, 1918, a relatively unknown German named Oswald Spengler wrote from Munich to a friend that he had completed a book that
was to be published later in the year. Since 1911 Spengler had been
engaged in writing and rewriting his book, which he believed "will
surely enter contemporary literature like an avalanche into a shallow
lake." The work had been long and tiring, what Spengler called "a sort
of walk to execution," and, although he was by nature a confident even
arrogant man, now that the date of publication was at hand he was
apprehensive. "But believe me," he wrote, "I regard the book with
mixed feelings. I cannot summon up the joy of an author. I am much
more clearly conscious of failings in the design, the style, and the
arrangement than I am of the significance of the ideas. As the result of
internal and external pressures, loneliness, lack of inspiration from
others or from journeys and experiences, I did not reach the level of performance which I felt I ought to attain."

In the spring of 1918 the book, entitled *Decline of the West*, was
published. It was a startling success. By 1922, when Spengler brought
out a second volume, the first had sold approximately 36,000 copies,
while by 1926 sales passed the 100,000 mark. *Decline of the West* was
translated into French, Spanish, Italian, English, Russian, and Arabic.
In 1926 an American edition of the first volume was published, and this

[1]Reprinted by permission from "Song" from W. H. Auden: *Collected Shorter Poems
1927-1957* (Random House, Inc., 1967).

was followed two years later by the second volume. Within fifteen years 21,000 copies of the work had been sold in the United States, and Spengler had become a well-known figure in intellectual and semi-intellectual circles throughout the Western world.

Decline of the West was a staggering monster of a book. It was almost 1,200 pages long, a swirling, repetitious, exasperating study, full of awesome insights, irritating and unsupported suppositions, great chunks of esoteric knowledge, and questionable hypotheses. As a critic remarked, Spengler "gives us a feeling of dizziness," and large numbers of educated men have engaged in a long struggle to refute Spengler and correct what they regarded as his errors of fact and of interpretation. Spengler's popularity offended many, and they reacted against what they regarded as his pessimism, his shallowness, and his incompetence. Spengler was condemned as wild and reckless, and many dismissed the German as one who happened to have published his book at a time when his gloomy and oversimplified interpretation appealed to those who had undergone the ghastly experience of the First World War. As a French scholar wrote: "In the twenties Spengler offered the wares that at that time were most in demand: a certain pathos, a determined anti-intellectualism, a heroic notion of destiny, anti-aestheticism, the thrill of being a mere human being before the broad majesty of History. . . . This is what gave Spengler his success: not the success of an analytical and deductive historian, but the success of a prophet, of a magician, of a visionary perfectly adapted to the needs of a troubled Germany. . . ."

The objections to Spengler's historical interpretation were valid. He did not possess the specialized knowledge to handle the great task he had set himself. He did make great, sweeping guesses about the past, and he did not hesitate to predict the future in a way that stunned more careful men. Moreover, his condemnation of those who disagreed with him as "simpletons, charlatans, or pedants" was hardly designed to stimulate calm and reasoned discussion of his book. Spengler often was guilty of forcing any recalcitrant fact or theory to fit into his set scheme of interpretation. Also, at times, he wrote nonsense. For example, he stated that "the male livingly experiences Destiny," while "the female, on the contrary, is herself Destiny." In the same way, in the attempt to show how men of various societies differ from each other, he stressed such foolishness as that "Western man looks up, the Russian looks horizontally over the broad plain."

Unfortunate as such lapses are, they do not touch the core of Spengler's argument or meet the problem he posed for Western civilization. A contemporary of his remarked that the response to Spengler's book showed that "a deep and secret wound had been probed," as though an unwelcome guest had pried into family secrets and had then presented these failings for all to see. As Spengler himself wrote, in the *Decline of the West* he attempted to determine "the state of West Europe and America as at the epoch of 1800 to 2000" and to discuss the "decline of the West-European Culture which is now spread over the entire globe." In this discussion he questioned many of the important ideas held by Western men. He denied the concept of progress, he ridiculed any idea that the West was a unique civilization that could in some way escape its fate, and he rejected what he thought of as "an unbridled optimism" that robbed Western man of any knowledge of his true condition. In a letter of 1914 he had written that "what lies before us is unfortunately equally unconsoling," and the message of his book was one that could only be depressing to Western man.

At the heart of Spengler's thought is the idea of destiny, and this is, in fact, the key to understanding what he is saying. What Spengler meant by destiny was that man's fate was directed by forces outside his control and that there is no way by which an individual or a society can escape what has been foreordained. As he wrote, "Everything depends on our seeing our position, our destiny, clearly, on our realizing that though we may lie to ourselves about it we cannot evade it." There is a pattern to life and to history that cannot be changed, no matter how men might will otherwise, and history is "a drama noble in its aimlessness, noble and aimless as the course of the stars, the rotation of the earth, and alternance of land and sea, of ice and virgin forest upon its face. We may marvel at it or we may lament it — but it is there."

Spengler was convinced that evidence of this law of destiny could be found in the world of nature where nothing escapes the cycle of life and death but moves steadily along a fated path. Man and his accomplishments are part of this natural pattern and are controlled by its laws. "I see world history as a picture of endless formations and transformations, of the marvellous waxing and waning of organic forms," he wrote, and everything goes through an organic cycle of birth, maturity, and death. Because of his illusions of progress and his belief in the unending improvement of his institutions, Western man thinks that he and his society can avoid the inevitable end and cannot conceive of his own disappearance. But this way of looking at ourselves as something unique, outside nature, is false. "The ground of West Europe is treated as a steady pole, a unique patch chosen on the surface of the sphere for no better reason, it seems, than because we live on it — and great histories of millennial duration and mighty far-away Cultures are made to revolve around this pole in all modesty." In Spengler's view, this egocentrism "is a quaintly conceived system of sun and planets," and no matter how much we may claim priority for ourselves and our beliefs, they are emphatically not "eternal" or "universal." As he wrote "the future of the West is not a limitless tending upwards and onwards for all time toward our present ideas." Rather, the West is "but a single phenomenon of history, strictly limited and defined as to form and duration."

Through his study of other societies that had existed on the earth, Spengler believed that he had discovered a process that applied to all men's efforts and that provided an insight into what would happen in the West. The history of mankind expresses itself through forms that Spengler called cultures. These come into being when a group of people accept a common spiritual commitment and are largely united through a certain general acceptance of a way of looking at the world and at themselves. Every culture has what is basically a religious outlook, "an instinctive, dream-sure logic of all existence" that surpasses "the logic of understanding and of things understood." Members of such a culture possess a "stronger, fuller, and more self-assured life" and claim the right to exist, "regardless of whether its right would hold before a tribunal of waking consciousness." They are creative, intuitive people who grasp the spirit of the age and are at one with the highest aspirations of their society. They possess a feeling of unity and fullness, an awareness of their potentialities as members of the culture in which they participate.

Each culture, as it develops, has its own unique spirit and differs from every other culture. "I see no progress, no goal, no path for humanity," writes Spengler, and men in one culture are cut off from those in another. "There are no eternal truths. Every philosophy is the expression of its own and only its own time." All institutions and beliefs are applicable only to the particular culture in which they appear and in which they develop. They cannot be transferred from one culture to another, and even concepts of time and space are set according to the culture of which they are a part. Cultures are even geographically confined and may not be carried from one part of the world to another, nor can one culture ever borrow anything of consequence from another. Politics, art, and religion are meaningful only if in tune with the general "spirit" of one culture, and "truths are only truths in relation to a particular mankind." There is no common humanity, and we cannot speak of such things as the spirit of man or appeal to a common human nature.

Yet, in Spengler's view, all cultures do have one thing in common. And that is the pattern of their development and decline. "Every culture passes through the age-phases of the individual man. Each has its childhood, youth, manhood, and old age," and a culture dies when it has "actualized the full sum of its possibilities in the shape of peoples, languages, dogmas, arts, states, and reverts into the proto-soul." All cultures eventually end as what Spengler called civilizations. This is the inevitable course that must be taken. "For every Culture has its own

Civilization. . . . The Civilization is the inevitable destiny of the Culture. . . . Civilizations are the most external and artificial states of which a species of developing humanity is capable. They are a conclusion, thing-become succeeding the thing-becoming, death following life, rigidity following expansion, intellectual and the stone-built, petrifying world-city following mother-earth. . . . They are an end, irrevocable, yet by inward necessity reached again and again." Civilizations are the sterile petrifications of cultures. Here facts take the place of intuition, art and literature decline, and men abandon their intuitive sense of time and space. "The period of Civilization is that of the victory of city over country, whereby it frees itself from the grip of the ground, but to its own ultimate ruin. Rootless, dead to the cosmic, irrevocably committed to stone and to intellectualism." Life is no longer "heavy with Destiny, blood, sex," but has become artificial and contrived, while men are attracted to a superficial religiosity and engage upon immature speculations.

The most pertinent part of Spengler's book was the application of his theory of culture and civilization to the Western world. Spengler argued that Western society, or what he called the Faustian outlook, as a distinctive culture had appeared in Europe around 1000. At this time Western man had adopted the idea of limitless space and a conception of time as something stretching into infinity. This had been a period of "rural intuition," a stirring of the spirit and a grasping of the reality of the Western situation. By the fourteenth century the West had entered its "Summer" period, a time of "ripening consciousness," which lasted until the late seventeenth century. "Autumn" had come to the West in the eighteenth century, when there appeared what Spengler called "the intelligence of the city," the "zenith of strict intellectual creativeness." The "Winter" of the West had set in near the middle of the nineteenth century. Then there was the "dawn of Megalopolitan civilization," and "extinction of spiritual creative force," and the appearance of "ethical-practical tendencies of an irreligious and unmetaphysical cosmopolitanism."

Thus Western man had entered upon his last days. "The crisis of the nineteenth century was the death-struggle" of Western society, and modern man can only live artificially because "the cosmic beat in his being is ever decreasing, while the tensions of his waking-consciousness become more and more dangerous." We are in a time of "existence without inner form," a time of "luxury, sport, nerve-excitement: rapidly changing fashions in art." The West can no longer produce anything original. Art has become nothing but a "tedious game with dead forms," and everywhere we find "only industrious cobblers and noisy fools, who delight to produce something for the market, something that will 'catch on.' " All the great reaches of the spirit are now beyond Western man. "Of great painting or great music there can no longer be, for Western people, any question. Their architectural possibilities have been exhausted these hundred years."

Perhaps the best indication of the decline of the West was that it had become what Spengler referred to as a civilization of "Cosmopolis," a city society, divorced from the earth that nurtured man. "The stone Colossus 'Cosmopolis' stands at the end of the life's course of every great Culture," wrote Spengler. The citizens of the city are rootless, spiritless people, and contemporary man had become nothing but "a new sort of nomad, cohering unstably in fluid masses, the parasitical city dweller, traditionless, utterly matter-of-fact, religionless, clever, unfruitful." Nor was it possible to do anything about our situation. Spengler assures us that "no wretchedness, no compulsion, not even a clear vision of the madness of this development, avails to neutralize the attractive force of these daemonic creations. The wheel of Destiny rolls on to its end; the birth of the city entails its death." We are in the age of spiritual drift, of a sterile and meaningless existence with no goal in sight and no purpose to which we may pledge our lives.

And what of the future? The decline will continue. The West will become increasingly a mass society, "which rejects the culture and its matured forms, lock, stock, and barrel." We will become people without any sense of values, disdaining "every sort of form, every distinction of rank, the orderliness of property, the orderliness of knowledge." The mass age is upon us, and mass man "recognizes no past and possesses no future." His appearance heralds "the passing of a history over into the historyless." Everything is as good as everything else, and "the mass is the end, the radical nullity." The political expression of this period will be what Spengler called "Caesarism," a form of "government which, irrespective of any constitutional formulation that it may have, is in its inward self a return to thorough formlessness." The decaying civilization will drift into a "second religiousness," which will exhibit itself in various primitive sects but without real feeling for the human situation or without integrity. Then the end. "In a few centuries from now there will no more be a Western culture." The West, as other previous societies, will disappear, leaving only some relics and some monuments for the curious eyes of future peoples.

Spengler, in answering his critics, argued that he was not a pessimist; he was only reporting what he believed to be the direction of history. As he wrote: "It is not our fault that we are living in the early winter of complete civilization and not in the midsummer of a ripe culture." In his later and minor publications, *Prussianism and Socialism*, *Man and Technics*, and *Year of Decision*, Spengler continued to defend his interpretation and to stress that he could only report what he thought to be the case. And, in his view, the facts were overwhelming. In *Man and Technics*, he argued again that "the mechanization of the world has entered a phase of highly dangerous over-tension. The picture of the earth with its plants, animals, and men has altered. In a few decades most of the great forests have been turned into newsprint. Innumerable animal species have been extinguished. All things organic are dying in the grip of organization." Spengler had concluded *Decline of the West* with the statement that "We have not the freedom to do the necessary or to do nothing. And a task that historic necessity has set will be accomplished with the individual or against it." In a similar way, the best that Spengler could offer was his statement in *Man and Technics*, where he wrote that it is "our duty to hold onto the lost portion, without hope, without rescue, like that Roman soldier whose bones were found in front of a door in Pompeii, who, during the eruption of Vesuvius died at his post because they forgot to relieve him."

There is much in Spengler's analysis that is offensive. He was, in many ways, a snob, and he gave full vent to his prejudices. Time and time again his hatred of the French and the Americans, of any form of democracy and of internationalism, expresses itself in ways that can hardly claim to be balanced. His glorification of the "soil" and of rural life is pathetically naive, while his easy dismissal of the bulk of mankind as a "mob" or a "mass" grates upon the nerves. He tends toward full, sweeping statements that take for granted what should be proved. For example, his argument that "mankind is a zoological quantity" is at once too broad and too narrow to mean much as a working definition of humanity. In the same way, when he speaks of "cosmic flowings" or points out that what a perceptive observer needs is "the power of seeing and not that of calculating, depth and not intellect," or says that one must be able "instinctively to see through the movements of events," we can only grasp dimly what it is he has in mind.

Yet attacks upon Spengler have often been far from the mark. Careful culling of Spengler's writings can produce statements supporting Hitler and the Nazis. But basically Spengler had little sympathy with what he thought of as the absurd theories of the fascists. In the nineteen-twenties at the time that Hitler was making his first attempt to overthrow the German government, Spengler remarked critically: "National politics are regarded as a form of inebriation. Crowds of youths were inspired by colors and badges, by music and processions, by theatrical promises and amateur appeals and theories." In 1932, shortly before Hitler came to power, he wrote: "The pathfinder must be a real hero, not an operatic hero. A ship is in a parlous state if the crew are drunk in a storm." During his last years Spengler was not looked upon favorably by the

Nazis, and it is likely that his sudden death in 1936 saved him from serious trouble.

More important, Spengler did stress some things about the Western world that cannot be denied. There has been the appearance of what must be called "primitive" or "pseudo-religious" values that violate the premises of Western life. He saw that politics in the Western world were becoming less relevant to the problems of Western man and, in too many cases, had "reduced themselves to a simple choice between technical expedients." He saw the implications for the creative mind in a world of mass culture and what has been called the "phonyness" of so much of contemporary life. He noticed the despair and the emptiness of so much of our existence, and *Decline of the West* "formulates more comprehensively than any other single book the modern *malaise* that so many feel and so few can express."

Spengler posed several important questions for twentieth-century Western man. Pride, a sense of progress, and a belief in the uniqueness of the West had provided much of the stimulus for the creation of the contemporary world. But in the twentieth century this optimism and self-centered egotism was often more of a hindrance than a help in confronting the problems of the day. The self-generated conviction that everything would automatically improve tended to blind Western man to the truth of his condition. A great deal of the drift in Western society was related to this empty optimism and to this belief in automatic progress.

There is also a point worth pondering in Spengler's argument that there can be no blending of one culture into another. It had been largely believed in the West that Western values and Western methods could be transferred to other parts of the world, and that men of various cultures could find a common ground upon which to stand. But Spengler denied this. His view that civilizations are separated by insurmountable barriers means that a dialogue between them is impossible and that consequently there is no general concept of humanity. Each man is locked in his civilization and is a victim of the destiny of his birth. The world applicability of Western values thus disappears, and the West becomes only another civilization, carrying on with its own special tasks but largely without importance to the rest of the world. The Western mission thus becomes aimless, and Westerners, as all others who in the past had hoped to extend their civilization beyond its original limits, are certain to fail.

Sigmund Freud

Contemporary Western man has been described in many ways. He has been characterized as a political man. He has been thought of, and has thought of himself, as a religious man. During the last century and more it has been common to depict him as an economic man. Each of these descriptions tells us something important about Western society, and each provides an insight into the nature of Western civilization. In the twentieth century a new dimension was added to our concept of ourselves and our world. It became possible to speak of a citizen of the West as a psychological man. A new way of looking at ourselves and at our problems became available with the development of modern psychology. And the one person most responsible for this new insight was undoubtedly Sigmund Freud.

Freud was born in 1856 in what is now Czechoslovakia. While still a child his family moved to Leipzig and then to Vienna, where Freud was to spend almost all of his long life. He was educated at the University of Vienna and became a physician. After engaging in the study of histology, pharmacology, anatomy, neuropathology, and hypnosis, Freud dedicated himself to psychological research. After 1900, in a series of essays and longer works that runs into numerous volumes, he created his masterpiece of interpretation. In works such as *The Interpretation of Dreams*, *Three Essays on the Theory of Sexuality*, *Totem and Taboo*, and many others, he opened the door upon a new perspective of the human condition, and in his clinical study of dreams and the inferences he drew about human sexuality he redefined our concept of man and civilization. He was attacked by many for his emphasis upon the incredible and fantastic realities that lay beneath the apparently calm surfaces of our lives, and his ideas, in his time and since, have been interpreted and reinterpreted by a host of disciples and opponents. In 1923 it was discovered that Freud had cancer of the jaw. Thereafter, for sixteen years, he was forced to undergo painful treatment, including thirty-three operations. But during this time he continued to write and to carry on his work. In 1938, when Germany annexed Austria and brought Vienna

338

under the control of the Nazis, Freud, a Jew and a hated "decadent" intellectual, was forced to depart the country where he had lived for more than seventy years and took refuge in London. Here he fought a less and less successful fight against his afflictions, and his life became, as he described it, "a little island of pain floating in a sea of indifference." In September, 1939, he died.

Sigmund Freud is best known for his psychological studies and his clinical research. But he was much more than a narrow specialist. Throughout his work there runs a broad thread of commentary upon cultural problems, and many of his clinical findings become in retrospect a series of footnotes upon the general condition of Western life. Freud was not a student of history or of politics or of philosophy. But he had a fantastically fertile mind and a quick sense of the ambiguity of human life. He once wrote a friend, perhaps a bit facetiously: "I am not really a man of science, but an observer, not an experimenter, and not a thinker. I am nothing but by temperament a *conquistador* — an adventurer, if you want to translate the word — with the curiosity, the boldness, and the tenacity that belong to that type of being." In his later years, this adventurous quality led him to ponder the wider problems of civilization and to bring his specialized knowledge to bear upon these matters. In 1935, in a "Postscript" to his *Autobiographical Study*, he wrote: "My interest, after making a long detour through the natural sciences, medicine, and psychotherapy, returned to the cultural problems which had fascinated me long before, when I was a youth scarcely old enough for thinking." The result of this consideration was the publication of two relatively short but stimulating books: *The Future of an Illusion* in 1927 and *Civilization and Its Discontents* in 1930. Of the latter book Freud himself remarked: "It deals with civilization, consciousness of guilt, happiness, and similar lofty matters. . . ." And he added: "In writing this work I have discovered afresh the most banal truths."

Freud's analysis of the problems of civilization was influenced by his interpretation of man's nature and the limitations imposed by that nature. He had no lofty view of the basic human material, and his message was never comforting. He saw the individual as crippled by his past and trapped by a series of erotic illusions. The character of men is controlled by certain immutable elements. Among these are sexuality, the "most unruly of all instincts," heredity, organic constituents that limit our efforts, and the burdens of "silence, solitude, and darkness." As Freud himself once said, his writings cannot provide "comfort and refreshment for the reader," and he had no religious faith to offer or any consoling philosophy. "The fact is as it is. Human life is a grim, irrational, humiliating business." Or, as he expressed it at another time: "Life . . . is too hard for us; it entails too much pain, too many disappointments, too many impossible tasks." A student of Freud's life and activities has written: "Freud was not hopeful; nor was he nostalgic. Retrospectively, he treasured no pagan or primitive past. He looked forward to no radically different future."

Many, if not most, commentators upon the general topic of man and civilization assume that the individual and his society have an identity of interests and that their goals are similar. Freud, however, saw the individual as inevitably and permanently alienated from his society and in continual conflict with it. In order to participate in a civilization, men renounce a part of themselves — of their freedom, of their instinct for gratification, of their right to live a life unencumbered by societal restrictions. Civilization is indeed established through a series of surrenders on the part of individuals. In this sense, a sacrifice of oneself is the beginning of civilization, which is based upon coercion and "instinctual repression." The individual is thus caught in the struggle between two forces — the unregenerate instincts and the overbearing culture. It is possible to have some sort of compromise between these forces but no resolution; and always a person becomes something less because of his membership in a civilization. As Freud expressed it, civilization is basically a struggle "between the instincts of life and the instincts of destruction, as it works itself out in the human species. This struggle is what all life essentially consists of and so the evolution of civilization may be simply described as the struggle of the human species for existence." Within the civilization the character of any individual will be determined by the way in which he has balanced the demands of his driving instincts and those of restraining society.

Freud admitted that the individual gained by being a member of a civilization. But a price had to be paid. Civilization was coercive and not liberating. "The liberty of the individual is no gift of civilization. It was greatest before there was any civilization, though then, it is true, it had for the most part no value, since the individual was scarcely in a position to defend it. The development of civilization imposes restrictions on it, and justice demands that no one shall escape these restrictions." In fact, Freud argued that "what we call our civilization is largely responsible for our misery, and that we should be much happier if we gave it up and returned to primitive conditions." But this, of course, is impossible. We could not survive in a primitive world, and "all the things with which we seek to protect ourselves against the threats that emanate from the sources of suffering are part of that very civilization."

According to Freud, the individual is always cheated by his civilization. And Freud holds out no hope for any change in this condition. "Restriction of freedom" is characteristic of any civilization, and the "replacement of the power of the individual by the power of the community constitutes the decisive step." Society is not able "to compensate the individual for his expenditure in instinctual renunciation. It is consequently left to the individual to decide how he can obtain enough compensation for the sacrifice he has made to enable him to retain his mental balance. On the whole, however, he is obliged to live psychologically beyond his income, while the unsatisfied claims of his instincts make him feel the demands of civilization as a constant pressure upon him."

Much of what Freud wrote on the problem of civilization he meant to apply as a common description of civilizations in general. Yet he was primarily interested in his own society, and he was convinced that Western civilization possessed certain characteristics that made the strain between the individual and the group more severe and the dangers more immediate. The more complicated a civilization becomes, and Western civilization was fantastically complicated, the greater the tensions that are built up among its members. The more complex a civilization, the more its members are required to make additional adaptations in order to keep the society functioning. But the more adaptations that are made, the more discontent that is engendered, and the more people who find it impossible to adapt and thus develop hostility toward "particular forms and demands of civilization" and ultimately "against civilization itself." The coercive power of the community is continually increased in order to maintain the civilization, and this power is used increasingly to make the citizens conform to restrictions of greater and greater complexity. Inevitably, many people find it impossible to accept these new restraints, and become non-members or even opponents of the civilization. In 1909 in a lecture he gave during a trip to America, Freud expressed this fear of the future of Western society. "The claims of civilization make life too hard for the greater part of humanity." There may be limits to men's ability to adjust to a refined civilization, and finally, in desperation at their failure and wounded by the burdens placed upon them, many members of that civilization become its enemies and thus threaten its continued existence.

Freud had no ready and easy solutions to this dilemma of Western civilization. His argument basically was that "the important thing is not to be cured, but to live with one's ailments." The way in which this was accomplished was to look at oneself, at life, and at Western civilization for what they were and to recognize the reality of our condition as Western men. Freud was primarily a rationalist, even though he knew the limitations of rationality and the difficulty of living by intellect. As has been said of him: "Reason cannot save us, nothing can; but reason can mitigate the cruelty of living, or give sufficient reasons for not living." Or, as he himself argued, "we have no other means of controlling our instinctual nature but our intellect." The human brain may not be an all-powerful instrument; but it is the best available, and the only hope is that we may understand our situation even if we cannot change it.

One thing that the human intellect can do is to see illusions about our life and our civilization for what they are and thus abandon them. One of these illusions that Freud attacked was the Christian religion of his day and ours. In his opinion, early Christianity had served a beneficial purpose as one of the coercive agents holding Western civilization together. As Freud wrote: "Religion has clearly performed great services for human civilization. It has contributed much towards the taming of the asocial instincts." But it could no longer, in the modern world, fulfill this function. God, who, for Freud, had been "a bloody mountain deity," the "awesome figure of the primal father, the missing link between anarchy and culture," had become only "a model man, compounded of the highest moral sentiments and sweet reason." Christian morality no longer was a coercive instrument and had merely become a problem in neurosis, and to identify religion and civilization was to threaten civilization itself. The decay of religious feeling was certain to result in hostility to any religiously identified civilization, and as religion became discredited as a meaningful explanation of life, civilization is pulled down and "your world collapses." Civilization needs prohibitions, but "we risk making observance dependent upon belief in God." There are, of course, risks in any movement away from religion, but Freud refused to accept the argument that "men are completely unable to do without the consolation of the religious illusion, that without it they could bear the troubles of life and the cruelties of reality." It is "humiliating to discover how large a number of people living today, who cannot but see that this religion is not tenable, nevertheless try to defend it piece by piece in a series of pitiful rearguard actions."

The belief that Western civilization was dependent upon the Christian religion was, for Freud, an illusion that could be compared to a "childhood neurosis." We should cease putting forward religious precepts as the justification for Western civilization, and "civilization runs a greater risk if we maintain our present attitude to religion than if we give it up." Religious faith was being destroyed by events in the Western world, and it was best if this fact were faced. Particularly, Freud felt that large numbers of what he would have called the "uncivilized" were kept under restraint by the proscriptions of Christianity, which they assumed were still in effect. "Civilization has little to fear from educated people and brain-workers. In them the replacement of religious motives for civilized behaviour by other, secular motives would proceed unobtrusively." But "it is another matter with the great masses of the uneducated and oppressed, who have every reason for being enemies of civilization." Such people made up what Freud called "these dangerous masses," which "must be held down most severely and kept most carefully away from any chance of intellectual awakening, or else the relationship between civilization and religion must undergo a fundamental revision." When these people discovered that religion was an illusion and that the world was not organized along Christian principles, they would suddenly be freed from all restraints and would vent their hostility against the civilization that had misled them. It would then, in Freud's opinion, be much better if "we were to leave God out altogether and honestly admit the purely human origin of all the regulations and precepts of civilization." Freud quoted with approval one of Heinrich Heine's poems stating that Heaven should be left to the "angels and the sparrows" while man assumed responsibility for the earth upon which he lived and died.

In the same manner Freud argued that our lack of perfectibility must be recognized, as must the limits of our abilities. "We may expect that in the course of time changes will be carried out in our civilization so that it becomes more satisfying to our needs and no longer open to the reproaches we have made against it. But perhaps we shall also accustom ourselves to the idea that there are certain difficulties inherent in the very nature of culture which will not yield to any efforts at reform." Or, as Freud put it at another time, we should "familiarize ourselves with the idea that there are difficulties attaching to the nature of civilization which will not yield to any attempt at reform." The demands of our civilization are harsh and unending, and for our participation we shall pay and pay and pay. Any unrealistic attitude, any belief that we can escape our condition, can only weaken the human personality and make life impoverished and uninteresting. Civilized life then becomes "as shallow and empty as . . . an American flirtation, in which it is understood from the first that nothing is to happen, as contrasted with a Continental love affair in which both partners must constantly bear its serious consequences in mind." Even the ultimate reality — death — must be faced, and some concept of the meaning of death must be incorporated into Western civilization. As Freud asked: "Should we not confess that in our civilized attitude toward death we are once living psychologically beyond our means, and should we not rather turn back and recognize the truth? Would it not be better . . . to give a little more prominence to the unconscious attitude toward death which we have hitherto so carefully suppressed?" Perhaps Freud's recommendation could be best summed up in his own pithy words: "But surely infantilism is destined to be surmounted. Men cannot remain children forever; they must in the end go out into 'hostile life.'"

Freud's concept of inevitable struggle between man and his civilization and the terrible price we pay for participating in our civilization is not a palatable one. It is much more comfortable to hold to a belief consisting of self-confidence and consolation and to maintain that it is only by accident that we find ourselves unable to realize our fondest dreams. Yet Sigmund Freud sensed some of the deep contradictions in Western society and pointed to some of the dangers to Western civilization that were present in the twentieth century. He saw that the machinery of that civilization was, in important respects, hostile to individuals. Western man had tended to live on what Freud called "moral inflation," and this tendency must "ultimately induce moral depression." Out of frustration and anguish many were prepared to cast off all cultural restraints and to live without the controls of civilization. Freud looked upon this tendency with horror and with prophetic insight as to its consequences. In 1923, in a letter to a French friend, he wrote: "A great part of my life's work . . . has been spent trying to destroy illusions of my own and those of mankind. But if this one hope cannot be at least partly realized, if in the course of evolution we don't learn to divert our instincts from destroying our own kind, if we continue to hate one another for minor differences and kill each other for petty gain, if we go on exploiting the great progress made in the control of natural resources for our mutual destruction, what kind of future lies in store for us?" Freud was always interested in large questions, and he saw that the end of Western man could be something very different from what most Westerners imagined. "The fateful question for the human species seems to me to be whether and to what extent their cultural development will succeed in mastering the disturbance of their communal life by the human instinct of aggression and self-destruction." Conditions were different from what they had been before, and "men have gained control over the forces of nature to such an extent that with their help they would have no difficulty in exterminating one another to the last man."

Sigmund Freud never overestimated the capacities of Western men. He knew them well — their weaknesses, their failings, and their petty and coarse thoughts that they dared not admit. He saw, too, that recent historical events had presented the prospect of strains more severe than any ever experienced by Westerners. But once men recognized their condition and the threats facing them, they could be admired, and Freud never abandoned his membership in the human race, or in Western civilization. Western men were awesome creatures.

> Their scientific knowledge has taught them much since the days of the Deluge, and it will increase their power still further. And, as for the great necessities of Fate, against which there is no help, they will learn to endure them with resignation. . . . As honest smallholders on this earth they will know how to cultivate their plot in such a way that it supports them. But withdrawing their expectations from the

other world and concentrating all their liberated energies into their life on earth, they will probably succeed in achieving a state of things in which life will become tolerable to everyone and civilization no longer oppressive to anyone.

SUGGESTIONS FOR FURTHER READING

The number of books on World War I is without end. Cyril Falls, The First World War *(1960),* Barrie Pitt, 1918: The Last Act *(1962), and Barbara* Tuchman, The Guns of August *(1962), are good, reliable reading. On the general effects of the war, the following may be consulted:* E. H. Carr, The Twenty Years' Crisis, 1919-1939 *(1939),* Pierre Renouvin, War and Aftermath, 1914-1929 *(1968), and* L. Martin, Peace without Victory *(1958). Three recently published books on the torment of German politics during the nineteen-twenties are* Andreas Dorpalen, Hindenburg and the Weimar Republic *(1964),* Francis Carsten, The Reichswehr and Politics: 1918-1933 *(1966), and* Louis Snyder, The Weimar Republic from Ebert to Hitler *(1966).* Rudolph Binion, Defeated Leaders. The Political Fate of Caillaux, Jouvenel, and Tardieu *(1960), is an excellent study of French politics of the time.*

The historical demoralization of the immediate postwar period is dramatically told by Robert G. L. Waite in his Vanguard of Nazism: The Free Corps Movement in Postwar Germany, 1918-1923 *(1952).* David Caute's Communism and the French Intellectuals 1914-1960 *(1964) discusses the historical dilemma of the French intellectual community, while Peter Gay's* Weimar Culture: The Outsider as Insider *(1968) is a brief but fascinating account of artistic effort in the midst of political breakdown.* Walter Laqueur and George L. Mosse, eds., The Left-Wing Intellectuals between the Wars, 1919-1939 *(1966), is instructive.*

H. Stuart Hughes' Oswald Spengler: A Critical Estimate *(1952) is a balanced and interesting discussion of the author of* Decline of the West. *Additional stimulating comment may be found in Erich Heller's "Oswald Spengler and the Predicament of the Historical Imagination," The Disinherited Mind (1957), and in Bruce Mazlish, "Spengler," The Riddle of History (1966). The best study of Freud as a political, social, and cultural commentator is Philip Rieff's* Freud: The Mind of the Moralist *(1959).* Ernest Jones' The Life and Work of Sigmund Freud *(1953-1957) is the basic biography, while Lionel Trilling's* Freud and the Crisis of Our Culture *(1955) and* Bruce Mazlish' Psychoanalysis and History *(1963) contain stimulating interpretations.*

Guernica detail, Pablo Picasso, 1937, on extended loan by the artist to the Museum of Modern Art, New York.

10

Totalitarianism

1917   The first totalitarian secret police force, the Cheka (Extraordinary Commission for Combating Counter-Revolution and Sabotage), established by Bolsheviks in Russia in December.

1918-
1919   Russian decrees legalizing labor camps for political opponents. Camps were not used extensively until 1930's when camp population may have been between five and six million.

1919   Formation of the Italian fascist party by Benito Mussolini.

1919   Formation of the National Socialist German Workers' Party (Nazis).

1921-
1922   Russian Communists forcibly suppressed opposition parties and forbad the formation of "factions" inside or outside Communist party.

1922   "March on Rome" by Mussolini and his fascists. Seizure of the Italian government.

1923   Adolf Hitler's "Beer Hall Putsch" in Munich, an unsuccessful attempt to seize control of Bavarian government.

1924   Murder of Italian socialist Giacomo Matteotti, who had written *The Fascists Exposed*, a book containing evidence of violence and illegal acts by fascists.

1925   Formation of the first French fascist party.

1926   Proclamation in Italy of the corporate state. In 1932 Mussolini provided a well-known definition of the corporate state: "The fascist conception of the state is all-embracing; outside of it no human or spiritual values may exist, much less have any value."

1929	Imperial Fascist League founded in Britain.
1930-1932	In Russia a series of measures to tighten political control. Free movement of labor restricted, unemployment relief abolished ("there was no more unemployment"), prison sentences for violation of labor discipline, death penalty for theft of state property, and introduction of internal passports for all citizens.
1932	Formation of the Falange, the most important Spanish fascist group.
1932	British Union of Fascists formally launched.
1933	Hitler became chancellor of Germany.
1934	Assassination of Sergei Kirov, an important Communist political figure, in Russia set the stage for the Stalinist Terror of the 1930's.
1934	Riots in Paris were at least partially sparked by fears of a fascist attempt to overthrow the government.
1935	The Nuremberg Laws "for the protection of the racial purity of the state" adopted in Germany. Reduced Jews to status of second-class citizens. In 1938 the campaign against the Jews was intensified.
1935	Italy invaded Ethiopia. Protests of Western democracies were ignored, and by 1936 Italy had occupied the country.
1936	Formation of Jacques Doriot's French Popular Party, the most important French fascist group.
1936	Formation of the Berlin-Rome Axis, an alliance of the two important fascist powers.
1936	First of the important purge trials in Russia.
1936-1939	Spanish Civil War.
1936	Formation of a Popular Front government in France. The Popular Front was a coalition of radicals and socialists and was supported by the Communists. Basis of Popular Front was the unity of liberal and left-wing groups against fascists in international affairs. Popular Front government fell in 1937, and the alliance ended in 1938.
1937	A large number of Russian military leaders were purged by Stalin.

1938	German invasion and annexation of Austria.

1938-1939	German pressure and British-French appeasement resulted in the destruction of Czechoslovak republic.

1939	Italian conquest of Albania.

1939	German attack upon Poland began World War II. At the time Hitler told his generals: "What weak Western European civilization thinks about me does not matter."

T he nineteen-thirties and early nineteen-forties have been called the Age of Fear, the Years of the Dictators, the End of European History. The newspaper headlines, the books, and the speeches of the time all indicated a general European political collapse. The newsreels show endless waves of marching, uniformed men and wildly gesticulating orators haranguing cheering crowds of people. The emotions and hatreds unleashed by the First World War had not been arrested and together with new grievances and animosities created a dark wave of revolution that ultimately was to engulf the continent.

There seemed a fatal direction to events in the years immediately following World War I. Variations of Western democracy and Western liberal institutions, which had been established with mixed success in various parts of Europe, went under one after another. In 1922 Benito Mussolini, with his political doctrine of "action not talk," authority and discipline, seized control of Italy. Arguments over boundaries and ethnic controversies prompted political instability in central Europe. The democratic government of Germany was continually harassed by powerful groups pledged to its destruction. In England and France social discontent, a lack of political leadership, and at times near-treason made it difficult for the most important democratic countries to master the growing disorder.

In the nineteen-thirties a severe and persistent economic depression undermined confidence in democratic politics. Small and large landowners, white- and blue-collar workers, economically distressed shopkeepers and wealthy industrialists, intellectuals and professional men, the young, the middle-aged, and the old — all felt the attraction of mass movements that promised an end to the apparent muddle, drift, and sterility of liberal constitutionalism. Powerful Communist parties in France and Germany — supported by and controlled from the Soviet Union — presented themselves as alternatives to democracy. But the most threatening of the anti-democratic movements were the various fascist groups. With their semi-military organizations such as the Black Shirts and the Storm Troopers, a disregard for law, a devotion to a single strong leader, and rabble-rousing demagogic slogans, the fascists introduced widespread violence and turmoil into European politics.

The Victory of Fascism

Fascist success in several European countries produced a crisis of political confidence. Although he was basically a buffoon, a vicious political clown, Mussolini was taken seriously by European political leaders and appeared as a continual threat to international stability. In 1936 the Spanish fascist Francisco Franco, with the help of Italy and Germany, led a rebellion against the republican government and three years later succeeded in establishing a fascist state. Fascist adventurers lurked in every European country, and all dreamed of overthrowing a government and seizing political power.

The serious threat, however, appeared in Germany. There a large number of anti-democratic parties flourished. One of these, the National Socialist German Workers' Party (Nazis), was organized in 1919. Adolf Hitler was party member number 55 and soon became the recognized leader. Hitler turned the party into a mass movement that used both legal and illegal methods in its struggle against the German government. In 1932 the Nazis became the largest party in the German parliament. In early 1933, as a result of political intrigue, mass support, and the weakness of his opponents, Hitler became chancellor, in effect the ruler of Germany.

Within a short period of time, Hitler assumed dictatorial powers. Emergency decrees suspended the constitutional guarantees of free speech, free press, and right of assembly. Opposition political parties were outlawed, all workers' organizations were brought under Nazi control, persecution of the Jews began, concentration camps were established, and universal military training was introduced. In 1934 Hitler became President of Germany, although he preferred the title *Der Führer* (The Leader).

Hitler's political success in Germany had an almost immediate effect on European international affairs. Ten months after he became chancellor, Germany withdrew from the League of Nations, the international peace organization that had been created following World War I. In 1935 he repudiated the terms of the Versailles treaty that called for

German disarmament, and a year later the German army occupied the Rhineland, a demilitarized zone between France and Germany.

Using the threat of war and aided by satellite Nazi parties in Austria, Czechoslovakia, and Poland, Hitler now began a campaign of blackmail against Germany's neighbors and indirectly against France and England who were pledged to support the independence of the smaller European countries. And his campaign succeeded. In 1938 Germany invaded and then annexed Austria, and the Sudeten region of Czechoslovakia was occupied. In early 1939 the remainder of Czechoslovakia was brought under German control. German pressure on Poland was steadily increased, and on September 1 German armies attacked. Two days later England and France honored the guarantee they had given the Poles and declared war on Germany.

Poland, which was also attacked from the east by the Soviet Union, was overwhelmed. In the spring of 1940 the German armies struck in the west, and Denmark, Norway, Belgium, the Netherlands, and France were conquered and occupied. Rumania and Hungary became German satellites, and in 1941 Yugoslavia and Greece were overrun, Russia was invaded, and war was declared on the United States. By the summer of 1942 Hitler had become the greatest conqueror in European history. He controlled the continent, and his armies were deep inside Russia and in north Africa.

Only those who endured it can adequately describe what the Nazi conquest of Europe meant. Frenchmen, Belgians, Danes, and others were subjected to a humiliation never before experienced. Large numbers of Europeans were reduced to near-slavery, all semblance of legality disappeared, and former beerhall agitators, small-time thugs, and intellectual and historical have-nots had the power of life and death. The standard of living fell, cultural life came to a halt, and torture, imprisonment, and mass executions became common occurrences.

Ultimately, the military might of the United States, the Soviet Union, and England defeated Germany. But this victory was accomplished only by widespread bombing of European cities and military campaigns that spared few parts of the continent. The results of the war have been summarized by the historian Martin Gilbert. "Whatever Europe achieved in science, culture, or medicine, in technology or scholarship, between 1900 and 1939, more was destroyed in the six years of war than such achievements could easily compensate for." Gilbert also points out the international results of the war and its consequences for Europe. "In 1939 there were four Great Powers in Europe: Germany, France, Italy, and Great Britain; and three outside Europe: Russia, the United States, and Japan. In 1945 there were only two Great Powers, Russia and the United States."

The Totalitarian Doctrine

It was against the background of these events leading up to and including the Second World War that there appeared in the Western world the political doctrine of totalitarianism. This was perhaps the single significant contribution of the first half of the twentieth century to Western political thought. In some ways totalitarianism was a projection of many of the ideas of the late eighteenth and nineteenth centuries. But it was also a radical departure from what could be called the Western traditional view of man and his society. It was recognizable, and yet it was strange. It could be looked upon as a logical development of Western history and also as a stone-bottom refutation of that history.

It is not easy for many, particularly Americans, to grasp the essential characteristics of totalitarianism. It offends against what we regard as our morality and our common sense, and neither the philosophies nor the actions of the totalitarians fit within our usual political frame of reference. As a student of the subject has stated, totalitarianism "cannot be comprehended through the usual categories of political thought," and its crimes "cannot be judged by traditional moral standards or punished within the legal framework of our civilization."

Definitions of totalitarianism abound. Some of these are naive, and some are misleading. Here are three that are to the point. Richard Lowenthal argues that totalitarianism has four principal characteristics: monopolistic control of the state by the ruling party wherein no opposition is tolerated; control of all forms of social organization; control of all channels of communication such as the schools and the press; and "the removal of all legal limitations on state power." Zbigniew Brzezinski goes a little deeper with his definition: "Totalitarianism is a system in which technologically advanced instruments of political power are wielded without restraint by centralized leadership of an elite movement, for the purpose of effecting a total social revolution, including the conditioning of man, on the basis of certain ideological assumptions proclaimed by the leadership in an atmosphere of coerced unanimity of the entire population." In a clear description of the way in which totalitarianism operates in practice, Robert Conquest provides a definition within the context of one totalitarian society. "The Soviet State and Party," he writes, "impinge upon the population in three ways: in their conditions of living, where the State is responsible for the organization of the economy; in their conditions of thought, in that the State directly or indirectly prescribes the information and culture which will be available for citizens; and in direct action through the laws and instruments of compulsion."

These are good definitions. They stress the ultimate nature of totalitarianism, and they fit the circumstances of totalitarian action. There have been two authentic forms of totalitarianism in this century: the Nazi dictatorship in Germany after 1938 and the Bolshevik dictatorship in Russia since the early nineteen-thirties. There were, of course, important differences between the two forms, but there were also amazing similarities. Both were total, all-embracing, coercive philosophies. Both aimed at a political triumph that was irreversible, and each argued that "outside of it no human or spiritual values may exist, much less have any value." Both sought "to pulverize all existing social units in order to replace the old pluralism with a homogeneous unanimity patterned on the blueprint of the totalitarian ideology." Both relied upon an intolerant political philosophy, upon charismatic appeals, and upon terror as the final instrument of control. Both demanded an absolute and unconditional loyalty — a single allegiance to which a man must sacrifice every other claim upon his heart and mind. Both pressed toward a catastrophic "final solution," which would see the destruction of all opposing ideas. Vladimir Lenin, the founding leader of Russian Bolshevism, was a scholar and a cultured man. Adolf Hitler was a crude, basically uneducated street-corner orator. Lenin projected a vision of a brotherhood of man, without conflict or inequality. Hitler dreamed of a narrower human community where the racially pure would deliver the world from the disease of mongrelization. It can be safely predicted that Lenin, who died in 1924, would have looked upon Hitler as an unprincipled ruffian, a piece of historical refuse. Hitler, in his turn, regarded the Communists as the carriers of a virulent historical plague, a collection of subhumans who should be exterminated in company with his other enemies. But Communist and Nazi alike were totalitarians, and they met each other at various places in their historical journeys.

Communism

The attraction of Communist totalitarianism in the nineteen-twenties, nineteen-thirties, and even later for many Europeans cannot be denied. Communism struck a responsive chord with many of those — workers, intellectuals, artists — who had a long history of frustration and disappointment with the liberal Western world. Those who had suffered a series of real or imagined defeats saw Communism as a reconciling force that would heal their historical and philosophical wounds. Terrifying doubts would be resolved, and one could rest secure that he was engaged in some great and moving historical project that had none of the inconsistencies, the contradictions, and the ambiguities that haunted Western life. A great part of Western radicalism appeared worn-out by the twentieth century, and Communism offered a new hope and a new promise. Those who have been described as "rebels against tyranny and oppression" saw in Communism a method whereby they might escape into a "higher freedom." Others who possessed a "mixture of religious mysticism and animal gregariousness for human solidarity" found a way whereby they might join a new human community. Still others who were "anxious for efficiency and intelligent organization" discovered an answer to the waste and suffering of disorganized capitalism and the laissez-faire society.

Twentieth-century Communism claimed to be the political manifestation of Marx's philosophy and thus had special attraction for many who saw Marxism as a logical development of a powerful Western intellectual tradition. Marxism appeared to combine the strong elements of German idealistic philosophy, French radicalism, and an interpretation of industrial organization. It set forth a method for understanding what was happening in the world, a system for decoding the secrets of history. Moreover, in the chaos following the First World War, Marxian Communism provided assurance that one was on the side of the future. It was a way whereby one did not need to concern himself about the details of the journey into that future but could be assured that all he had to do was to support Communism. As the German poet and playwright Bertolt Brecht wrote:

> He who fights for Communism must be able to fight and not to fight; to speak the truth and not to speak the truth; to render services and to refuse services; to keep promises and not to keep promises; to incur danger and to avoid danger; to be recognizable and unrecognizable. He who fights for Communism has of all virtues only one: that he fights for Communism.

For many this was enough to quiet any nagging doubts about the type of society that was being built under the banner of Marxism in Russia. If the goal was great enough, then the lack of certain political niceties could be excused. Many in the West rejected the politics and institutions of their own countries and gave their allegiances to Russia, the home of the true faith. Frenchmen, Germans, Englishmen, Americans, and others accepted the discipline laid down by the Russian Communist leaders and pledged themselves to forward the political aims of the Communist fatherland. "It is much better to be ruled by Stalin than by a pack of half-witted and half-hearted social-democrats," argued a British historian (living in Britain it must be admitted), and an English newspaper could say that the power of the Russian political police may be "regrettable" but is "historically speaking, of secondary importance." It was usually admitted that personal liberty had been suppressed, but this was excused in light of the great historical task upon which Russia was engaged. The lies, the forgeries, and the cruelties of Communist totalitarianism were ignored in the name of the purposefulness of history and the determination to support some dynamic political doctrine that would cleanse the old world of its filth and its disgrace.

Nazism

Nazi totalitarianism made its appeal to the broad stream of nihilism that was coursing through Western life in the twentieth century. It built upon no established intellectual tradition, but was, in fact, a refutation of any attempt to arrive at a rational understanding of history. George Lichtheim correctly noted that millions of Germans longed for something that "would rid them at one blow of all the perplexities afflicting the modern world: Capitalism, Communism, liberalism, democracy, plutocracy, newspapers, elections, big-city life — the whole complex rigmarole of contemporary urban civilization." Hitler himself argued that his was not a political or economic revolution but "a revolution of attitudes and feelings." Nazism was a doctrine designed for the cynical, the totally alienated, those who had given up trying to make sense of their condition, those who acknowledged despair as the motivating fact in politics. Its appeals were primarily predatory, basically to the harshest instincts, and it scorned any real attempt to intellectualize its program. As Alfred Rosenberg, the man who usually passes for what the Nazis regarded as a philosopher, put it: "The life of a race or a people is not a philosophy that is logically developed and consequently is not a process that grows according to natural laws; it is the construction of a mythical synthesis, or activity of soul, which cannot be explained by rational inferences or made comprehensible by exhibiting causes and effects." Nazism substituted hysteria for rationality, the hallucination of racism for any logical interpretation of human society, the rantings of the demagogue for ordered political discourse. Many saw Nazism as a defense against what they regarded as destructive radical political movements or as a choice they could make to block the success of their own political opponents. Thus even some Frenchmen were prepared to cry "Rather Hitler than Blum," because the French politician Leon Blum was a Jew, a socialist, and an intellectual.

Totalitarian Power

In both Russia and Germany the totalitarian movements demanded and exercised absolute power. Lenin wrote that "dictatorship is power, based directly upon force, and unrestricted by any laws." And the Bolshevik state was built according to this principle. All opponents, whether of thought or deed, were ultimately declared enemies and were either destroyed or forced to depart the country. Nothing escaped the attention of the political authorities, and the power of some men over other men was unchecked. Those in charge were not bound by any "elaborate set of rules," or, in fact, by any rules at all. Power was so tightly held that even the official Marxist doctrine could be manipulated and changed at will. It has been truly pointed out that "Lenin's Marxism presents the anomaly of being at once the most dogmatic assertion of orthodox adherence to the principles of the master and at the same time the freest rendering of it on points where circumstances required its modification."

In a similar way the Nazis claimed all power in Germany and in all areas that fell under their control. Independent politics, philosophy, and economics ceased to exist. Law was what Adolf Hitler and his associates declared it to be, and there was no appeal from their judgment. Everything was subordinated to the single truth expressed by Hitler, and there was no other authority to which one might refer for direction. The courts, industry, educational institutions, newspapers, and even the military services were stripped of any independence and were made instruments of Hitler's will. Politics as we usually think of it came to an end, and there was in Germany no effective way one could oppose the state or escape it. Silence was the only refuge, and even this was dangerous if the state declared such withdrawal offensive. If one did not accept the official doctrine, he had no claim to existence, and a leading Nazi bluntly ordered that opponents were to be regarded "not as individuals but as carriers of tendencies endangering the state and therefore beyond the pale of the national community."

Totalitarianism and Western Civilization

Communists and Nazis unceasingly expressed their hatred for each other. But the great enemy of the totalitarian state is what has been called the pride of Western civilization — the free-thinking, independent citizen. The totalitarians have announced "their utter contempt for the liberal aspects of the democratic tradition — freedom of discussion and dissent, protection of minorities and partial interests, security of individual rights under the rule of law." In 1934, Hitler declared that one of the aims of the Nazi party must be the "elimination of private citizenship," and in Germany and Russia any claim to identity in the sense of being a person who looks to himself for his purposes and his justification was made a criminal offense against society. There was no place in a totalitarian state for the autonomous individual. The psychologist Bruno Bettelheim, who was himself an inmate in a German concentration camp, has defined personal autonomy: "One's sense of identity, the conviction of being a unique individual, with lasting and deeply meaningful relations to a few others; with a particular life history that one has shaped and been shaped by; a respect for one's work and a pleasure in one's competence in it; with memories peculiar to one's personal experience, preferred tasks, tastes, and pleasures — all these are at the heart of man's autonomous existence."

It is this autonomous existence that totalitarianism is determined to destroy. A Nazi official wrote in 1938: "There are no more private citizens." And a short time later, another Nazi could say that "the only person who is still a private individual is somebody who is asleep." The individuality of the human personality is declared an aberration of the human condition, and everyone is required to drown himself in the doctrine. Outside of history man is nothing. Outside of race he is nothing. Outside of the class struggle he is nothing. Even death is destroyed as a meaningful individual experience, and there is only "organized oblivion." Men are reduced to a pulplike substance, so manipulated and conditioned that they are not even conscious of their enslavement. The ultimate aim of totalitarianism has been described by Hannah Arendt.

> Total domination, which strives to organize the infinite plurality and differentiation of human beings as if all of humanity were just one individual, is possible only if each and every person can be reduced to a never-changing identity of reactions, so that each of these bundles of reactions can be exchanged at random for any other.

To serve its ends totalitarianism relies upon force, and a horrifying criminality is an integral part of totalitarianism. The political police are turned loose upon the people and operate almost unrestrained by any controls and become a shadowy, threatening power within the state. One month after seizing power in Russia, the Bolsheviks established the Cheka — the Extraordinary Commission for the Struggle against Counterrevolution and Sabotage. This action set the pattern, and no totalitarian society has been able to exist without a horde of secret police. In Nazi Germany there was the Gestapo. In Russia, the name was continually changing — from Cheka to GPU to OGPU to NKVD to MVD to MGB to KGB. But the intent was always the same — to terrorize and control the population. Totalitarian leaders and many of those who serve them are murderers, sadists, members of a political underworld who kill without thought and without regret. Even when they claim to act on behalf of a great historical purpose, they remain men who shoot others in the back of the head, kick people to death, and look on without compassion as other human beings writhe in pain. A Frenchman, writing in the nineteen-fifties, put very well the open and secret criminal behavior of totalitarianism: "We were looking for sophisticated psychological and sociological interpretations; partly true, no doubt, but the essential truth was that men were tortured in their flesh."

Those who believe, in spite of all its failings, in the open, questioning, tolerant, and humane Western society must regard totalitarianism as a deadly enemy. The liberal Western society has many weaknesses. It is not as just as it should be, nor as free. But it is nonetheless true that the "contrast between limited freedom and total suppression is fundamental, as is that between limited sense and utter nonsense." Different patterns of economic organization, political arrangements, and even styles of life are acceptable parts of Western history. Totalitarianism, however, cannot be accommodated within the context of Western civilization. It violates too many assumptions of that civilization. It dismisses difference of opinion as nothing but "opportunism, eclecticism, and absence of principle," and it sets itself in opposition to what it describes as "the old vicious freedom" whereby Western man makes his hesitating but unfettered search for the meaning of his existence. Totalitarianism denies the value of the search for truth and, in fact, refuses to accept the idea that objective truth exists. In 1936, at Heidelberg University, the German Minister of Education said: "The old idea of science based on the sovereign right of abstract intellectual activity is gone forever. The new science is entirely different from the idea of knowledge that found its value in an unchecked effort to reach the truth." Such a statement refutes over two centuries of allegiance to the belief that the highest task of Western man was to use his intellectual power, unconfined by any preconceived notions, to unravel the mystery of himself and his world. For all its claims to intellectual certitude and tough-mindedness, totalitarianism is a new form of primitivism, complete with obscure rites, incantations, and an emphasis upon the dark, inscrutable ways of history. As Albert Camus wrote, revolutionary totalitarianism "contrives the acceptance of injustice, crime, and falsehood by the promise of a miracle." What a man does and what a man is are no longer of any importance.

Perhaps the greatest offense of totalitarianism is that it denies any meaning to what we think of as the spirit of man. Over fifteen centuries ago, Saint Augustine said: "Man is a great deep." There is little in the present Western world to remind one of Augustine. But his words speak to us. They hint at a part of man that is beyond measurement, beyond organization, beyond classification, and they define the awesome and tangled situation in which we find ourselves as we make our way from day to day, from month to month, and from year to year. They also suggest that the human condition consists of an essence, however ill-understood, as well as a history and that there is something in men that if violated will turn human beings into objects and make life itself an absurdity. The sacrifice of this essence to any ideology, any historical necessity, obliterates our humanity, and men without Augustine's "great deep" are not men at all.

The experience with Nazism frightened Western man out of his wits and showed him what this alternative to the liberal society meant. In theory, at least, totalitarianism had appeared to many as a possibility in the West. As the Frenchman Albert Camus wrote in his "Letters to a German Friend" in 1943: "For there is always something in us that yields to instinct, to contempt for intelligence, to the cult of efficiency. Our great virtues eventually become tiresome to us. We become ashamed of our intelligence, and sometimes we imagine some barbarous state where truth would be effortless." And then Camus continued: "But the cure for this is easy; you are there to show us what such imagining would lead to, and we mend our ways." As totalitarianism showed its true form, there was a rallying to decency and to the often-abused and often-ridiculed values of liberal democracy. An English writer stated during World War II that he could only give two cheers for democracy, not the usual three — but, as he said, in the circumstances two were enough.

There was also an increasing suspicion about Communist totalitarianism. Russia, as a victor in the war, gained immense prestige and influence. And there were strong Communist parties in many of the Western countries. But there was also an awareness of the inhumanity and the intellectual shoddiness of Communism. Some of the anti-Communist fears produced an unhealthy hysteria and promoted near-panic in parts of the West. But the instinctual opposition to Communism was sound. Ideologies had decreasing appeal, and more and more people were prepared to accept the argument put forward by the English philosopher Bertrand Russell following his visit to Russia in 1920: "I went to Russia as a Communist; but contact with those who have no doubt has intensified a thousandfold my own doubts, not as to Communism in itself, but as to the wisdom of holding a creed so firmly that for its sake men are willing to inflict widespread misery." The ruthless imposition of Communism upon the people of central Europe dulled the appeal of Communism in the West. Moreover, it became apparent in the nineteen-fifties and nineteen-sixties that the Russians themselves were finding the harsher aspects of Communist totalitarianism unacceptable and that there was some possibility that the Communist doctrine and practice would be modified.

Yet totalitarianism had shaken Western man's confidence in himself and his society. The grisly experience had scarred the spirit, and no one was certain that under some new social, political, or economic strain something akin to totalitarianism might not again appear. It was a new, terrible knowledge that Camus spoke of in 1946 when he said that "the poison which impregnated Hitlerism has not been eliminated; it is present in each of us." And the same point was stressed again by Camus in his novel *The Plague* when he had a character say: "I know positively . . . that each of us has the plague within him; no one, no one on earth is free from it. And I know, too, that we must keep endless watch on ourselves lest in a careless moment we breathe in somebody's face and fasten the infection on him. What's natural is the microbe. All the rest — health, integrity, purity (if you like) — is a product of the human will, of a vigilance that must never falter. The good man, the man who infects hardly anyone, is the man who has the fewest lapses of attention. And it needs tremendous will-power, a never-ending tension of the mind, to avoid such lapses."

Some of the important particular aspects of totalitarianism are illustrated by the following three chapters from its history. Adolf Hitler was the most charismatic, most dedicated, most ideologically oriented of the totalitarians, and he demonstrated the destructive nihilism that underlay one of the great totalitarian movements of this century. The Auschwitz extermination camp was a terrifying example of what was to be found as Europe went down the totalitarian path. George Orwell was probably the best known of all those commentators who saw what totalitarianism meant and who attempted to interpret it for his fellow citizens of the Western world.

Adolf Hitler

Adolf Hitler was born in the small town of Braunau on the frontier of Germany and Austria on April 20, 1889. He was the son of a minor Austrian customs official, and as a young man went to Vienna, apparently to become an artist. He failed and drifted down into the world of the flophouse, the itinerant worker, the beerhall debater. He became a violent anti-semitic, an equally violent opponent of the bourgeois middle-class ethic, and a perceptive student of the emotions and hatreds that move men. In 1913 he left Vienna for Munich, and in 1914 enlisted in the German army. After World War I ended, he became a member of one of the many small revolutionary parties then so common in Germany and created the Nazi organization. After becoming Chancellor in 1933, he crushed the trade unions, destroyed any liberal opposition, brought the powerful industrial interests, which at one time hoped to use him, under control, bullied the churches into acceptance of his position, and finally even triumphed over the army. His hold on the party which he headed, upon those who served him, was unquestioned. He was too strong for any individual or group of individuals, and his program for Germany was introduced and carried out over only the feeblest of objections. He imprisoned thousands of his own people and drove many of the most intelligent and most cultured of Germans out of their native land. He swept aside all opposition and exercised political power that had never been at the command of any individual in the long history of Western Europe. And he carried Germany to the height of international military power and became master of an area that stretched two thousand miles from the French Atlantic coast to the Volga River and from the Arctic Ocean to the Mediterranean.

And what was the result of all this success, all these triumphs? After Hitler was gone, a continent lay in ruins, almost every family in mourning, every city haunted by the memory of the dark hours of the Nazi control. A shame hung so heavy that no one, not even the most nationalistic German, has dared to erect a monument or dedicate a memorial to Europe's greatest conqueror. His was a powerful and sweeping revolution, but it left nothing but remorse and revulsion. "The great revolutions of the past, whatever their ultimate end, have been identified with the release of certain powerful ideas: individual conscience, liberty, equality, social justice." But not Hitler's. He left nothing but a spiritual and historical dustbowl, a curse, and the smell of blood.

It is easy to dismiss Hitler as a madman. But such an interpretation fails to account for his true importance. He combined in one person so many of the suspicions, the grievances, the animosities that had plagued Western civilization since the late-eighteenth century. All the important expressions of distrust and hatred of contemporary Western civilization — the polite and not-so-polite anti-semitism of large numbers of people, the basic loathing of free intellectual effort, the dissatisfaction with middle-class liberalism, the revolt against a complex and complicated industrial society — appeared in Hitler in an exaggerated and terrifying form. He embodied "all the cruel impulses, the irrational beliefs, the atavistic prejudices, the memories and fears" of the frustrated and disappointed. He exemplified the revenge of millions against the Western world for having robbed them of their certainties, their sense of security, and their belief in their own superiority. He identified himself with all those who had been left out. As the Englishman George Orwell wrote of him: "The fact is that there is something deeply appealing about him. One feels it again when one sees his photographs. . . . It is a pathetic, doglike face, the face of a man suffering under intolerable wrongs. . . . The initial, personal cause of his grievance against the universe can only be guessed at; but at any rate the grievance is there. He is the martyr, the victim, Prometheus chained to the rock, the self-sacrificing hero who fights single-handed against impossible odds."

Hitler's appeal was wide and deep. Like a magnet he drew all those who were prepared to substitute a caricature of Western civilization for its substance. He was what "nationalism, militarism, authoritarianism, the worship of success and force, the exaltation of the state and politics devoid of humanity lead to, if they are projected to their logical conclusion." In a world ripped by controversy and doubt, where the complexity of society was felt by many to be a burden, Hitler offered the simple explanation and the simple solution. As he himself said: "I have the gift of reducing all problems to their simplest foundations," and he never allowed any hated "objective" fact or any complication to stand in the way of arriving at a simple explanation and a simple way of action. For him, nationalism was simple, war was simple, race was simple. And because he cut through all the complications, the harrowing doubts and ambiguities, he succeeded in carrying out what has been termed "a mobilization of the disaffected."

Hitler was really a symptom of the cancer that had been growing in Western civilization for a very long time and which in the nineteen-thirties and nineteen-forties reached its virulent stage. He was the enemy within the gates, and he was dedicated to the destruction of Western society. It is important to realize that Hitler's aim was, in spite of all talk about being a shield of the West against Asian Russia, to put an end to a world he hated and despised. This is why all attempts to appease Hitler failed. The British Prime Minister, Neville Chamberlain, assumed that he could carry on business with Hitler. But there was no business to conduct. Hitler's purpose was not to win a war or even to conquer territory. It was to smash a civilization. "They regard me as an uneducated barbarian," he once said. "Yes, we are barbarians. We want to be barbarians. It is an honorable title. We shall rejuvenate the world. This world and this civilization are near their end." He once informed Benito Mussolini, the Italian fascist leader, that the last 1,500 years of European history, the years between Attila the Hun and himself, had been a mere interruption of human development, which "is now about to resume its forward march." So the West was to come to an end and was to be replaced by a new form of society — what Winston Churchill called "a new Dark Age, made more sinister and more protracted by the lights of perverted science."

Hitler was a true revolutionary. He was dedicated to the changing of the human condition. He was attempting to create a new structure of authority, and to impose a new vision of man. He expected to bring about a new ruling elite, a new morality, a new life. He never made any secret of his desires, nor did he hestitate to implement his plans. Unfortunately, too many dismissed his proposals for a civilization to replace that of the West as mere ravings, the frothings of one who was demented.

Hitler rejected the Western emphasis upon individuality and intelligence. "Providence has ordained me," he said, "that I should be the greatest liberator of humanity. I am freeing man from the restraints of an intelligence that has taken charge; from the dirty and degrading self-mortification of an illusion called conscience and morality, and from the demands of a freedom and personal independence which only a very few can bear." According to Hitler, men did not desire to be free, nor did they wish to be left to make their own decisions about the important issues of their lives. All efforts in the past to force man to be free had been against human nature, for people "have a simple way of thinking and feeling, and anything that cannot be fitted into it disturbs them." There was no great cry for liberty on the part of Western men. On the contrary, men wished for some kind of security, some way of casting off the burden of decision. "The masses of the people prefer the ruler to the suppliant and are filled with a stronger sense of mental security by a teaching that brooks no rival than by a teaching which offers them a choice. They have little idea of how to make such a choice and are prone to feel that they have been abandoned." Or, as he said on another occasion, people "feel little shame at being terrorized intellectually and are scarcely conscious of the fact that their freedom is abused."

Hitler thus envisaged a new type of community in which there would be no place for the kind of individual liberty and conscience that had for so long been the aim of Western politics. With Hitler there was to be no temporary suspension of liberty; rather, it was, in any recognizable form, to disappear altogether. "A very large measure of individual liberty is not necessarily the sign of a high degree of civilization. On the contrary, it is the limitation of this liberty, within the framework of an organization which incorporates men of the same race, which is the real pointer to the degree of civilization attained." An emphasis upon liberty was a sign of decadence, and the individual in himself had little value. "To the Christian doctrine of the infinite significance of the individual human soul and of personal responsibility, I oppose with icy clarity the saving doctrine of the nothingness and insignificance of the individual human being, and of his continued existence in the visible immortality of the nation."

Humanity was for Hitler a form of coarse material that could be manipulated at will. There was no need to take into account any violation of individual rights or feelings, and brutality and terror could be used freely against individuals in order to create the new order. In fact, people respond to such methods. "Brutality is respected. Brutality and physical strength. The plain man in the street respects nothing but brutal strength and ruthlessness — women, too, for that matter. The people need wholesome fear. They want to fear something. They want someone to frighten them and make them shudder and submit. Why babble about brutality and be indignant about torture? The masses want it. They need something that will give them the thrill of horror." Hitler knew the value of such brutality and terror, and they were part of his politics. "Terror is the most effective political instrument," he boasted. "I shall not permit myself to be robbed of it simply because a lot of stupid, bourgeois mollycoddlers choose to be offended by it." Any worthy political leader must approach his task without fear or without regard for the individual. Conscience had no place in his book, and, as he said, it "is a Jewish invention. It is a blemish, like circumcision." In a directive for young Germans he set forth one of his goals. "A violently active, dominating, intrepid, brutal youth — that is what I am after. Youth must be all these things. It must be indifferent to pain. It must have no weakness or tenderness in it. I want to see in its eyes the gleam of pride and independence of the beast of prey. I shall eradicate the thousands of years of human domestication. Then I shall have in front of me the pure and noble natural material. With that I shall create the new order." And he concluded with a refutation of what had been regarded as the proper occupation of youth. "I will not have intellectual training. Knowledge is the ruin of young men."

Hitler never made any secret of what he proposed to put in place of the destroyed Western civilization. The distinguishing feature of men was to be their race. This was what set one man off from another, and one nation from another. The Germans, as the superior race, were to be the rulers, and all other national groups were to be subordinate in varying degrees. "We do not intend to abolish the inequality of man; instead, we shall deepen it and create insurmountable barriers which will turn it into law. There is no equal right for all. We will have the courage to make this denial the basis of all our actions, and to acknowledge it openly."

And then Hitler went on to state a rejection of any sense of fraternity or real community of men. "No other nation has equal rights with the Germans. It is our task to place other nations in subjection. The German people are called upon to give the world a new aristocracy."

What was to happen to those who were conquered by the Germans? Some were to be more favored than others and were to be allowed to pursue menial tasks and exist at a secondary level of society although never to be in a position to threaten German supremacy. But many were to be regarded as *Untermenschen*, subhumans. These — the Jews, Slav intellectuals, and in fact, anyone so defined by the Germans — were to be exterminated. Others were to be allowed to exist as animals, without education, without ambition, and without aspirations. They should know enough German to understand orders. They should know enough geography to understand that Berlin is the capital of the world. They should practice contraception to reduce their birthrate and be denied the use of hospitals in order to increase their deathrate. But "our guiding principle must be that these people have but one justification for existence — to be of use to us economically."

This was the doctrine that made Adolf Hitler a new kind of conqueror. Prior to him defeat had meant disgrace and humiliation and territorial penalties. Now the defeated paid with his life. There were no limited conquests, and the non-German peoples of the West — as others — had no right even to exist. Anything opposing Hitler was to be destroyed, and, because he was himself in opposition to the West, it was doomed. Lewis Carroll's Queen may have cried "Off with his head." With Hitler the deed was done. Rotterdam was bombed into ruins. Leningrad was to be destroyed and its surrender was not to be accepted. Moscow was to be levelled so that nothing could ever live there. Paris was to be put to the torch rather than to be allowed to fall into enemy hands. Hitler demanded the destruction of Warsaw, even when the city could put up no resistance. His anti-semitism was translated into the physical destruction of all Jews — a Final Solution that aimed at the absolute disappearance of a certain group of people. His emotions were heightened by the sights of suffering and death. He watched films of his opponents strung up with meathooks through their throats, and he relished thoughts of the sky dark with smoke, shells falling on cities, and people lying in blood. A German general has described him on such occasions: "His eyes popped out of his head. He was suddenly seized by the lust for blood."

Hitler did as he said: "Let us go back to primitive life, the life of the savages." For him it was world power or ruin. "We shall drag the world down with us — a world in flames." He expected to be the gravedigger of the West, and he engaged in what has been described as the "purposeless but gleeful destruction of life and property, and all those values of civilization which the German Nazi, though he sometimes tries painfully to imitate them, fundamentally envies and detests." In his last days as he was being hunted to earth, he was like an animal living in the dark. He settled into places called "Fort Wolf" and "Eagle's Nest" and finally from the middle of January, 1945, in a bunker buried fifty feet below the ground in Berlin. Here, as the Russian armies broke in upon the city, he continued to spew his hate. He sentenced people to death, disowned the Germans because they had not been capable of carrying out the task he had assigned them, and looked with satisfaction upon what he had done to Europe. In the political testament that he wrote shortly before committing suicide on April 30, 1945, he called for everlasting hatred, for death over life, for a continuation of the struggle against the Jews, and for the winning of territory in the east.

Words are weak instruments to use in summing up Hitler. Yet here is how one of the leading authorities on Hitler described him. "The passions which ruled Hitler's mind were ignoble: hatred, resentment, the lust to dominate, to destroy. His career did not exalt but debased the human condition, and his twelve years' dictatorship was barren of all ideas save one — the further extension of his own power and that of the nation with which he had identified himself. Even power he conceived of in the crudest terms: an endless vista of military roads, S. S. garrisons and concentration camps stretching across Europe and Asia." And this description may be followed by one by another qualified historian. "No word he ever uttered even so much as touched the human spirit. His views on art were worthless. He did not know the meaning of humanity. Weakness he despised, and pity (being sympathy with weakness) he despised also. . . . And if he despised physical weakness he also, in others, hated moral strength. . . . And as for the purpose of human life, that futile quest which nevertheless is an index of humanity, it was for him merely that Germans should be the masters of the world. . . . He was a complete and rigid materialist, without sympathy or even tolerance for those immaterial hopes or fears or imaginations or illusions which, however absurdly, cast a faint ennobling gleam on the actions of mankind."

Auschwitz

Auschwitz, or as it is known in Polish, Oswiecim, is a relatively insignificant small town near the Vistula River, west of Cracow and south of Warsaw. It has little historical importance save as the town that gave its name to a place where something horrifying happened more than twenty-five years ago. As Rudolf Höss, whose own name was closely connected with that of Auschwitz, said in 1946 after the end of World War II: ". . . Auschwitz. That was far away. Somewhere in Poland." There are still stone buildings, barbed wire, brick chimneys, and railroad tracks. And there is a brooding silence, except when the wind blows through the wire or when visitors speak.

Auschwitz became more than a place on the map. Hans Kremer, who had been a professor at Münster University and who was hanged in Cracow in 1947 for his activities at Auschwitz, recorded in his diary, "we are at *anus mundi*" — which we might roughly translate as the rectum of the world. And he was right. A young German has written: "If you want a picture of contemporary man, you must imagine a dog urinating on Diderot's monument." Auschwitz provided such an obscene desecration of all Western man's tradition of reason and humanity and compassion. It has been said that the Antarctic is a place of God without man. Auschwitz was a place of man without God. Here the Jews called to Yahweh, the Catholics to the Virgin Mary, the Protestants to Jesus. And there was no answer. The Italian writer Carlo Levi puts the question: "Have you ever seen women weeping over bars of soap? These were all that remained of their husbands and brothers and sons and lovers. This is the way the human adventure ends. This is the slice of life. A bar of soap." At Auschwitz the lie was given to the belief of Western man that his life had dignity and meaning.

There is an enormous literature on Auschwitz. There are many pictures of the camp as it is now and even some of how it was then. We can look at the cordons of wire, at the young and the old standing beside the railway cars, at the mutilated victims, at the crematoria, at the piles of corpses being burned, at the final separation of men from their wives and children. We can also examine pictures of those who directed the activities at Auschwitz. The named and the nameless, the participants in this awesome dance of death, seem reminders of some terrifying dream. But the facts are real, and the history of Auschwitz is a burning, stinking part of our heritage.

Soon after coming to power in Germany the Nazis established concentration camps. Into these camps were herded those who were regarded as threats to the Nazi rule. The camps were designed to degrade and humiliate opponents and to break their spirit. Torture, segregation, and death were instruments used to rid Germany of the recalcitrant and the stubborn. Intellectuals, socialists, Communists, and churchmen were torn away from their families and their communities and placed in camps where they were terrorized, forced to submit to indignities, and reduced from contributing members of society to nameless, regimented nonentities, engaged in monotonous, useless labor and at the mercy of brutal and vindictive guards. The camps were to show the superiority of the Nazis and to re-educate the inmates so that with their spirits broken they would oppose the regime. By 1939, when World War II began, approximately 300,000 Germans had been confined to such camps.

In 1940 a new type of camp was inaugurated by the Germans. Death and the threat of death had always been part of the concentration camp system. But death was the principal aim of the new extermination camps. Designed to rid Europe first of the Jews and then of other undesirables that fell into German hands in the course of the war, these camps were located in eastern Europe, in areas that had been overrun by the German armies. There were a number of these camps, and they were effective as "death factories." Figures of actual killings are only approximate, but estimates give some idea of the magnitude of the task undertaken by the Germans. The total number of victims at the camp at Belzec was close to 600,000; at Sobibor, near 250,000; at Treblinka, 700,000; and at Chelmno, more than 300,000. The camps were regarded as places of no return, and they largely succeeded in satisfying this purpose. For example, of the over 34,000 Dutch people deported to Sobibor from March to July, 1943 we know of only nineteen (sixteen women and three men) who survived to return to the Netherlands.

The largest and most important of these extermination camps was Auschwitz. Construction on the camp was begun in the spring of 1940, and the first members of the prison staff arrived in May of that year. A month later the camp received its first prisoners. Ultimately Auschwitz became a vast establishment, covering an area of eighteen square miles. It consisted really of thirty-nine camps in all, divided into three main groups. There was Auschwitz I, the main camp, including the

administrative headquarters. Auschwitz II, officially known as Birkenau, was for the destruction of prisoners. Auschwitz III, or Buna, was a
labor camp. About 2,000 Germans were posted to Auschwitz to adminis-
ter the camp, and "the extermination of millions was planned to function like a machine."

It is impossible to say with any absolute accuracy how many people
were sent to Auschwitz. Höss himself admitted that between two and
two and one-half million people were slain, while a Russian survey has
put the figure at four million. One careful scholar has contended that a
little less than a million souls perished in the camp from all causes —
disease, shootings, starvation, and gassings. The Germans did keep a
record of registrations, but this is highly unreliable. Particularly in the
last days of its operation, there was a great deal of confusion in the camp,
and a host of records was destroyed. But, whatever the figure, the camp
was organized to dispose of a continually increasing number of people.
The trains thundered across the continent to the end of the line at Auschwitz and ran on almost a time-table schedule. Thus between July 19 and
July 31, 1942, eight trains left France and in August of that year thirteen.
Each train carried approximately one thousand people, packed like so
much merchandise into the cars. Passenger trains took the Dutch across
Germany — 750 miles in forty hours — and on one occasion 900 Dutch
lunatics and mentally retarded children were packed onto a cattle train
and hustled to Auschwitz. Between 250,000 and 300,000 Hungarian
Jews were gassed or shot at Auschwitz in the summer of 1944 and all
within the space of forty-six days. The victims were from a multitude of
countries, with the largest number being Polish and Hungarian Jews.

Upon arrival at Auschwitz, inmates were plunged into a mad world,
into what a commentator has called "a hell in which fiends, themselves
damned, inflicted endless, pointless sufferings of a horrible ingenuity
upon defenseless souls." Auschwitz was utter degradation, a studied,
cold-blooded system of inhumanity. Inmates were destroyed as human
beings before being killed, and every possible indignity was inflicted
upon the prisoners. Men, women, and children were sexually abused,
used as guinea pigs for medical experiments, and beaten as one would
beat a carpet or a piece of dough. The world of Auschwitz was a world
of men standing with their testicles smashed and the blood running
down their trouser legs, of people put into what was called a standing
cell and eating their own excrement before they starved to death, of
women who had their fallopian tubes and their wombs filled with
injections of various kinds and then being subjected to x-ray treatment.
It was a world without law or understanding or meaning. As Höss, the
camp commandant, once announced: "Only what is ordered is allowed.
Anything not ordered is forbidden and will be severely punished." But

no one knew what was allowed, and there was no hope of appeasing the authorities or protesting against their acts.

The purposeful crowding reduced all to worse than animals. There were seldom less than 30,000 people in Birkenau, and at times there may have been as many as 70,000. In the women's camp, thousands shared a single latrine barracks and slept on tiered bunks, three or four or six to a bunk. There were no sanitary facilities — no soap, no towels, no tooth-brushes, no toilet paper. Here is a description of camp life.

> Crowds fighting for a drop of water from taps that barely drip; crowds fighting for a few moments' use of the primitive closets already running over with excrement; five or six men attempting to share one blanket in the depths of a Polish winter; starving crowds fighting for their food; crowds of women trying to find their clothes in the darkness of their huts when suddenly ordered on parade, and, not infrequently, being set upon by Alsatian dogs; crowds of dying, too many for the mock-hospital; crowds of corpses, too many even for the massive incinerators; crowds, everywhere crowds, being screamed at and struck and harried by the supervisors and the guards and always, save in some of the torture-chambers, the sight and sound and smell of these huge masses of human beings, the great majority of them starving, filthy, and sick. So constant was the shuffling of feet between the huts, that in all those square miles no blade of grass grew.

And, of course, there was ultimately death. The life expectancy of a new arrival was a matter of weeks, and one survived longer than that by chance. After all, as one of those in charge of the camp said: "Life had no value. To kill a man was nothing, not worth talking about." Many died at the hands of the guards, and many fell victim to disease and starvation. But the official way of death at Auschwitz was by gas.

The installations at Auschwitz were combination units, each of which contained an anteroom, a gas chamber, and an oven. People were herded into the anterooms and told that they were to take showers. They were instructed to undress and to hang their clothes on hooks, being careful to remember the numbers of the hooks so that they could later reclaim their clothing. They then walked into the "shower room," and the doors were bolted shut after them. The gas was injected into the room through small openings in the ceiling, and after approximately thirty minutes the victims were dead, lying in a grotesque pile of tangled bodies. The doors were then opened, the gas cleared out, and special squads of prisoners, wearing gas masks, hurried in and jerked the bodies out of the "shower room" and into the ovens for burning. The largest of the gas chambers was 250 square yards in area and capable of holding up to 2,000 at one time. Höss claimed that the five crematoria could burn 12,000 bodies a day. But this appears to have been an exaggeration, and some have argued that little more than a thousand could be disposed of in this way. Whatever the facts as to the efficiency of the crematoria, they could not keep up with the number of those killed, and piles of corpses were often burned in huge incineration pits, shallow, broad ditches that were covered up once the bones had been burned. From both the crematoria and the incineration pits came the haze that settled over the camp, while "the stench of burning flesh blanketed the country-side for miles around, and dark, fatty smoke wafted across the sky."

The great majority of victims at Auschwitz were Jews. But Auschwitz was not only designed for the extermination of Europe's Jewish population. In the early fall of 1944, when the complete destruction of the Jews was in sight, plans were under way to enlarge the camp. Extermination camps were to be a permanent part of Hitler's Europe, and there is little doubt that ultimately members of one national group after another would have found themselves in Auschwitz and similar places. The dynamics of Nazi totalitarianism, with an emphasis upon racial superiority and an indifference to the claims of any individual to life, required "death factories." The shutting down of Auschwitz would have come only on that day when there was no inferior human material, no *Untermenschen*, left to offend against German purity and Nazi politi-cal philosophy.

Who were those in charge of this death operation? Some of them were pathological criminals, murderers, sexual deviates, and many of the supervisors used in the women's part of the camp were hardened prostitutes dredged up out of the German underworld. The majority were, however, not members of what is usually regarded as the criminal class. They had been businessmen, engineers, foresters, construction workers, butchers, lawyers, dentists, pharmacists. Some were young men who had lived in the environment created by Hitler and the Nazis and found at Auschwitz only the last of a series of brutal assignments that had been given them. Included also were a number of physicians who not only selected the arrivals for dispatch to work gangs or to death but also carried out the unbelievable experiments upon prisoners. Some saved an occasional prisoner by giving him special assignment. But all became brutes. And none failed to participate in the undertaking. They did their jobs. They all supported and accepted the purpose of the camp, which was stated coldly by a lieutenant as a welcome to some new arrivals. "I tell you it is not a sanatorium you have come to but a German concentration camp from which the only exit is up the chimney. If anybody doesn't like it, he can go and throw himself against the high ten-sion wires straight away. If there are any Jews on the convoy, they are not entitled to live more than two weeks; priests have one month of life and the remainder three months."

In November, 1944, with the advancing Russian armies close at hand, the order was given that the camp at Auschwitz should be dismantled. Prisoners were to be shipped to other camps inside Germany itself, records were to be destroyed, and the site was to be abandoned. On January 17, 1945, the last roll call at Auschwitz was taken. There were 54,651 prisoners on hand. Two days later, about 52,000 of these were marched out of Auschwitz to the west. They walked through the bitter cold and were then transported in open trucks. Thousands appear to have died or to have been shot along the way. A handful escaped. The remainder were delivered to new camps, where a French prisoner there described them: "It was impossible to extract from their lips their names, much less their date of birth. Kindness itself had not the power to make them speak. They would only look at you with a long expressionless stare. If they tried to answer, their tongues could not reach their dried-up palates to make a sound. One was aware only of a poisonous breath appearing to come from entrails already in a state of decomposition."

Russian advance patrols arrived at Auschwitz on January 26. The number of prisoners liberated was 2,819, people who had been spared apparently because of the panic that had overtaken the German guards. The Russians also found part of the legacy of Auschwitz: 369,000 men's suits, 836,000 women's coats and dresses, large amounts of false teeth, and a great deal of women's hair. This was all material that had not yet been shipped to Germany for use in the war effort. Other things — sad mementoes — were also found that gave some indication of what had happened in the camp. One of the moving reminders was a dented tin bowl, probably the receptacle from which some prisoner drank his watery soup. On the bowl someone had scratched a rough picture of a boat riding on some waves. Over the picture was written in English the words: "Don't forget the forlorn man." It was an obituary worth remembering.

After the war many of those who had served in Auschwitz were run to earth. Hans Schwarzhuber was hanged in Hamburg, Josef Kramer was executed at Lüneburg, Gerhard Palitsch killed himself, and Marie Mandel was executed at Cracow. Some vanished, and some were even brought to trial as late as 1963. Höss himself disappeared after the defeat of Germany in the spring of 1945 but was discovered by the British a year later. After testifying at the Nuremberg Trials he was turned over to the Poles. His trial there lasted ten months. In April, 1947, he was taken back to Auschwitz, and "there hanged upon a gallows especially built so that the last sight to meet his eyes would be the camp he had created and administered." Several years before, Lieutenant Mussfelt, the crematorium chief at Auschwitz, had said to some of the occupants of the camp: "Good evening, children, you are all going to be killed very soon, but after that it will be our own turn."

What was the meaning of Auschwitz? Historical interpretation large-ly fails for there was something here that cannot be comprehended by the human mind. Over twenty years after the last inmate had left Ausch-witz the German writer Peter Weiss visited the camp and wrote of his impressions. "This is where they walked, in the slow procession, coming from all parts of Europe, this is the horizon which they still saw, these are the poplars, these the watch-towers, with the sun reflected in the window-panes, this is the door, through which they went into the rooms that were bathed in glaring light, and in which there were no show-ers, only these squared metal columns, these are the foundation walls between which they died in the sudden darkness, in the gas which streamed out of the holes. And these words, this knowledge, they tell us nothing, explain nothing. Only heaps of stone remain, overgrown with grass. Ashes remain in the earth, ashes of those who died for nothing, who were torn from their homes, their shops, their workshops, away from their children, their wives, their husbands, lovers, away from all everyday things, and flung into something incomprehensible. Nothing is left but the total meaninglessness of their death."

George Orwell

There have been many excellent studies of totalitarianism. His-torians, philosophers, theologians, political scientists, and psycholo-gists have all had their say and have attempted to explain the how, what, and why of totalitarian theory and practice. One man, however — the Englishman George Orwell — is perhaps more commonly identified as a commentator on totalitarianism than anyone else. There were many students of totalitarianism who were more learned than Orwell, as there were many whose interpretations were more profound, more analytical, more philosophically satisfying. But Orwell had the literary talent, the temperament, and the imagination necessary to strike to the heart of the subject and to place his description in a dramatic and memorable context.

George Orwell was born in 1903 in Bengal, the son of a British official. He was educated in England and then served as a member of the Indian Imperial Police in Burma from 1922 until 1927. He returned to England and supported himself as best he could — as a dishwasher, a school teacher, a shopkeeper — while he struggled to become a writer. During the nineteen-thirties he published four novels, *Burmese Days, A Clergyman's Daughter, Keep the Aspidistra Flying,* and *Coming Up for Air.* He also wrote three books — *Down and Out in Paris and London, The Road to Wigan Pier,* and *Homage to Catalonia* — that were more or less based upon his personal experiences. He was author of many political and literary essays, some of which — "How the Poor Die," "Politics vs. Literature," Politics and the English Language," "Charles Dickens," and "Inside the Whale" — are near-classics. In 1937 he went to Spain to fight against the fascists who were attempting to overthrow the Spanish republic. During World War II he was rejected for military service because of a lung affliction and spent the war years as a radio broadcaster and a pamphleteer. In 1945 he achieved world-wide recognition when he published his political fable *Animal Farm.* Four years later his famous fictional description of the totalitarian society of the future, *Nineteen Eighty-Four,* appeared. He died in 1950.

Orwell was not a great novelist, nor was he an accomplished historian. As a critic has pointed out: "He was a novelist who never wrote a satisfactory novel, a literary critic who never bothered to learn his trade properly, a social historian whose history was full of gaps." But, as the same critic continues: "Yet he matters. For as polemic his work is never anything less than magnificent; and the virtues which the polemic demands — urgency, incisiveness, clarity, and humor — he possessed in exactly the right combination." Orwell was the political journalist at his best. He had an eye for the false and the pretentious, and he was never taken in. He had no sympathy with what he called "the damned impertinence of these politicians, priests, literary men, and what-not," and he was never trapped by slogans, hair-splitting justifications, or consoling excuses. He knew what he liked and what he hated. "My starting point is always a feeling of partisanship, a sense of injustice," he said. "I write because there is some lie that I want to expose, some fact to which I want to draw attention, and my initial concern is to get a hearing." He was a committed man, and the strength of his writing was directly related to this sense of commitment. Near the end of his life he wrote: "And looking back through my work, I see that it is invariably where I lacked a political purpose that I wrote lifeless books and was betrayed into purple passages, sentences without meaning, decorative adjectives, and humbug generally." This was a fair enough self-analysis.

Orwell himself argued that "every line of serious work that I have written since 1936 has been written, directly or indirectly, against totalitarianism." This claim was not quite true, but it did indicate the important focus of his efforts. He wrote at a time when the liberal, democratic world appeared to be crumbling. The important historical facts in the nineteen-thirties and early nineteen-forties were "bombs, aeroplanes, tinned food, machine guns, putsches, purges, slogans, gas masks, submarines, spies, provocateurs, press censorship, secret prisons, aspirins, Hollywood films, and political murder." Others might turn away from such reality, but not Orwell. The overriding consideration of political existence was that "Hitler is a criminal lunatic, and he has an army of millions of men." A new type of violence, a new type of brutality, had made its appearance in the Western world, and all the traditional patterns of conduct were being destroyed. A way of life was coming to an end. "Since about 1930," Orwell wrote, "the world has given no reason for optimism whatever. Nothing is in sight except a welter of lies, hatred, cruelty, and ignorance, and beyond our present troubles loom vaster ones which are only now entering into the European consciousness."

The popularity of his last two books, *Animal Farm* and *Nineteen Eighty-Four*, has often obscured the fact that the totalitarian societies described there are really a logical development of what Orwell believed had happened to the Western world during the earlier years of the twentieth century. The totalitarianism of *Nineteen Eighty-Four* was not a sudden and unexpected catastrophe. It had roots in the conditions of modern life and was the logical conclusion of the way in which Western man was living. Sinister influences had brought about a mutation in his political, intellectual, and physical environment, and Orwell's earlier books were attempts to identify these influences and to show the effect they have upon human beings.

It has been pointed out by many that Orwell had a quarrel with the modern world. He was not impressed by what he called an "essentially fat-bellied version of progress," and he believed that under the name of progress the world was becoming more inhuman, more foreign to men as a place to live. The habitat was being changed, and changed in a way that threatened to destroy what Orwell regarded as the essence of the human character. The increasingly organized, highly efficient society was, for all its claims to the contrary, providing a hostile environment. Orwell once wrote: "The machine has got to be accepted, but it is probably better to accept it rather as one accepts a drug — that is, grudgingly and suspiciously. Like a drug, the machine is useful, dangerous, and habit-forming. The oftener one surrenders to it, the tighter its grip becomes." The continual mechanization of life was producing a world that Orwell described as "slick and stream-lined, everything made out of something else. Celluloid, rubber, chromium-steel everywhere, arc-lamps blazing all night, glass roofs over your head, radios all playing the same tune, no vegetation left, everything cemented over, mock-turtles grazing under the neutral fruit-trees."

In such a mechanical, cold environment, people were being victimized, and Orwell's early novels portrayed the situation of people at the mercy of their surroundings. In *Burmese Days* Flory is the victim of the "dirty work of Empire at close quarters," of "the hollowness, the futility of the white man's domination in the East." Gordon Comstock in *Keep the Aspidistra Flying* is the victim of grinding poverty and unrealized ambitions. Tubby Bowling in *Coming Up for Air* is the victim of a vulgarized society. The modern world was forcing the individual human being to lead "a kind of cadging, toadying life," and there seemed an institutional and historical animosity to any sense of decency, any independent intellectual judgment, any expression of individual integrity.

In Orwell's view modern society stimulated brutality. Men were being conditioned to violence, and there was a growing indifference to cruelty, suffering, and pain. No one any longer seemed to care what happened to other people. "In the chaos in which we are living, even the prudential reasons for common decency are being forgotten. Politics, internal or international, are probably no more immoral than they have always been. But what is new is the growing acquiescence of public opinion in the face of the most atrocious crimes and sufferings, and the black-out memory which allows blood-stained murderers to turn into public benefactors overnight."

One of the important indications of what was happening in the Western world was, in Orwell's opinion, the abuse of language. In many ways Orwell's writings could be summed up as a diatribe against men's misuse of the power of speech. A flabby, contorted vocabulary had become the instrument whereby men expressed their knowledge of themselves, and the language was being sucked empty of any real meaning. Men seemed afraid to speak correctly of what was happening, and Western political language had become nothing but "euphemism, question-begging, and sheer cloudy vagueness." The important line between truth and falsehood was being obliterated, and "I have the feeling that the very concept of objective truth is fading out of the world." Orwell had an enviable talent for identifying this propensity for masking reality behind an ersatz language, and in one of his most important essays he gave some haunting examples of this reduction of language — the method by which we communicate our experience — to an absurd meaninglessness.

"Defenceless villages are bombarded from the air, the inhabitants driven out into the countryside, the cattle machine-gunned, the huts set on fire with incendiary bullets: this is called *pacification*. Millions of peasants are robbed of their farms and sent trudging along the roads with no more than they can carry: this is called *transfer of population* or *rectification of frontiers*. People are imprisoned for years without trial, or shot in the back of the neck or sent to die of scurvy in Arctic lumber camps: this is called *elimination of unreliable elements*."

If the modern world was one of blind mechanization, of brutality, and of an indifference to truth, what will be the result? For Orwell, there seemed only one answer. In 1939 he wrote: "Almost certainly we are moving into an age of totalitarian dictatorships — an age in which freedom of thought will be at first a deadly sin and later on a meaningless abstraction. The autonomous individual is going to be stamped out of existence." What Orwell called "our civilization" was going to be swept away and replaced by "something so different that we should scarcely regard it as human. . . ." In *Coming Up for Air,* he provided a description of what lay in store as the West moved surely into a "kind of hate-world, slogan-world. The coloured shirts, the barbed wire, the rubber truncheons. The secret cells where the electric light burns night and day and the detectives watch you while you sleep. And the processions and the posters with enormous faces and the crowds of a million people all cheering for the Leader till they deafen themselves into thinking that they really worship him, and all the time, underneath, they hate him so that they want to puke."

This was the world of the future that Orwell described in his last novel. *Nineteen Eighty-Four* is a grim, horrifying book. It is part parable, part historical prediction, part political tract. It is "the expression of a mood, and it is a warning. The mood it expresses is that of near despair about the future of man, and the warning is that unless the course of history changes, men all over the world will lose their most human qualities, will become soulless automatons, and will not even be aware of it." In Orwell's novel the European adventure has come to a gritty end. There is nothing left but meanness and oppression and lies and fake appeals. Suspicion, alienation, and acquiescence have become the principal characteristics of life. Those in positions of power have discovered the secret of "tearing human minds to pieces and putting them together again in new shapes of their own choosing," and the individual is spied upon, continually lectured, controlled, and forced to conform. Political power is used "to narrow the range of human consciousness," "to narrow the range of thought," and all those refractory, individualistic attitudes — affection, loyalty, joy — have been replaced by a shoddy patriotism, hate, and devotion to abstract and contradictory principles.

In his novel Orwell presents the picture of a society where any concept of truth has disappeared. Even the past is continually changing, so that what was true yesterday is no longer so today. The past, present, and future are manipulated, and no sense of reality exists. Orwell argued that "totalitarianism demands, in fact, the continuous alteration of the past, and in the long run probably demands a disbelief in the very existence of objective truth." In *Nineteen Eighty-Four* men accept without protest or any sense of being abused the most flagrant degradation of language. Words no longer have any real meaning. Thus society is controlled by four ministries: The Ministry of Truth, which concerns itself with news, entertainment, education, and the fine arts; the Ministry of Peace, which conducts the war; the Ministry of Love, which maintains law and order; and the Ministry of Plenty, which is responsible for economic affairs. Over everything rules the mysterious, all-powerful party, with its three slogans: War Is Peace; Freedom Is Slavery; Ignorance Is Strength. There is no way in which anyone can escape the control of the society, and the human mind has been tamed to docility and conditioned responses. Men are no longer citizens but subjects, and they have accepted this new status. They are capable of *crimestop*, the ability to stop short when there is the possibility of having a dangerous thought. They are also capable of *blackwhite*, the ability to know and to believe that black is white, and of *doublethink*, the power of holding two conflicting beliefs simultaneously and to accept both of them.

But those in positions of power require more than mere outward acceptance of their authority. The principle of the ruling party is that "power is in inflicting pain and humiliation." All self-respect, all independent judgment, all doubts must be eliminated. The human personality has been pulverized, and the party demands the utter degradation of reason, the surrender of all claims to self-engendered opinions, the sacrifice of any unique individual quality. All hope of, and in fact all knowledge of, a life different than that under the control of the party must be abandoned. As one of the party members tells Winston Smith: "If you want a picture of the future, imagine a boot stamping on the human face — forever." Ultimately only that person can survive who is "in the end utterly penitent, saved from himself, crawling to our feet of his own accord. . . ." Absolute acceptance of what is said and done is required, and all conflicting loyalties or allegiances must be given up. Everyone must accept the practice that Orwell put in a couplet:

> Under the spreading Chestnut tree
> I sold you and you sold me —

In the end the principal character Winston Smith wins through to a true understanding of what is demanded of him. He becomes a hollow man, a human cipher, squeezed empty and spiritually emasculated. He becomes part òf the totalitarian landscape. As Orwell ends his novel: "He had won the victory over himself. He loved Big Brother."

In the years since the publication of *Nineteen Eighty-Four*, many critics have argued that George Orwell's analysis of totalitarianism was overly dramatic and superficial. It has been pointed out that his talent for the striking and memorable phrase and his emphasis upon the shocking episode have obscured the more subtle aspects of totalitarianism. He had, his critics say, too simple a view of politics, and his own pessimism forced him over the edge into overdrawn exaggeration.

These criticisms are just. But Orwell also saw something that has too often escaped the attention of students of totalitarianism. When one works his way through the political, historical, social, and economic interpretations of totalitarianism, he arrives at the rather simple Orwellian truth. Basically, totalitarianism is a nasty and obscene doctrine. Orwell's own view of politics may be reduced to what is essentially a cliché — men must be decent. And he meant by decency that behavior that takes into account the feelings and personalities of other people. What made life worthwhile was ultimately "the bedrock decency of a human being." If this disappeared, nothing else really mattered, and "either power politics must yield to common decency or the world must go down into a nightmare of which we can already catch some dim glimpses."

Others might attack totalitarianism as an economic or historical idea. But Orwell was a cranky defender of decency, and totalitarianism violated what he thought of as the essence of the human condition of Western man. He once expressed this condition in terms that made him the eternal enemy of all those who would do dirt upon us. "The essence of being human is that one does not seek perfection, that one is sometimes willing to commit sins for the sake of loyalty, that one does not push asceticism to the point where it makes friendly intercourse impossible, and that one is prepared in the end to be defeated and broken up by life, which is the inevitable price of fastening one's love upon other human individuals."

SUGGESTIONS FOR FURTHER READING

Good studies of the historical background of totalitarianism are Martin Gilbert, The European Powers 1900-1945 *(1965), Ludwig Dehio,* Germany and World Politics in the Twentieth Century *(1959), and Elizabeth Wiske-*

mann, Europe of the Dictators, 1919-1945 *(1966). Walter Laqueur and George L. Mosse, eds.*, International Fascism, 1920-1945 *(1966), contains some interesting items, and Eugen Weber's* Varieties of Fascism *(1964) is a careful, rich study. The impact of totalitarianism can be examined in Martin Gilbert,* Britain and Germany between the Wars *(1964), and Margaret George,* The Warped Vision: British Foreign Policy 1933-1939 *(1965). H. Stuart Hughes,* The Obstructed Path: French Social Thought in the Years of Desperation, 1930-1960 *(1968), is a fine piece of intellectual history.*

General discussions of the theory of totalitarianism are Hannah Arendt, The Origins of Totalitarianism *(1951 and later editions), Adam Ulam,* The New Face of Soviet Totalitarianism *(1963), and Zbigniew Brzezinski,* Ideology and Power in Soviet Politics *(1962). Two of the more specialized studies that have something important to say are Harold Swayze,* Political Control of Literature in the USSR, 1946-1959 *(1962), and David Schoenbaum,* Hitler's Social Revolution: Class and Status in Nazi Germany, 1933-1939 *(1966). Robert Conquest's* The Great Terror: Stalin's Purge of the Thirties *(1968) is a vast compilation of facts and ideas.*

Material on Hitler abounds. Alan Bullock's Hitler, a Study in Tyranny *(1952 and later editions) is the basic biography. H. R. Trevor-Roper's* The Last Days of Hitler *(1947) is a brilliant, fascinating report, and his edition of* Hitler's Secret Conversations *(1953) provides an insight into Hitler's ideas and motivations. Hermann Rauschning's* The Revolution of Nihilism *(1939) is still worth reading.*

There are some valuable reports of personal experiences in concentration camps. The best of these are Bruno Bettelheim, The Informed Heart: Autonomy in a Mass Age *(1960), and Alexander Solzhenitsyn,* One Day in the Life of Ivan Denisovich *(1963). Gerald Reitlinger's* The Final Solution: The Attempt To Exterminate the Jews of Europe, 1939-1945 *(1953) is a good survey, as is Raul Hilberg's* The Destruction of the European Jews *(1961). Constantine Fitzgibbon's "Auschwitz and the Camp Commandant," in* Encounter *(April, 1960), is a short review of the career of Rudolf Höss, the commanding officer at Auschwitz.* The Death Factory: Document on Auschwitz, *by Ota Kraus and Erich Kulka (1966), contains some nerve-shattering facts and photographs. The motion picture* The Pawnbroker *is a dramatic presentation of what it meant to be a survivor of Auschwitz.*

The best source for Orwell is Orwell himself. Animal Farm *and* 1984 *are necessities, as are some of his essays, now collected in several readily available volumes. A recently published, four-volume* Collected Essays *(1968), edited by Sonia Orwell and Ian Angus, is full of wonderful things. Richard Rees,* George Orwell: Fugitive from the Camp of Victory *(1961), and George Woodcock,* The Crystal Spirit: A Study of George Orwell *(1966), are good secondary sources.*

Man of Peace, Leonard Baskin, 1952, by permission of the artist.

11

The Present Situation

1945 The end of World War II

1945 Delegates from fifty nations met in San Francisco to organize the United Nations.

1945 Vannevar Bush issued his *Science: The Endless Frontier*. Recommended the creation of a government–sponsored foundation in the United States for the support of basic research in science. In 1950 Congress established the National Science Foundation.

1945 The Frenchman Jean-Paul Sartre initiated the periodical *Modern Times*, which through the following years became identified with existentialism, probably the most important philosophical movement in the postwar Western world.

1945- The Nuremberg Trials. Nazi leaders were brought to trial by the
1946 victorious powers.

1946 Operation of the first electronic high-speed digital calculating machine.

1946 France adopts the Fourth Republic.

1946- The "Welfare State" introduced into Britain. Large sections of the
1949 economy were brought under state ownership and control, including the Bank of England, the coal industry, civil aviation, public transport, and the generation, supply, and distribution of electricity. The principal welfare measures were the National Insurance Act and the National Health Service.

1947 Word automation coined to define "self-powered, self-guided, and correcting mechanism."

1947	The Indian subcontinent achieved independence of British rule and became the sovereign states of India, Pakistan, and Ceylon. In the following years Burma, Malaya, and Indonesia in Asia became independent.
1947	George Kennan's famous article in *Foreign Affairs* set forth the arguments in behalf of a policy of containment as an answer to Russian international pressures.
1947-1948	Severe tensions between the Western countries and Russia appeared. The Communist coup in Czechoslovakia and the Russian blockade of Berlin in 1948 put pressure upon the West.
1948	The Marshall Plan initiated whereby the United States provided money for the reconstruction of West Europe's industry. The Plan was both idealistic ("Our policy is directed not against any country or doctrine but against hunger, poverty, desperation and chaos") and a realistic international policy designed to buttress Western Europe against Soviet influence.
1949	The North Atlantic Treaty tied the United States to the states of Western Europe in a military alliance.
1949	Establishment of a German Federal Republic in West Germany. In 1955 West Germany became a sovereign state.
1949	Victory of the Chinese Communists resulted in the end of Western political and economic influence in China.
1950-1952	Creation of an international authority for the production of coal and steel in France, West Germany, Italy, Belgium, the Netherlands, and Luxembourg.
1950-1953	The Korean War. An attack by North Korea on South Korea brought a United Nations force (largely American) into the war in support of South Korea. The armistice agreement in 1953 left the boundary between the two countries where it had been in 1950.
1953	A model developed for the structure of DNA that accounted for the transmitting of a variety of genetic information.
1953	Electronic computers with feedback mechanism made possible the field of cybernetics — "the study of control and communication in the animal and the machine."

1953   First performance of Samuel Beckett's *Waiting for Godot* in Paris. *Godot* was the most important illustration of the "drama of the absurd" as it appeared in the postwar Western world.

1954   French abandoned the attempt to pacify their colonies in Southeast Asia. Laos and Cambodia were given independence. Vietnam was divided into two separate countries. The United States assumed support of South Vietnam and became increasingly involved in the struggle between North and South.

1954   The Americans exploded a hydrogen bomb.

1954   The first of a number of important Supreme Court decisions in the United States that struck down patterns of segregation based upon race. A convenient date marking the beginning of the Negro revolution.

1955   Raymond Aron's *Opium of the Intellectuals*. The most influential of a number of statements arguing against the application of historical "ideologies" to the contemporary world.

1956   Tunisia and Morocco became independent of French control.

1956   First full-scale use of nuclear fuel to produce electricity.

1956   Following upon Egypt's nationalization of Suez Canal, British, French, and Israeli armies invaded Egypt, but were forced to withdraw under pressure from the United States and Russia.

1956   William Whyte's *The Organizational Man*, the best-known if not the most profound description of what many regarded as the typical Western personality.

1957-   Widespread immunization began against polio. This was only
1960   one of the dramatic developments in medicine in the postwar period. Antibiotics, a continually lowering infant mortality, the science of gerontology, advances in the understanding of mental retardation, and organ transplants, among others, were bringing about a medical revolution.

1957   Treaties of Rome brought about (in 1958) the creation of the European Economic Community (the Common Market) consisting of France, West Germany, Italy, Belgium, the Netherlands, and Luxembourg.

1957   The Gold Coast became the independent state of Ghana in Africa. The liquidation of the African colonial empires, with the exception of the Portuguese, followed.

1957	Beginning of the "space age" with the launching of the first man-made satellite by the Soviet Union. In 1961 Juri Gagarin became the first human being to orbit the earth in a satellite.
1958	Establishment of the Fifth French Republic with Charles de Gaulle as president. The republic was brought about by the strains produced by the struggle with Algeria. In 1962 Algeria became independent.
1961	Pope John XXIII issued the encyclical *Mater et magistra*, a call for social justice throughout the world. In 1963 John issued *Pacem in terris,* stating that those interests uniting men were more important than those dividing them and calling for a concentrated effort to find ways to peace.
1963	The United States, Russia, and other nations signed a treaty prohibiting the testing of nuclear devices in the atmosphere.
1967	First artificial production of DNA (deoxyribonucleic acid), the basic chemical controlling growth and heredity.
1967	First human heart transplant.
1969	Men successfully land on the moon.

On April 25, 1945, American and Russian troops met at the town of Torgau on the Elbe River in central Germany. Not quite two weeks later, representatives of the German army surrendered, and World War II was over in Europe. Hitler had been defeated, but at a staggering cost. Behind the Russian army stretched a thousand miles of desolation through eastern Europe and on into the Soviet Union. Crowds of refugees clogged the roads, and the cities were in ruins. In eastern Germany, Poland, eastern Slovakia, and Hungary countless numbers died of exposure and disease or were murdered by undisciplined Russian troops.

The suffering and dislocation in Western Europe was less. But in the wake of the victorious American and British armies was destruction and discouragement aplenty. Rotterdam, Cologne, Cherbourg, and many other cities had been reduced to dark, rubble-strewn, and forlorn husks. Industry was at a standstill, commerce was reduced to a pathetic level, and the great wealth of Western Europe was gone. The peoples had been freed from German control. But this had been accomplished largely by American and Russian power. There was relief that the war was over, but the past had been so dreadful and the future was so clouded that there were few who could muster a whole-hearted joyous response at the liberation. European and American scholars were busy writing books with titles such as *The Passing of the European Age* and *Farewell to European History*, and there were general expressions of the opinion that European civilization was at an end. The German theologian Dietrich Bonhoeffer, who was executed by the Nazis near the end of the war, wrote shortly before his death a sentence that could have applied to all Europe: "One may ask whether there have ever before in human history been people with so little ground under their feet." Without any doubt in his own judgment, the American General Douglas MacArthur had stated bluntly as early as 1944: "Europe is a dying system. It is worn out and run down. . . . The lands touching the Pacific with their billions of inhabitants will determine the course of history for the next ten thousand years."

Europe in 1945

It is difficult for us to remember now or to imagine what Europe was like in 1945. As the German novelist Heinrich Böll has written, "not twelve years separate 1945 from 1957, but centuries, abysses of diverse contemporaneity. . . ." And if there is an immeasurable historical gap between 1945 and 1957, that gap is even greater between 1957 and 1970. Event has followed upon event, change upon change, with such rapidity that even the recent past moves away from us with the speed of light.

Yet there is some justification in regarding 1945 as the beginning of a distinctive historical period. Many of the conditions of our lives are rooted in the response that was made to the problems existing at the end of World War II. In 1945 the political boundaries of Western Europe were largely restored to what they had been in 1940, and when one looked at a map it appeared very similar to what it had been in 1918. But the historical changes were significant and substantial. Germany was an occupied wasteland, and the Germans had been removed from participation in the political, economic, and intellectual life of the West. Western influence in eastern Europe had been so weakened that within a few years the West was to be more alienated from the Russians, the Poles, the Hungarians, the Czechs, and the Rumanians than it had been for three centuries. The great colonial empires of the British, the French, and the Dutch were in disarray and seething with revolt. Even the human composition of the continent had changed in important respects. Large numbers of East Europeans left their homes and sought a new life in the West. For the first time in almost two thousand years the majority of Jews, a group that had contributed so much to European culture, lived outside Europe. Many important participants in European intellectual life — Albert Einstein, Thomas Mann, Arturo Toscanini, and countless others — had left Europe for the United States, and this bleeding away of many of the most talented and energetic Europeans was to continue.

Each of the important European national societies had been crippled. For England, World War II meant the acceleration of the process of decline in power that had been going on since the turn of the century. Her lonely struggle against the Nazis in 1940 and the early part of 1941, when she had appeared as the single beacon of hope to millions of enslaved peoples, had been, as Winston Churchill said, "her finest hour." But the cost of heroism had been prohibitive. Churchill had promised the English people "blood, sweat, and tears," but the war demanded more than that. The great British overseas investments were diminished, her industrial capacity had shrunk, and her ability to influence the course of historical events was limited. Throughout the nineteenth and into the twentieth centuries England had been the great balance wheel in Western society, a force for sanity and for a rough international equality. Now, although she was a titular victor in the war, she did not have the strength to carry out this historical function. In June, 1945, Churchill wrote in a memorandum to the British Foreign Office:

> It is beyond the power of this country to prevent all sorts of things at the present time. The responsibility lies with the United States, and my desire is to give them all the support in our power. If they do not feel able to do anything — then we must let matters take their course — indeed, that is what they are doing.

The end of the war found France internally divided and, in some measure, demoralized. Shamed by her defeat in 1940 and suffering from memories of the German occupation, France endured a crisis of confidence. André Malraux remarked that "we are back at the year zero," and the intellectual pessimism that had been so much a part of French thinking since the late nineteenth century appeared to be the prevalent attitude. French military and political leaders had been disgraced, and French history, so rich in memories and glories, seemed without direction. Immediately following the war France was forced to endure the pitiful sight of some Frenchmen accusing others of treason. There were over 160,000 treason trials, of which 27,000 resulted in acquittal and 45,000 in dismissal of charges. But 88,000 people were condemned as traitors, and the notorious collaborators were executed. An understandable weariness permeated the country. The Nazi Josef Goebbels had predicted that even if Germany were defeated, Western Europe would be "engulfed in chaotic political and social confusion which would only represent a preparatory stage for the coming Bolshevization." To large numbers of Frenchmen his prediction seemed on the verge of coming true.

For Germany 1945 was the null-point. Occupied by enemy armies, her cities destroyed, her people scattered and scraping among the ruins, Germany was only a geographical expression. She was divided among the conquerors into zones and lost control of her affairs. Pell-mell the Germans were expelled from central and eastern Europe. By the late nineteen-forties the eight-hundred-year German attempt to colonize to the east had ended, and there were no substantial numbers of Germans living east of Germany and Austria. The Russian occupation of eastern Germany meant the end of Prussian influence in German affairs. The Prussian military and landowning aristocracy was destroyed, and famous old German cities such as Koenigsberg, Breslau, and Danzig lost their German populations, and were even renamed. Millions of Germans fled to the West. Over a million German soldiers were prisoners of war, and thousands of these were to be executed or were to die in captivity during the next few years. Survival for Germans became a matter of reliance upon the charity of the victors and the black market. There was no longer any national dream of greatness but only the bare-bone reality of everyday objects, a reality expressed so well in Günter Eich's poem "Inventory."

> This is my cap.
> this is my coat.
> here is my shaving kit
> in a linen bag.
>
> A tin is my plate
> my mug.
> I have scratched my name
> in the tinplate.
>
> This is my notebook
> this is my groundsheet
> this is my towel
> this is my thread.

One nation in the West was in a unique position. "At night across the Atlantic the great cities of America blazed like modern cathedrals of Providence, warm with human kindness and golden optimistic light, full of a dynamic and strong people who were untouched by despair." The Americans appeared to have become the inheritors of everything that was left of Western civilization: the wealth, the liberties, the sciences, the arts. The divergence of American history from that of Europe seemed more pronounced than ever. Unmarked by enemy action, the Americans had during the war created an overpowering military force and had built up a fantastic industrial machine. As soon as the war ended, American armed forces were drastically reduced, and in the minds of many America seemed prepared to withdraw again across the ocean.

European Recovery

But this was not to happen. Instead there was to be an even closer unity of the Western world, and events after 1945 were to bring together, some were to say force together, the various national societies of the West. For twenty years after 1945 three great problems of common concern were to create unity, and also strain, in Western life. These were: the question of reconstruction and security; the demolition of the great colonial empires; and the search for new values and new identities in Western civilization itself. The response to these three problems was to introduce what we must call the contemporary Western civilization of the second half of the twentieth century.

The reconstruction of Western Europe and the security of the Western people were, in the decades following the end of World War II, to be part of the answer of the West to the threat of Russia and Russian Communism. There is some controversy about who was responsible for what came to be known as the Cold War. But there is no question that Russian power, Russian Communist ideology, and general European weakness constituted a threat to the West European countries. It was soon evident after 1945 that wherever the Russian army went the result was a brutal imposition of Soviet institutions and Soviet control. As the Russian dictator Josef Stalin told the Yugoslav Milovan Djilas: "This war is not as in the past; whoever conquers a territory also imposes on it his own social system. Everyone imposes his own system as far as his army can reach. It cannot be otherwise."

There were many, in 1945 and after, who disputed that the Russians posed any threat. An English visitor to Russia, in the early nineteen-fifties, could say:

> I asked myself frequently, while I was in Russia, whether one was conscious of any curtailment of personal liberty. In the round of daily life, I could not see that it differed much from our life. . . . If one was law-abiding, and if one conformed, one could live in peace and comfort. . . . I did not myself talk politics while I was in Russia, not because I was deliberately refraining, but because I do not normally discuss them in England, for I am not interested in party politics.

They always seem to me to be, like sanitation, necessary but not a civilized subject for conversation.

This was one point of view. But here is another English attitude expressed by Malcolm Muggeridge: "I realized that, for me at any rate, freedom was a condition of life — freedom to think what I like, say what I like, read what I like, make what jokes I like, and form such judgments as my own poor wits, freely exercised, may provide." All evidence indicates that this type of activity is incompatible with the Soviet system, so far as we have seen it in operation. Yet it is at the heart of the Western idea of the proper life.

The elements of disaster were present in Western Europe: a huge Russian army near at hand, large Communist parties in several Western countries, a discouraged people, and a substantial number of Westerners who, for one reason or another, were prepared to accept what they regarded as a cleansing revolution. In addition, the economic and social disorders and the political weakness showed no sign of improvement. What is usually regarded as the moment of crisis occurred in February, 1947. The British, who had traditionally supported the independence of various countries in many parts of the world, announced that they could no longer assist the Greek and Turkish governments to resist the pressures of internal Communist revolt and external Russian threats. On March 12, in a historic decision, President Harry Truman announced that the United States would undertake the burden of protecting Greece and Turkey.

This step was followed by a series of American-initiated actions designed to guarantee the political integrity and stability of that part of Europe not under the direct control of Russia. Three months after assuming the responsibility for Greece and Turkey, the United States proposed what was called the Marshall Plan, the providing of financial support for European economic reconstruction. In all, between 1948 and 1952 this economic aid amounted to approximately thirteen billion dollars given to sixteen European countries. The Europeans themselves showed an amazing ability to recover, with the result that when the plan was terminated, industrial production had reached or had surpassed the levels of the prewar years. In 1949 this economic program was underpinned by the creation of the North Atlantic Treaty Organization, a military alliance whereby the United States, Canada, England, France, Iceland, Belgium, the Netherlands, Luxembourg, Norway, Denmark, Italy, and Portugal pledged themselves to common defense efforts. In 1952 Greece and Turkey joined the alliance, and in 1955 West Germany.

Another important development, at least in part traceable to Russian pressure, was the decision to rebuild that part of Germany under Western control and to bring the Germans back into the Western community. There was, of course, strong opposition expressed by many West Europeans to any idea of a revived Germany, and especially a Germany that might become a military power. And this opposition was understandable. But without Germany, Western Europe would be perpetually condemned to weakness and isolation. Some plan for Germany had to be adopted, and there was no alternative but to place some trust in the Germans themselves. As the American George Kennan wrote: "If Germany cannot be accorded reasonable confidence in these coming years, then I would know of no promising solution to the entire problem of Europe. To assume that such confidence cannot be given is to cut ourselves off in advance from possibilities that may be vital to our very survival." So the decision was made. The American, British, and French occupation zones were combined, and step by step what we now recognize as West Germany was created. In 1949 the German Federal Republic was established, and in 1955 became an independent state. And the gamble was remarkably successful. Germany has shown little inclination to revert to militarism, a revived Germany has added appreciably to Western power and prosperity, and the Germans have exhibited the capacity to participate as important contributing members of the Western society.

By the early nineteen-fifties Western Europe had largely recovered from the physical damage of the war and had regained a measure of confidence. There were still persistent and dangerous problems in every Western country, but the death of Stalin in 1953 and discernible if ambiguous changes within the Soviet Union brought some easing of international tensions and reduced the pressure upon the Western world, at least in Europe. The external threat from Russian Communism was no longer an all-consuming problem for the West.

Yet there was one element in any international controversy that made hollow any talk about Cold War and defense of the West. On August 6, 1945, in the last days of World War II, the United States had dropped an atomic bomb on Hiroshima in Japan. On August 9 a second bomb had fallen on Nagasaki. A new dimension to man's destructive capacity had been added, and since that summer day over twenty years ago all people on earth have been living under the threat of the sinister mushroom cloud. Eighty thousand people died at Hiroshima, and by the early nineteen-fifties both the United States and Russia were producing the hydrogen bomb, which was many times more destructive than the device used in Japan. These new weapons forced men to think the unthinkable: the absolute termination of the human race. They also introduced a terrifying downward spiral in man's ability to protect himself against his own creations. Ironically, the greater the military power of a nation, the less security it achieved. Jerome Wiesner and Herbert York put the dilemma this way: "Ever since shortly after World War II the military power of the U.S. has been steadily increasing. Throughout this same period the national security of the U.S. has been rapidly and inexorably diminishing. . . . The military power of the U.S.S.R. has been steadily increasing since it became an atomic power in 1949. Soviet national security, however, has been steadily decreasing. . . ."

Thus far the ultimate catastrophe has been avoided, perhaps because a common mortality is the final irrefutable argument. Moreover, the nature of nuclear warfare rendered obsolete many of the time-honored and valued attributes of Western man. What did bravery mean in the face of irradiation burns or the birth of deformed children? Ernest Hemingway had spoken of the virtue of "grace under pressure." Such a statement was a childish obscenity to anyone standing in the blast area of a nuclear explosion. A certain masculine boldness had been a much-admired part of Western history. Now the phrase "die like a man" struck many as nothing but a piece of absurd bravado. Although at the time of his death he did not know of nuclear warfare, and was, in fact, speaking to a more general philosophical problem, Bonhoeffer was almost historically prophetic when he wrote that "the ultimate question for a responsible man to ask is not how he is to extricate himself heroically from the affair, but how the coming generation is to live." Several years ago Robert Jungk wrote a book entitled *Children of the Ashes*, an examination of the inhabitants of Hiroshima, where the first atomic bomb had exploded. He pointed out that those who did not die by blast, fire, or radiation were known in Japan as the survivors. To a greater or lesser extent, every person alive in the world remains, thus far, a survivor.

The End of Colonialism

Even as the search for security was going on in Europe, the Western world was being forced to accommodate itself to the disintegration of the European colonial empires. In the years preceding World War II there had been revolts in the colonies, but in retrospect the period between 1918 and 1939 appears as the golden autumn of imperialism. In Hong Kong, Singapore, Djibouti, Zanzibar, Bombay, and elsewhere Europeans seemed as confident of the rightness of their presence as in the nineteenth century. Kenya, for example, has been described in the nineteen-thirties as "an enclave of Victorian paternalism, where an Englishman, divorced from the annoyances of modern political theory, might live the life of a gentleman-farmer." There were, of course, continual statements that ultimately the colonial relationship should change and that even within the empires there should be no obstacles to the welfare and progress of the subject peoples. In 1921 Churchill said: "I think there is only one ideal that the British Empire can set for itself, and that is that there should be no barrier of race, colour, or creed which would prevent any man by merit from reaching any station if he is fitted for it." Such an attitude was accepted by many, but the practical way of achieving such welfare and progress, and particularly of independence, remained a mystery. To a great extent the words of Lord Lugard in 1923 expressed the general opinion of the European colonial powers. "The danger of going too fast," Lord Lugard warned, "with native races is more likely to lead to disappointment, if not to disaster, than the danger of not going fast enough."

World War II sent shock waves throughout the colonial empires. The victories of the Japanese in French Indochina, Burma, Malaya, and Indonesia affected the position of Britain, France, and the Netherlands in a part of the world where they had previously been unchallenged. After the war the European powers attempted to reassert their rule, and the result was a series of painful, futile, and desperate efforts at the show of military force. From the late nineteen-forties there was a continual rearguard action as the Europeans abandoned one position after another, first in Asia and then in Africa. The British fought in Malaya, in Cyprus, and in Kenya, while the French engaged in a savage attempt at pacification in Indochina and Algeria. But the desire for independence by the colonial peoples was too great, and the price of retaining the empires was too high. A. P. Thornton has pointed out what it would have taken for the British to remain an imperial power:

> The mobilization of a standing army in India; the marshalling of "flying squadrons" of military police to deal with colonial "brush-fires"; an involvement in a bitter quarrel with the United States, for whom Britain was no match; and a withdrawal from any effective participation in the United Nations Organization. Britain would also have been compelled to spend untold sums of money, money which she did not have and which no one would have lent her; and she would have had to drain the country of the manpower so desperately needed to set the lurching domestic economy back if not on its feet at least on its knees.

So, with surprisingly good grace the British gave up the empire. It was not easy. In India, for example, civil war had broken out between Hindus and Moslems, and the country seemed on the verge of disintegration. But, as one observer has written, "England had a wolf by the ears. It required great courage to simplify and falsify the problem, to ignore those complications, to disregard the snapping jaws and quietly let go of the ears. It was dangerous and courageous; it was the right thing to do."

A little over two years after the end of the war, the British left, and in February, 1948, a farewell parade for the last British troops in India was held. The members of the First Battalion of the Somerset Light Infantry prepared to embark for home. "The bands played *God Save the King*; the Somerset Light Infantry presented arms in a Royal Salute and the bands played *Bande Mataram*, which six years before had been the rallying song of the insurrection; the King's Colour and the Regimental Colour were trooped through the Gateway of India, the bands played *Auld Lang Syne*." Following India, a host of other former colonies achieved independence: Burma, Ceylon, and Malaysia in Asia and then, later, the African states such as Ghana, Nigeria, Kenya, and numerous others.

The French, too, were forced to retire grudgingly. A fruitless struggle in Indochina was abandoned in 1954. Soon thereafter France found herself involved in what was a part-colonial, part-civil war in Algeria. There the brutal effort to crush a native revolt produced deep divisions within France. Weak political leadership and a lack of support by the civilian population left the army isolated and frustrated and produced the threat of a military revolt against the government. Stewart Easton has described the dilemma of the embattled French army in Algeria. "These soldiers came to regard themselves as the sole repository of French honor, of a different class, almost a different race, from the politicians and petty bourgeois in France who understood nothing of such things and were prepared to abandon Algeria and their countrymen simply because the war was expensive and damaging to their world position and for other civilian reasons." It was the army that was instrumental in bringing Charles de Gaulle to power in France in 1958. But de Gaulle sensed that the war could not go on and succeeded in extricating France from Algeria and, in fact, managed to retain French influence if not power in large parts of what had been French colonial Africa.

The end of empire has not meant, however, the end of the Western presence in Asia and Africa. In reality, what we have seen in the past twenty years is both a shrinking and an expanding Western influence. Political control has disappeared, but the legacies of European institutions, often fragmented and often modified, have been more lasting than one would have expected. Bureaucracies, educational institutions, and commercial arrangements are modelled after Western patterns, and Asians and Africans have shown a continuing and lively interest in what have been called "the wonderful boxes of tricks" of the Westerners. Through technology and cooperative programs the impact of the West has carried deeper into the native cultures since the decline of imperial rule than before. It is difficult to judge the ultimate effect of this

Western impact. The results of Western influence are not always beneficial, and some of the shabbier aspects of our own society have been exported. The French anthropologist Claude Lévi-Strauss has complained that as we travel about the world we see "the filth, our filth, that we have thrown in the face of humanity." And he goes on: "the islands of the South Seas, for instance, have become stationary aircraft-carriers; the whole of Asia has been taken sick; shanty-towns disfigure Africa; commercial and military aircraft fly across the still 'virgin' but no longer unspoilt forests of South America and Melanesia. . . ."

Lévi-Strauss may be correct. But, for better or for worse, a continually shrinking world forces the West ever closer to Asia and Africa. The West is amazingly rich, and much of Asia and Africa is depressingly poor. But this poverty is a Western as well as an Asian or African problem, and there is no possibility of the West becoming a small, restricted area of the planet, bulging with wealth, and surrounded by a "sea of ravenous, multiplying, and encroaching" people. In addition, the outgoing, outward-looking spirit of the West cannot be confined to the narrow limits of Europe and North America. One of the strongest characteristics of Westerners is their belief that "they ought to be busy in the world, guiding, influencing, and setting an example — and that if they are not doing so, mankind is being deprived of much sage counsel and advice." There are dangers in this attitude, and it can become offensive. But it is also a guarantee against indifference and a sterile turning inward that would condemn the West, along with the non-Western world, to a stifling and catastrophic future.

As the search for political security and the emergence of a new noncolonial Asia and Africa were taking place, something else of major importance was going on in the West. We were, in the words of the French philosopher Gabriel Marcel, "laying utterly bare . . . our human condition." Historical and cultural accumulations were being stripped away with fantastic speed, and definitions of Western man and Western civilization that had been accepted as beyond dispute were being questioned. Almost daily each person was being charged, in the words of the German playwright Peter Weiss, "To turn yourself inside out and see the whole world with fresh eyes."

The New Science and Technology

Perhaps the most striking of the changes taking place in the West, and the one most easily observed, was the new and different scientific and technological revolution of the second half of the twentieth century. Giant research institutes — factories of knowledge — are bringing about a scientific explosion. We are flying to the moon, transplanting hearts and kidneys, and are well on the road to creating in the laboratory a living human cell. New sources of heat and light are being developed, and new methods of transportation and communications are reducing space and time to what many regarded as almost absurd measurements. Computers are not only being designed to store and retrieve information but to "think," and plans are underway to farm the ocean bottoms. We are acquiring the tools that will involve changes in the way we live perhaps as important as those which took place in neolithic times when men began to settle into lasting communities and to till the earth. Zbigniew Brzezinski warns that "Most of the change that has so far taken place in human history has been gradual — with the great 'revolutions' being mere punctuation marks to a slow, elucible process. In contrast, the approaching transformation will come more rapidly and will have deeper consequences for the way and even perhaps for the meaning of human life than anything experienced by the generations that preceded us." Professor Brzezinski assures us that within a few short years we shall be able to control the sex of children, to affect intelligence through the use of drugs, to modify the human personality, and to create new forms of social control.

This is "progress" with a vengeance. This new revolution promises riches, leisure, and unthought-of mastery over nature. It also, in its apparently uncontrollable surge, is sweeping us into the future. Since the eighteenth century a great part of Western man's history has been his attempt to free himself from what he regarded as the restrictions and burdens of the past. But now the past was not only being left behind; it was being obliterated, and within a short time it may be as impossible for us to imagine what life was like in 1900 as it is now for us to place ourselves in the position of the man living in the year 1000. In 1925 the American F. Scott Fitzgerald published his novel *The Great Gatsby*. At the end of the novel the narrator stands and looks out over the New York countryside.

> And as the moon rose higher the inessential houses began to melt away until gradually I became aware of the old world here that flowered for Dutch sailors' eyes — a fresh, green breast of the new world. Its vanished trees, the trees that made way for Gatsby's house, had once pandered in whispers to the last and greatest of all human dreams; for a transitory, enchanted moment man must have held his breath in the presence of this continent, compelled into an aesthetic contemplation he neither understood nor desired, face to face for the last time in history with something commensurate to his capacity for wonder.

Fitzgerald could still imagine what the disappeared world must have been like, and to sense its closeness to him. We will undoubtedly find it increasingly difficult even to conjure up a memory of the past. As Wright Morris wrote forty years after the publication of *The Great Gatsby*: "It may have mattered to Gatsby, but not to us, that the dream was already behind him, where the dark fields of the republic rolled on under the night. We *know* it is behind us."

It is the unthinking, mechanical, inexorable nature of this change that many find so threatening. In the eighteenth, nineteenth, and early twentieth centuries Western men assumed that they could direct change and create plans for the future. But as Michael Harrington noted in his *The Accidental Century*: "Where these conscious revolutionists of the past proposed visions that outstripped reality, the unconscious revolutionists of the present create realities that outstrip their vision." The Frenchman Raymond Aron argues that all human characteristics save that of adaptation are being destroyed, and that we are enduring "the crushing and startling technical superiority of arms, organization, and production over personal qualities." Many of those involved in these scientific and technological changes have expressed concern. Lévi-Strauss makes a wistful and moving complaint. "I have little taste for the century in which we live. It seems to me that the present tendency is on the one hand man's total mastery over nature and on the other hand the mastery of certain forms of humanity over others. My temperament and my tastes lead me far more toward periods which were less ambitious and perhaps more timid but in which a certain balance could be maintained between man and nature, among the various and multiple forms of life, whether animal or vegetable, and among the different types of culture, of belief, of customs, or of institutions." In 1965 the scientist Max Born put the matter in an even more startling context and raised the question of whether the price being paid for scientific advance was not excessive. "I am haunted," he wrote, "by the idea that this break in human civilization, caused by the discovery of the scientific method, may be irreparable. Though I love science I have the feeling that it is so much against history and tradition that it cannot be absorbed by our civilization." And Born goes on. "The political and military horrors and the complete breakdown of ethics which I have witnessed during my life may not be a symptom of an ephemeral social weakness but a necessary consequence of the rise of science — which in itself is one of the highest intellectual achievements of man."

Political and Cultural Change

But scientific and technological change was only the most obvious alteration in the conditions of Western life. Political ideas and institutions were being subjected to increasing criticism. Representative government, the right to vote, and liberal constitutions were being questioned as valid expressions of political life, and much of our political activity seemed to many archaic and irrelevant. "Our political vocabulary," a French commentator has observed, "has a strong resemblance to those old novels that people no longer read; it is no longer suitable for modern times and the realities of the present; we use words that are old, vague, and out-of-date." It was something along the same line that moved the late Robert Kennedy to say in addressing a group of South African university students in 1966: "Obstacles of this swiftly moving planet will not yield to obsolete dogmas and outworn slogans. They cannot be moved by those who cling to a present that is already dying. . . ."

There is little question but that drastic changes in our political and cultural lives are coming. New patterns of sexual behavior, new attitudes toward work, new standards of aesthetic judgment are easily discernible. Yet even as these changes appear more and more obvious, there is an increasingly desperate clinging to the past and the present by those whose beliefs, positions, and peace of mind are threatened. As Hannah Arendt has noticed, "The end of a tradition does not necessarily mean that traditional concepts have lost their power over the minds of men. On the contrary, it sometimes seems that this power of well-worn notions and categories becomes more tyrannical as the tradition loses its living force. . . ." In the apparent wilderness of the present, many call for a return to the rocklike verities of the past. They are, in the words of Vladimir Nabokov, ever "hunting out the things which had once been fresh and bright but which were now worn to a thread, dead things among living ones; dead things, shamming life, painted and repainted, continuing to be accepted by lazy minds serenely unaware of the fraud."

Such a response is understandable, and one can sympathize with those who hold it. But it is difficult to fault J. P. Corbett who, in his *Europe and the Social Order*, suggested that "all such harkening back to the peculiar glories of the European past in order to find a basis for the European present is an illusion. It rests upon conditions which do not obtain and appeals to forces which do not exist." There is an ambiguity in contemporary life, a striking indiscriminate quality that jars on the nerves of those who long for a more measured and stable world. In his novel *The Sins of the Fathers*, published in 1960, the German writer Christian Geissler describes the room of his hero, and the description could pass for much of what we see as we look about us. The room has some books — the writings of Lenin, the Bible, German constitutional law, Hitler's *Mein Kampf*, a popular edition of myths and legends, three old volumes of logic, and fifty paperback volumes of comic strips. There are also some coat hooks and some cheap pictures. One of these is of a nude woman, one of a Negro singer behind a microphone, one of an

Indian woman carrying a baby on her back, and one, the largest of all, of a tightly embracing couple mounted on horseback, the horse flying over the rooftops.

What is one to make of this conglomeration? Does it express the apparent confusion of our lives and our civilization? There is certainly a lack of focus that is probably more pronounced than ever before in Western civilization. And it is easy to criticize this eclecticism. But the French philosopher Maurice Merleau-Ponty speaks with rare insight when he writes: "We should be careful. What we call disorder and ruin, others who are younger live as the natural order of things; and perhaps with ingenuity they are going to master it precisely because they no longer seek their bearings where we took ours. In the din of demolition, many sullen passions, many hypocrisies or follies, and many false dilemmas will disappear. Who would have hoped it ten years ago?"

In fact, it could be argued that in spite of the decline in the effectiveness of traditional appeals and injunctions the moral content of Western life is greater than ever before. The second half of the twentieth century seemed a time of increasing moral fury that attacked everything — manners, customs, and laws — that offended against what were regarded as the general principles of decency and an honest facing of our situation. This new morality had little to do with concepts of traditional proper conduct. It claimed, rather, to speak to the substance instead of the letter of behavior and was impatient with what were regarded as fraudulent claims and any kind of political or intellectual posing. There was a rumbling, and particularly among many of the younger members of Western society, of moral outrage at the falsities and cruelties that had become embedded in Western civilization. This new morality was unstructured and tended to grow up around Western institutions rather than express itself through them, and thus created political and social instability. Many observers have believed that this uninstitutionalized morality is excessive, and some like the scholar Michael Polanyi have warned against the nihilism that will result from this demand for absolute moral content. Polanyi argues that this moral fervor "has in our lifetime outreached itself by its inordinate aspirations and thus heaped upon mankind the disasters that have befallen us." Moral passions must be controlled or they will bring about an anarchy that will be unbearable.

Polanyi and others are certainly correct in their belief that excessive morality poses dangers. Yet in the face of a basically structural amorality, or even immorality, that modern bureaucratic societies encourage and the mouthing of tired phrases that pass for wisdom, there is a refreshing quality about those who protest untiringly against shoddy practice and shoddy ideas. And the moralists have been remarkably successful. Almost every important statement about Western politics or society must be couched in moral terms to be accepted, and because of the moral basis upon which so much of Western civilization depends, the moral argument is irrefutable. In March, 1967, Pope Paul VI issued an encyclical, which in part read: "When so many people are hungry, when so many families suffer from destitution, when so many remain steeped in ignorance, when so many schools, hospitals, and homes worthy of the name remain to be built, all public or private squandering of wealth, all expenditures prompted by motives of national or personal ostentation, every exhausting armaments race becomes an intolerable scandal." The "scandal" is a moral one, and the recent attempts to cope with poverty, with racial injustice, and with cultural deprivation have been largely motivated by moral commitment.

What the result of this moral commitment will be it is impossible to say. We have become aware in recent years that our view of the continuity of our civilization has been naive and misleading. Deeply embedded in Western thought — as exemplified by the attempts of men such as Hegel, Marx, Tocqueville, and Spengler — is the belief that we can somehow discern the basic direction of the present and thus predict the future. This confidence in historical inevitability has been, as the sociologist Robert Nisbet pointed out so clearly in 1968, "the basis of all that we call philosophy of history and social developmentalism. From it has come the widely accepted notion that there is an entity called civilization or culture, that this entity obeys certain imminent principles of growth in time, that the continuity of time is roughly the same as the continuity of this growth, that past, present, and future have not merely a chronological relation but a genetic relation, and that through sufficient study of the past and the present it is possible to foresee the future simply by extending or extrapolating ongoing processes."

As Nisbet maintains, this belief that the present follows the past and the future the present is only true in a chronological way. He quotes with approval Émile Durkheim's statement that "it is impossible to conceive how the stage which a civilization has reached at a given moment could be the determining cause of the subsequent stage. The stages that humanity successively traverses do not engender one another." Such an argument seems particularly appropriate in the second half of the twentieth century. Our contemporary Western civilization is not only a different phase, it is probably a different experience, and what is called modernity separates us irrevocably from the past. Long ago, in 1905, the French writer Charles Péguy remarked that "the little culture that exists in this modern world is itself essentially modern." He went on to say that "it is that much more mortal, that much more exposed to death because it is less profound, less ingrained in the heart of man." Péguy's first statement is undoubtedly true. His second is impossible to evaluate and is similar to many other seemingly profound but actually quite meaningless descriptions of our cultural situation. We often hear that we are now living in a mass age. If what is meant here is that the age-old and traditional distinctions between people have broken down, that our political and social institutions are being forced to accustom themselves to the demands of vast numbers of people, that new cultural forms are being created in order to fill the needs of people who have historically been passive, if not dumb, participants — then we are indeed in a mass age. But we have no models that can indicate what the effect of this will be, and we are ill-served by those who make dire predictions based upon an examination of a past that has little relevance.

It is convenient for us to divide our history into stages. That part of our history that began roughly in the eighteenth century probably ended in the middle of the twentieth. The past is, of course, still with us, and as Samuel Beckett, one of the West's most important contemporary playwrights, put it: "Yesterday is not a milestone that has been passed, but a daystone on the beaten track of the years, an irremediable part of us, within us, heavy and dangerous." But the new conditions of our civilization separate us from what has gone before in a way that is strikingly different. Never has a civilization before been world-wide and thus vulnerable to influences and activities in every part of the world. Never has a civilization so largely mastered nature and thus destroyed any mystical connection that might hold man to his surroundings. Never has a civilization so taken to its heart the belief in the legitimacy of human betterment. The citizen of Western civilization is a new type of individual, a new type of human personality, freed from tribal and geographical restraints, and with the possibility of being truly intellectually free. It is a sometimes forgotten fact, and one whose implications are impossible to predict, that women in contemporary Western civilization are the first to be biologically and culturally freed, and with that freedom a previously muted one-half of the human race will certainly play a dynamic and revolutionary role in the future. Western man is without caste or class alignments, without a serious regard for ceremonial functions, without dogma, and without transcendentally oriented assignments. All this is new, frightening, and challenging.

In 1940 Winston Churchill, in the face of disaster, became Prime Minister of Great Britain. Churchill was a man of another time, a time that has disappeared. Yet he had a sense of the living reality, and he expressed this in one of the first speeches he made to Parliament on assuming office. "It is not given to human beings," he said, "happily for them, for otherwise life would be intolerable, to foresee or to predict to any large extent the unfolding course of events. . . . History with its flickering lamp stumbles along the trail of the past, trying to reconstruct its scenes, to revive its echoes, and kindle with pale gleams the passions of former days." And then Churchill asked the rhetorical question: "What is the worth of all this?" He implied that there is little to be gained as a practical guide by attempting to look to the past for direction. What then is to be done? Churchill made no appeal to religion, or to nationalism, or to progress. His answer was personal. "The only guide to a man," he continued, "is his conscience; the only shield, because we are so often mocked by the failure of our hopes and the upsetting of our calculations; but with this shield, however the fates may play, we march always in the ranks of honour."

The attitudes of three perceptive commentators illustrate individual responses to our present condition. The Frenchman André Malraux has been a man of action and a man of thought and has participated in many of the important historical occurrences of the century. The Russian Boris Pasternak was a powerful voice from the rim of the Western world that spoke to our hopes and fears. Albert Camus was perhaps the most popular and influential of those who at the halfway point of the century attempted to make sense of Western man and his circumstances.

André Malraux

On the American frontier in the nineteenth century there was a well-known phrase used to describe a man who had looked further and had gone farther than others. It was said that he had seen the elephant. In the twentieth century such a description could be applied to the Frenchman André Malraux. He has been a political activist, a perceptive world traveller, a gifted novelist, and a stimulating art critic. He has participated in wars and revolutions, has explored the jungles of Cambodia and the deserts of the Near East, has fought with the Communists and against them. Malraux has been a man of action who has attempted to intellectualize his experiences, and the titles of his books — *The Temptation of the West* (1926), *The Conquerors* (1928), *The Royal Way* (1930), *Man's Fate* (1933), *Days of Wrath* (1935), *Man's Hope* (1937), *The Voices of Silence* (1951) — indicate what it has been like to live in our times.

André Malraux was born in Paris in 1901. He was too young to participate in World War I, but he exhibited the intellectual restlessness so characteristic of the Western world in the postwar years. During the nineteen-twenties many Americans fled their own country and sought the excitement of Europe. For Malraux, however, Europe itself was what he called "the constellation of despair," "a charnel-house of dead values," a place where two voices competed with each other: "One sang the glory of God; the other questioned it in hollow tones." In his first important book, *The Temptation of the West*, Malraux stressed the emptiness of European civilization. "Europe, great cemetery where only dead conquerors sleep, whose sadness is deepened by the pride taken in their illustrious names — you leave me with only a naked horizon and the mirror of solitude's old master, despair."

Disillusioned with Western society, Malraux turned from Europe to Asia, and his novels present us with a rich interpretation of twentieth-century Europeans in the Far East. His fictional characters are, however, not military or bureaucratic imperialists, but men driven by "the demons of action." Some have gone to the East in search of wealth, some to lose themselves in the darkness of Asian eroticism, and some to participate in the national awakening of China. But all are determined to assert themselves in a way denied them in Europe. In *The Conquerors* Pierre Garine sees in the Chinese Communist revolutionary movement an opportunity to "tie oneself to a great action of some kind, not to let go of it, to be haunted and intoxicated by it." In *The Royal Way* Perken is obsessed by the idea of creating an empire in southeast Asia where he will have unlimited power and unlimited freedom of action. In *The Walnut Trees of Altenburg* Vincent Berger becomes involved in a grandiose effort to create a new Turkish empire, a "union of all Turks throughout Central Asia from Adrianople to the Chinese Oasis on the Silk Trade Route." As Berger writes of his undertakings: "It was mixed up with the need to get away from Europe, the lure of history, the fanatical desire to leave some scar on the face of the earth, the attraction of a scheme to which he had contributed not a few of the fine points, the comradeship of war, friendship."

Malraux made his first trip to Asia in 1923 in search of some ruined temples in what was then French Indochina. The facts of this and many of his subsequent activities are somewhat in dispute, for Malraux has been reticent about commenting upon his personal life. But he did make his way through the Cambodian jungle and did discover some Khmer temples. He was accused of the theft of statuary by the French colonial administration and was sentenced to three years' imprisonment. The case against him was dismissed, and he was released. He returned to Paris, but in 1925 went again to Indochina, where he became involved in support of a native liberation movement. Within a short time he was in China and was at least an observer and may have been a participant in the revolutionary uprisings in Canton and Shanghai. In 1928 he returned to France, and with the exception of some brief visits to Japan, India, Iran, and the Yemen desert, his days as a European adventurer in Asia were over.

Malraux had not spent a great deal of time in the East, but his experiences there left their mark upon his work and upon his life. As he himself once said, "it is my obsession with other civilizations that has given my own civilization and probably my life their special accent." The going out to Asia had been a traumatic episode. H. Stuart Hughes remarks that Malraux's early writings illustrate "the cultural shock — which hit Europeans when they realized that their own values depended on a sense of history which was unique to their culture and which barred them from the idea-world of the timeless cultures of the East." The answers for which Western men searched could not be wrung from the jungles, the cities, or the wise men of Asia. Instead, the European was destroyed by the East and was left with only his erotic illusions, his pathetic mementoes, and his failures. In *The Conquerors* Garine conquers nothing and wears himself out in his pursuit of action. In *The Royal Way* the jungle becomes "a vast mirror of emptiness," where Perken's dream of empire ends in defeat and death. In *Man's Fate* Ferral's plans for a great economic enterprise that will give him wealth and power come to nothing, and in *The Walnut Trees of Altenburg* Vincent Berger is almost beaten to death by an Islamic madman.

So André Malraux returned to Europe and confronted the history that he had hoped to escape. The consideration of the problem of "one man and his destiny" would now be carried out in Western surroundings, among Western men. Certainly Malraux is referring to his own experience when in *The Walnut Trees of Altenburg* Vincent Berger, possessed still by the idea of a great Turkish empire, begins to dream of Europe. "Oh for the green of Europe! Trains whistling in the night, the rattle and clatter of late cabs." When Berger returns to France he is struck by the "infinite possibilities of human life," by a sense of "a poignant liberty." As he enters Marseilles harbor he is conscious of the "agonizing sense of freedom," and as he watched "the shadows glide in the faint odor of cigarettes and absinthe," he "suddenly felt delivered."

In the nineteen-thirties Malraux wrote novels, made speeches, signed manifestoes, participated in mass meetings, and fought against the rising threat of fascism. His novel *Days of Wrath* was the first important French report on the new German prison camps. Two days after the Spanish Civil War began in 1936 he was in Spain to take part in the struggle against Franco. He was one of the founders of the World League against Anti-Semitism and a member of the International Committee To Aid Victims of Hitler's Fascism. In 1940 he volunteered as a private in the French tank corps and in June was captured by the Germans. He escaped later in the year and soon thereafter joined the French underground resistance movement. In the spring of 1944 he was again captured but was freed when Paris was liberated. In 1945 he became Minister of Information in General Charles de Gaulle's provisional government but left this post when de Gaulle withdrew from politics. He returned to political life in 1958 as Minister of Information and then as Minister for Cultural Affairs in the Fifth French Republic following de Gaulle's coming to power in that year. His last novel, *The Walnut Trees of Altenburg*, was published in 1943. After World War II he published various studies on art, the most important of which were *Saturn, An Essay on Goya* (1950), *The Psychology of Art* (1947-1950), *The Voices of Silence* (1951), and *The Metamorphosis of the Gods* (1957).

Malraux's writing reflects the violence of the world in which he has lived. He portrays men with nails driven through their shoulders, heads with mouths cut from ear to ear, prisoners burned alive in locomotive boilers. Knives are thrust into flesh, bodies are beaten into pulp, and gassed soldiers cough up their lungs. For many readers the most dramatic and even memorable episodes from his work are those that show his characters confronting pain and death: Perken in *The Royal Way* dying of his infected leg and in his final moment saying, "There is no death . . . There is only I . . . I . . . who am dying"; Katow in *Man's Fate*, slowed by his wounds, limping toward his end; Vincent Berger in *The Walnut Trees of Altenburg* realizing that he has breathed the fatal gas and filled with "a forlorn hatred against everything that had prevented him from being happy."

But Malraux's novels are more than mere adventure stories, full of blood and slaughter. His principal characters are intellectuals, and his writing is heavy with historical speculation. From his first novels to his great books on art, in his actions and his comments, Malraux has concerned himself with the problem of how Western man can make sense of his historical predicament. He has stressed the most important questions of his time. How do we escape our overwhelming feeling of historical and individual absurdity? What is the meaning of death in our civilization? How do we satisfy our longing for some form of fraternity? How do we carry on what he calls our "struggle against humiliation"?

For Malraux, these problems have taken on a new dimension in the twentieth century. He writes that "every day the incapacity of modern civilization for giving form to any values becomes more apparent." The Western mind "desires to construct a plan of the universe and give it an intelligible form, that is, to establish between the unknown and the known a relation capable of bringing to light things that have been obscure." Western man's history encourages him to believe that he can dominate his surroundings and enforce his desire upon the world. Yet the very world that the Westerner has created has brought about his own alienation, and each man is locked in solitude. The ties that hold men together and thus explain their common situation have snapped, and "our civilization is the first not to know the communion, be it sentimental or metaphysical, that links man to his neighbor, to all forms of suffering, all forms of life."

Perhaps the most dramatic presentation of this theme of isolation and alienation appears in *The Walnut Trees of Altenburg* in the discussion of European intellectuals held at an old abbey. A group of men have gathered to debate the question: "Is there something given upon which we can base the notion of man?" The discussion is dominated by one of Malraux's great fictional creations, the anthropologist Möllberg, who has devoted a great part of his adult life to the study of Africa and has attempted to impose upon the world an interpretation that would fit man into his surroundings. But he has been defeated by Africa, "the succession without end of days under the dusty firmament of Libya or the heavy, gray sky of the Congo, the tracks of invisible animals converging toward the water-holes, the migration of famished dogs under the empty sky, the hour when all thought becomes weariness, the gloomy thrust of giant trees in prehistoric boredom. . . ." His manuscript, entitled "Civilization as Conquest and Destiny," has been scattered by the African winds, and the pages "are hanging from the lower branches of various types of trees from the Sahara to Zanzibar."

As a result of his experiences, Möllberg has returned to Europe convinced that there is no meaning to the human enterprise and that the life of man is as insignificant as that of termites. Men cannot communicate their experience to each other or from one cultural setting to another. Basically, "man is a chance element, and fundamentally speaking, the world consists of oblivion." According to Möllberg, "there's no better way of concentrating on man than looking at an ant-hill." Or, as he puts it in another way, the idea of "man is a myth, an intellectual's dream about peasants." He sums up his argument with a refutation of the value of any speculation about the meaning of human history. "The less men partake of their civilization, the more they resemble each other. . . . But the less they partake of it, the more they fade away. The permanence of man can be conceived, but it is a permanence in nothingness."

Möllberg's argument reduces Western civilization to a meaningless historical spasm. Moreover, Malraux had in his previous work often seemed to agree with Möllberg. In *The Temptation of the West* he wrote: "More or less distinct, the idea of the impossibility of grasping any reality whatsoever dominates Europe." Garine, in *The Conquerors*, says, "I don't think of society as evil — and thus capable of improvement — but as absurd." In 1927, in an essay entitled "On European Youth," Malraux stated: "Our epoch . . . does not dare reveal the core of its thought, which is nihilistic, destructive, fundamentally negative."

Yet from the early nineteen-thirties there was in Malraux's writing a suggestion that while Möllberg's contention that life is meaningless cannot be refuted by rational argument, it is wrong. In *The Walnut Trees of Altenburg*, the actions and thoughts of Vincent Berger are set against those of Möllberg. Berger believes that the basic aspects of human experience are "mysteries that cannot be elucidated but only revealed," and when Möllberg insists that the permanence of man is a permanence in nothing, Berger answers softly: "Or in the fundamental?" What Berger and his son a generation later propose is a concept of man as a creature struggling against chaos and a crushing destiny and in that struggle showing man's "age-old familiarity with misfortune" and his equally "age-old ingenuity, his secret faith in endurance, however crammed with catastrophes, the same faith perhaps as the cavemen used to have in the face of famine." Men in the twentieth century know what their lives are. "We know that we did not choose to be born and that we did not choose to die; that we did not choose our parents; that we can do nothing about the passage of time; that between us and universal life there is a sort of gulf. When I say that every man is deeply conscious of the existence of destiny, I mean he is conscious, and almost always tragically so — at least at certain moments — of the world's independence of him." But men do not need to submit to the fatality of existence. And in their struggle against their animal destiny, they use "human means to burst the human condition" and thus carry out a "humanization of the world." The power of human creation, of the interpretation of experience, transcends the material of life. "The greatest mystery is not that we have been flung at random among the profusion of matter and that of the stars. It is that in this prison we have drawn from within ourselves images powerful enough to deny our nothingness."

This refutation of Möllberg is given dramatic form in what is often regarded as the most important part of the novel, and perhaps of all Malraux's works. During World War I Vincent Berger, as a German officer, participates in the first attempt to use poison gas against the Russian army on the eastern front. The gas is launched, and then the German soldiers attack. Suddenly those remaining behind in the trenches see the German soldiers returning across the battlefield, each one carrying a stricken Russian on his back. The horror and inhumanity of the new weapon had been too much, and a soldier protests that "man was not born to moulder." The Russians are no longer enemies but only common victims of an inhuman force. Berger realizes that in this act of simple men he has received an answer to Möllberg's pessimistic analysis. He thinks again of his home: "Right up to the shining, blue sky climbing slope with its now renewed smell of trees, the smell of box and balsam still dripping from the shower. . . . He was standing before the great copse of walnut trees." He confronts his destiny. He hurries out and picks up a gassed Russian and in this fatal act asserts his liberty and his choice. He has, at the crucial moment, made "the discovery of a simple sacred secret."

With the publication of *The Walnut Trees of Altenburg* Malraux concluded his career as a novelist. And in looking at the work of almost twenty years it is possible to see that Malraux had considered and rejected most of the common ways of describing Western civilization. To interpret that civilization historically is self-defeating, for "every historical attempt to render the past intelligible makes of it an evolution or a fatality, charged with hope or death for those to whom the explanation is addressed." History is continually saying that certain things had to happen or should have happened, and confuses what is only part of man with the whole. In *Man's Hope* Malraux has a character say that "man engages only a small part of himself in an action, and the more the action claims to be total, the smaller is the part of man engaged."

Malraux also rejects politics as an explanation of the human situation. Western politics is not "a reality" but only "a sentiment," and political leaders continue to think in terms of "ourselves and the enemy" and not in terms of "ourselves and the destiny of the world." Politics ultimately becomes only a matter of gestures. Political activity leads only to confusion, and because political conflicts can never be resolved, man's sense of fraternity is threatened. Politically motivated men are basically men of action who wish to do something. The problem for Malraux, however, is to be something. And in this quest politics is irrelevant.

Nor will Malraux accept the argument that science can provide any understanding of the deeper levels of experience. We do not reach a knowledge of man by "scratching" in search of "secrets." As Vincent Berger says, "It's our old struggle against the devil . . . which makes us confuse our knowledge of men with our knowledge of his secrets." Freedom and fraternity cannot be explained by scientific experimentation, and scientific knowledge is always questionable because "we can hardly ever foresee the really important actions of those nearest to us." What then does express our civilization? What supports any idea of fraternity and Malraux's belief that "we must have a world we can understand"? Malraux's answer is "breathless, oracular, and elliptical," and is given in full form in the large, rambling, turgid volumes on art that he wrote in the late nineteen-forties and in the nineteen-fifties. These books are full of fantastic insights and plagued by irritating obscurities and redundancies. But in them he does develop what can be called a cultural interpretation of Western civilization. For Malraux the most important evidence that life has meaning, that men can transform fate into freedom, is art. Art is "a symbol that expresses man's collective and eternal struggle to transcend the conditions of his servitude." Through art man overcomes his sense of powerlessness and subjects the world to his design. And through his interpretation he establishes a relationship with other men and escapes isolation. In a unique and awesome way art allows men to "possess" the pain and emptiness and horror of their lives. Art dominates "its subject-matter, instead of being dominated by it," and "every masterpiece . . . tells of a human victory over the blind force of destiny. . . ." Malraux illustrates his point when he writes that "life is a tale told by an idiot, full of sound and fury, signifying nothing. But *Macbeth* signifies something." Shakespeare, by imposing his genius upon the raw material of life, has brought order and significance out of chaos.

Art is the style of a civilization, the single great creative effort that tells us the most about man's attempts to understand his life and his society. It is an "invincible dialogue with the past and the future," and points toward the new world that is always in the making while retaining the memory of the past that is being destroyed. It frees man, and it is a way whereby one can live in the absurd without accepting the absurd. In *The Voices of Silence* Malraux gives a dramatic example of how art rectifies the fatality and destiny of history and "humanizes" the world. He writes of the destruction of Germany as World War II ended, and how the creative artist is the only one who can interpret the disaster. "In the past of art, Sumer, Thebes, Nineveh, and Palenque have come to mean to us only the hymns arising from their abysmal darkness; the sordid annals of Byzantium are effaced by the majesty of Christ Pantocrator, the dust and squalor of the steppes by the gold plaques, the lazar houses of the Middle Ages by the Pietàs. I saw the fetishes of the Nuremberg Museum justify their age-old leer as they gazed down at the last wisps of smoke curling up from the ruins, through which a girl on a bicycle, carrying a sheaf of lilac, steered an erratic course amid the singing Negro truck drivers; yet had there been an art of the prison-camp incinerators, only that day extinguished, it would have shown us not the murderers, but the martyrs."

Malraux's cultural interpretation is a rich and powerful one. It is also easy to criticize. Malraux has been justifiably called an elitist, and his indifference to the day-to-day, at times squalid but necessary political, economic, and organizational activities that make up so much of our lives is distasteful. Art is certainly a powerful, perhaps the most powerful, expression of a civilization. But, in Malraux's interpretation, individual human beings are ignored in a scheme that stresses the creative efforts of society, and men live and die primarily to furnish the materials through which the artist may achieve a "higher degree of proud awareness." Malraux himself has written that "we know that our peace is as vulnerable as the preceding ones, that democracy carries in it capitalism and totalitarian police, that science and progress permit atomic bombs, that reason fails to give an account of man." With all this one can only agree. Yet Malraux implies that there is little we can do about these dangers. Freedom and fraternity, those two great elements of Malraux's thinking, are really reserved only for a few men with the multitude to follow dumbly after.

Yet Malraux has something of value to say to us. We do tend to become enamoured with a purely descriptive interpretation of ourselves, and we assume that we can define our lives and our civilization by careful measurements and what are often superficial political and historical judgments. We show little talent for the theme of "action and art, history and vision, involvement and transcendence." Malraux has argued that "the European heritage is tragic humanism," and if he is correct, most present-day interpretations have been far from the point. Malraux does show us one way whereby a man may, in Kyo's words in *Man's Fate*, "conquer without betraying himself," whereby we may "measure all things by the duration and intensity of a single human life." Art does escape the national, linguistic, and institutional barriers that separate men from each other. In 1948 Malraux said: "There are irreducible political conflicts; but it is absolutely false to say that cultural conflicts are irreducible by definition." The facts of the past and even the present are quickly forgotten; it is the creative act that is permanent. Art, architecture, literature — these activities catch the heartbeat of a civilization, resolve the confusion of contradictory facts, and crystallize the best hopes and aspirations. "A culture survives," Malraux writes, "not because of what it actually was; it interests us in virtue of the notion of man that it describes or of the virtues it transmits. . . ." Put simply, our dreams of what our civilization is may be more important than the reality of our experience. The Western idea of freedom, for example, may be more meaningful than the actual practice of that freedom. Our vision of order and our sense of reality may be more significant than the order and reality that exists. Malraux's definition is not complete, but it is worth pondering.

Boris Pasternak

In November, 1957, the translation of a Russian novel was published in Italy. Entitled *Doctor Zhivago*, the book was an immediate international success, and the Italian edition was followed by translations published in Germany, England, the United States, France, Sweden, and many other countries. The author of *Doctor Zhivago* was Boris Pasternak, a sixty-seven-year-old poet whose previous writings had been known only to a small group of specialists in Russian literature. The appearance of the novel made Pasternak a world-famous figure and also involved him in an acrimonious controversy within Russia that lasted until his death in 1960. In 1958 Pasternak was awarded the Nobel Prize for Literature. Violent opposition by Russian officials to *Doctor Zhivago*, however, forced Pasternak to refuse the award, and the greatest Russian novel of the twentieth century has not yet been published in the Soviet Union.

Boris Pasternak was born in Moscow in 1890, and he grew up in a world that now seems eons away from us. His family belonged to that brilliant circle of Russian intellectuals who combined the best of both West European and Russian cultures. His father, Leonid Pasternak, was an accomplished artist, the friend of Sergei Rachmaninoff, Alexander Scriabin, and Anton Rubinstein, and the painter of their portraits. Another friend was Leo Tolstoy, whose "spirit pervaded our whole house." One of Boris' early memories was of an evening concert given by his mother, a well-known musician, in the family home. "The room was in a cloud of smoke. The candles blinked as if the smoke hurt their eyes. They played glittering scales of light on the polished mahogany of the violin and the 'cello. The piano was black and so were the suits of the men. The necks and shoulders of the ladies rose out of their low-cut dresses like flowers out of a festal bouquet. The smoke rings blended with the grey hair of two or three elderly people."

As a boy and as a young man, Boris Pasternak participated in a cosmopolitan atmosphere. When he was sixteen he visited Berlin with his parents and later wrote of this experience: "I settled down quickly in Berlin, went for walks through its endless streets, spoke German with an imitation Berlin accent, breathed a mixture of the smoke of the steam engines, the smell of the gas lamps and beer froth, and I listened to Wagner." In 1909 he began the study of law at Moscow University, later changing to the study of philosophy. In 1912 he attended the University of Marburg in Germany for a term and then made a trip to Italy. By this time he had also become interested in literature and was associated with several of the literary groups then blooming in Russia. In 1914 his first volume of poems entitled *A Twin in the Clouds* was published.

The First World War and the triumph of the Bolsheviks in Russia brought an end to the world that Boris Pasternak had known. Large numbers of the Russian intelligentsia emigrated, and increasingly throughout the nineteen-twenties, nineteen-thirties, and nineteen-forties those brilliant, creative Russians associated with Pasternak's early life fell upon evil days. Ivan Bunin, Vladislav Khodasevich, and many others died in exile. Alexander Blok died from anemia and starvation in 1921, and in that same year Nikolai Gumilev was shot for counter-revolutionary activity. Sergei Esenin, Vladimir Mayakovsky, and Marina Tsvetaeva committed suicide. Osip Mandelshtam was arrested and disappeared, apparently starving to death in a prison camp. A dull terror gradually settled over Russia, and everything was forced into the rigid pattern of political orthodoxy. As a young Russian was to write in the late nineteen-fifties: "So that prisons should vanish forever, we built new prisons. So that all frontiers should fall, we surrounded ourselves with a Chinese wall. So that work should become a rest and a pleasure, we introduced forced labor. So that not one drop of blood be shed any more, we killed and killed and killed."

But Pasternak survived. His second volume of poetry, *Above the Barriers*, was published in 1917. This was followed by *My Sister, Life* (1922), *Themes and Variations* (1923), *The Year 1905* and *Lieutenant Schmidt* (1927), an autobiographical prose work *Safe Conduct* (1931), and another volume of poems *Second Birth* (1932). Then for many years Pasternak published no more original work, although he did his highly praised translations of Goethe, Schiller, Shelley, and Shakespeare. He was subjected to intense criticism by Soviet officials and was effectively silenced. In his *Sketch for an Autobiography*, written in 1956, Pasternak made only a general but illuminating comment at the end of the volume on what life was like at this time. "I have now come to the end of my autobiographical sketch. To continue would be exceedingly difficult. . . . One would have to write about it in a way to make the heart stop beating and the hair stand on end." Yet he did not disgrace himself, and as the critic and poet Robert Conquest has said, Pasternak had "an immense moral toughness, an ability to sit it out year after year in the face of the overwhelming pressures of the vast and insistent machinery of power."

Pasternak began writing what was to become *Doctor Zhivago* at the end of World War II in 1945. He believed that a new chapter in the human adventure was beginning and that a new vision of life must come from the catastrophic events of the first half of the twentieth century. As he wrote. "A war is not a game of chess. It cannot simply end with the victory of white over black. Something new must come out of it. So many sacrifices cannot have been in vain." Pasternak apparently felt a personal responsibility to bear witness to the tragedy of modern life and to cast up an interpretation of what had happened since he had been a boy in the eighteen-nineties. "So then I said to myself, you must stand up straight before your own name. It seemed to me that I first had to earn the name I had won, not by poetry, but by prose, by something that might well cost more labor, more effort, more time, and whatever else." Writing on the novel stopped in 1950 when the paranoid suspicions of Stalin made it appear unlikely that any literature save that acceptable to the party line would be published. In 1953, after Stalin's death, Pasternak again took up his task, and the book was finished in 1955. He believed that he had succeeded in his efforts to portray what he called the "realities and truths of naked time." He once said to a questioner: "You have the right to ask me whether I believe what I have written. My answer is yes, I have borne witness as an artist; I have written about the times I lived through." Or as he stated in terms that he certainly hoped would apply to himself: "The significant writer of his epoch (and I want no other besides him) is a revelation, a representation of the unknown, unrepeatable uniqueness of living reality. What else is originality if not a cultural event having its source in the world's absolute reality?"

Doctor Zhivago is set against the background of the First World War and the Russian Revolution. The central character is a young Russian physician, Zhivago, a product of the brilliant intellectual and cultural world of prerevolutionary Russia, who finds himself a participant in and an observer of the events of the first three decades of the twentieth century. He serves in the war, returns to Moscow in the early days of the revolution, and after a period flees with his family to the Russian countryside in order to survive. Here he is separated from his family, which ultimately leaves Russia, is forced to join a partisan band during the Russian civil war, and finally returns to Moscow, where one day on a crowded streetcar he has a heart attack and dies. Throughout the novel there is hunger, murder, suffering, and the confusion and chaos of events that defy explanation or understanding. The times were those when, as Pasternak wrote, "the whole human way of life is being destroyed and ruined. All that's left is the naked human soul stripped to the last shred, for which nothing has changed because it is always cold and shivering and reaching out to its nearest neighbor, as cold and lonely as itself."

Of course, *Doctor Zhivago* is more than a historical novel. It is a great love story, complete with the wracking pain of an intense emotion aroused by the affection of a man for a woman, and speaking to "the riddle of life, the riddle of death, the enchantment of genius, the enchantment of beauty." It is also a story of the historical controversy between Zhivago and Antipov-Strelnikov. Here the names of the two characters are indicative. Zhivago comes from the Russian word "life," "live," and Strelnikov from the Russian word "cannonade," "volleying," "shooting" — by inference one who is an activist, one prepared to set himself as the judge of mankind and who dreams of "drawing his sword in defense of life and so of avenging it." As Zhivago believes in the sacredness of life and in the self-renewing and self-transforming of existence, so Strelnikov is prepared to force humanity into the measure of some doctrine that will at one stroke abolish all evils, overcome all obstacles, and achieve a great historical breakthrough to absolute justice. Most important of all, perhaps, *Doctor Zhivago* is a story of a creative personality, of a man who develops a sublime vision of life and casts up this vision for all to see.

Although events related in *Doctor Zhivago* took place half a century ago, the novel speaks more to the future than it does to the past. And it is this focus upon the future condition of Russians and non-Russians alike that converts *Doctor Zhivago* into a piece of world literature, a cultural and historical commentary that addresses itself to Americans, Englishmen, Germans, Frenchmen, and others as well as to Russians. Pasternak himself was turned toward the future not the past. In 1958, he said: "On the whole, in our age, people are having a new attitude toward life. During the nineteenth century it was the bourgeoisie who ruled. Mankind sought security in money, land, and things. Today mankind has realized that there is no security in property. This applies not only to Russians. In this era of world wars, in this atomic age, the values of things change in the human conception. We have learned that we are the guests of existence, travellers between two stations. We must discover security within ourselves. During our short span of life we must find our own insights into our relationships with the existence in which we participate so briefly. Otherwise, we cannot live! This means, as I see it, a departure from the materialistic view of the 19th century. It means a reawakening of the spiritual world, of our inner life — of religion. I don't mean religion as a dogma or as a church, but as a vital feeling. Do you understand what I mean?"

Boris Pasternak was no mystic. He wrote, "I have become a realist, and for that I am grateful." But the reality of which he spoke was not a careful and mechanical description of static order, an arithmetic sum of actions and circumstances. In a letter written in 1959 to the English poet Stephen Spender, Pasternak pointed out that in the nineteenth century reality was identified with "the incontestable doctrine of causality, the belief that objectivity was determined and ruled by an iron chain of causes and effects, that all appearances of the moral and material world were subordinate to the law of sequels and retributions." Such a view of reality implied a predictability and assumed that it was possible to observe the passage of time and the sequence of events as a series of separate, almost photographic, images, each distinct and leading from one to another in what would appear to be a natural order. In Pasternak's opinion this was a cramped and erroneous interpretation. Rather, he believed that we should regard "nature and universe themselves not as a picture made or fastened on an immovable wall, but as a sort of painted canvas roof or curtain in the air, incessantly pulled and blown and flapped by an immaterial unknown and unknowable wind." From this point of view reality was a "developing, passing by, rolling and rushing," and we must look at our lives and our history "as if reality itself had freedom and choice and was composing itself out of numberless variants and versions." Only in this way could we avoid seeing things as "a cardboard-opera situation," only in this manner could we catch a sense of what was real, of what Pasternak called "the ground-rhythm of an epoch."

As a young man and as an old, Pasternak in his writing protested against the staleness and the sterility of our usual view of ourselves and our experience. Our vision of our possibilities has been warped by slogans, by empty social and political concepts, by a lack of understanding of and feeling for the human situation. "I also from my earliest years," Pasternak wrote, "have been struck by the observation that existence was more original, extraordinary, and inexplicable than any of its separate astonishing incidents and facts. . . ." Pasternak was convinced that the twentieth century had seen the end of one historical epoch and the birth of another and that the challenge of the new times must be grasped. Too often our view of our history consisted of nothing but "immature fantasies," daydreams based upon "school-boy escapades." Again and again Pasternak stated his belief that there was little of the old intellectual furniture of the past that could be dragged into the last half of the twentieth century. He respected the past and knew well his connection with it. But what was now over was over. "The proclamations, the tumult, the excitement are over. Now something else is growing, something new. It is growing imperceptibly and quietly, as the grass grows. It is growing as fruit does, and it is growing in the young. The essential thing in this epoch is that a new freedom is being born." In 1958, in a letter, Pasternak wrote that "a completely new era is beginning, with new tasks and new demands on the heart and on human dignity, a silent age which will never be proclaimed and allowed voice but will grow more real every day without our noticing it." To superimpose an old-fashioned interpretation upon the fluidity of the times was to insure disaster. In January, 1960, a little over four months before his death, Pasternak stated: "I am weary of this notion of faithfulness to a point of view at all cost. Life around us is ever-changing, and I believe that one should try to change one's slant accordingly — at least once every ten years. The great heroic devotion to one point of view is alien to me — it is a lack of humility."

When in 1956 Russian editors rejected *Doctor Zhivago* for publication, they stated that after reading the manuscript their thoughts were "alarming and grave." They wrote: "The spirit of your novel is the spirit of nonacceptance of the socialist revolution." Basically the instincts of the editors were sound. Pasternak's novel was a statement of nonacceptance of any all-embracing, all-answering doctrine that was hostile to the individual and claimed to speak for man rather than allowing him to speak for himself. In *Doctor Zhivago* Pasternak has a character say: "Every herd is a refuge of mediocrity, regardless of whether it claims allegiance to Solovyev, Kant, or Marx. Only lone individuals seek the truth, and they break with all those who do not value it highly enough. Is there anything on earth that deserves allegiance? Such things are few indeed." Pasternak was a great subversive, a great opponent of all those who believe that man can be manipulated and molded into any desired shape. He threatened all those who have an inbred hostility toward the undetermined, the uncertain, the original. In a speech of 1931, Pasternak had said: "The times exist for man, not man for the times."

Pasternak had a vision of freedom as an end in itself and a belief that the creative springs of mankind would not dry up. He was also convinced that twentieth-century man had only dimly grasped the implications of this freedom and this creativity. Pasternak did not scorn the machinery of life. What he did argue was that beyond the organization, the planning, the progress, there still was "The matter nearest to creation — The themes of freedom, life, and fate." He once said that if you wished to know what life was you must "multiply hell by paradise," and he feared that the unique quality of living in the twentieth century was slipping away from us. We tend to look outside ourselves, and Pasternak put this thought in one of his finest stanzas:

> It is not some upheaval or uprising
> Can lead us to the new life we desire —
> But open truth and magnanimity
> And the storms within a soul afire.

Or, as he wrote:

> Of life, not as pretenders live —
> In emptiness, with many fears,
> But give your heart to vast horizons
> And hear the call of future years.

Albert Camus

The 1957 Nobel Prize for Literature was awarded to the French writer Albert Camus. The selection was a popular one, although Camus himself spoke of his "bewilderment" and of "a kind of panic" when he was notified of the honor. At age forty-four he was the second youngest man ever to have received the prize. The official citation read that Camus was the recipient of the award because of "his important literary production which with clear-sighted earnestness illuminates the problems of the human conscience of our times." In his speech accepting the prize, Camus referred to those "times," and in so doing he summed up what he believed was the history of his generation. He spoke of "more than twenty years of absolutely insane history," and of "blighted revolutions, misguided techniques, dead gods, and worn-out ideologies." He also said: "Probably every generation sees itself as charged with remaking the world. Mine, however, knows that it will not remake the world. But its task is perhaps even greater, for it consists of keeping the world from destroying itself." And he mentioned what he regarded as the burden carried by men of his day: "They have had to forge for themselves an art of living through times of catastrophe, in order to be reborn, and then to fight openly against the death-instinct that is at work in our time."

Camus was born into what he called "this century of fear" in 1913 in Mondovi, Algeria, then a part of France. His father, who had migrated from Alsace, was a laborer, and his mother was an illiterate woman who spoke with difficulty. Later in his life Camus remarked that an intellectual has an obligation to speak for those who cannot speak for themselves, and he wrote that he would achieve nothing until he placed "at the center" of his work "the admirable silence of a mother and the effort of a man to find some form of justice or love that would counter-balance that silence." Camus was a year old when his father was killed in World War I. The family moved to the city of Algiers, where Camus lived in near-poverty with his mother, his grandmother, his uncle, and his brother, and where his mother worked as a charwoman. His university career and his plans to become a teacher ended when it was discovered at the age of seventeen that he had tuberculosis. After a variety of occupational undertakings, he became a journalist. At the outbreak of World War II in 1939 he volunteered for the French army. He did not believe in war, but he was convinced that "one collaborates or one fights." He was, however, rejected because of ill health and spent the greater part of the next few years in Algeria. In 1942 he went to France where he was to live more or less permanently the rest of his life. He became a member of the French resistance movement and a writer for the resistance newspaper *Combat*. After the war he was an editor and then engaged in full-time writing. In January, 1960, he was killed in an automobile accident.

Camus has been regarded by many as the most significant moral and historical commentator in the Western world in the nineteen-forties and nineteen-fifties. His novels — *The Stranger* (1942), *The Plague* (1947), and *The Fall* (1956) — and his essays, the most important of which were published in books entitled *The Myth of Sisyphus* (1942), *The Rebel* (1951), and *Resistance, Rebellion, and Death* (1960), aroused widespread response. His intellectual honesty, his insights into the historical and philosophical dilemma of contemporary Western society, and his moral courage gave him a unique standing, particularly with the young, who discovered in him one of the few men of the previous generation with whom they could identify. Neither a foolish optimist nor a discouraged crank, Camus appeared as a clear-eyed and generous-spirited man who scorned humbug and complacency. He spoke directly about the world in which he was living and of the hopes and fears of his contemporaries. More than perhaps any other writer of his time he succeeded in describing what has been called "modern man and his torment, his sin and his grandeur."

One of the primary reasons for Camus' popularity was that his thought, action, and writing were individual responses to what he saw and experienced. He called things by their proper names, and he refused to substitute political and historical abstractions for the clearly recognized, everyday reality. To those weary of contorted philosophical explanations and cloudy historical interpretations, Camus' personal approach was refreshing. Hayden Carruth in his stimulating *After The Stranger* noted that Camus seemed a voice speaking from the ruin of the world and crying out: "No, no more. We have had our fill. No more fictive absolutes, no more dandyism and cruelty. Away with them!" Camus himself once wrote: "I can feel this heart inside me, and I conclude that it exists. I can touch this world, and I also conclude that it exists. All my knowledge ends at this point. The rest is hypothesis." There was the individual and the world, and the placing of abstractions of any kind between them was to distort reality. A sense of what is actually happening disappears, and men "forget the present for the future, the fate of humanity for the delusion of power, the misery of the slums for the mirage of the eternal city, ordinary justice for the empty promised land. They despair of personal freedom and dream of a strange freedom of the species. They reject solitary death and give the name of immortality to a vast collective agony. They no longer believe in the things that exist in the world and in living man."

What did Camus see as the rock-bottom reality from which there was no escape? Here is a question he put in one of his postwar essays: "Do you know that over a period of twenty-five years, between 1922 and 1947, 70 million Europeans — men, women, and children — have been uprooted, deported, and killed?" That was reality. "Just beyond Villeneuve," he writes in another essay, "opposite a grove of poplars, the truck stopped, the soldiers leaped to the ground and commanded the men to get out and go toward the woods. A first group of six left the truck and started toward the trees. The machine guns immediately cracked behind them and mowed them down. A second group followed, then a third. Those who were still breathing were put out of their pain by a final shot." That also was reality. "Foreign tanks, police, twenty-year-old girls hanged, committees of workers decapitated, scaffolds, writers deported and imprisoned, the lying press, camps, censorship, judges arrested, criminals legislating, and the scaffold again." Once more the reality. The concentration camps at Dachau and Buchenwald, the burning flesh of Hiroshima, the slave prisoners in Russia, the mutilation of Frenchmen by Algerians and Algerians by Frenchmen — these are the unadorned true experiences that cannot be obscured by any historical interpretation. Shortly before his death Camus wrote: "We have a right to think that truth with a capital letter is relative. But facts are facts. And whoever says that the sky is blue when it is gray is prostituting words and preparing the way for tyranny."

But Camus was not a writer who derived morbid satisfaction from listing the specific horrors of the world. The important thing was that, in spite of their staggering effects, individual and collective actions in the twentieth century did not reflect any discernible order or purpose. Experience was incoherent and incongruous, and all demands for clarity and understanding are denied. In brief, underlying the history of modern Western man was a basic absurdity. There was no ultimate meaning to our lives, no explanation for the presence of evil or pain or death. In *The Myth of Sisyphus* Camus gave a clear definition of what he understood by this absurd quality. "A world that can be explained even with bad reasons is a familiar world. But, on the other hand, in a universe suddenly divested of illusions and lights, man feels an alien, a stranger. His exile is without remedy since he is deprived of the memory of a lost home or the hope of a promised land. This divorce between man and his life, the actor and his setting, is properly the feeling of absurdity."

For Camus, the general absurdity of the world must be accepted. The world must be recognized for what it is, and "I continue to believe that this world has no ultimate meaning." But, as he wrote in 1938, "to assert the absurdity of life cannot be an end in itself, but only a beginning. . . . It is not the discovery that interests us, but the consequences and the rules of action that one draws from it." The question Camus posed was whether it was possible in an absurd world to discover a purpose for life. In September, 1945, in an article in the newspaper *Combat*, he put the problem in these words: "For the coexistence of a philosophy of negation and a positive morality illustrates the great problem that is painfully disturbing the whole epoch. In a word, it is a problem of civilization, and it is essential for us to know whether man, without the help either of the eternal or of rationalistic thought, can unaided create his own values." In 1946, in a speech at Columbia University in New York City, he spoke again along the same lines. We have learned, he said, "that we cannot accept any optimistic conception of existence, any happy ending whatsoever. But if we believe that optimism is silly, we also know that pessimism about the action of man among his fellows is cowardly."

Camus realized that a variety of interpretations could be drawn from the general absurdity of our condition, and he devoted a substantial part of his efforts to refuting what he regarded as erroneous conclusions. In particular he had life-long quarrels with two ideas that presented themselves as resolutions to the problems posed by the absurd. One of these quarrels was with any religious interpretation, or what he thought of as a form of supernatural consolation. The other was with the doctrine that history itself would provide an answer to our present dilemma as it unfolded in the future.

A religious explanation of the world rests upon a belief that what is inscrutable to men is part of a divine mystery and that our lack of under-standing is only the result of our ignorance and sin. The world's evil must be accepted, and we must resign ourselves to inexplicable pain and injustice. Camus choked on this interpretation. He could not reconcile himself to evil or resign himself to injustice. For him there was no salva-tion save in this world, and answers to the dilemma of the world must be provided in the here and now and not deferred to God's time and place. "Historical Christianity postpones to a point beyond the span of history the cure of evil and murder, which are nevertheless experienced within the span of history." As he put the argument in a ringing ques-tion: "Who would dare to assert that eternal happiness can compensate for a single moment's human suffering?" In *The Plague*, Dr. Rieux, cer-tainly speaking for the author, remarks that "until my dying day I shall refuse to love a scheme of things in which children are put to torture." Belief in a consolatory religion is only a way whereby one may use the excuse that God, not man, is responsible for the world. Then one may claim with sanctimonious hypocrisy that the poor will always be with us, that suffering is God's will, and that evil must be endured. In any argument between God and man, Camus chooses man. As the theme of *The Plague* might be expressed: "All I maintain is that on this earth there are pestilences and there are victims, and it's up to us, so far as possible, not to join forces with the pestilences."

But if the answer to our situation could not be found in the mystery of religion, neither could it be discovered in history. Camus was an outspo-ken opponent of what is called historicism — the belief that there is a historical current to men's affairs that tends toward some great future goal and that the pain, violence, and crime of the present may be excused because history will ultimately set things aright. The crimes of today are justified in light of a golden future, and "values are only to be found at the end of history. Until then there is no suitable criterion on which to base a judgment. One must act and live in terms of the future, and all morality becomes provisional." If one acts in the name of history, he is excused from all restraint, and a belief in a "golden age, postponed to the end of history. . . justifies everything." Present-day cities may be destroyed in the belief that better cities will be built, and present-day man may be sacrificed in the name of the perfect man of the future. Those who speak of the destiny of the nation, of the absolute validity of a political belief, of the unquestioned faith in a historical interpretation are all expressing a belief in historicism.

Camus regarded such attitudes as blasphemies, as interpretations that threatened the very existence of men. To rely upon history was a form of fatalism, and we "blindly embark down this tunnel" without knowing what we will confront at the end. Concepts such as justice, innocence, and liberty may be defined as one wishes. The result is "cynicism," "conformity and opportunism," "individual terror and state crime." In the name of history some men are given unlimited power over others, and individuals are molded to fit the demands of the historical task. "The sky is empty, the earth delivered into the hands of power without principles." Efficiency and strength become the only measures of success, and the stronger enforces his will upon the weaker. And, in spite of all its demands and its promises, historical philosophy never delivers. The goal is continually pushed further and further into the future, and the pressures upon men are continuous and unending.

In addition to his rejection of a religion of consolation or a blind faith in the values of history, Camus also opposed those who, ravaged by despair, had yielded to the temptations of nihilism. If one could believe in nothing, then nothing deserved belief, and there were many in the twentieth century who adopted the principle of "absolute rebellion, total insubordination, sabotage on principle." Dostoievsky's famous remark that "if God does not exist, everything is permitted" had been accepted as an invitation to abandon any kind of moral judgment and to act out of frenzy. In 1945, in his "Letters to a German Friend," Camus wrote of this condition of mind: "You never believed in the meaning of this world, and you therefore deduced the idea that everything was equivalent, and that good and evil could be defined according to one's wishes. You supposed that in the absence of any human or divine code the only values were those of the animal world — in other words, violence and cunning." In such a desert of amorality, each man became a law to himself, at once a potential victim and a potential executioner.

In place of nihilism, of a religious explanation, and of a faith in the historical future, Camus puts a human-centered, present-oriented program. He often expressed his attitude (he protested against calling it a philosophy) in simple, explosive statements. "The earth remains our first and last love." "There is only one original rule of life today. To learn to live and die, and, in order to be a man, to refuse to be a god." "Real generosity toward the future lies in giving all to the present." "When I come to look for what is fundamental in myself, I find a taste for happiness." "The world is beautiful, and outside it there is no salvation." "I loathe none but executioners." "Dreams change from individual to individual, but the reality of the world is common to us all." "I have a sense of the sacred and do not believe in a future life, that is all." In his novel *The Fall* appears an awesome statement of Camus' attitude: "I'm going to tell you a great secret, my friend. Don't wait for the last judgment. It's taking place every day."

There is a deceptive simplicity in statements such as these, and many object that there is little here but a form of literary moralizing. They protest that everyone would agree with what Camus is saying and that he is largely voicing a series of clichés. To such an argument the answer of Camus would surely be that everyone agrees and then acts to the contrary. It is this indifference to what should be the moral content of Western civilization that has brought us to what Camus calls "the death of freedom, the triumph of violence, and the enslavement of the mind." He once wrote two sentences that point up this discrepancy between what everyone says he believes and his actions. "That is why the era which cares to claim that it is the most rebellious that has ever existed only offers a choice of various types of conformity. The real passion of the twentieth century is servitude."

Camus is often thought of as the great modern rebel against the conditions of Western life. But it is important to understand what it was that he was rebelling against. Western civilization has consisted of political power, industrialization, technology, and organization. It has also consisted of the search for truth and freedom. Camus believed that in this century power and freedom often came into conflict, and that Western men were divided into those who gave primacy to one or the other. He expressed this difference in his "Letters to a German Friend": "For you Europe is an expanse encircled by seas and mountains, dotted with dams, gutted with mines, covered with harvests. . . . But for us Europe is the home of the spirit where for the last twenty centuries the most amazing adventure of the human spirit has been going on. It is the privileged arena in which Western man's struggle against the world, against the gods, against himself reached its climax." He once expressed the belief that the greater part of Western civilization consisted of destructive, repressive elements. However, there was a quarter-truth "called liberty. And liberty is the way, and the only way, of perfectibility. Without liberty heavy industry can be perfected, but not justice or truth." In 1956 he wrote: "The defects of the West are innumerable, its crimes and errors very real. But in the end let's not forget that we are the only ones who have the possibility of improvement and emancipation that lies in free genius."

One must, therefore, be a rebel against those forces in Western society that act against life and liberty. But this rebellion must not be based upon resentment or envy, or can it be an instinctual glorification of the passions. Nor is it the rebellion of the dandy who watches himself in the mirror while he performs. True rebellion combines courage and intelligence, and must be based upon a compassion for one's fellowmen, "without which the world is never anything but a vast solitude." It must always be on behalf of life but not in defiance of it. Such a rebellion is, at best, an unequal struggle, and in 1948 Camus said: "I have nothing but reasonable illusions as to the outcome of the battle. But I believe it must be fought." At his best, the rebel is one who says no, but whose refusal is not a renunciation.

Camus' thinking stresses a certain negative approach to the problems of Western civilization. He basically argued that it is impossible to know what the truth is. On the other hand, we can know what is false. We may not know what God is. But we do know that he is not man and he is not science or the organized political society. It is perhaps indicative that in *The Plague* Dr. Rieux does not argue so much on behalf of life but rather says that "I've never managed to get used to seeing people die." Camus himself once said that "if I feel so great a solidarity with so many students, for example, it is because we are all confronted with the same problem. . . ." In 1951 he scorned the description of himself as one of the masters of the young generation. "A master, already! But I don't claim to teach anybody! Whoever thinks this is mistaken. The problems confronting young people today are the same ones confronting me, that is all. And I am far from having solved them. I therefore do not think that I have any right to play the role you mention. . . . What are young people looking for? Certainties. I have not many to offer them. All I can say definitely is that there is a certain order of degradation which I shall always refuse. I think that this is something which they feel. Those who trust me know that I shall never lie to them." The best that could be done was to enroll in "the service of truth and the service of freedom."

SUGGESTIONS FOR FURTHER READING

Challenging studies of World War II are Chester Wilmot's The Struggle for Europe *(1951), Eugen Kogon's* The Theory and Practice of Hell *(1951), and A. and V. Toynbees'* Hitler's Europe *(1954). Chapters in Koppel S. Pinson,* Modern Germany: Its History and Civilization *(1966), Paul A. Gagnon,* France since 1789 *(1964), and Martin Gilbert,* The European Powers, 1900-1945 *(1965), are good, short summaries. The political and international history of the West since the war may be examined in John Lukacs,* Decline and Rise of Europe *(1965), Charles Yost,* The Insecurity of Nations *(1968), G. F. Hudson,* The Hard and Bitter Peace: World Politics since 1945 *(1967), Theodore Geiger,* The Conflicted Relationship: The West and the Transformation of Asia, Africa, and Latin America *(1967), L. J. Halle,* The Cold War as History *(1967) and Ludwig Dehio,* Germany and World Politics in the Twentieth Century *(1959). Robert Heilbroner's* The Future as History *(1959) is particularly valuable for Americans.*

Intellectual and general cultural aspects of the contemporary West are

discussed in Norman N. Greene, Jean-Paul Sartre: The Existentialist Ethic
(1960), Robert Waelder, Progress and Revolution *(1967), Gabriel Vahanian,*
The Death of God: The Culture of Our Post-Christian Era *(1961), R. J.
Forbes,* The Conquest of Nature: Technology and Its Consequences *(1968),
Frederick J. Hoffman,* The Mortal No: Death and the Modern Imagination
(1964), Fred L. Polak, The Image of the Future *(1961), Nigel Calder, ed.,* The
World in 1984 *(1965), Stephen R. Graubard, ed.,* A New Europe? *(1964), and
Michael Polanyi "Beyond Nihilism," in K. A. Jelenski, ed.,* History and Hope
(1962).

Temptation of the West, Man's Fate, The Voices of Silence, *and* The
Walnut Trees of Altenburg *are probably Malraux's most important writings. The translation of his recently completed* Memoirs *was published in
1968. The best collection of factual material about Malraux is still Janet
Flanner's "The Human Condition,"* The New Yorker *(November 6 and 13,
1954). W. M. Frohock's* André Malraux and the Tragic Imagination *(1952),
Charles D. Blend's* André Malraux: Tragic Humanist *(1963), David Wilkin-
son's* Malraux: An Essay in Political Criticism *(1967), and Denis Boak,*
André Malraux *(1968), provide various interpretations. David Caute, in*
Communism and the French Intellectuals, 1914-1960 *(1964), has an interest-
ing chapter on Malraux.*

The study of Pasternak must begin with Doctor Zhivago. *The* Autobiogra-
phy *is also important. Robert Conquest's* The Pasternak Affair: Courage of
Genius *(1961) is an excellent study, while Richard Pipes, ed.,* The Russian
Intelligentsia *(1961), contains the text of the letter from the editors of* New
World *upon rejecting* Doctor Zhivago *for publication in the Soviet Union.
Two of the many articles discussing Pasternak that are worth examining
are John Strachey, "The Strangled Cry,"* Encounter *(December, 1960), and
N. Nilsson, "We Are the Guests of Existence,"* The Reporter *(November 27,
1958).*

Camus' The Stranger, The Plague, The Fall, The Rebel, *and two collec-
tions of his essays —* The Myth of Sisyphus *and* Resistance, Rebellion, and
Death *— are easily secured. There is a great deal of commentary on Camus.
Philip Thody,* Albert Camus: A Study of His Work *(1957), John Cruick-
shank,* Albert Camus and the Literature of Revolt *(1960), and Emmett
Parker,* Albert Camus: The Artist in the Arena *(1965), are good. A valuable,
although usually overlooked discussion appears in Heinz Politzer, "The
True Physician: Franz Kafka and Albert Camus,"* Franz Kafka: Parable and
Paradox *(1966).*

Buffalo II, Robert Rauschenberg, 1964, from the collection of Mr. and Mrs. Robert B. Mayer.

12

The Idea of America

Western civilization is commonly identified with Europe. When we speak of Western history, Western philosophy, or Western literature, we are usually referring to European history, philosophy, or literature. The recognizable characteristics of the modern Western world — industrialization, nationalism, democracy, science — are rooted deep in the European experience. Most of our cultural concepts — the methods by which we describe ourselves and our surroundings — are derived from Europe. Our religions, our languages, and our habits have been indelibly marked by their European origin.

In the second half of the twentieth century, however, Europe is no longer the only significant source of influential Western political and scientific ideas, as she is no longer uniquely instrumental in the development of morals and tastes. The new technology, the new revolutionary movements, the new forms of industrial and business organization, the new patterns of behavior, the new cultural interpretations, the new sense of history that are transforming the contemporary Western world are not particularly European. Much of what we see as the explosive, threatening or promising future is closely related to what we can call the idea of America. Eldridge Cleaver was only dramatizing an obvious situation when he wrote in 1968 in *Soul on Ice*: "It is not an overstatement to say that the destiny of the entire human race depends upon the outcome of what is going on in America today." And then he went on to rub in his point. "This is a staggering reality to the rest of the world; they must feel like passengers in a supersonic jet liner who are forced to watch helplessly while a passle of drunks, hypes, freaks, and madmen fight for the controls and the pilot's seat."

Some aspects of this American influence are almost too obvious to mention. American military power and political "clout" are perpetually on parade. American banks, soft-drink companies, distribution centers, and supermarkets — or their facsimiles — are ubiquitous. American influence is probably more persuasive than that ever exerted by one nation upon others. If Marshall McLuhan is right, and the world is becoming one great "global village," then it is likely that a good part of that world conglomeration will exhibit American characteristics. Since 1945 the United States has dominated the West in a way that no European nation could even dream of. Almost every important undertaking in which the West has engaged has depended upon American power and wealth, and as T. R. Fyvel has remarked, the American dominance was "much more than U.S. armed power within NATO, behind whose shield an affluent Europe could become the summer playground of the young. U.S. support assured the peace of West Berlin and at the same time of Israel; U.S. economic and military strength provided an answer to Soviet missiles, and at the same time provided wheat for the masses of India and aid in general for the Third World; U.S. institutions doled out grants for research and U.S. universities took in European academics; behind most Western endeavors, in fact, there stood support in the shape of the dynamic, democratic optimism of the U.S."

Military, economic, and organizational power is an important part of the idea of America. But power alone cannot create a way of life. The old saying that one may conquer on horseback but cannot live in the saddle is still true. The substance of the idea of America must involve a genuine spiritual and intellectual contact with the new and still largely strange world that the Americans have helped create. In 1929 Edmund Wilson spoke to the essence of the problem when he stated that "It is up to American writers to try to make some sense of their American world — for their world is now everybody's world." Some years later Leslie Fiedler made a similar argument when he wrote that the American writer could no longer escape being "the recorder of the encounter of the dream of innocence and the fact of guilt, in the only part of the world where the reality of that conflict can still be recognized."

Fortunately, there is more to the idea of America than military and economic power. In 1961, in his *The Invention of America*, Edmundo O'Gorman pointed out that the mere discovery of the New World brought about a drastic change in the way men looked at themselves and their environment. The earth was suddenly bigger, more diverse — and more exciting — than previously thought. "But this revolution went even deeper; the world having ceased to be considered as a sort of cosmic jail, man was able to picture himself as a free agent in the deep and radical sense of possessing unlimited possibilities in his own being, and as living in a world made by him in his own image and to his own measure. Such is the profound meaning of this historical process that implies modern man's contempt for and his rebellion against the fetters which he himself had forged under pressure of archaic religious fears."

What O'Gorman stresses is that, contrary to our usual habit of saying that America was discovered by Europeans, the reality of our history indicates that America was "invented" by Americans. In this process of invention, we have drawn heavily upon Europe. But we have never accepted Europe as "the self-appointed judge and model of human behavior." As O'Gorman writes, the American had a choice of two ways of relating to Europe. "The first consists of adapting himself as closely as possible in all respects to the model which has been set up for him. This is the road of imitation, which, at best, can only produce a copy, necessarily inferior to the original model. The second consists in trying to realize on his own and at his own risk the possibilities implied in the way of living exemplified by the model, with due regard to personal circumstances and idiosyncrasies. This is the road of originality, which allows the possibility of exceeding the model."

The idea of America can thus best be seen as the extension of certain aspects of European history, which have then in America assumed distinctive characteristics. If we should try for a single word that could express this process, it might be well to settle on modernization. It is important, however, to realize what we mean by such a term in the context of American life. Too often, modernization is identified with mechanization — one of its most obvious and startling manifestations. But American modernization is much more than the creation of machines and the organization of a society's physical energies. It is a radical hostility to institutions that claim a right to existence on grounds other than performance. It is a rejection of any "aristocracy founded on brains, culture, and blood." It is a belief, in spite of all "documented" evidence to the contrary, that the "common" opinion of "common" people is a valid indication of a worthwhile purpose. It is the demand for an "open" society — no secrets, no closed cultural or political cabals that are designed to shield anyone or anything from public scrutiny. It is the argument that the individual happiness of its members is the overriding goal of a healthy society. It is a suspicion of abstract and complex historical generalizations that are divorced from observable, day-to-day reality and postpone the present in favor of some theoretical future. It is, in William James' words, "the belief that something is doing in the universe, and that novelty is real." It is ultimately what Hazel Barnes calls "the irreducible reality of the free individual conscience."

All of this, of course, is related to the European concepts of rationality, humanity, and liberality. But in America this modernization appears without the institutional framework and the historical memories that have traditionally conditioned the European response to modernity. The intellectual interpretations that are so much a part of European history and which are expressed by the vocabulary developed by Europeans are not applicable to America. We often use words such as Bourbon, bourgeoisie, fascist, Marxist, and existentialist. But when we think carefully we know that we have with such words said little meaningful about American life. Deep and dense speculations about the past and the future are the elements of the great European pondering upon the human situation. But the American has trouble relating himself to the past — even his own — or in creating a philosophy of the future. There is not, and probably cannot be, in America anything similar to German *Kultur* — the powerful expression of a continuing nationalistic folk spirit that provides cultural security — or to French *civilisation* — a deep historical confidence in a set of intellectual and cultural values that come from the past, permeate the present, and extend into the future. Wright Morris may be correct when he says that in America "nostalgia rules our hearts while a rhetoric of progress rules our words." But "nostalgia" and "a rhetoric of progress" can hardly pass as a valuable historical interpretation. In 1968 Stow Persons wrote of contemporary America that the "past and the future radiate out from the present as measured by a series of changes, and both are increasingly obscure as they recede from the present." Americans do lack a sense of history and have been markedly unsuccessful in establishing cultural or historical forms that could express their experience.

Yet Americans have an almost pathetic urge to see their condition in terms of European interpretations. The great cultural and intellectual forms developed in Europe fascinate us. Thus we often adopt archaic historical and institutional concepts that are inappropriate to American life — as they are becoming less and less relevant to Europe itself. Good examples of this attitude are attempts to define our actions in terms of a Christian purpose, to establish some recognized standard of cultural judgment, and to forward the idea of a homogeneous society.

There may have been some historical justification for Europeans in the sixteenth and seventeenth centuries to see themselves as carriers of organized Christianity throughout the world and to attempt to mold the planet to Christian purposes. But America's efforts to play the role of Christian agent and to take over God's tasks have been particularly embarrassing. We can perhaps understand, if not excuse, the argument in 1898 of a United States Senator that "We must not renounce our part in the mission of our race, trustee, under God, of the civilization of the world. . . . God . . . has marked us as His chosen people, henceforth to lead in the regeneration of the world." But what can be said of the statement of a former secretary of state who could only thirty years ago say that America's historical duty toward China was to help her develop "toward the ideals of modern Christian civilization," or of that of a well-known American publisher who identified what he called the American century with the will of God? What rubbish, what puerile ideas! The awesome and consuming thrust of the organized Christian interpretation of life that was such an important part of European civilization has been blunted in the United States. Catholicism has played a far different role here than in Europe, while American Puritanism, whatever its one-time influence on intellectual life, degenerated into a crabbed and narrow view of the nature of this country. The most prevalent form of American religious expression, as it has influenced national behavior, has probably been pietism, which has, however, been institutionally fragmented, has lacked intellectual content, and has been involved in everything from the justification of slavery to the censorship of books and movies.

Christianity, of course, still provides a treasured interpretation of life for many Christian Americans. As Judaism does for American Jews and Mohammedanism for American Muslims. But these religious feelings cannot be translated into terms of national power and national purpose, nor can America act the part of "Defender of the Faith," as if she were some sixteenth-century European monarchy. As Charles L. Sanford has written recently, the attempt to combine theology and national politics in the United States has been near-disastrous: "It is no wonder that Americans have been so often blind to their self-interest in the conduct of foreign affairs, so easily deceived by their own rationalizations, so hesitant to employ military or economic sanctions to enforce their principles and policies, so quick to preach pious doctrine without regard to immediate practical consequences, and so susceptible to moods of cynicism and despair when their high expectations and noble intentions collapse in the wreckage of ignoble results."

Some Americans also hanker after what they regard as the European allegiance to a clearly defined system of cultural values that is protected from vulgarization by a class of men possessing distinctive training, background, and special insights. Into the present, the European outlook has been deeply influenced by the status accorded the Herr Professor, the cultural commissar, the intellectual mandarin. And there have been efforts to establish cultural guardians in the United States. But they have not found the climate congenial. Ezra Pound dismissed such claimants as "fusty old crocks" who "pretended to look after American culture," and his argument has gained general support. There is in America hostility to any idea of an elite, and Michael Harrington expresses a common American attitude when he writes: "The most benign elites will not simply rob people of civil liberties in a subtle way. They will also make a mess of things."

This opposition to any system of political or cultural guardians is not, as many have argued, primarily an expression of a deep-seated American anti-intellectualism (although there is more than enough of this particular form of idiocy in American life). It is rather a refusal to accept the European idea of culture as something that is almost "sacred" and that must be protected by and restricted to a learned aristocracy and fenced off from the "masses." There is a rejection of claims to precedence based upon any appeal to cultural superiority, and in fact, a suspicion that the usual European idea of a life of culture may itself be spurious.

The idea of America is also incompatible with the European concept of a homogeneous society. We often speak loosely of common American traditions that have created the American character. We read that the American consciousness was formed by Puritanism or by the business ethic or by the frontier experience. But when we look closely at these interpretations, we see that they do not fit the circumstances of American life. The consciousness of some Americans was formed by one or another of these influences, but none of them can claim to express the idea of America. Americans have varied historical memories, different standards of behavior, and even dissimilar loyalties and allegiances. The at least partially successful attempt to impose a common life style on Americans has been a horrible mistake and has robbed our national existence of much of its richness and excitement. What is usually and tritely called the "melting pot" view of our society is an aberration of the idea of America. Thus American schools, political organizations, and social conventions have strained to impose upon American life a flat, empty commonality, based upon what Edward L. Thorndike, perhaps the most influential American educator, called "the more clean, decent, just, and kind," or what we recognize now as the emptiest of cultural descriptions. Until recently it was possible to read newspapers, listen to political speeches, watch movies, and attend school without being reminded that there were in this country American Jews, American Catholics, American blacks, American Japanese, American Greeks, Italians, Chinese, native Indians, and hosts of other people who were living, working, and dying here as almost forgotten citizens.

Perhaps there was some justification in the relatively homogeneous European national societies for the belief that a French minister of education should be able to tell at any one time what all the French students in a particular class were studying in common, as perhaps the aim of British cultural conditioning was to turn every English boy into a Tory or a Liberal. Perhaps there was, and is, in Europe such a thing as a French character, a British character, or a German character, although David Riesman has warned that "the study of national character indeed seems to be an Alice-in-Wonderland croquet game." But any attempt to define the American character is certain to fail. The conglomerate nature of America is too pronounced, and American national life must be looser, more free, more mobile, more tolerant than has ever been the case with a European society.

This secularly oriented, pragmatic, equality-minded, "open" American idea, with its confidence in modernity, is perhaps the major cultural influence in the contemporary Western world. The manifestations of this idea are destroying the older European institutions and interpretations and undercutting the conditions of European life. Attitudes and behavioral patterns generated by America seep around and then overwhelm traditional customs, and because these influences are not institutionalized or even formulated, defenses against them are unsuccessful. Michael Harrington gives an excellent example of the way the force of the idea of America works when he writes: "Teen-agers are an authentic, unprecedented social type . . . which was invented in the United States and then exported all over the world." Laws, customs, and even frantic appeals to the past or to some cultural verity are helpless before such a revolutionary influence. Hannah Arendt once wrote that what America lost "through the failure of thought and remembrance was the revolutionary spirit." Michael Harrington, however, says that America "is the most radical country in the world." Professor Arendt is a learned philosopher who has thought long and well upon many matters. But she is seeking in America for something that is not there — some philosophical image of revolution that can be embodied in a philosophy of history. Mr. Harrington is more modest. He sees that because its appeal cuts into all levels of society and carries with it no requirement for ideological commitment the idea of America is an irresistible revolutionary surge unleashed in the modern Western world.

It is true, of course, as many have been quick to point out, that Americans themselves are the great betrayers of the idea of America. To be at all acceptable, American society must exhibit what has been termed "a climate of veracity," the relatively close relationship of words and facts. Because they have little else to fall back on, Americans must, as the poet Wallace Stevens said, live on "the bread of faithful speech." We have the words, but one has only to look at the shocking poverty, the intellectual delinquency, the vulgar expressions of economic affluence, the cruel discrimination, the unbearable combinations of superficiality and pedantry in order to realize the extent of our failure. A Manus islander told the anthropologist Margaret Mead that "from Americans we learned that it is only human beings that are important." But what the islander learned from us, we ourselves frequently forget. Too often, as F. Scott Fitzgerald wrote, the American is "like a little boy left in a big house, who knows that now he could do anything he wanted to do, but found that there was nothing that he wanted to do." We commit impossible-to-imagine crimes against our environment, and Wright Morris writes: "the green dream burned over, the clear streams polluted, the natural beauty corrupted beyond repair." Our cultural life tends to peter out in one ridiculous charade after another. R. P. Blackmur says that we have been engaged in "wrestling with God, with the self, with the conscience, and above all in our latter day with our behavior." And we have, to a lesser or greater extent, failed in every respect. We swing violently from a foolish belief in inevitable progress to an equally unwarranted gloomy prediction of decline. We show an amazing propensity for being taken in — by the charlatan, the vulgarian, the exhibitionist — and we seem the continual victims of "overblown unconceived philosophy, technicolor melodramatics, and a staggering ignorance." At times we even appear to be ready to give up and join in the chorus of Saul Bellow's *Dangling Man*:

> Hurray for regular hours!
> And for the supervision of the spirit!
> Long live regimentation!

And our failures create disorientation and confusion in Europe and in other parts of the world. We do give the impression of being a predatory national society, of showing the American "will to power, cloaking itself in idealism." We fall into the habit of regarding Western Europe and the rest of the world in terms of real estate, as if the earth were ours to dispose of as we wished. In the late nineteen-sixties our difficulties in Vietnam, our domestic racial crisis, our disorder and confusion sapped American self-confidence and introduced ugly and violent forces into our political and social lives. But the effects of our troubles were not confined to the United States. Disappointment in America and a feeling that Americans had lost their way were responsible, to an important extent, for the political malaise, the suspicion, and the moral confusion that have appeared in Western Europe. American floundering has called into question the legitimacy and even the value of the new Western society that has been created since the end of World War II. Because Western Europe looks at its future in terms of its interactions with the United States, American disasters raise fears about that future.

Temporary and even ultimate failure (the first a certainty and the second at least a possibility), however, cannot rob the idea of America of significance. It is a true blossoming of Western civilization and must be the major source of answers to many of the important questions being posed in the West: How do we reconcile our capacity for creating powerful organizations with our determination to enjoy the widest possible freedom? How are the increasing demands of an increasing number of people to participate in political, economic, and social decisions to be met? How can the energies, talents, and the aspirations of the young contribute to a society whose history and culture they regard with suspicion and even hostility? How can we rid ourselves of those old phobias about race, those old fears about the mass society, those old dangers of a runaway technology, those old nightmares of war?

In the new Western world the American, as Eric Larrabee says, "must learn to do without the European model, while the European must take account of the wider range of perspective and concern that Americans have opened up to him." The idea of America will undoubtedly be modified in Western Europe, transformed by European genius, and then returned to America to enrich our own lives. And there will be nothing extraordinary in such a course of events in that historical partnership that has been established between Western Europe and America. It is instructive to look at an example of some of the influences that created the idea of America. We traditionally date the United States from 1776. This was the year of the American Declaration of Independence, which contains the basis for what we can call the American concept of the modern democratic revolution. It was also the year of important developments in James Watt's steam engine, the instrument for the industrialization of the West, of Adam Smith's *Wealth of Nations*, a plea for the freeing of Western man's energies from traditional restrictions, and of Jeremy Bentham's *A Fragment on Government*, a statement that the search for happiness on this earth was the aim of life. These great monuments stood at the beginning of modern Western history, and they were products of Europe. The ideas contained in them were taken by the Americans, extended and developed, and then returned to Europe. Henry David Thoreau said: "I must walk toward Oregon and not toward Europe." The American has walked to the west across the continent. But he has also returned to Europe, not as a suppliant or a poverty-stricken borrower, but as an active participant in a wider Western civilization. And the result has been described by O'Gorman: "To us it seems that we no longer have two distinct worlds, one young and promising, the other old and dying, but that a new historical entity has been formed, which may well be called Euro-American and in which the great ocean of ancient geography undergoes its last transformation; it has been converted into the new *Mare Nostrum*, the Mediterranean of our day." In much the same way, the late J. Robert Oppenheimer once said that he had to believe in the reality of Western history, of his role in it, and his responsibility for it, because "I am too much a Jew, much too much a Christian, much too much a European, far too much an American."

Index of Proper Names